Smith's Canadian Gazetteer

$9.50

Revd Offees
May 2 1844

SMITH'S
CANADIAN GAZETTEER;

COMPRISING

STATISTICAL AND GENERAL INFORMATION RESPECTING
ALL PARTS OF THE UPPER PROVINCE, OR

CANADA WEST:

DISTANCE TABLES;
GOVERNMENT AND DISTRICT OFFICERS AND MAGISTRATES IN EACH DISTRICT,
LIST OF POST OFFICES, WITH THEIR DISTANCES FROM SOME OF THE
PRINCIPAL TOWNS,
STAGE AND STEAMBOAT FARES; PRINCIPAL HOTELS AND TAVERNS;
RATES OF TOLL ON THE WELLAND CANAL AND SOME OF THE PRINCIPAL HARBOURS,
LISTS OF EXPORTS, QUANTITY OF CROWN LANDS FOR SALE IN EACH TOWNSHIP,
NAMES AND ADDRESSES OF LAND AGENTS AND FORWARDERS,
THE LEADING FEATURES OF EACH LOCALITY AS REGARDS SOIL, CLIMATE, &C,
WITH THE AVERAGE VALUE OF LAND

WITH A MASS OF OTHER DESIRABLE AND USEFUL INFORMATION FOR
THE MAN OF BUSINESS, TRAVELLER, OR EMIGRANT

THE WHOLE COLLECTED FROM THE BEST AUTHORITIES, VERIFIED BY PERSONAL OBSERVATION AND
INQUIRIES, DURING NEARLY THREE YEARS DEVOTED TO THE SUBJECT, IN WHICH TIME THE
AUTHOR VISITED EVERY DISTRICT, TOWN, AND VILLAGE, IN SEARCH OF INFORMATION

WITH A

MAP OF THE UPPER PROVINCE,

COMPILED EXPRESSLY FOR THE WORK, IN WHICH ARE LAID DOWN ALL THE
TOWNS AND PRINCIPAL VILLAGES

BY
WM. H. SMITH.

*Dedicated by Permission to Lord Metcalfe, late Governor General
of British North America*

TORONTO
PUBLISHED FOR THE AUTHOR, BY H. & W. ROWSELL.
1846.

Price 10s.

ROWSELLS AND THOMSON, PRINTERS, TORONTO

TO

THE RIGHT HONOURABLE

CHARLES THEOPHILUS BARON METCALFE, G. C. B.,

Late Governor-General of British North America, &c &c &c

THIS WORK

IS, BY PERMISSION, MOST RESPECTFULLY INSCRIBED,

BY HIS LORDSHIP'S

MOST OBEDIENT

AND MOST HUMBLE SERVANT,

The Author.

Toronto, July 1st, 1846.

PREFACE.

In compiling this, the first Gazetteer of Canada West, I was induced to undertake the task by the great ignorance which I found to exist respecting the Province, not only amongst persons in Great Britain, or newly-arrived emigrants, but even amongst many of those who had been for years resident in the country, and from ascertaining that the various, contradictory, and occasionally false accounts given to emigrants on their arrival, respecting distant localities, frequently led them to alter their original intentions respecting their destination, and often induced them to leave the Province altogether, and settle in the United States. This I found to be the case myself, on my arrival in Canada, when I was told that I should find the western borders of the Province a complete wilderness—that on the River St. Clair, for instance, there was a marked difference between the appearance of the country on the American and on the British side—that on the former all was bustle and activity, fine farms and flourishing orchards, while on the Canadian side nothing was to be seen but uncleared forest—and that the Western District was very sickly. In travelling by stage, during the winter of 1844, from London to Chatham, one of my fellow passengers, who had been for some years in the Province, told me that he was going to Chatham, from whence he intended to cross over the river to Detroit, and he was astonished when informed, that to reach Detroit, he would have to travel *fifty miles* farther! Again, during the last year, I remember seeing amongst the articles in the newspapers respecting the western railroads, Windsor and Sandwich spoken of as *being on the River St. Clair!*

Respecting the natural productions and capabilities of the Province, I have found also quite as much misinformation. Many persons, for instance, have been quite surprised to hear that marble was plentiful in the Province; and one individual told me, as a very great secret, that he had made what he considered a most valuable discovery, that in the course of his explorations about Lake Huron and the Georgian Bay, he had discovered a quarry of white marble, but he thought the secret so valuable that he would not tell the situation in which he had found it.

To collect materials for the first Gazetteer of any country, (which in itself implies that it is a Gazetteer of a *new* country,) may truly be called "the pursuit of knowledge under difficulties," which may be supposed to be the reason that although it is now three hundred years since the first settlement was made in Canada, no one has hitherto had sufficient resolution to undertake and carry through the task. These difficulties arise principally from the obstructions and inconveniences of travelling in remote places, and from the difficulty in many localities of collecting authentic information. The latter difficulty is caused not so much by the unwillingness of parties to give what information they possess as from apathy on the subject, and I have found the most trouble in gaining information from those places that were lagging in the back ground—the inhabitants appearing to view me as one who had come "to spy the nakedness of the land," and being unwilling to have themselves and their neighbourhoods dragged before the public. And in all such instances there appeared to be a great want of spirit and enterprise amongst them. In all those places, on the contrary, where the inhabitants were industrious, enterprising, and desirous of seeing their particular locality prosper, I have had no difficulty in arriving at any information I required. From those government and district officers, to whom I have found it necessary, in the course of my inquiries, to apply for information, I have invariably received all the assistance in their power, (with two or three exceptions only, one of these refused me the information I required, on the ground that "he was not *obliged* to give information to every one who asked for it." On mentioning his conduct to some of his townsmen, the reply I received was, "you should have shown him a shilling, and he would have given you the information fast enough." Another had the conscience to refuse me a list of the qualified magistrates in his district, unless I paid him a quarter of a dollar for each name! (153 in number), and I was consequently obliged to procure the list from the Secretary's Office, at Montreal,) and I take this opportunity of returning to them my best thanks for their kindness and courtesy.

In collecting together such a mass of information, extending over so great a surface of country, (and which information it was also necessary to condense as much as possible), it is not unlikely that some few inaccuracies may have crept in, but I believe the work will be generally allowed to be as correct as it was possible for a work of the kind to be made. Some two or three places of small consequence have been necessarily omitted, as Merrickville, on the Rideau Canal, which I passed through in the night, and Bath, on the St Lawrence, which, on account of the badness of the weather, I was unable to visit. I wrote to the postmaster of the latter place, (as the most public man in a village), requesting him to favour me with the statistics of the village, but he had not the politeness to answer my letter.

In the prosecution of my object, I have spared neither trouble, expense, nor personal fatigue, and, in the course of my travels, I have walked over more than three thousand miles of ground, through both the heats of summer and the snows of winter, and having completed my labours, like a mariner starting on a voyage of discovery, I launch my bark upon the waters, trusting to the winds and waves of public opinion to waft it safely into port,—(put the profits into his pocket, he means.—PRINT DEV),—with the confident expectation that my exertions to make the Province better known and appreciated, will be supported as they should be, by all who must necessarily, directly or indirectly, benefit by my researches.

THE AUTHOR.

CANADIAN GAZETTEER.

ADDINGTON.

A County in the Midland District : comprises the townships of Amherst Island, Camden, Ernestown, Kaladar, Sheffield, and Anglesea. For the purposes of representation in the House of Assembly, it is united to the county of Lennox.

ADELAIDE.

A Township in the London District : is bounded on the east by the township of Lobo ; on the south-east by Carradoc and Ekfrid ; on the north by Williams; and on the west by Warwick and Brooke. In Adelaide 32,272 acres are taken up, 4,025 of which are under cultivation. The east branch of Bear Creek runs along the east and south-east border of the township, and the River Aux Sables touches its northern boundary. Adelaide contains excellent land, and some good farms. The villages of Adelaide and Katesville are situated in the township, and there are one grist and two saw-mills in the township. Four hundred and fifty acres of crown lands are open for sale in Adelaide, at 8s. c'y per acre.

Population in 1842, 1234.

Ratable property in the township, £15,283.

ADJALA.

A Township in the Simcoe District: is bounded on the north by the township of Tossorontio; on the west by Mono; on the south by Albion; and on the east by Tecumseth. In Adjala 20,793 acres are taken up, 2929 of which are under cultivation. There is a swamp extending across the township, south of its centre, on both the north and south of which there is some excellent land, level, with good hard timber. There are some good farms in the township. This, and Tossorontio which joins it, are long, narrow townships. On the town line, between Adjala and Mono, the land is hilly and sandy. There are lime-stone quarries on the line. There are 4,000 acres of crown lands for disposal in Adjala, at 8s. c'y per acre, to purchase which application must be made to the Crown Lands Agent at Barrie. There are two saw mills in the township.

Population in 1842 (since when no census has been taken), 890.

Ratable property in the township, £8,948.

ADMASTON.

A Township in the Bathurst District : is bounded on the north-east by the township of Horton, on the north-west by Bromley; on the west by unsurveyed lands; and on the south-east by Bagot and Blithefield. In Admaston 11,206 acres are taken up, 679 of which are under cultivation. This township, which was originally called Kenmare, is but little settled. The River Bonne Chaur runs across the centre of the township, and there are several large lakes scattered over it. Seventy-four thousand six hundred acres of Crown lands are open for sale in Admaston, at 8s. c'y per acre. There is one saw-mill in the township. Population not yet returned.

Ratable property in the township, £3,534.

ADOLPHUSTOWN.

A Township in the Midland District ; is bounded on the north-east by the township of Fredericksburgh ; and on the west and south-west by the Bay of Quinté. In Adolphustown 11,343 acres are taken up, 6,662 of which are under cultivation. A portion of the Bay of Quinté divides the township into two. There is a small settlement in the south of the township, on the bay, where is a court-house, for holding township meetings, and an Episcopal church. In the centre of the township are a Quaker meeting-house, and a Methodist chapel. There are some good farms in the township, and four saw-mills.
Population, 671.
Ratable property in the township, £16,102.

ADOLPHUSTOWN.

A small Village in the township of Adolphustown, situated on the Bay of Quinté, contains about 100 inhabitants

ALDBOROUGH.

A Township in the London District is bounded on the north-east by the township of Dunwich , on the north-west by the River Thames; on the south-west by Orford, and on the south-east by Lake Erie In Aldborough 15,593 acres are taken up, 3,519 of which are under cultivation The south of the township contains some good land, but the north is very hilly and broken. There are many wet patches in it, and much of the timber is swamp elm. Most of the settlers are poor they are principally Highland Scotch. A road called " Furnival's Road," is cut out through the township, from Lake Erie to the River Thames, which it reaches about half a mile below Wardsville. There are four saw-mills in the township
Population in 1842, 737.
Ratable property in the township, £9,853.

ALBION.

A Township in the Home District is bounded on the east by the townships of King and Vaughan, on the north by Adjala and Tecumseth; on the south-west by Caledon and Chinguacousy , and on the south-east by the Gore of Toronto. In Albion 41,829 acres are taken up, 10,000 of which are under cultivation. The north and north-east of the township are hilly and broken, with a great deal of pine land ; in the south of the township the land is better, and there are some good farms There are four grist and two saw mills, and two distilleries in the township
Population of Albion in 1842, 2,154.
Ratable property in the township, £26,279

ALFRED

A Township in the Ottawa District is bounded on the south-east by the townships of Longueil and Caledonia , on the north by the Ottawa, and on the south-west by Plantagenet In Alfred 6,320 acres are taken up, 682 of which are under cultivation This is a triangular-shaped township, which is but little settled There is one saw-mill in the township Ten thousand eight hundred and sixty-five acres of crown lands are open for sale in Alfred, at 8s. c'y per acre.
Population, 220.
Ratable property in the township, £3,069.

ALNWICK

A Township in the Newcastle District; is bounded on the east by the township of Percy; on the north-west by Rice Lake; and on the south by Haldimand.

This is a triangular-shaped township, which as yet contains only an Indian settlement, called Aldersville.

Near Rice Lake, and about fifteen miles north-east from Cobourg, is a settlement of Mississaga Indians, who, previous to the year 1826, were Pagans, wandering in the neighbourhood of Belleville, Kingston and Guananoque; and were known under the name of the Mississagas of the Bay of Quintè. In 1826 & 27, between two and three hundred were settled on Grape Island, in the Bay of Quintè, six miles from Belleville, where they commenced planting, and where schools were established by a Wesleyan Methodist Missionary for their instruction. On this island they resided eleven years, subsisting by agriculture and hunting. Their houses were erected partly by their own labour, and partly at the expense of the Methodist Missionary Society; the number, at length, amounted to twenty-three, besides which, they had a commodious building for religious service and schools, another room for an infant school, a hospital, a smithy, a shoemaker's shop, and a building for joiners' and cabinet work. These however were relinquished, to be sold for their benefit in 1830, when they removed to their present location, which was granted to them by Sir John Colborne. It contains 2,000 acres, which is divided into lots of twenty-five acres each. The village, or street, which is called Aldersville, is about a mile and a half in length; it contains thirty six houses, six barns, a saw-mill, and a large school-house, in which divine worship is performed, all erected under the direction of the Indian Department, out of the annuity of £642 10s to which this band is entitled for the surrender of a vast tract in the rear of the Johnstown and Midland Districts. Of the thirty-six dwelling houses, twenty-two are framed, and the remainder are of square logs, all of commodious size. the barns are framed, of forty by thirty feet in dimensions. These Indians are 233 in number; each family has at least half its lots of 25 acres cleared; and several have nearly the whole under cultivation. The total quantity cleared is between 360 and 400 acres. Their stock consists of eight yoke of Oxen, two horses, eleven cows, twenty-one heifers and calves, and a number of pigs and poultry. They possess eight ploughs, six harrows, three carts and waggons, and twelve ox-sleighs.

When on Grape Island, a cabinet maker, blacksmith, shoe maker, and occasionally a tailor, were employed by the Methodist society, to instruct these Indians in their several trades. Although it was found difficult to keep the scholars at their work, and considerable losses were sustained in the undertaking, yet the Indians shewed unusual ingenuity, and gained considerable knowledge in those branches, which has been of much use to them since their settlement at Alnwick, where no shops have yet been erected.

For four years past, a school, on the manual labour plan, has been in operation. This system combines elementary instruction with domestic economy. The girls are taught reading, writing, arithmetic, and geography, together with house-keeping, spinning, knitting, needle-work, and the management of a dairy. in the latter department are seven cows. The boys are taught in the same branches as the girls, and in English grammar, and in the business of farming. For this purpose, a model farm of fifty acres in extent is provided. The scholars, twelve in number, are boarded and lodged in the mission family, and clothed at the expense of the Missionary Society. They are all clad in cloth spun by the Indian girls. During four years past, thirty-one girls and fourteen boys have received instruction in this school.

Two hundred and fifty acres of Crown lands are open for sale in the township, at 8s. c'y per acre.

ALBERT PORT.

A Village in the township of Ashfield, situated on the Ashfield River at its entrance into Lake Huron, nine miles above Goderich. Albert has one tavern. Population about 40.

The government agent for disposing of Crown lands, Mr. J. Hawkins, resides here.

ALLENBURG.

A Village in the township of Thorold, situated on the Welland Canal, 8 miles from St. Catherine's. It possesses a town-hall for public meetings
Population about 500.
Professions and Trades —One grist mill, one saw ditto, carding machine and cloth factory, candle factory, pipe factory, four stores, two taverns, one waggon maker, one cabinet maker, one blacksmith and one baker.

AMARANTH

A Township in the Wellington District is bounded on the east by the township of Mono, on the north by Melancthon, on the west by Luther; and on the south by Garrafraxa. In Amaranth 2,710 acres are taken up, 351 of which are under cultivation. This township is as yet but little settled. Fifteen thousand and fifty acres of crown lands are open for sale in it, at 8s. c'y per acre.
Population in 1841, 105
Ratable property in the township, £1,295.

AMELIASBURGH

A Township in the Prince Edward District: is bounded on the north and east by the Bay of Quinté, on the west by Weller's Bay (with the exception of the north-west corner, where it joins the township of Murray, and a small portion of the south-east corner, which is bounded by Sophiasburgh); and on the south by Lake Consecon, Consecon Creek, and the township of Hillier. Ameliasburgh contains 40,466 acres, 15,217 of which are under cultivation. Two portions of the bay, which are bordered by marsh, extend for some distance into this township. A creek, also bordered by marsh, runs across the township, north of the centre, from west to east, and a small lake, called Roblin's Lake, is situated about the centre of the township. There is a ferry established across the bay from this township to Belleville. Population in 1841, 2,115, many of whom are of Dutch extraction. There are two grist and three saw-mills in the township.
Ratable property in the township, £40,400.

AMHERST ISLAND

An Island in Lake Ontario, situated opposite the township of Ernestown, so called from the Earl of Amherst; the name originally given it by the French, being "Isle of Tanti." It was originally granted by the Crown to Sir John Johnston, for military services. The upper portion of it has been settled about 70 years, and the remainder about 25 years. The principal part of the island is now owned by the Earl of Mountcashel. The land is generally of very good quality, and the tenants are in comfortable circumstances. The steamboats touch here on their passages to and from Trent and Kingston. Amherst island forms a township of the Midland District; 13,387 acres of land are taken up in the island, 5030 of which are under cultivation. There is a Post Office on the island, and an Episcopal Church. There are also on the island, one physician and surgeon, one store, two taverns, three ship-builders, five tailors, seven shoemakers, five carpenters, twelve weavers, two blacksmiths.
Population, 1104.
Ratable property, £11,185

AMHERSTBURG.

A garrison Town, in the township of Malden, in the county of Essex: sixteen miles from Sandwich, on the Detroit River. It was commenced in the year 1798, soon after the evacuation of Detroit. The situation is good, but most of the streets are rather narrow. The banks of the river, both above and below the town, but particularly the latter, where the river emerges into Lake

Erie, are very beautiful; the sweet-briar bushes, with which the banks are studded, are here remarkably fine. Several handsome houses are built on the banks below the town. About a mile below the town, near the entrance of Lake Erie, is a chalybeate spring; which is said to resemble the waters of Cheltenham, in England. A fort called Malden, capable of accommodating a regiment, is situated about half a mile above the town, on the river; it was rebuilt in 1839, and is at present occupied by three companies of rifles. Sir Chas. Metcalfe in the year 1845 granted a charter to the town of Amherstburg to hold a fair twice a year.

A plot of land containing about 100 acres, (being the military reserve,), outside the town, is perfectly cleared of timber, and forms a fine large common, which is very convenient for the inhabitants of the neighbourhood, for grazing. The steamboats; London, from Buffalo to Detroit; Gore, from Windsor to Goderich and Penetanguishine, and Brothers, from Chatham, touch here regularly. The latter leaves Amherstburg every Tuesday, Thursday, and Saturday mornings, at half past seven o'clock, for Detroit and Chatham. Fare to Detroit $\frac{1}{2}$, to Chatham $2\frac{1}{2}$. And many of the American steamers stop here to take in wood. Amherstburg contains 985 inhabitants, of this number 174 are people of colour. There are five churches and chapels, viz. Episcopal, Catholic, Presbyterian, Methodist, and Baptist, the latter for coloured people, and a news and reading room, a market place, and court house have recently been erected.

Post office, post every day.

List of Professions and Trades.—Two physicans and surgeons, one lawyer, two breweries, two auctioneers, two asheries, one steam grist and saw mill, one carding machine and woollen manufactory, one soap and candle manufactory, two tanneries, three schools, fourteen stores, six blacksmiths, three bakers, three saddlers, five waggon makers, eight shoemakers, four tailors, one tinsmith, one watchmaker, two painters, ten taverns, one tobacconist, one notary public, two butchers, inspector of flour and pork; four large schooners are owned here. Principal tavern, the "British North American."

EXPORTS FROM AMHERSTBURG FOR THE YEAR 1844.

Quantity	Description.	Estimated value.
12,600 bushels	wheat	£2580 0 0
1,500 do	potatoes	75 0 0
2,500 do	Indian corn	250 0 0
100 barrels	pork	250 0 0
300 do	potash	1500 0 0
10 do	lard	30 0 0
200 hogsheads	tobacco	1500 0 0
2,000 lbs	hams	50 0 0
50,000 lbs	raw hides	375 0 0
45,000 lbs	standard staves	450 0 0
50,000 feet	black walnut lumber	125 0 0
	furs	36 10 0

Total value of exports.. £7221 10 0

ANCASTER.

A Village in the township of Ancaster, situated on the plank road, about six and a half miles west from Hamilton. It was formerly a place of considerable business, but the rapid growth of Hamilton has thrown it into the shade; it is, however, beginning partially to recover itself through the enterprise of some of its inhabitants. Part of the village was destroyed by fire during 1845. It is intended to erect a cloth factory during the present year.

Population, about 150, who have an Episcopal Church and a Presbyterian do. There are also a grist and saw mill, one physician and surgeon, one lawyer, one tannery, a foundry and manufactory for making carding and other machines, two stores, two groceries, two taverns, one blacksmith, two tailors, two shoemakers.

Post Office, post every day.

ANCASTER.

A Township in the Gore District, is bounded on the south-east by the townships of Barton and Glanford, on the north by Flamborough West and Beverly; and on the south-west by Onondaga and Brantford. In Ancaster, 41,850 acres are taken up, 17,952 of which are under cultivation This is a triangular-shaped township, is well-settled, and contains some fine farms The villages of Dundas and Ancaster are situated in it, and there are also two grist and six saw mills in the township.

Population in 1841, 2930

Ratable property in the township, £68,212.

ANDERDON

A Township in the county of Essex, is bounded on the north by the township of Sandwich; on the west by the Detroit river, on the south by the township of Malden; and on the east by the township of Colchester. In Anderdon 5675 acres are taken up, of which 1159 are cultivated The river Canard runs through the township, and enters the Detroit River about midway between its northern and southern boundaries Soil fertile The banks of the river are well settled In the south-west of the township are three valuable lime-stone quarries, part of which belong to the Indians, and are leased to private individuals Large quantities of lime are exported, giving employment to a great number of hands during the burning season One person alone exported during the year 1844, 5000 barrels of lime, and 270 toise of stone; and the aggregate amount exported, would probably be fully half as much again

There are in the township, two asheries There is a good tavern on the Sandwich road, about two miles above Amherstburg

Population, 608

Ratable property in the township, £4772

ANTRIM

A small Village in the township of Howard, on Lake Erie,—the shipping-port for the surrounding neighbourhood,—contains storehouses for storing produce for shipment, a tavern, &c Vessels are occasionally built and repaired here. Antrim is three and a half miles from Morpeth

ARTEMISIA.

A Township in the Simcoe District, is bounded on the north by Euphrasia; on the west by Glenelg; on the south by Proton, and on the east by Melancthon This township has been added to the Simcoe District since 1844; it is only just laid out, and is not yet opened for sale.

ARTHUR.

A Village in the township of Arthur, at the commencement of the Government settlement on the Owen Sound road, twelve miles above Fergus, on the Canastoga, a branch of the Grand River. Contains 22 inhabitants.

ARTHUR.

A Township in the Wellington District, is bounded on the east by the township of Luther, on the north by Egremont; on the west by Minto; and on the south by Maryborough and Peel This township has only lately been laid out, and no return has yet been made from it. There are as yet but few settlers in it.

ASPHODEL.

A Township in the Colborne District, is bounded on the east by the townships of Seymour and Belmont; on the north by Dummer; on the west by Otonabee; and on the south by the River Trent. In Asphodel 18,441 acres are taken up, 3,315 of which are under cultivation. Much of the land in this township is covered with pine. The village of Norwood is situated in the east of the township, and there are also one grist and two saw-mills, and one distillery. Asphodel is principally settled by Irish Catholics Seven hundred and fifty acres of crown lands are open for sale in the township, at 8s c'y per acre.

Population.

Ratable property in the township, £10,314.

ASHFIELD.

A Township in the Huron District, belonging to the crown Is bounded on the north by crown lands, on the west by Lake Huron, on the south by the township of Colborne and on the east by Wawanosh. This township possesses a fine climate and excellent soil, and is settling very fast. Nearly every lot along the lake shore is taken up. A town plot, comprising 600 acres, is laid out at the entrance of the River Ashfield into Lake Huron. The village is called Albert. A creek enters the lake at the north-west corner of the township. The River Ashfield enters the township at its north-east corner, runs nearly south till within about four miles of the south boundary, then makes a sharp bend, and runs west-south-west till it reaches the lake. In Ashfield 3,722 acres are taken up; of which 228 are under cultivation There is in the township one saw-mill.

Population 266.

Ratable property in the township, £1,325 6s.

Government price for land in this township, 8s currency per acre.

ATHOL

A Township in the Prince Edward District, is bounded on the north by the township of Hallowell, on the East by Marysburgh, and on the south and west by Lake Ontario. Athol contains 22,154 acres, 9760 of which are under cultivation. A bay, called "East Lake," stretches nearly across the north of the township, from south-west to north-east, it is connected with Lake Ontario by means of a small channel A range of high sand banks separates the body of the bay from the lake The village of Bloomfield is situated in the north of this township. There are two water-grist and two saw mills, and one steam-grist mill in Athol.

Population in 1842, 1454

Ratable property in the township, £23,429.

ATHERLY.

A Village in the towship of Mara, laid out in 1843, by Captain Creighton, just below the narrows of Lake Simcoe. There are but few settlers in it at present. There is some fine land in the neighbourhood

AUGUSTA.

A Township in the Johnstown District, is bounded on the east by the township of Edwardsburgh; on the north by Oxford and Walford, on the west by Elizabethtown; and on the south by the river St. Lawrence In Augusta, 44,313 acres are taken up, 17,823 of which are under cultivation. The land bordering on the St. Lawrence, in this township, is generally good; but the back of the township contains much poor land. In Augusta, there are 250 acres of Crown lands for sale. There are six saw mills, one grist mill, and four distilleries in the township. The town of Prescott is situated in the south-east corner of the township, on the St. Lawrence.

Population, 5474.
Ratable property in the township £69,169, which includes the town of Prescott.

AYLMER.

A Village in the township of Malahide, on the Talbot road, twelve miles from St. Thomas, pleasantly situated on Catfish creek, in the midst of a rolling country. It was commenced in 1835, and now contains about 260 inhabitants, who have a neat Baptist chapel.

Post Office, post three times a-week.

Professions and Trades—One physician and surgeon, two tanneries, three stores, three taverns; one ashery and saleratus factory, one watchmaker, two cabinet makers, two saddlers, four blacksmiths, three waggon makers, one tinsmith, four tailors, three shoemakers.

AYR

A Village in the west of the township of Dumfries, situated on Smith's creek, or river Nith, ten miles from Galt. It was laid out in 1839. Population, 230. Ayr contains two churches, Presbyterian

Post Office, post once a-week.

Professions and Trades—One grist mill, fulling mill and carding machine, one tannery, two stores, one blacksmith, two shoemakers, two tailors, one cooper, two carpenters.

BAGOT AND BLITHEFIELD.

Townships in the Bathurst District, which, being but little settled, are at present united together. Bagot lies to the north-east and Blithefield to the south-west They have been formed out of the township of Madawaska; and are bounded on the north-east by McNab; on the north-west by Adamston; on the west by unsurveyed lands, and on the south-east by Levant and Darling. In Bagot and Blithefield 9,172 acres are taken up, 1,020 of which are under cultivation. In Bagot 65,900 acres, and in Blithefield 30,150 acres of crown lands are open for sale, at 8s. currency per acre There is one saw-mill in the township. There is no return of population for these townships.

Ratable property in the township, £4,047.

BALDOON.

A Settlement in the township of Dover, which was originally made under the auspices of the Earl of Selkirk, who caused a road to be cut out from the settlement to the river Thames The situation, however, was not well chosen, being too low, and liable to ague, consequently it has not increased very fast, or made much progress in improvement.

BALSAM LAKE

A Lake in the north-west of the Colborne District The most northerly of a chain of lakes running through the Colborne and Newcastle Districts.

BARTON.

A Township in the Gore District; is bounded on the east by the township of Saltfleet, on the north by Lake Ontario and Burlington Bay; on the west by Ancaster; and on the south by Glanford. In Barton, 15,392 acres are taken up, 8993 of which are under cultivation. This township is small, but it is well settled, and a large portion of it is under cultivation. The land is generally good, although the soil on the banks of the lake and bay is light. Timber,—maple, black walnut, beech, oak, &c, with a small quantity of pine. The town of Hamilton is situated in the township, on Burlington Bay. There are one grist and five saw mills in the township

Population in 1841, 1434.

Ratable property in the township, £13,873.

BARTONVILLE.

A small Settlement in the township of Barton, situated on the St. Catherine's road, four miles from Hamilton. It contains two taverns and about ten houses.

BARRIE.

So called after Commodore Barrie, the District town of the Simcoe District: is beautifully situated at the head of Kempenfeldt Bay, in the township of Vespra, thirty-two miles from Holland Landing, and forty miles from Penetanguishine. Barrie was first settled in the year 1832; in 1837 it contained about twenty-eight families. In 1843 the county of Simcoe, until then part of the Home District, was declared a separate district, with Barrie for its district town. Since then it has increased rapidly. The situation was well chosen and is healthy. Should the contemplated canal from the bay to Lake Huron, through Willow Creek and the Nottawasaga River, ever be formed, Barrie, which is now truly in the woods, will have uninterrupted water communication with the St. Lawrence. At present, the road from Barrie to the Holland Landing, is, in the spring and fall, almost impassable for waggons. The road to Penetanguishine is much better, running for the most part along a stony ridge of land. The mail, during the spring and autumn, is carried on horse-back; and through the summer, partly on horseback, and partly by water. A new steamboat, the "Beaver," was launched during the summer of 1844: she is an excellent boat, and has good accommodation. The banks of the bay have a rather sombre appearance, being almost totally devoid of clearing: most of the timber on the banks is pine. Town lots, of a quarter of an acre, in the old survey (or original town-plot) are in the hands of private individuals, and sell at from £20 to £50, some higher. An addition has lately been made to the town-plot, and the lots in the new survey sell at from £5 to £12 10s. each; they are mostly in the hands of the Crown. The public buildings are the jail and court-house. The jail is a handsome stone building; the court-house is of brick, and has *no beauty* to boast of; the two cost the district nearly £9,000. There are three churches and chapels: viz. one Episcopal and two Methodist. There is an excellent district school (where private pupils are taken); a mechanics' institute, and a cricket club.

The inhabitants are principally English, Irish and Scotch, and number about 500.

The following government and district offices are kept in Barrie: Judge of District Court, Sheriff, Clerk of Peace, Registrar, Inspector of Licenses, Crown Lands Agent, District Clerk, Clerk of District Court, Deputy Clerk of Crown.

Professions and Trades.—One physician and surgeon, one lawyer, six stores, three tanneries, one surveyor, three taverns, four blacksmiths, one waggon maker, one baker, one saddler, one cabinet maker, one watchmaker, six shoemakers, three tailors, two butchers, one bank agency "Upper Canada."

Agent for Home District Mutual Fire Insurance Company.—W. B. Smith.

Steamboat Fares:—

    To Holland Landing...... 8s. 9d. c'y.   To Orillia ...... 8s. 9d.
    To ditto by Orillia ....11s. 3d.   Shorter distances in proportion.

Principal Tavern.—"The Queen's Arms."

BARRYFIELD.

A Village in the township of Pittsburg, situated on the Cataraqui Bay, opposite Kingston. It is irregularly built on a rising ground, having a blue limestone foundation. From the high ground in the neighbourhood of the village, on which Fort Henry is situated, a fine view may be obtained of the bay, Lake Ontario, Kingston, and the surrounding country. Barryfield contains about 300 inhabitants, two small stores, three taverns, two blacksmiths, and one shoemaker.

BASTARD.

A Township in the Johnstown District ; is bounded on the north-east by the township of Kitley , on the north-west by South Burgess and the Rideau Lake ; on the south-west by South Crosby ; and on the south-east by Lansdowne. In Bastard, 40,422 acres are taken up, 10,484 of which are under cultivation. This is a well settled township, containing good farms ; much of the land is of excellent quality, but that portion bordering on the lake is poor and mostly stoney , and there is considerable pine in the township   In Bastard, 900 acres of Crown lands are open for sale, at 8s. per acre.   There are two grist and five saw mills in the township
Population in 1842, 3058.
Ratable property in the township, £33,364

BATHURST

A Township in the Bathurst District ; is bounded on the north-east by the township of Drummond ; on the north-west by Dalhousie ; on the south-west by Sherbrooke , and on the south-east by Burgess.   In Bathurst, 32,635 acres are taken up, 8725 of which are under cultivation.   The south branch, and a smaller stream, called the middle branch, of the Mississippi, run through the north-west of the township from south-west to north east ; they unite in the north corner of the township   The south branch, soon after its entrance into the township, expands into a small lake.   The river Tay, a branch of the Mississippi, stretches across the south-east border of the township, at the eastern corner of which it is joined by Grant's Creek   The base of the north of the township is principally marble, varying in colour from pure white to dark grey. The south of the township is granite   In the south of the township is an iron mine, the ore of which is said to be very rich   There are some good farms in the township   Three thousand five hundred acres of Crown Lands are open for sale in Bathurst, at 8s. currency, per acre.   There are five grist and nine saw mills in the township
Population in 1842, 2307
Ratable property in the township, 26,858.

BATHURST DISTRICT.

Consists of the counties of Lanark and Renfrew, which are united so far as relates to representation in the Legislative Assembly, and return one member. The Bathurst District is bounded on the north by the Ottawa river, and is also watered by the Mississippi river and lakes, the Madawaska river, and the river Bonne-Chaur; besides numerous small streams scattered over it, and it is thickly studded with lakes, varying in size   Beds of marble, of various shades of colour, from pure white to dark grey, extend through the townships of Lanark, Dalhousie and North Sherbrooke, and from thence into the Midland District. Fine white freestone and limestone are abundant in the district , and also granite, which however, has not yet been brought into use , and rich iron ore has been discovered within a few miles of Perth   Much of the land in the district is of good quality.   Timber—a mixture of hardwood and pine.   The settlers are generally industrious and thriving ; many of them are Scotch. Perth. the district town, is a flourishing place, with many good buildings.   Four hundred and eighty thousand two hundred acres of Crown lands are open for sale in the Bathurst district, at 8s. currency, per acre , to purchase any of which, application must be made to the Crown lands' agent at Perth.

Population in 1842, 21,672 ; since when it has probably increased one-fifth,

The following abstract from the assessment rolls will show the rate of increase and improvement in the district :—

Date.	No. of Acres Cultivated.	MILLS. Grist.	MILLS. Saw.	Milch Cows	Oxen, 4 years old, and upwards.	Horned Cattle, from 2 to 4 years old.	Amount of Ratable Property.
1842	74228	22	34	7241	2748	3530	No Return.
1843	81999	23	39	8121	3036	3882	£263,691
1844	87809	21	43	8541	3068	3041	276,063

Government and District Officers in the Bathurst District :

OFFICE.	NAMES.	RESIDENCE.
Judge of District Court, and Judge of Surrogate Court	John G. Malloch	Perth.
Sheriff	Andrew Dickson	Pakenham.
Clerk of Peace	John Macdonald	Perth.
Treasurer	T. M. Radenhurst	Do.
Inspector of Licenses	A. Leslie	Do.
Crown Lands' Agent	Do.	Do.
Registrar of County of Lanark	Alex. McMillan	Do.
Superintendent of Schools	Rev. —— Mann	Do.
District Clerk	Robert Moffatt	Do.
Clerk of District Court, and Deputy Clerk of Crown	Chas. S. Sache	Do.
Warden	Daniel McMartin	Do.
Coroner	Thos. Brooke	Do.

Number of Common Schools in operation in the District.—Bathurst, twelve; Beckwith, nine; Burgess, two; Dalhousie, six; Darling, two; Drummond, sixteen; North Elmsley, eight; Horton, three; Lanark, twelve; Montague, nine; McNab, seven; Pakenham, four; Ramsay, twelve; North Sherbrooke, one; Bagot, two; Bromley, two; Pembroke, one; Westmeath, two. Total 110.

BAYHAM.

A Township in the London District: is bounded on the east by the townships of Houghton and Middleton; on the north by Dereham; on the west by Malahide; and on the south by Lake Erie. In Bayham, 40,192 acres are taken up, 7,907 of which are under cultivation. Big Otter Creek enters the township near its north-east corner, runs south-west to its western border, where it enters the township of Malahide, makes a semicircular bend, and re-enters the township of Bayham, and runs a south-east course till it reaches Lake Erie. This is one of the finest mill streams in Canada, and there is a large quantity of fine pine on its banks. The village of Richmond is situated in Bayham, on Talbot Street. There are three grist and twenty-five saw mills in the township.

Population in 1842, 2,250.

Ratable property in the township, 34,591.

BAYFIELD.

A Village on Lake Huron, at the entrance of the River Bayfield, twelve miles below Goderich. It was laid out in 1834, by the Baron de Tuylle, who purchased the land of the Canada Company. The banks of the river and lake are here about sixty or seventy feet high. Bayfield has two taverns.

Population about 150.

BAYFIELD RIVER.

Takes its rise in the great swamp north of the Huron Tract, runs through the townships of McKillop and Tuckersmith, divides the townships of Goderich and Stanley, and enters Lake Huron twelve miles below Goderich, at the village of Bayfield

BEACHVILLE

A Village in the township of West Oxford, situated on the east branch of the River Thames, 5 miles west from Woodstock, on the plank road. It contains nearly 300 inhabitants. Churches and chapels, three viz Episcopal, Catholic and Methodist.

Post Office, post every day.

Professions and Trades —One grist mill, two saw ditto, carding machine and fulling mill, distillery, two stores, two taverns, one fanning mill maker, one chair factory, two tanneries, one cabinet maker, two waggon makers, two shoemakers, two blacksmiths and two tailors.

BEAMSVILLE.

A Village in the township of Clinton, situated on the St. Catharine's road, twenty-two miles from Hamilton. Much has been written respecting a spring in the neighbourhood, which is said to freeze over during the hottest part of the summer, and to thaw in the winter When in the neighbourhood during the last winter, I was unable to visit the spot, but I was informed by a gentleman living at Beamsville (and who I believe to be good authority), that he had visited the place frequently, and that there was in reality *no spring whatever* there. He stated, that the supposed spring was situated in a cave, in the side of the mountain, the bottom of which is about four feet below the level of the ground; that the only water in the cave is that deposited by continual drippings from the roof above; that he has frequently visited the cave in summer, and has on such occasions dug lumps of ice out of the crevices in the rocks which form the floor of the cave. That he has on all such visits found the bottom of the cave thickly covered with dead leaves (which must have been blown in), and which he has had to remove before getting at the ice, and he supposes the ice to be formed during the winter, and preserved through the summer, as in an ice-house But he has never visited the place during the winter, to ascertain the fact, nor does he know any one who has This, however, seems a rational explanation of a circumstance that at first view would appear rather a singular phenomenon. The cave is about two miles east from the village, and about three-quarters of a mile from the road There are three churches and chapels in the village, viz Presbyterian, Methodist and Baptist. Population about 250. Post office, post every day.

Professions and Trades —One physician and surgeon, four general stores, two hardware ditto, two taverns, two foundries, one of which has a steam engine, one bookseller and druggist, one tannery, one chair maker, one baker, one saddler, two blacksmiths, one cabinet maker, two tailors, two shoemakers, three waggon makers.

BEAR CREEK,

Or River Sydenham is divided into two branches The east, or principal branch, takes its rise in the township of Lobo or London, runs through the south east of Adelaide, the north-west of Mosa, enters Zone near its north-east corner, and leaves it near the south-west corner, after which it runs nearly due west, through the townships of Dawn and Sombra, till it reaches the Chenail Ecarté, or "*Sny Carte,*" as it is commonly called, a branch of the River St. Clair. The north branch takes its rise in the township of Warwick, and runs southwest across the township of Enniskillen, and to about the centre of the township of Sombra, where it makes a bend, and runs due south till it reaches the east branch, the two forming what is called the "Forks" of Bear Creek, which is about nine miles from the River St. Clair.. Some of the best land in Canada is situated in the townships bordering on the river After getting a few miles above the forks, the land becomes rolling, and heavily timbered, and the banks higher; but below the forks there is a considerable extent of marsh and prairie, which although useful enough for grazing cattle, is too liable to produce ague to make it a fit neighbourhood to settle in, particularly for European emigrants. Both branches are navigable for large vessels the east branch about nine miles, and the north about five miles above the forks, the water ranging in depth from ten to twenty five feet. At the forks is a hole about forty feet in depth.

BEAVERTON.

A Village in the township of Thorah, on the bank of Lake Simcoe, contains about half a dozen houses. The steamboat "Beaver" touches here, but cannot approach the shore, the water on the bank being too shallow

Post Office, post twice a-week

BECKWITH

A Township in the Bathurst District, is bounded on the north-east by the township of Goulburn; on the north-west by Ramsay, on the south-west by Drummond, and on the south-east by Montague In Beckwith, 36,671 acres are taken up, 8131 of which are under cultivation. The Mississippi lake fills up a large portion of the west corner of the township Just above the lake on the Mississippi river. is a village, called Carleton Place; and in the south-east of the township is a village, called Franktown In the south-west of the township are fine white freestone quarries. In Beckwith, 6100 acres of Crown lands are for sale. There are one grist mill, one saw do, and two distilleries in the township

Population in 1842, 1898.

Ratable property in the township, £25.419.

BEDFORD

A Township in the Midland District, is bounded on the east by South Sherbrooke, and North and South Crosby, on the north by Oso, on the west by Hinchinbrooke; and on the south by Loughborough and Pittsburg. In Bedford, 8990 acres are taken up, 1389 of which are under cultivation. A lake in the north-east of the township, is called Wolf Lake, and a number of lakes, varying in size, most of which are connected together by means of small streams, are scattered over the south of the township. Bedford is but little settled, much of the land being of poor quality; the timber principally pine. There are four saw mills in the township Eight thousand acres of Crown lands are open for sale in Bedford, at 8s. currency, per acre

Population, 552.

Ratable property in the township, £4626.

BELLAMY, or NORTH AUGUSTA

A Village situated in the east of the township of North Augusta; it contains about fifty inhabitants, one store, two taverns, one ashery, one tannery, one blacksmith.

BELLE RIVER.

Takes it rise in Gosfield, and forms the dividing boundary of the townships of Maidstone and Rochester, running in nearly a straight line from south to north. It is several feet deep for some miles before entering the lake.

BELLE POINT.

A small point of land, in the south-west corner of Mersea, jutting out into Lake Erie.

BELLEVILLE.

The District Town of the Victoria District, is situated in the south-west corner of the township of Thurlow, on the Bay of Quinté, 50 miles west from Kingston, It is a bustling, thriving little town, and a place of considerable business The greater portion of the town lies rather low ; but it possesses many good buildings It was incorporated in 1835, and now contains 2040 inhabitants. The jail and court house is a handsome stone building, and is erected on a rising ground in the rear of the town There are seven churches and chapels, viz., Episcopal (brick), Catholic (stone), two Presbyterian, three Methodist, (one of which is of brick)

The Kingston and Toronto stages pass through the town daily ; and, during the season, a steamboat calls daily, on its passage to and from Trent and Kingston. These boats stay every night at Picton

Two weekly newspapers are published here, the " Belleville Intelligencer," and " Victoria Chronicle." There is a fire company, with two engines, and a hook and ladder company

Post Office, post every day.

The following Government and District offices are kept in Belleville :—Judge of District Court, Sheriff, Clerk of Peace, Treasurer, Registrar of County of Hastings, Inspector of Licenses, Crown Lands' Agent, Collector of Customs, Inspector of Potash. District Clerk, Clerk of District Court.

Professions and Trades—Five physicians and surgeons, seven lawyers, two grist mills, one steam saw mill, three water do, three cloth factories, one paper mill, one planing machine, three foundries, two breweries, three tanneries, one ashery, one soap and candle factory, one pail factory, two axe factories, eighteen dry goods stores, fourteen groceries, seventeen taverns, two surveyors, two auctioneers, one chair factory, three chemists and druggists, two booksellers, two printers, five saddlers, three watchmakers, four waggon makers, two livery stables, one furrier, six painters, four hatters, twenty-one tailors, twenty-two shoemakers, eight blacksmiths, one gunsmith, four tinsmiths, six cabinet makers, two confectioners, two barbers. Bank agencies, " Montreal," and " Commercial." Principal tavern, " Munro's "

In consequence of the short-sighted policy of some of the merchants in Belleville, who refused to allow any account of the produce shipped from the place to be published, on the plea, that the exports were so large, that the publication of their amount would immediately cause the town to be inundated with fresh stores, to the loss of the merchants already established there, I am unable to give any list of exports from Belleville, with the exception of potash, the returns of which I obtained from the inspector

Quantity of Potash shipped from Belleville, during the year 1844......2711 brls.

    Stage fare to Kingston   £0 10 0
    Do to Cobourg......... . 0 12 6

BELMONT.

A Township in the Colborne District is bounded on the east by the township of Marmora, on the north by Methuen, on the west by Dummer ; and on the south by Seymour. In Belmont, 2670 acres are taken up, 365 of which are under cultivation. This is a poor township, and much of it unfit for cultivation, being rocky. A large lake, with its branches, occupies a considerable portion of the centre and east of the township In Belmont, 4837 acres of Crown lands are open for sale at 8s currency, per acre.

Population, —

Ratable property in the township, £1159.

BENTINCK.

A Township in the Wellington District ; is bounded on the east by the township of Glenelg, on the north by Sullivan, on the west by wild land ; and on the south by Normanby. This township has only lately been surveyed and laid out, and no return has yet been made from it

BERLIN.

A Village in the township of Waterloo, nine miles from Galt; contains about 400 inhabitants, who are principally Germans. A newspaper is printed here, called the "German Canadian," and there is a Lutheran meeting-house
Post Office, post twice a-week.

Professions and Trades —One physician and surgeon, one lawyer, three stores, one brewery, one printing office, two taverns, one pump maker, two blacksmiths.

BERTIE.

A Township in the Niagara District, is bounded on the east and north-east by the Niagara river; on the north by the township of Willoughby; on the west by Humberstone, and on the south by Lake Erie. In Bertie, 33,320 acres are taken up, 12,498 of which are under cultivation. This is an old-settled township. The village of Waterloo, and Fort Erie, are situated in Bertie, on the Niagara river; and trere are two grist and seven saw mills in the township.

Population in 1841, 2318, who are principally Pennsylvanian Dutch, and their descendants.

Ratable property in the township, £36,066.

BEVERLY.

A Village situated in the south-west corner of the township of Bastard, contains about sixty inhabitants, grist and saw mill, and carding machine, one store, one tavern

BEVERLY.

A Township in the Gore District; is bounded on the north-east by the township of Flamboro; on the north by Puslinch, on the west by Dumfries; and on the south by Ancaster. In Beverly, 52,159 acres are taken up, 16,332 of which are under cultivation. This is a well settled township, possessing fine farms. The land varies in quality, some parts being heavy, with hardwood timber, and others light soil, with pine timber There are two or three excellent mill streams in the township, on which are one grist and eleven saw mills.

Population in 1841, 2684.

Ratable property in the township, £67,488

BEXLEY.—(*See* FENELON)

BIDDULPH.

A Township in the Huron District, is bounded on the north and north-east by Usborn and Blanshard; on the west by Stephen and McGillivray; and on the south-east by London. Biddulph is laid out in the form of a triangle A branch of the Sable river runs through the township Biddulph contains 40,748 acres, 23,308 of which are leased or sold, of which 1740 acres are under cultivation.

Population, 1009.

Ratable property in the township, £8354 12s.

BIG ISLAND —(*See* SOPHIASBURGH)

BINBROOK

A Township in the Niagara District, is bounded on the east by the township of Caistor; on the north by Saltfleet, on the west by Glanford, and on the south by Seneca. In Binbrook, 17,477 acres are taken up, 6357 of which are under cultivation This is a small, well-settled township The Welland river runs through the south of it There are three saw mills in the township.

Population in 1841, 712.

Ratable property in the township, £23,279.

BLANDFORD.

A Township in the Brock District; is bounded on the east by the township of Blenheim; on the north by Wilmot, on the west by Zorra; and on the south by Oxford. In Blandford, 13,109 acres are taken up, 2653 of which are under cultivation The timber of Blandford is principally pine. In the south of the township, on and about the line between Blandford and Blenheim, are several ponds or small lakes, varying in size from 50 to 200 acres, and surrounded by considerable swamp. The town of Woodstock is in the south-west corner of the township.

Population of Blandford, 733, who are principally emigrants from Europe.
Ratable property in the township, £10,224.

BLANSHARD.

A Township in the Huron District, is bounded on the north-east by Fullarton and Downie, on the north-west by Usborne. on the south-west by Biddulph; and on the south-east by Nissouri The north branch of the river Thames runs through this township Blanshard contains 50,396 acres, 26,468 of which are leased or sold, of which 619 are under cultivation. There are in the township one grist mill and one saw mill.

Population, 972.
Ratable property in the township, £7821

BLENHEIM

A Village in the township of Harwich, recently laid out by Colonel Little, on the road leading from Chatham to the Rond'Eau, at the point where it crosses the Talbot road Distant from Chatham, ten miles, and from the Rond'Eau, four and a half The situation is healthy, being on a gravelly soil, at an elevation of 117 feet above the level of the lake. It contains a tavern. Village lots are sold at from £5 to £7. 10s.

BLENHEIM

A Township in the Brock District; is bounded on the east by the township of Dumfries; on the north by Wilmot, on the west by Blandford; and on the south by Burford In Blenheim, 35,985 acres are taken up, 10,882 of which are under cultivation A large swamp extends across the township, dividing it into two portions. The land on the north side of the swamp is good, with hardwood timber, and on the south side the land is poor, timber principally pine. The village of Princeton is situated in the south of the township, near the centre. of the town line between Blenheim and Burford; and the village of Canning, near the south-east corner. There are one grist and fourteen saw mills in the township

Blenheim contains a mixed population of 1772
Ratable property in the township, £29,615.

BLOOMFIELD.

A Village in the north of the township of Athol contains about one hundred inhabitants, who have two Quaker meeting houses There are in the village two grist and saw mills, carding machine and woollen factory, and two stores.

BOGART-TOWN —(See KING)

BOIS BLANC ISLAND.

A long, narrow Island in the Detroit River, opposite Amherstburg. It contains about 230 acres of land, all of which are fit for cultivation. It *was* thickly wooded, but the timber was cut down, during the rebellion, in order to give the forts a greater command of the channel on the American side. There are three block-houses on the island, which are garrisoned by British soldiers. On the south point of the island, which commands a view of Lake Erie, is a light-house.

BOND HEAD.

A small Village in the township of West Gwillimbury, six miles west from Bradford. It contains about 100 inhabitants, who are principally Highland Scotch; two stores, two taverns, two wheelwrights, one tannery, two blacksmiths, two shoemakers, one tailor.

Post Office, post once a-week.

BOND HEAD.

A Village and Shipping-place on Lake Ontario, one and a half miles from the village of Newcastle ; contains about fifty or sixty houses, which are very much scattered , about one-third of which are unoccupied , no store open ; one tavern open ; two or three shut up. There is a considerable quantity of marsh about the harbour. There is in the village an Episcopal Church, and a grist mill

Exports from Bond Head Harbour during 1844

Wheat	24,000 bushels.
Oats	950 do.
Flour	2,065 barrels.
Pork	28 do.
Potash	50 do.
Pearlash	41 do.
Whiskey	82 do.
Lumber	70,000 feet.
Butter	10 kegs.
Lard	6 do.
Potatoes	290 bushels.
Oxen	4

BOND'S LAKE

A small Lake situated close to Yonge street, partly in the township of Whitchurch, and partly in King. It is twenty-two miles from Toronto.

BOSANQUET.

A Township in the Western District , is bounded on the east by the townships of Williams, McGillivray and a small portion of Stephen , on the north-west by Lake Huron ; and on the south by Warwick and Plympton. In Bosanquet, 3490 acres are taken up, 295 of which are under cultivation Bosanquet originally formed a portion of the Huron Tract, but it has been since added to the Western District. The river Aux Sables divides the township from Williams and McGillivray on the east, and Stephen on the east and north. At the northern extremity of the township it makes a sudden bend, and then runs parallel with Lake Huron, at an average distance of half a mile, for ten miles, when it enters the lake. Mud Creek enters the river at about a mile from its mouth ; and Lake Burwell, which is in fact two lakes connected together by a narrow gut, is situated about three miles from Lake Huron, in the triangle formed by the bend of the river , its northern extremity is about three miles from the north boundary of the township , it is about four miles long, by about two broad, and is surrounded by a considerable extent of marsh , it has never been surveyed. A ridge of sand hills, about three miles wide, extends from the mouth of the Sable river to the extremity of the township. There is a great deal of low, swampy land on the borders of the river, for about two miles from its mouth. A point of the coast, called " Kettle Point," about five miles below the mouth of the Sable river, has excited considerable curiosity, from its being constantly on fire.

The land in the south of the township is of fine quality. For the first four miles above Plympton, the banks of the lake are high , afterwards they become low and rocky, up to Kettle Point ; and then they become low and sandy.

After leaving Kettle Point, the timber is principally pine. A saw mill was established at the north bend of the river, soon after the first settlement of the district. There is an Indian reserve near Kettle Point, and another about three miles above.

No separate census has yet been taken of this township.

Ratable property in the township, £1418.

BOUCHER'S MILLS, OR SUTTON MILLS.

A small Village in the township of Georgina, about two miles from Lake Simcoe, and twenty-three miles from Holland Landing; contains about one hundred inhabitants. There are in the settlement, a grist and saw mill, tannery, store, tavern, one blacksmith, and two shoemakers.

BOWMANVILLE.

A Village in the township of Darlington, situated on the eastern road, nine miles east from Oshawa. The village is prettily situated, being built on the sides of two hills, with a mill stream running through the hollow which divides the village. It contains about 500 inhabitants; churches and chapels, five, viz., Episcopal, Free Church, Congregational, Canadian Wesleyan, and Christian.

Post Office, post every day.

Professions and Trades.—One physician and surgeon, one grist mill, one oatmeal do., one tannery, one distillery, one carding machine and cloth factory, one axe factory, one ashery, seven stores, four taverns, one brewery, one druggist, one pottery, two waggon makers, three blacksmiths, one chair factory, two bakers, two watchmakers, six shoemakers, six tailors.

BRADFORD.

A Village in the township of West Gwillimbury, 4 miles from Holland Landing, and twenty-two from Barrie. The road from the Landing to Bradford passes over the Holland river, and a large swamp bordering it, where a causeway has been constructed nearly a mile in length, with a floating bridge in its centre. The road between the two places has been macadamised, and a toll-gate placed on it. Bradford was laid out in the year 1830, and it now contains 250 inhabitants. Churches and chapels, two; Presbyterian and Methodist.

Post Office, post three times a-week.

Professions and Trades.—One steam saw mill, one tannery, one distillery, three stores, three taverns, two blacksmiths, two cabinet makers, two tailors, two waggon makers, one gunsmith, one saddler, one pump maker, two shoemakers.

BRAMPTON.

A Village in the township of Chinguacousy, situated on the Centre road, in the south of the township; contains about 150 inhabitants.

Post Office, post twice a-week.

Professions and Trades.—Two stores, one tavern, one tannery, one cabinet maker, two blacksmiths, two tailors.

BRANTFORD.

A Town in the township of Brantford, situated on the Grand River, 23½ miles from Hamilton. It was laid out by the crown in 1830, and is a place of considerable business. A canal, two miles and a-half in length, has been constructed from Brantford to below the falls of the Grand River, which will be capable of admitting and allowing vessels drawing three feet and a-half water to reach the town. The fall in the river between the town and the termination of the canal, is about twenty-three feet, which has been overcome by means of three locks. During the last two seasons, a steamer ran regularly three times a-week from the entrance of the canal to Dunnville (fare $1½). The Western road runs through the town. Brantford contains eight churches and chapels, viz., Episcopal,

Presbyterian, Catholic, two Methodist, Baptist, Congregationalist, and one for coloured people; also a Fire Company with an engine, and a Mechanics' Institute. A weekly newspaper is published here, the "Brantford Courier."
Population about 2,000   Post Office, post daily.

Professions and Trades —Three physicians and surgeons, four lawyers, three grist mills, carding machine and fulling mill, foundry, two surveyors, two breweries, four distilleries, twenty-one stores, one soap and candle factory, fourteen taverns, two druggists, one printer, twelve groceries, two watchmakers, three tinsmiths, seven tailors, ten shoemakers, five painters, five cabinet makers, two livery stables, one gunsmith, one tobacconist, one marble factory, three barbers, two ladies' schools, two do. for boys, three bank agencies—"B. N. America," "Montreal," and "Gore."

Principal Taverns —"Clements," "Irish's," and "Matthews."
Land Agent.—Jas R Buchanan.

BRANTFORD.

A Township in the Gore District, is bounded on the east by the townships of Ancaster and Onondaga; on the north by Dumfries, on the west by Burford, and on the south by Oakland In Brantford 58,035 acres are taken up, 42,273 of which are under cultivation This is a fine township, containing good land, and numerous well cultivated farms A larger amount of land is under cultivation in Brantford, in proportion to the quantity taken up, than in any other township in the province. The Grand River runs completely through the township, on which, in about the centre of the township, is situated the flourishing town of Brantford, and the settlement of Mount Pleasant is in the south of the township In the west of Brantford much of the land is of that description called oak plains, light land, easy of cultivation, and under proper management, growing superior wheat   There are six grist mills and six saw mills in the township.
Population in 1841, 5199.
Ratable property in the township, £114,437

BRIDGEPORT.

A Village in the township of Waterloo, opposite Glasgow, contains about 100 inhabitants, one store, one ashery, one tavern, one blacksmith.

BRIGHTON

A Village in the township of Murray, formerly called Newcastle, situated on the eastern road, twenty-four miles east of Cobourg, contains a population of about 200.
Post Office, post every day.
Professions and Trades.—Grist-mill, tannery, ashery, two stores, two taverns, one saddler, one shoemaker, one tailor.

BRITANNIA.

A Settlement in the north of the township of Nepean, situated on the Ottawa River. It has only lately been laid out, and contains very few houses.

BROCK

A Township in the Home District ; is bounded on the east by the township of Mariposa , on the north by Thorah , on the west by Georgina and Scott ; and on the south by Reach. In Brock, 38,368 acres are taken up, 7667 of which are under cultivation   The Black River runs through nearly the centre of the township from south to north. Brock contains a fair proportion of good land, and is becoming well settled. There are two grist and three saw mills in

the township. One thousand acres of Crown lands are open for sale in Brock, at 8s. currency, per acre.
Population in 1842, 1541.
Ratable property in the township, £20,787.

BROCK DISTRICT.

Consists of the county of Oxford, which returns a member to the House of Assembly, and comprises the townships of Blandford, Blenheim, Burford, Dereham, Nissouri, North Oxford, East Oxford, West Oxford, Oakland, Norwich, East Zorra, and West Zorra. This is a fine district, containing excellent land, most of it high, and much of it rolling; and many well cultivated farms. It is watered by branches of the Grand River, the Thames, Otter Creek, and Catfish Creek, besides numerous small streams scattered over the district. The soil of the district varies much in quality; but a large portion of it is good land, fit for cultivation. The Brock District is settled principally by emigrants from Great Britain and Ireland, many of them English. Improvements have been going on slowly, but gradually; and some of the most beautifully situated farms in Canada are to be found in the neighbourhood of Woodstock, the district town. There are no Crown lands for sale in this district.

Population of the Brock District in 1842, 16,271; since when it has probably increased one-fifth.

The following abstract from the assessment rolls will show the rate of increase and improvement in the district:—

Date.	No. of Acres Cultivated.	MILLS. Grist.	MILLS. Saw.	Milch Cows.	Oxen, 4 years old, and upwards.	Horned Cattle, from 2 to 4 years old.	Amount of Ratable Property.
1842	67397	13	46	6790	2941	3924	£220,335
1843	......	...	...	......	......	......	......
1844	83046	15	53	7248	3357	3944	250,344

Government and District Officers in the Brock District:

OFFICE.	NAMES.	RESIDENCE.
Judge of District Court	D. S. McQueen	Woodstock.
Sheriff	James Carroll	Do.
Clerk of Peace	Wm. Lapenotiere	Do.
Judge of Surrogate Court	Do.	Do.
Registrar of do.	John G. Vansittart	Do.
Treasurer	H. C. Barwick	Do.
Registrar of County	James Ingersoll	Ingersoll.
Inspector of Licenses	John G. Vansittart	Woodstock
Crown Lands' Agent	John Carroll	Zorra.
District Clerk	W. Lapenotiere	Woodstock
Clerk to District Court	John G. Vansittart	Do.
Deputy Clerk of Crown	Do.	Do.
Coroners	S. J. Stratford & J. Turquand	Do.
Warden	Geo. W. Whitehead	Burford.
District Superintendent of Schools	Geo. Hendry	Woodstock.
Auditors	Jno. McF. Wilson & V. Hall	Do.

In consequence of the absence of the Superintendent, I was unable to procure a list of the schools in this district.

BROCKVILLE.

The District Town of the Johnstown District, in the county of Leeds, situated on the St Lawrence, fifty-six miles east from Kingston, the eastern road passing through it. It was laid out in 1802, and is now incorporated. This is a handsome town, most of the houses and other buildings being constructed of stone, many of which have cut fronts Being situated on a bed of lime stone, this material is found the cheapest that can be used for building, and its general adoption gives the town a very substantial appearance. Granite is also to be obtained in the immediate neighbourhood of the town, but being harder to work is not at present used The court house and jail is a handsome stone building There are six churches and chapels, viz, Episcopal, Catholic, Presbyterian, Methodist, Baptist and Congregational, all of which are of stone. During the season, the steamboats call here regularly, on their passages to and from Montreal and Kingston. A road is constructed from this place to Perth, the capital of the Bathurst District, which is about 40 miles north-west Two newspapers are published here weekly, the "Statesman," and the "Brockville Recorder." On an island, or rather rock, in the St. Lawrence, opposite the town, is a block house, where there are stationed a few rifles.

Population 2111.

Post Office, post every day

The following government and district offices are kept in Brockville Judge of District Court, Sheriff, Treasurer, Clerk of Peace, Registrar of County of Leeds, do of Surrogate Court, Collector of Customs, Inspector of Licenses, Superintendent of Schools, Clerk of District Court, District Clerk, Deputy Clerk of Crown

Professions and Trades.—Three physicians and surgeons, seven lawyers, one grist mill, eighteen stores, four tanneries, two asheries, one bookseller, one brewery, one foundry, two printers, two saw mills, three chemists and druggists, ten taverns, four waggon makers, four blacksmiths, two tinsmiths, two gunsmiths, two watchmakers, two saddlers, six tailors, eight shoemakers, three cabinet makers, six groceries, two hatters, four bakers, three painters, two bank agencies —" Montreal," and "Commercial"

Forwarders and Commission Merchants.—Sanderson & Murray, H. & S. Jones.
Land Agent.—Andrew N. Buell.
Principal Tavern —"Wilson's."

BROMLEY.

A Township in the Bathurst District; has been divided off from the township of Ross, and is bounded on the north-east by Ross; on the north-west by Stafford, on the west by unsurveyed lands, and on the south-east by Admaston. In Bromley 9614 acres are taken up, 770 of which are under cultivation This township is as yet but little settled, and 41,500 acres of Crown Lands are open for sale in it. There is one saw mill in the township

Population not returned.

Ratable property in the township, £3399.

BRONTE.

A small Village in the township of Trafalgar, on the Lake Shore Road, seven miles from Wellington Square, situated on the Twelve-mile Creek. It contains about 100 inhabitants, grist and saw mills, one store, two taverns, one waggon maker, one blacksmith, one cabinet maker

BROOKE.

A Township in the Western District, is bounded on the east by Adelaide and Mosa; on the north by Warwick, on the west by Plympton and Ennis-

killen; and on the south by Zone. In Brooke 3412 acres are taken up, 404 of which are under cultivation. The north branch of Bear Creek runs through the north-west corner of the township. This township is as yet but little settled: there are some wet places in it, but a large proportion of the land is of good quality. Fifteen thousand seven hundred acres of Crown lands are open for sale in Brooke, at 8s. currency per acre. There is one grist and one saw mill in the township.
Population, 169.
Ratable property in the township, £1602.

BROWNSVILLE.

A small Village in the township of King, one mile and a half north-east of Lloydtown, contains about sixty inhabitants. There are in Brownsville one grist and saw mill, one tavern, one store, one blacksmith.

BURFORD.

A Township in the Brock District; is bounded on the east by the townships of Brantford and Oakland; on the north by Blenheim, on the west by Oxford and Norwich; and on the south by Windham. In Burford 39,255 acres are taken up, 13,683 of which are under cultivation. The north of the township consists principally of oak plains—a description of land easily cultivated, and, under proper management, growing excellent wheat. In the south of the township the timber is mostly pine. There is a large swamp near the south-east corner. There are one grist and nine saw mills in the township.
Population in 1842, 2,314.
Ratable property in the township, £35,856

BURGESS, SOUTH

A Township in the Johnstown District; is bounded on the north-east by the township of South Elmsley, on the north-west and west by the Rideau Lake; and on the south-east by Bastard. In South Burgess 3,226 acres are taken up, 294 of which are under cultivation. This is a very small township, and it is but little settled. One thousand three hundred acres of Crown lands are open for sale in South Burgess, at 8s. currency per acre.
The population of Burgess is included in that of Bastard, no separate return having been made.
Ratable property in the township, £1,228

BURGESS, NORTH.

A Township in the Bathurst District, is bounded on the north-east by the township of Elmsley, on the north-west by Bathurst, on the south-west by North Crosby; and on the south-east by the Rideau Lake. In Burgess 12,273 acres are taken up, 2,167 of which are under cultivation. There are several large lakes in the township, the principal of which are Pike Lake, Salmon Lake, Ottley's Lake, and the Rideau Lake. Much of the land bordering on the lakes is poor and stoney. Three thousand one hundred acres of Crown lands are open for sale in North Burgess, at 8s. currency per acre. There are two saw mills in the township
Population in 1842, 553
Ratable property in the township, £7,047

BURLEIGH

A Township in the Colborne District, is bounded on the east by the township of Methuen, on the north by unsurveyed lands, on the west by Harvey; and on the south by Dummer. Salmon Lake and Stoney Lake, portions of the chain of lakes that runs through the District, separate the township from Dummer; and numerous small lakes are scattered over the township. Burleigh is at present but little settled, and no return has yet been made from it. Forty-eight thousand and twenty-one acres of Crown lands are open for sale, at 8s. currency per acre.

BURLINGTON BAY.

A Bay at the western extremity of Lake Ontario, about five miles and a half long, and about three miles and three quarters broad in its widest part In shape it is nearly triangular, with its base towards the lake A long, low ridge of sand nearly separates it from the lake; and in order to make it accessible, a canal has been formed from the lake, through the bar, to enable vessels to reach Hamilton, and, through the Desjardins Canal, Dundas. There is a considerable marsh at its western extremity, through which the Desjardins Canal has been constructed. The old works being out of repair, and inefficient, great improvements have been made in the canal. it has been enlarged by dredging, and the piers have also been much improved. From the commencement of the work up the 1st July, 1844, £18,539 11s. 2d have been expended on it; and the gross revenue arising from tolls on the canal, from 1st February, 1844, to 31st January, 1845, amounted to £2933. The town of Hamilton is situated near the south-western extremity of the bay.

The following are the Rates of Toll at the Burlington Bay Canal —

DESCRIPTION OF ARTICLES	QUANTITY.	RATES.
Steamboats (weekly)		10s. 0d.
Do. (semi-weekly)		5 0
Do. (daily)		2 6
Sailing craft under 10 tons		Free.
Do. 10 tons and under 50		5 0
Do. 50 tons and upwards		10 0
Wheat	Per bushel	0 0½
Flour	Per barrel	0 2
Whiskey	Do.	0 6
Pork	Do.	0 6
Ashes	Do.	1 0
Salt	Do.	0 3¾
Butter	Do.	0 9
Do	Per keg	0 4½
Lard	Do.	0 4½
Do.	Per barrel.	0 9
Beer	Do.	0 6
Beeswax	Do.	0 9
Plaster of Paris	Do.	0 6
Cider	Do.	0 3
Oil	Do.	0 9
Lumber	Per 1000 feet	0 10
Square Timber	Do.	2 6
Shingles	Per 1000	0 3
Ploughs	Each	0 6
Potatoes	Per bushel	0 1¼
Apples	Do	0 0¼
Stone	Per toise	0 3
Peas and Oats	Per bushel	0 0½
Merchandize	Per cwt	0 3
West India Staves	Per 1200 ps.	2 6
Pipe Staves	Per 1000	10 0
Pig Iron	Per cwt	0 1
Coal	Do.	0 1

BURWELL LAKE

A Lake in the township of Bosanquet, or rather two lakes connected together by a narrow gut, situated about three miles from Lake Huron, in the triangle formed by the bend of the River Sable, its northern extremity is about three miles from the north boundary of the township. It is about four miles long by about two in breadth; and is surrounded by a considerable extent of marsh. It has never been surveyed.

BYTOWN

The District Town of the Dalhousie District; situated in the north-east corner of the township of Nepean, on the Ottawa River. It is divided into two portions, called Upper and Lower Bytown, the former is the most aristocratic, the latter the most business portion of the town. The lower town has been long settled the upper town has been more recently erected, and is situated about half a mile higher up the river, and on considerably higher ground. The land on which the upper town is erected, together with a portion of that comprising the lower town, was purchased some years since for the sum of £80, and is now computed to be worth some £50,000 or £60,000. The Rideau Canal enters the Ottawa River just above the lower town, where eight handsome locks have been constructed to overcome the fall in the river.

The scenery about Bytown is, next to that at the Falls of Niagara, the most picturesque of the inhabited portion of Canada. The Chaudiere Falls, a short distance above the upper town, are very beautiful. Just below the falls, a handsome Suspension Bridge has been constructed over the Ottawa, which connects Upper with Lower Canada.

Bytown is principally supported by the lumber trade. On the Lower Canadian side of the river, slides have been constructed to facilitate the passage of the rafts. Here all timber brought down the river, which has been cut on Crown lands, is measured, and the owner enters into a bond for the payment of the duties at Quebec. The town is fast improving in appearance, and several handsome stone buildings are already erected. The Barracks are in a commanding situation, on the highest part of the bank of the river, between the upper and lower town, and are garrisoned by a company of Rifles.

The inhabitants of the lower town are about one-third French Canadians, the remainder are principally Irish.

Churches and chapels in the lower town, five, viz., Catholic, Free Church, two Methodist, and Baptist. In Upper Bytown, three, viz., Episcopal, Presbyterian, and Methodist. The Jail and Court House are of stone. Two Fire Engines are kept, one in the upper, and one in the lower town. There is a "Commercial Reading-room," supported by subscription, and a "Mercantile Library Association."

A Fair is held at Bytown on the second Tuesday in April, and the third Wednesday in September. Three newspapers are published here weekly—the "Ottawa Advocate," "Bytown Gazette," and "Packet."

During the season, a steamboat plies daily between Bytown and Grenville, in Lower Canada, leaving Bytown in the morning, and returning from Grenville in the evening. And comfortable boats of a good size, ply on the Rideau Canal, between Bytown and Kingston, but, as they are generally engaged in towing barges, there is little dependance to be placed on their regularity.

Population of Bytown, about 7000.

Post Office, post daily. The mail is conveyed to Kingston on horseback.

The following Government and District Offices are kept in Bytown:—Judge of District Court, Sheriff, Clerk of Peace, Judge of Surrogate Court, Treasurer, Registrar of Surrogate Court, District Clerk, Clerk of District Court, Coroner, Collector of Timber Duties

Professions and Trades.—In Upper Bytown: three lawyers, two grist mills, two saw mills, three foundries, fourteen general stores, two lumber merchants

stores, two druggists, one printer, five blacksmiths, two saddlers, seven shoemakers, four tailors, three cabinet makers, one tinsmith, one butcher, one baker, one barber, one waggon maker, four taverns, one ladies' school. Three Bank agencies—"Montreal," "Upper Canada," and "Bank of British North America." In Lower Bytown : one physician and surgeon, four lawyers, thirty-two stores, six tanneries, two breweries, two druggists, one soap and candle factory, two printers, thirty-five taverns, fifty groceries, twenty beer shops, six saddlers, fourteen shoemakers, six tinsmiths, six tailors, three watchmakers, seven butchers, eight bakers, four cabinet makers, one coach maker, one turner, four waggon makers, two hatters, seven schools. Two Bank agencies—"Commercial," and "City Bank of Montreal"

Principal Taverns—Upper Town : "Dalhousie Hotel," and " Exchange." Lower Town : " British Hotel," and " Ottawa House."

Forwarders.

Hooker, Henderson & Co.
Sanderson & Murray,
Macpherson, Crane & Co.
H. & S. Jones,
Quebec Forwarding Company,
John Egan & Co.
} Storehouses at Canal Wharf.

Land Agent—Christopher Armstrong

Steamboat Fares.—To Grenville (exclusive of meals) ... 10s. 0d.
Do.   To Kingston (meals included) 27 6

Quantity of Timber brought down the Ottawa, during the year 1844, with its estimated value :—

White Pine, 52,864 pieces, being 3,700,480 feet, at 6d. ... £92,512 0 0
Red Pine, 92,874 pieces, being 3,529,212 feet, at 10d 147,050 0 10
Oak and Elm, 160 pieces, being 5440 feet, at 7d. 158 13 4
Saw Logs, 79,853, each 4s. 2d. 16,636 0 10

£256,356 15 0

Amount of duty on the above, £23,805 9s. 3d.
The Free Timber, or that cut on private lands, may be
  estimated at about one-third of the above, or 85,399 7 2

Making together £341,756 2 2

CAISTOR

A Township in the Niagara District ; is bounded on the east by the township of Gainsborough ; on the north-east by Grimsby and Saltfleet, on the west by Binbrook ; and on the south by Seneca and Canboro. In Caistor 9,738 acres are taken up, 2,636 of which are under cultivation. The Chippawa, or Welland River, runs through the south of the township. There are 1 grist and four saw mills in the township. Inhabitants principally Canadians and Americans, 599 in number.

Ratable property in the township, £9,071.

CALEDONIA.

A Village in the township of Caledonia, in the Ottawa District, five miles south from the Ottawa River, and nine miles from L'Orignal. This is the situation of the "Caledonia Springs" which are now generally well known in Canada, by reputation at least. The village owes its existence altogether to the situation of the springs, the discovery of which has been the sole cause of the formation of the settlement. There were but two or three houses in the place, which were kept for the reception of visitors to the springs, till the property came into the possession of the present proprietor in 1836, who immediately commenced improving the situation, by clearing and building. The

D

springs were secured from the drainings of the land, cleaned out, and encased. A large hotel has been built for the reception of visitors, capable of accommodating 150 persons, and a bath house; and a circular railroad has been laid down round the grounds for the amusement of invalids. There are also in the village two churches, stores, saw mill, post-office, a resident physician, three taverns, and other boarding houses, and a small paper called "Life at the Springs," is published weekly. The principal tavern, the "Canada House," is kept by the proprietor of the springs. There are four springs in the place, called the Saline, Sulphur, Gas, and one more lately discovered, called the Intermittent. The Caledonia water is bottled and exported

The following is an Analysis of the Waters of the different Springs:

SALINE SPRING —ONE QUART OF WATER.

Chloride of Sodium	108,22
Do. Magnesium	2,01
Sulphate of Lime	1,28
Carbonate of Lime	2,00
Do Magnesia	5,12
Do Soda	,82
Iodide of Sodium	,38
Vegetable Extract	,61
Grains	120,44

ONE HUNDRED CUBIC INCHES OF THE GAS FROM THE GAS SPRING, ANALYZED, IS AS FOLLOWS

Light Carburetted Hydrogen	82,90
Nitrogen	6,00
Oxygen	1,56
Sulphuretted Hydrogen	4,00
Carbonic Acid	5,54
Cubic inches	100,00

INTERMITTENT SPRING.
Sp Gr. 1,0092
In Imperial Pint . Grains, 123,04

Carbonate of Magnesia	7,437
Carbonate of Lime	2,975
Sulphate of Lime	1,788
Chloride of Sodium	98,925
Chloride of Magnesium	11,916
Iodide of Sodium, 3 in a gall.	
Bromide of Sodium, 1,7 in do.	
Grains	123,04

Gases, { Light Carburetted Hydrogen. Carbonic Acid Gas. Sulphuretted Hydrogen

GAS SPRING —ONE QUART OF WATER.

Chloride of Sodium	89,75
Do. Magnesium	1,63
Do Potassium	,55
Sulphate of Lime	1,47
Carbonate of Lime	2,40
Do. Magnesia	2,50
Do. Soda	1,00
Do. Iron	,03
Iodide of Sodium	,35
Resin, a vegetable extract	,52
Grains	100,20

Gases, { Carbonic Acid. Sulphuretted Hydrogen. Nitrogen.

WHITE-SULPHUR SPRING.—ONE QUART OF WATER.

Chloride of Sodium	60,42
Do. Magnesium	,64
Sulphate of Lime	,68
Carbonate of Lime	,82
Do Magnesia	3,60
Iodide	
Vegetable Extract, &c.	,30
Grains	66,46

Gases, { Carbonic Acid .. 3,20 Sulphuretted Hydrogen 6,14

Cubic inches... 9,34

CALEDONIA.

A Township in the Ottawa District, is bounded on the east and south-east by the townships of Hawkesbury West and Kenyon, on the north by Longueil;

and on the north-west by Alfred and Plantagenet. In Caledonia 8111 acres are taken up, 1594 of which are under cultivation This township is as yet but little settled. It is principally known and visited for its Mineral Springs, the water of which is bottled and exported under the name of "Caledonia Water" 18,481 acres of Crown Lands are open for sale in Caledonia at 8s currency per acre. There are one grist and two saw mills in the township.

Population, 714.

Ratable property in the township, £7,087.

CALEDONIA.

A flourishing Village on the banks of the Grand River, twenty miles from Brantford, fourteen from Hamilton, and twenty-three from Port Dover; principally situated in the township of Seneca, with a small portion on the opposite side of the river, in the township of Oneida The two portions of the village are connected by means of a handsome swing bridge across the river. Caledonia was laid out as a village by the Crown, about two years since, and the village of Seneca was included in the town plot The plank road from Hamilton to Port Dover passes through the village Stages run daily to Hamilton and Port Dover, and a mail runs three times a week to Dunnville, and from thence to St. Catharines A settlement, called "Little Caledonia," (where is a grist mill, and saw mill with two saws), is situated about a quarter of a mile distant

Population, including Little Caledonia, about 300.

Post Office (in Oneida), post daily

Professions and Trades.—One physician and surgeon, five stores, three taverns, two groceries, one saddler, two waggon makers, two cabinet makers, three blacksmiths, three shoemakers, three tailors, two bakers

CALEDON

A Township in the Home District; is bounded on the north-east by the township of Albion; on the north by Mono, on the north-west and south-west by Garafraxa and Erin; and on the south-east by Chinguacousy In Caledon 43,661 acres are taken up, 9,307 of which are under cultivation The north of the township is hilly and broken, with a considerable quantity of pine; in the south the land is much better, and the timber principally hardwood There are some good farms in the township. There are three grist-mills and one saw-mill in the township. Four hundred acres of Crown lands are open for sale in Caledon, at 8s. c'y per acre.

Population in 1842, 1920.

Ratable property in the township, £25,587.

CAMBRIDGE

A Township in the Ottawa District; is bounded on the north-east by the township of Plantagenet, on the north-west by Clarence; on the south-west by Russell; and on the south-east by Finch In Cambridge 2879 acres are taken up, 161 of which are under cultivation The "Petite Nation" River runs through the centre of the township from south to north Cambridge is as yet but little settled, and 10,800 acres of Crown lands are open for sale in the township at 8s. currency per acre. There is one saw-mill in the township.

Population in 1842, 108.

Ratable property in the township, £963

CAMDEN.

A Township in the Western District, is bounded on the north-east by the township of Zone; on the north by Zone and Dawn, on the south-west by Chatham; and on the south by the River Thames In Camden 6300 acres are taken up, 1295 of which are under cultivation. This is a small township, containing excellent land, and it is becoming settled fast. A good road has been

made through the township, from the Western Road to Bear Creek. There is one grist mill and one saw mill in Camden
Population, 316
Ratable property in the township, £4029.

CAMDEN EAST.

A Township in the Midland District, is bounded on the east by Portland; on the north by Sheffield; on the west by Richmond; and on the south by Ernestown and a small portion of Fiedericksburg. In Camden 70,207 acres are taken up, 19,248 of which are under cultivation A lake, called Mud Lake, is situated a little east of the centre of the township, and one, called Vardy Lake, in the south-east corner A mill stream runs through the south of the township, on which are several grist and saw mills There is a quarry of fine marble near the centre of the township. Camden is well settled, and contains some good farms. The land varies in quality. Timber—hardwood, intermixed with pine The village of Newburgh is situated in the south-west of the township; and Clark's Mills a little south of the centre of the township. There is a Presbyterian Church a little west of Newburgh There are four grist and fourteen saw mills in the township Six hundred acres of Crown lands are open for sale in Camden, at 8s. currency per acre.
Population, 4788.
Ratable property in the township, £56,195

CANASTOGA RIVER

A branch of the Grand River, takes its rise in the lands west of Wellesley and Peel, runs through the south-west corner of Peel, and the north-east corner of Wellesley, and joins the Grand River in the south-east of Woolwich.

CANARD'S RIVER.

A Stream; different branches of which take their rise in the townships of Sandwich and Colchester, it runs through the township of Anderdon into the Detroit River. In Anderdon, a branch of it unites with a creek, which then runs through the township of Malden into Lake Erie.

CANBORO'.

A Township in the Niagara District, is bounded on the east by the township of Moulton; on the north by Caistor and a small portion of Gainsborough; on the west by Seneca and Cayuga; and on the south by the Grand River. In Canboro' 15,804 acres are taken up, 3876 of which are under cultivation. The land on the banks of the river is generally rolling. Timber principally hardwood, amongst which is fine white oak of a large size. A branch of the Welland River flows through the north of the township. There is one grist mill in the township.
Population in 1841, 663.
Ratable property in the township, £11,430.

CANBORO'.

A small village in about the centre of the township of Canboro', seven miles from Dunnville It contains about 100 inhabitants, two churches (Methodist and Baptist). Post Office, post twice a-week One saw mill, tannery, two stores, one tavern, one shoemaker, one blacksmith.

CANNING.

A small Village in the south-east corner of the township of Blenheim, situated on Smith's Creek. It contains about 120 inhabitants, grist mill, saw mill, tannery, one store, and one blacksmith.

CARLETON, COUNTY OF.—(*See* DALHOUSIE.)

CARRADOC.

A Township in the London District; is bounded on the north-east by the township of Lobo; on the north-west by Adelaide, on the south-west by Ekfrid; and on the south-east by the River Thames. In Caradoc, 29,399 acres are taken up, 5065 of which are under cultivation. The land of this township is generally good. Timber principally hardwood. The east branch of Bear Creek runs through the north of the township. The Indian village of Munseytown is in Carradoc, on the Thames, eight miles below Delaware. There is one grist mill and one distillery in the township.

Population in 1842, 972.
Ratable property in the township, £15,403.

CARTWRIGHT.

A Township in the Newcastle District; is bounded on the east by the township of Manvers; on the north by Mariposa, on the west by Reach; and on the south by Darlington. In Cartwright 15,128 acres are taken up, 1713 of which are under cultivation. The Scugog Lake takes up a large portion of the north-west half of the township, and the land bordering on it is generally poor, and mostly timbered with pine. There is one saw mill in the township. In Cartwright, 200 acres of Crown lands are open for sale, at 8s. currency per acre.

Population in 1842, 445
Ratable property in the township, £6063.

CAT ISLAND.

A small Island in Lake Huron, lying between Horse Island and the Isle of Coves.

CAVAN.

A Township in the Newcastle District, is bounded on the east by the townships of North and South Monaghan, on the north by Emily; on the west by Manvers, and a small portion of Clark, and on the south by Hope. In Cavan 52,128 acres are taken up, 15,277 of which are under cultivation. The township is well watered by numerous small streams running across it; it is well settled, and contains some good farms; timber principally hard wood. The village of Millbrook is situated a little south-west of its centre. There are four grist and seven saw-mills, and one distillery in the township. One thousand acres of Crown lands are open for sale in Cavan, at 8s c'y per acre.

Population in 1842, 3086.
Ratable property in the township, £39,304.

CAVANVILLE.

A small Settlement in the township of Cavan, 3½ miles from Millbrook. It contains an Episcopal church, one store, one tannery

Post Office, post twice a week.

CAYUGA.

A small Village in the township of Cayuga, pleasantly situated on the Grand River, fifteen miles above Dunnville. The road from Simcoe to the Falls of Niagara passes through the village. Cayuga contains about seventy inhabitants: one store, one grocery, three taverns, one blacksmith, two waggon-makers, one shoemaker, two tailors.

CAYUGA.

A Township in the Niagara District, is bounded on the east by the township of Canboro'; on the north-west by Seneca and Oneida; and on the south-west

by Rainham and Walpole. In Cayuga 14,871 acres are taken up, 3,666 of which are under cultivation. The Grand River flows through the township, on the banks of which are some good clearings. The timber on the Grand River, to within a short distance of the village of Cayuga, is mostly hard wood, much of which is white oak of a large size, in exporting which a profitable trade is carried on. Above the village of Cayuga the timber is principally pine, with a small quantity of hard wood intermixed. About four miles below Cayuga village, is a bed of white gypsum, situated close to the river. The village of Indiana is situated on the river, about two miles above Cayuga, and about six miles below the same village is a small Episcopal church.
Population in 1841, 837.
Ratable property in the township, £13,872

CEDAR CREEK.

A small Stream, which takes its rise in the township of Colchester, and enters Lake Erie in the south-west corner of Gosfield. On it is a saw-mill.

CHAMBERLAIN'S CORNERS.

A Settlement on the Perth road, in the township of Kitley, two miles north of Frankville It contains about forty inhabitants: one store, one tavern.
Post Office, post twice a-week.

CHANTRY ISLAND

A long narrow Island in Lake Huron, about one mile in length, opposite the entrance of Saugeen River.

CHARLESTON

A small Village situated in the north-east of the township of Yonge. It contains about 100 inhabitants one store, one tavern, one tannery, one shoemaker, one cooper.

CHARLESVILLE.

A small Village in the township of Osnabruck, situated on the St Lawrence, eighteen miles from Cornwall. It contains about 120 inhabitants, and one tavern.

CHARLOTTENBURG.

A Township in the Eastern District, is bounded on the north-east by the township of Lancaster, on the north-west by Kenyon; on the south-west by the reserve of the St Regis Indians, and on the south and south-east by the St. Lawrence In Charlottenburg 73,784 acres are taken up; 17,415 of which are under cultivation. The River Aux Raisins runs across the centre of the township from west to east The village of Martintown is situated in the west of the township, and the village of Williamstown in about its centre. The soil of Charlottenburg varies in quality, on the banks of the river it is generally poor, with pine timber. There are some good farms in the township. This is the best settled township in the Eastern District. There are four grist and six saw mills in the township.
Population, 4975; the principal part of whom are Scotch.
Ratable property in the township, £63,795.

CHARLOTTEVILLE.

A Township in the Talbot District, is bounded on the east by Woodhouse; on the north by Wyndham; on the west by Walsingham; and on the south-east and south by Lake Erie. In Charlotteville, 31,064 acres are taken up, 9,546 of which are under cultivation. This township contains a considerable quantity of pine. The villages of Vittoria and Normandale are situated in Charlotteville. There are three grist and seven saw mills, and two distilleries in the township.

Population in 1841, 1969, who are principally Canadians and Americans.

Ratable property in the township, £36,777.

CHATHAM.

The County Town of the County of Kent; pleasantly and advantageously situated on the River Thames, at the junction of the townships of Chatham, Raleigh, Harwich, and Dover East; and at the entrance of McGregor's Creek into that river: the portion of it situated on the north shore of the river being called Chatham North. This town was originally laid out by Governor Simcoe, who, while examining the valley of the Thames, on arriving at the spot on which Chatham now stands, was so much struck with its great natural advantages, that he immediately reserved 600 acres for a town plot. The town, however, may be said to have commenced only about fifteen years ago, since which time it has progressed rapidly, and now contains about 1500 inhabitants, and property has greatly increased in value, so much so, that a small town lot, which at the first settlement could have been worth but a mere trifle, was sold a short time since to a merchant at the *enormous advance* of 750 dollars.

This place was a garrison town during the rebellion, and contains barracks, but they are at present unoccupied

The new road from London to Amherstburgh passes through the town. Four-horsed stages, going eastward and westward, leave Chatham every day

The steamboat "Brothers," Captain Eberts, is owned here, and, during the season, leaves Chatham for Detroit and Amherstburgh every Monday, Wednesday and Friday, returning on the alternate days. The "London," Captain Van Allen (the fastest boat on the upper lakes) meets the "Brothers" at Detroit, and continues the route to Buffalo, touching at the intermediate ports on the Canadian side. The "London" is a beautiful boat; and, during the winter of 1844-5, the "Brothers" was overhauled, enlarged and refitted.

Chatham contains four churches and chapels; viz, Episcopal, Presbyterian, Secession, and Methodist: also, a Theatre, which is well attended, the performers being amateurs, and a cricket club.

A newspaper, the "Chatham Gleaner," is published here every Tuesday. Town lots of a quarter of an acre, and park lots varying from three to ten acres, are still to be purchased, the price varying according to situation The table of exports for the past year will give some idea of the trade of the town, as well as of the prosperity and industry of the surrounding neighbourhood.

List of Professions and Trades.—Five physicians and surgeons, one lawyer, one dentist, one steam grist mill, one water do, two saw mills, two breweries, three distilleries, one tannery, ten stores, four groceries, one pottery, one maltster, six tailors, two saddlers, three shoemakers, ten taverns, one printing office, one watchmaker, one gunsmith, eight blacksmiths, three cabinet makers, one hatter, one tinsmith, two carriage makers, one foundry, two bakers, one tallow chandler, two asheries, one livery stable, one bookseller and stationer, two bank agencies (Gore and Upper Canada), one land agency, three schools.

Principal tavern and stage house, the "Royal Exchange," at which is a reading and news room

Land agent, Abraham Steers.

Stage fare from Chatham to London, $3½; to Detroit, $2½. Steamboat fare from Chatham to Detroit, $2; to Amherstburg, $2½.

Chatham is sixty-six miles from London, and fifty miles from Detroit.

List of Exports from the Port of Chatham for the year 1844, with their estimated value when shipped.

Quantity	Description	Value
32,639 bushels	Wheat	£6,378 3 0
3,128 barrels	Flour	3,140 0 0
3,280 bushels	Peas	307 9 6
450 do	Oats	22 10 0
1,040 do	Barley	123 6 8
362 do	Indian Corn	34 16 5
970 do	Potatoes	40 12 6
74 barrels	Pot and Pearl Ash	368 8 0
	Lard and Butter	9 0 0
200 bushels	Cranberries	62 10 0
100 do	Timothy Seed	21 17 0
48,000 feet	Walnut Timber	148 0 0
167,000	Standard Staves	2,506 18 3
100,000	West India do	151 9 3
7,430 lbs	Hides	130 0 0
	Furs and Skins	2,005 0 0

Total value of exports from Chatham £15,450 0 7

CHATHAM

A Township in the County of Kent; is bounded on the north by Sombra and Dawn, on the south-west by the township of Dover, on the south-east by the River Thames; and on the north-east by Camden. Bear Creek runs through the north-east corner of the township. Chatham contains 17,119 acres, of which 3749 are under cultivation. The Canada Company possess 3400 acres in the township Soil—fertile. Timber—maple, black walnut, elm, oak, beech, &c. Chatham is getting well settled. About a mile back from the river is a considerable Scotch settlement.

Population, 799.

Ratable property in the township, £11,996.

CHINGUACOUSY.

A Township in the Home District; is bounded on the north-east by the township of Caledon and the Gore of Toronto; on the north-west by Caledon; on the south-west by Esquesing; and on the south-east by Toronto township. In Chinguacousy 74,977 acres are taken up, 26,266 of which are under cultivation. This is one of the best settled townships in the Home District, containing excellent land, and many good farms. The timber is principally hardwood, with a small portion of pine intermixed: the land mostly rolling. The River Credit runs through the south and west of the township, and the Etobicoke River through the east and centre Excellent wheat is grown in this and the adjoining townships There are one grist and seven saw mills in Chinguacousy.

Population in 1842, 3965

Ratable property in the township, £59,952.

CHIPICAN LAKE.

A small Lake in the township of Sarnia, about six acres in extent; two miles north of Port Sarnia. It is separated from Lake Huron by a ridge of high land.

CHIPPEWA

A large Village, situated partly in the township of Willoughby, and partly in Stamford, the two portions being divided by the Chippewa, or Welland River. That portion of the village situated in Stamford was laid out in 1816, and the portion in Willoughby about ten years since. Chippewa derives its greatest importance from its advantageous situation for ship building for the upper lakes; the mouth of the Welland River being a short distance above the Rapids of the Niagara River. The Niagara Harbour and Dock Company have a Shipyard here; many vessels have been built here, and a fine steamboat of 800 tons is now on the stocks, intended to be ready for service during the present season During the season, a steamboat runs from Chippewa to Buffalo; and the Canadian line of Stages from Buffalo to Detroit passes through the village. Churches and chapels, 3, viz, Episcopal, Presbyterian and Methodist. There are also barracks, with a company of Rifles.

Population, about 1000.

Post Office, post daily.

Professions and Trades —Shipyard, one steam grist mill, one steam saw mill, two physicians and surgeons, three distilleries, two tanneries, iron and brass foundry, tin and sheet iron foundry, seven stores, six taverns, one druggist, six groceries, two waggon makers, four blacksmiths, one hatter, two saddlers, four tailors, two bakers, five shoemakers, two cabinet makers, one gunsmith. One Bank agency, "Upper Canada"

Principal Taverns —"Steamboat Hotel," and "National."

CHURCHVILLE.

A Village in the township of Toronto; four and a half miles from Streetsville, and eleven and a half from Dundas Street, situated on the River Credit. Contains about 150 Inhabitants, and a Methodist chapel.

Post Office, post twice a-week

List of Professions and Trades —One grist and two saw mills, one tannery, one distillery, one tavern, two stores, two waggon makers, two blacksmiths, one tailor, one cabinet-maker, one shoemaker.

CLAREMONT.

A village in the township of Burford, situated on the plank road, about nine miles from Brantford. It contains about 150 inhabitants, and a church free to all denominations.

Post Office, post every day.

Professions and Trades —One physician and surgeon, two stores, one tavern, one cabinet maker, one waggon maker, two blacksmiths, one tailor, one shoemaker.

CLARENCE.

A Township in the Ottawa District is bounded on the north-east by the township of Plantagenet, on the north by the Ottawa River, on the south-west by Cumberland, and on the south-east by Cambridge. In Clarence 4,682 acres are taken up, 734 of which are under cultivation A branch of the "Petite Nation" River runs through the south of the township Clarence is but little settled, and there are 21,631 acres of Crown lands for sale in the township, at 8s. c'y per acre

Population 200.

Ratable property in the township, £2,524.

CLARKSVILLE.

A Village in the township of Camden, situated on the Napanee River, two miles above Newburgh. It contains about 200 inhabitants, who have an Episcopal Church, grist and saw mill, carding machine and cloth factory, one store, one tavern.

CLARKE, VILLAGE OF.—(*See* NEWTON.)

CLARKE.

A township in the Newcastle District is bounded on the east by the township of Hope, on the north by Manvers; on the west by Darlington; and on the south by Lake Ontario. In Clarke 49,449 acres are taken up, 19,000 of which are under cultivation. The villages of Newcastle and Newton are situated in the south of the township, on the Eastern Road, the village of Bond Head on the lake shore, and a small settlement called "Orono," about five miles north of Newcastle. This is an old settled township, containing good farms, many of which are rented out, the average rent being $2 per acre. The land near the coast is rather poor and stony, but it improves as you go back, it is rather hilly in parts. Excellent wheat is grown in this and the adjoining townships. There are two grist and thirteen saw mills in the township. Four hundred acres of Crown lands are open for sale in Clarke, at 8s. c'y per acre.

Population in 1842, 2,832.

Ratable property in the township, £47,970.

CLINTON.

A township in the Niagara District is bounded on the east by the township of Louth, on the north by Lake Ontario, on the West by Grimsby, and on the south by Gainsborough. In Clinton 23,378 acres are taken up, 10,605 of which are under cultivation. This is an old settled township, containing many good farms. There are one grist and six saw mills in the township.

Population in 1841, 2,122.

Ratable property in the township, £37,352.

COBOURG.

The District Town of the Newcastle District, in the township of Hamilton; is pleasantly situated on a gently rising ground, on the bank of Lake Ontario, 103 miles from Kingston, and 72 miles from Toronto. The town is incorporated, and the corporation limits extend for nearly two miles from the centre of the town. Cobourg is situated on a gravelly soil, and it is consequently dry, clean and healthy. The town is well laid out, possesses good streets, and many excellent buildings, and has a very flourishing appearance. A harbour has been constructed at an expense of £10,381 6s 3d, and a light-house erected at the end of the pier. Excellent planked side-walks extend in every direction for a distance of from one to two miles.

During the season, steamboats call daily on their passages to and from Kingston, Toronto, and Rochester (United States), and a stage leaves daily for Rice Lake, where it is met by the steamboat Forester, which conveys passengers to Peterborough, and the Toronto and Kingston stages pass through the town every day. During the winter, a stage leaves daily for Peterborough. A fair is held here on the second Tuesdays in April and October. The merchants have established amongst themselves a "Board of Trade," for the purpose of regulating the commercial affairs of the place, they have a news-room, where several papers are taken. There is also a Mechanics' Institute. Three newspapers are published here, viz, the "Church," "Cobourg Star," and "Canada Christian Advocate." Churches and Chapels six, viz, Episcopal, Presbyterian, Catholic, Congregational, Methodist, and Christian. In the Episcopal church is a very good organ. The Jail and Court House is a handsome stone building, situated about a mile and a-half from the town, on the Toronto road.

Victoria College was founded by the Wesleyan Conference; the institution was chartered in 1835, as an Academy, and by Act of Parliament, in 1842, was constituted a College, with power to confer degrees in the several arts and sciences—(the only degree yet conferred has been one in literature), it is supported partly by a legislative grant of £500 per annum, and partly by tuition fees. The building is handsome, and well situated, and cost nearly £10,000; it contains Library, Reading Room, Chapel, Laboratory, Lecture Rooms, &c. &c. Although the institution was founded by the Methodists, there is nothing sectarian in its character. The following periodicals are received at the Reading

Room, which are liberally forwarded by their several editors, the College being merely at the expense of postage: Church, Cobourg; British Colonist, Toronto; British Canadian, do.; Banner (Presbyterian), do ; Kingston News, Montreal Gazette; Willmer and Smith's European Times; Pilot, Montreal; Hamilton Gazette; Hamilton Journal and Express; Canada Gazette; Kingston Herald; Port Hope Gazette; Cornwall Observer; Brockville Recorder ; Niagara Chronicle; Belleville Intelligencer, Prince Edward Gazette, Woodstock Herald; British American Cultivator, Canada Christian Advocate (Episcopal Methodist), Peterboro Chronicle; Christian Guardian, Toronto; Methodist Quarterly Review, New York; Anglo American, do , Spectator, do ; Literary Garland, Montreal; Albion, New York; New Orleans Picayune, Christian Advocate and Journal, New York; Southern Christian Advocate, Charleston, Episcopal Recorder, Philadelphia. The boarders at the College at present number about thirty-five, and the day pupils about twenty.

A large cloth factory has been lately erected, for the manufacture of coarse cloth, tweeds, cassinett, blankets, flannels, &c.; when in full operation it will employ nearly 200 hands, and will be capable of turning out 850 yards of cloth per day. The building is of brick, and is five stories high, including basement.

The following government and district offices are kept in Cobourg. Judge of District Court, Sheriff, Treasurer, Inspector of Licenses, Collector of Customs. Registrar of County of Northumberland, District Clerk, Clerk of District Court, The office of the Clerk of the Peace is kept at Port Hope.

Post Office, post every day.

Population, 3,347.

Professions and Trades.—Six physicians and surgeons, seven lawyers, one steam grist-mill, two water do , two saw-mills, one cloth factory, one brewery, three distilleries, one ashery, one soap and candle factory, three tanneries, two foundries, twenty dry-goods stores, ten groceries, two hardware stores, twelve taverns, two druggists, three printers, three booksellers, two surveyors, five waggon makers, one hatter, two livery stables, one veterinary surgeon, two watch makers, three tinsmiths, five cabinet makers, ten tailors, two saddlers, four bakers and confectioners, eleven blacksmiths, one marble worker, one pail factory, four planing machines, one machine maker, fourteen shoemakers, three merchant tailors, two barbers, four butchers, three schools for boys, three ladies seminaries, two bank agencies—" Commercial," and ' Montreal."

Principal Taverns.—" North American," and "Globe."

Land Agent, S. Armour.

Stage fare to Peterborough during winter, ten shillings c'y., stage and steam-boat fare to do. during summer, seven shillings and six-pence.

EXPORTS FROM COBOURG DURING 1844, AND THEIR ESTIMATED VALUE.

Quantity	Description	Estimated value
49 barrels	Ashes	£ 245 0 0
7 "	Beef	11 0 0
37 "	Pot Barley	37 0 0
21,538¼ "	Flour	22884 0 0
243¼ "	Liquors	426 2 6
31½ "	Meal	31 10 0
656 "	Pork	1640 0 0
7 "	Peas	7 0 0
427 kegs	Butter	640 10 0
2085 cwt	Bran	208 10 0
44 m ft	Lumber	66 0 0
10 m	Staves, W. I.	45 0 0
5¼ m	" Standard	105 0 0
12 bundles	Shingles	3 0 0
		£26,353 10 6

COLBORNE DISTRICT.

Consists of the county of Peterboro', which returns a member to the House of Assembly, and comprises the following townships: Asphodel, Belmont, Burleigh, Bexley, Dummer, Douro, Ennismore, Emily, Eldon, Fenelon, Harvey, Methuen, Mariposa, Otonabee, Ops, Smith, Somerville, Verulam, and North Monaghan. This District is situated to the north of the Newcastle District; and has a chain of lakes running through the north and east of it, called Balsam Lake, Sturgeon Lake, Pigeon Lake, Shemong Lake, and Trout Lake; and the townships of Otonabee and Asphodel are bounded on the south by Rice Lake and River Trent. It is besides, watered by the Otonabee River, the Scugog River, and numerous small streams scattered over it; most of which discharge themselves into the lakes. Much of the timber on the lakes and rivers is pine, and a great trade is carried on in lumber; immense quantities of which are carried down the River Trent. The district is getting well settled, and land in the neighbourhood of Peterboro', the district town, is becoming valuable. Two hundred and sixty-four thousand nine hundred and twenty-eight acres of Crown lands are open for sale in the Colborne District, at 8s. currency per acre; to purchase any of which, application must be made to the Crown lands' agent, at Peterboro'.

Population in 1842, 13,706; since when it has probably increased one-fifth.

The following abstract from the Assessment Rolls will show the rate of increase and improvement in the district:—

Date.	No. of Acres Cultivated.	MILLS. Grist.	MILLS. Saw.	Milch Cows.	Oxen, 4 years old, and upwards.	Horned Cattle, from 2 to 4 years old.	Amount of Ratable Property.
1842	48910	14	17	4756	2789	2264	£159,003
1843	53340	13	24	4911	3007	2575	170,331
1844	58492	15	20	5214	2947	2550	180,245

Government and District Officers in the District:

OFFICE.	NAMES.
Judge of the District Court and Surrogate Court	B. T. McKyes.
Sheriff	W. S. Conger.
Registrar	Charles Rubidge.
Treasurer and Crown Lands' Agent	Frederick Ferguson.
Clerk of the Peace and Deputy Clerk of the Crown	W. H. Wrighton.
Clerk of the District Court and Registrar of the Surrogate Court	Thos. Fortye.
Inspector of Licenses	Thos. Milburn.
District Superintendent of Schools	Elias Burnham.
District Clerk	Walter Sheridan.

Coroners of the Colborne District:

NAMES.	RESIDENCE.
John Hutchison	Peterboro'.
John R. Benson	Smith.
Samuel Strickland	Douro.
Christopher Knowlson	Emily.
Francis Henderson	Do.
John McNabb	Peterboro'.

No. of Common Schools in operation in the Colborne District.—Asphodel, nine; Douro, four; Dummer, three; Emily, twelve; Ennismore, one; Fenelon, one;

Mariposa, seven, North Monaghan, four; Ops, eight; Smith, thirteen; Verulam, one; Otonabee, nine. Total, seventy-two.

COLBORNE.

A Township in the Huron District, is bounded on the north by Ashfield and Wawanosh; on the west by Lake Huron; on the south by the River Maitland, and on the east by the township of Hullett. The land, for from two to three miles back from the lake, and for half a mile on each side of the river, is poor, the soil of the rest of the township is good. Colborne contains 35,460 acres, 13,188 of which are leased or sold, of which 1558 are under cultivation.

There are in the township five saw mills, on creeks running into the River Maitland, and Lake Huron, and one distillery.

Population, 503

Ratable property in the township, £5831 2s.

COLBORNE HARBOUR.

A small Settlement on Lake Ontario, in the township of Cramahe, at the mouth of a small creek; it contains a grist and saw mill, carding machine and cloth factory, plaster mill, (the plaster being imported from the United States) and a burr mill stone factory.

COLBORNE.

A Village in the townships of Cramahe and Murray, the town line running through the village; situated on the eastern road, sixteen miles east from Cobourg, and one mile and a half north of Lake Ontario. A portion of the village called East Colborne, is built about three quarters of a mile to the east. Population of both portions, about 400. Churches and chapels, three, viz., Episcopal, Church of Scotland, and Methodist.

Professions and Trades.—One physician and surgeon, one lawyer, one distillery, one ashery, one foundry, six stores, two taverns, one chair and blind factory, one pottery, two saddlers, one waggon maker, four blacksmiths, three cabinet makers, one fanning mill maker.

COLCHESTER

A Township in the county of Essex, bounded on the north by the townships of Maidstone and Sandwich, on the west by Anderdon and Malden; on the south by Lake Erie, and on the east by Gosfield. It contains 21,530 acres, of which 5124 are under cultivation. About half the township is wet land, and requires considerable draining, the remainder is mostly good land. Timber, maple, beech, elm, oak, black walnut, butternut, chestnut, &c. A large quantity of iron ore is found in the south of the township, about three miles from the lake, which is taken to the furnace in Gosfield. A large marsh in the north of the township, called Hog Marsh, empties itself into the River Canard. There is a saw mill on Cedar Creek, and a tannery, ashery, and three stores on the lake shore. Colchester possesses an Episcopal church, built of stone, and a Baptist chapel. Colchester is well settled, containing 1422 inhabitants. The Canada Company possess about 9000 acres in this township, and 700 acres of Crown lands are open for sale in the township, at 8s. currency per acre.

Ratable property in the township, £18,723.

COLDWATER.

A Village in the township of Medonte, situated on the Coldwater River, thirty-one miles from Barrie, and fourteen miles from Orillia, The government road from Orillia to Sturgeon Bay passes through it. Coldwater contains a grist and saw mill, which are the property of the Indians, but are leased to a white settler; two taverns, one store.

COLLINGWOOD.

A Township in the Simcoe District; is bounded on the north by the Nottawasaga Bay; on the west by the townships of St. Vincent and Euphrasia, on the south by Ospry, and on the east by Nottawasaga In Collingwood 940 acres are taken up, 78 of which are under cultivation. This township is well watered, and possesses its share of good land. It has only just commenced settling, and there is as yet no return of its population. It was added in 1844 to the Simcoe District, having previously formed part of the Home District.
Ratable property in the township, £299.

COLUMBUS

A Village in the township of Whitby, situated on the plank road to Scugog, six miles north from Windsor It has been settled about eight years, and contains nearly 300 inhabitants There is a Methodist church in the village, and an Episcopal church a short distance west of it There are grist mills in the neighbourhood

Professions and Trades —One ashery, four stores, two taverns, two waggon makers, two tailors, two blacksmiths, four shoemakers.

CONSECON

A small Village, situated on Weller's Bay, partly in the township of Ameliasburgh, and partly in Hillier, at the mouth of Consecon Creek. It contains about sixty inhabitants, grist and saw mill, and Methodist chapel

COOK'S MILLS.

A small Settlement in the township of Crowland, four miles from Helmsport, containing about sixty inhabitants, one saw mill, carding machine and cloth factory, two stores, one tavern, one shoemaker.

Post Office, post three times a week.

COOK'S BAY.

The southernmost bay of Lake Simcoe it runs into the land, due south, for about eight miles, and is from two and a half to four miles wide The Holland River enters it at its south-west corner.

COOKSVILLE

A small Village in the north-west of the township of Williamsburg, about six miles from the St. Lawrence, contains about 100 inhabitants, two stores, three taverns.

COOKSVILLE

A Village in the township of Toronto, situated on Dundas Street, sixteen miles from Toronto, and two miles and a half from Port Credit. It was laid out about the year 1830, and contains about 185 inhabitants. There are three saw-mills in the immediate vicinity of the village.

Post Office, post daily.

Professions and Trades — One physician and surgeon, two stores, one tannery, two taverns, one watchmaker, one blacksmith, one saddler, one tinsmith, two waggon makers, four shoemakers, two tailors, one baker, one painter.

CORNWALL

The District Town of the Eastern District, in the township of Cornwall, and county of Stormont, pleasantly situated on the River St. Lawrence. The town is well laid out, and has some good streets, with many excellent stone and brick houses. The town was incorporated in the year 1834, and returns a member to the House of Assembly. The Cornwall Canal passes the town, lying between the town and the River St. Lawrence. This place was formerly called by the French inhabitants "Point Malin," on account of the difficulty they experienced in ascending that portion of the river with their "Bateaux." There is a handsome stone jail and court-house. Churches and chapels four, viz., Episcopal, Catholic, Presbyterian and Methodist. A newspaper is published here, the "Cornwall Observer." Population of Cornwall about 1,600

Post-office, post every day.

The following government and district offices are kept in Cornwall: Judge of District Court, Sheriff, Clerk of Peace, Treasurer, Inspector of Licenses, Collector of Customs, Crown Lands Agent, District Clerk, Clerk of District Court, Deputy Clerk of Crown

Professions and Trades—Three physicians and surgeons, eight lawyers, eight stores, one foundry, two tanneries, eight taverns, one druggist, one bookseller, one auctioneer, one printer, four bakers, six groceries, two tin-smiths, four blacksmiths, five tailors, two watchmakers, two butchers, three coopers, six joiners and carpenters, one hatter, two painters, one ladies' school, two bank agencies, "Commercial," and "Montreal" Principal Taverns, "Chesley's," and "Pitt's."

CORNWALL.

A Township in the Eastern District, is bounded on the north-east by the reserve of the St. Regis Indians, on the north-west by the township of Roxborough, on the south-west by Osnabruck, and on the south by the River St. Lawrence. In Cornwall 53,583 acres are taken up, 13,624 of which are under cultivation This is an old and well-settled township The town of Cornwall is situated in its south-east corner, and the villages of Moulinette, and Milleroche, and the settlement of St Andrews, are also in the township There are four grist and four saw mills in the township Population of Cornwall 3,907, who are principally English, Irish, and Scotch

Ratable property in the township, £65,632

CORUNNA

A Town in the township of Moore, five and a half miles below Port Sarnia; laid out in 1835 by the government The town-plot contains about 400 acres, but has at present very few settlers There is a saw and grist mill, supplied by a canal two miles long. The town-plot fronts on the River St Clair The road from Port Sarnia to Chatham passes through the town. Price of building lots, from six to twenty-four dollars.

COVES, ISLE OF.

An Island in Lake Huron, at the entrance to the Georgian Bay, about six miles from Cape Hurd The main channel from Lake Huron to the Georgian Bay, lies between the Isle of Coves and Cat Island.

CRAMAHE

A Township in the Newcastle District, is bounded on the east by the township of Murray, on the north by Percy, on the west by Haldimand, and on the south by Lake Ontario In Cramahe 48,332 acres are taken up, 15,473 of which are under cultivation The village of Colborne is situated near the south-west corner of the township, and the village of Brighton at its south-east corner, both on the eastern road. Presqu' Isle Harbour is situated partly in this township, and partly in the adjoining township of Murray. The land in the north of the township is not of very good quality, that in the south is better. Timber, principally hardwood. There are three grist and sixteen saw mills, and one distillery in the township.

Population in 1842, 3,200

Ratable property in the township, £45,681.

CREDIT, RIVER.

Takes its rise among the mountains of Caledon; makes its way through the townships of Chinguacousy, Esquesing, and Toronto, and enters Lake Ontario at the village of Port Credit, making many curves, and receiving several small streams in its course. This river has long been celebrated for its salmon fishing, immense quantities having been annually taken, in the spring, during their passage up the stream to deposit their spawn. But, from the great number of mills which have been erected on the river during the last four years, the fishing is destroyed, the salmon being unable to make their way over the dams. Immense quantities of lumber are sawn at the mills on the river, and shipped at Port Credit. Some of the scenery on the banks of the river is very beautiful.

CRIPP'S MILLS.—(See ERAMOSA).

CROSBY, NORTH.

A Township in the Johnstown District, is bounded on the north-east by the township of North Burgess; on the north-west by South Sherbrooke, on the south-west by Bedford, and on the south-east by South Crosby. In North Crosby 10,733 acres are taken up, 1,959 of which are under cultivation. This township is not much settled, some of the land is good, but a considerable portion is poor and stoney. One hundred and seventy-five acres of Crown lands are open for sale in North Crosby, at 8s currency per acre. There are one grist and two saw mills in the township.
Population in 1842, 863
Ratable property in the township, £7822

CROSBY, SOUTH.

A Township in the Johnstown District, is bounded on the north-east by the township of Bastard, on the north-west by North Crosby, on the south-west by Bedford and Pittsburg. In South Crosby 17,279 acres are taken up, 3,892 of which are under cultivation. A considerable portion of the centre and north of the township is taken up by a large lake called Mud Lake, through which the Rideau Canal passes. Much of the land in this township is poor and stoney. A large proportion of the timber in the township is pine. One hundred acres of Crown lands are open for sale in South Crosby, at 8s currency per acre. There are two saw mills in the township.
Population in 1842, 1,003
Ratable property in the township, £11,570

CROWLAND

A Township in the Niagara District, is bounded on the east by the township of Willoughby, on the north by Thorold and Stamford, on the west by Wainfleet; and on the South by Humberstone. In Crowland 15,220 acres are taken up, 6,670 of which are under cultivation. This is a small township, it is pretty well settled. There are two grist and two saw mills in the township.
Population in 1841, 973, who are principally Canadians, with a few Irish, Scotch and English
Ratable property in the township, £18,864.

CUMBERLAND

A Township in the Ottawa District, is bounded on the north-east by the township of Clarence; on the north-west by the Ottawa River, on the south-west by Gloucester; and on the south-east by Russell. In Cumberland 10,654 acres are taken up, 1,616 of which are under cultivation. A branch of the "Petite Nation" River runs through the township. There is one saw mill in the township. Cumberland is not much settled, and there are 14,081 acres of Crown lands for sale, at 8s. currency per acre.

Population in 1842, 713.

Ratable property in the township, £5,895.

DALHOUSIE DISTRICT.

Consists of the County of Carleton, which returns a member to the House of Assembly; and comprises the townships of Fitzroy, Goulbourn, North Gower, Gloucester, Huntley, March, Marlborough, Nepean, Osgoode, and Torbolton. This district, which is bounded on the north by the Ottawa River, is also watered by the Mississippi, the Rideau, and the Petite Nation Rivers. The Dalhousie District, being more dependant upon the lumber trade, than upon agricultural pursuits, advances but slowly. Much of the land in this district is of rather poor quality, being stoney and rocky. There is, however, a sufficient quantity that is fit for agricultural purposes. The larger portion of the inhabitants being engaged in preparing timber for the Quebec market, agriculture is neglected, and the consequence is, that provisions are dearer in Bytown than in any other town in Canada West. The Rideau Canal passes through the district.

(For the quantity of lumber brought down the Ottawa, see BYTOWN.)

Sixty thousand six hundred and eighty-four acres of Crown lands are open for sale in the Dalhousie District; to purchase any of which, application must be made to the Crown Lands' Agent, at New Edinburgh, near Bytown.

Population of the district in 1842, 19,612; since when it has probably increased one-fifth.

The following abstract from the Assessment Rolls will show the rate of increase, and improvement in the district:—

Date.	No. of Acres Cultivated.	MILLS. Grist.	MILLS. Saw.	Milch Cows.	Oxen, 4 years old and upwards.	Horned Cattle, from 2 to 4 years old	Amount of Ratable Property.
1842	42357	8	14	4718	1268	1821	£167,816
1843	47567	4	14	5208	1317	1694	189,892
1844	44146	5	16	......	......	......	166,210

Government and District Officers in the District:

OFFICE.	NAMES.	RESIDENCE.
Judge of District Court	Christ'r Armstrong	Bytown.
Judge of Surrogate Court	Do.	
Sheriff	Edward Malloch	Do.
Clerk of Peace	F. C. Powell (since resigned)	Do.
Treasurer	D. O'Connor	Do.
Inspector of Licenses	Arch. McDonell	Osgoode.
Clerk of District Court	B. Billings	Bytown.
Registrar of Surrogate Court	Do.	
District Clerk	G. P. Baker	Do.
Crown Lands' Agent	John Durie	New Edinburgh.
Warden	Hon. T. McKay	Do.
Coroners	J. Stewart	Bytown.
	John Ritchey	Do.
	W. Smyth	Gloucester.
	Thomas Sproule	Goulbourn.

In consequence of the absence of the Superintendent, I was unable to obtain any account of the schools in this district.

DALHOUSIE

A Township in the Bathurst District; is bounded on the north-east by the township of Lanark, on the north-west by Levant; on the south-west by Sherbrooke; and on the south-east by Bathurst. In Dalhousie 23,440 acres* are taken up, 8,112* of which are under cultivation. Two small branches of the River Clyde stretch across the north of the township, and the north branch of the Mississippi runs through the south of the township from west to east. At its entrance into the township it expands into a lake, containing about 1,200 acres, and its course is very tortuous and irregular. Several small lakes are scattered over the township. The base of a large portion of the north and east of the township is marble of different shades of colour, varying from pure white to dark grey. In Dalhousie 17,200 acres of Crown lands are open for sale, at 8s. c'y per acre. In the township are one grist and two saw mills.

Population in 1842, 1,258.

Ratable property in the township *£17,601.

* These include the township of Levant, no separate assessment having been made.

DARLING

A Township in the Bathurst District, is bounded on the north-east by the township of Pakenham, on the north-west by Bagot, on the south-west by Levant, and on the south-east by Lanark. In Darling 5,094 acres are taken up, 1,257 of which are under cultivation. The River Clyde runs through the south of the township from west to east, and a large lake called Wabalae, or White Lake, stretches across the north corner of the township, and a number of smaller lakes are scattered over the township. Darling is as yet but little settled, and in 1842 contained only 271 inhabitants. Thirty-four thousand eight hundred acres of Crown lands are open for sale in Darling, at 8s. c'y per acre.

Ratable property in the township, £3,088.

DARLINGTON, PORT

A Shipping Place on Lake Ontario, one mile and a half from the village of Bowmanville, it contains a few houses, storehouses for storing produce, and a tavern.

Exports from Port Darlington during 1844

Lumber	254,000 Feet.
Flour	6,927 Barrels.
Oatmeal	203 „
Whiskey	102 „
Pork	16 „
Corn Meal	12 „
Potash	11 „
Ashes	143 „
Butter	21 „
Potatoes	102 Bushels.
Wheat	2,300 „

DARLINGTON

A Township in the Newcastle District, is bounded on the east by the township of Clarke, on the north by Cartwright, on the west by Whitby; and on the south by Lake Ontario. In Darlington 55,205 acres are taken up, 19,364 of which are under cultivation. The township is well watered by numerous small streams running into the lake. The village of Bowmanville is situated in the south-east corner of the township on the eastern road. This is an old, well-settled township, containing good farms, many of which are rented out, the average rent being about $2 per acre. The land is of good average quality, much of it rolling, timber mostly hardwood. There are six grist and nine saw

mills, and one distillery in the township. Two hundred acres of Crown lands are open for sale in Darlington at 8s. c'y per acre.
Population in 1842, 3,500.
Ratable property in the township £51,124.

DAWN.

A township in the Western District; is bounded on the east by the township of Zone, on the north by Enniskillen, on the west by Sombra, and on the south by Chatham and Camden west. In Dawn 16,339 acres are taken up, 3,320 of which are under cultivation This is a fine township, containing excellent land; the soil is generally rich, and the timber the best kinds of hardwood—maple, black walnut, beech, elm, white oak, &c   Bear Creek runs through the south of the township, from east to west, it is navigable as far as the new settlement of Dresden, and from the immense quantities of white oak on its banks, a profitable trade is carried on in staves, large numbers of which are annually exported. The land in the west of the township is rather flat and low, but as you proceed up the creek it becomes more rolling The settlement of Dawn, or Taylor's Mills, is situated in the east of the township, on Bear Creek; and there is also a settlement of coloured persons on the river, situated about ten miles above the forks. They number about fifty families, and have 300 acres of land. The settlement commenced about three years since, and they have now sixty acres cleared and under cultivation, twenty more partially cleared, and they are clearing more fast, they appear to be very industrious. They have a school room (used as a chapel on Sundays), which is usually attended by about sixty pupils, half only of whom are children, and three teachers, one male and two female There is an ashery in the township There are some good farms in the township.
Population 940
Ratable property in the township, £10,898
Exports from Dawn during the year 1844, with their estimated value:
125 M West India Staves £437 10 0
17 M Butt Staves 191 5 0
1000 Bushels of Wheat 187 10 0
32,500 Feet Walnut Lumber 97 10 0
50 Barrels Pot and Pearl Ash 250 0 0

DAWN MILLS.

A Settlement in the township of Dawn, situated on the east branch of Bear Creek, fifteen miles from the forks, and five miles from the western road It is a pleasant, healthy situation; and a good road has been made to the River Thames At present the settlement only contains a grist and saw-mill, store and post-office (post twice a week), and about ten houses.

DAWSON'S BRIDGE.

A small Settlement on the Grand River, near the centre of the township of Dumfries, six miles from Galt, contains about forty inhabitants, one saw-mill, one store, one tavern, one blacksmith

DELAWARE

A Township in the London District, is bounded on the east by the township of Westminster, on the north and west by the River Thames, and on the south by Southwold. In Delaware 10,033 acres are taken up, 1,756 of which are under cultivation. This is a beautiful township, containing many fine situations for farms, or private residences, the scenery, particularly that on the banks of the Thames, having a very English appearance The soil is generally good and most of the timber hardwood there is some pine in the north of the township. The villages of Delaware and Kilworth, and the Indian settlement

Oneida, are in the township. There are two grist and three saw mills and one distillery in Delaware

Population in 1842, 468.

Ratable property in the township, £9,158.

DELAWARE.

A Village in the township of Delaware, on the western road, twelve miles west from London, beautifully situated on the River Thames, this is one of the prettiest spots in Canada, with much the appearance of an English village. The scenery of the surrounding neighbourhood is very picturesque, and resembling the grounds about some of the fine old country seats in England. A handsome bridge, 900 feet in length, has been constructed across the Thames, which is generally considered the finest work of the kind in Canada In the neighbourhood of Delaware are some fine farms, and the flats of the river form excellent grazing ground Delaware was first settled in 1832, it contains about 300 inhabitants, and a neat Episcopal church

Post Office, post every day.

Professions and Trades—One grist and saw mill, four stores, two taverns, one saddler, one cabinet maker, two waggon makers, two blacksmiths, four shoemakers, two tailors

Principal tavern, "Bullen's"

DEMORESTVILLE

A Village in the township of Sophiasburg, situated on the Bay of Quinté, opposite Big Island, which is reached by means of a bridge constructed across the bay It contains about 400 inhabitants, who have two churches, Presbyterian and Methodist. There are also in the village, three stores, two taverns, one waggon maker, one blacksmith, two tailors, two shoemakers.

Post Office, post three times a week

DERBY

A Township in the Wellington District, is bounded on the east by the township of Sydenham, on the north and west by unsurveyed lands, and on the south by Sullivan The Owen Sound Bay encroaches on its north-east corner. Derby has only lately been laid out, and no return has yet been made from it.

DEREHAM

A Township in the Brock District, is bounded on the east by the township of Norwich, on the north by Oxford, on the west by South Dorchester, and on the south by Malahide In Dereham 23,068 acres are taken up, 3951 of which are under cultivation Several branches of the Otter Creek run through the township Timber—pine, intermixed with hardwood The village of Tilsonburg is situated in the south-east corner There are one grist mill and two saw mills in the township

Population in 1842, 1014

Ratable property in the township, £14,243

DESJARDINS CANAL—(*See* DUNDAS)

DETROIT RIVER

Forms the western boundary of the County of Essex, in the Western District, dividing that portion of Canada from the United States. It receives the waters of the upper lakes from Lake St Clair, and discharges them into Lake Erie. It is about twenty-three miles in length, and from one to two miles wide. There are several islands in the river, varying in size, the principal of which are Bois Blanc, Fighting Island and Peach Island; and the scenery on its banks is very beautiful. Large quantities of fish are taken in the river (about 1200 barrels of Whitefish alone are generally taken annually), and the sportsman usually finds abundance of wild ducks, which breed in great numbers in the marshes bordering some of the islands, and portions of the coast. The towns of Sandwich and Amherstburgh, and the village of Windsor are situated on its banks.

On the bank of the river, a short distance above Amherstburg, is an Indian reserve occupied by Chippewas, Hurons, Munsees, and Shawnees. In the year 1790, when the council of the four nations, (Chippewas, Ottawas, Hurons and Pottawatamies), surrendered to the government the extensive tract of land in Western Canada, now known as the Huron District, they stipulated for a reservation of the hunting grounds then occupied by the Hurons and Wyandotts, which comprised 22,390 acres, extending about six miles along the shore of the Detroit River, and having a depth of seven miles. In the year 1836, in consequence of the encroachments of the whites upon these lands, and the desire which existed in that part of the country to be allowed to settle upon them, the government induced the Indians to surrender a large portion of their reserve, in trust, to be sold for their exclusive benefit. By a subsequent agreement, made in the next year by Sir F. Head, they resigned two-thirds of the reserve, the proceeds of one-third to be applied to their exclusive benefit, and those of the second and third for the general purposes of the Indians in Upper Canada. The portion of the reserve still remaining in their possession is about 8,000 acres in extent. Upon this are settled each on a separate farm, the Chippewas, and other Indians. The Munsees and Shawnees are chiefly migratory, but the few families who have become in some measure stationary, live on the reserve, but have not had separate farms assigned to them, nor erected any dwellings. The Hurons have thirty-four dwelling-houses, of which thirty-three are made of logs, and one is a very comfortable frame dwelling of two stories, for the erection of which they paid £250. They have also ten barns, of which four are framed, and twenty-three log stables. None of the Hurons live in wigwams, but the Chippewas, except their chief, who resides at Point Pelé, have no other habitations.

The land occupied by the Hurons is laid out in regular blocks of 200 acres each, which are selected for the several families by the chiefs. Among this tribe a man's children inherit his property, but if he leaves no children, his farm becomes at the disposal of the chief. He has not the power of conveying his interest to other members of his tribe, or to strangers. These Hurons have for a long time been engaged, more or less, in cultivating the land, but until a few years ago, they made little or no progress in husbandry; more recently however they have greatly and regularly extended their farms by clearing, and have improved in their mode of agriculture. Many of them are good farmers, and they are annually becoming more prosperous and happy. About twelve years ago, they had scarcely any agricultural implements but the hoe, they now possess nineteen ploughs, ten harrows and six fanning-mills; they have also twelve waggons and carts, fourteen sleighs, one caleche, and three carioles. They have cleared 259 acres, each male adult has a farm of 200 acres allotted to him, on which many have from fifteen to thirty acres under cultivation, the average is between seven and eight acres. Their stock consists of seven yoke of oxen, nine bulls, eight steers, twenty-seven cows, fifteen heifers, ninety-three horses, two hundred and ninety swine, and seventy-three geese. They have given up the chase in a great measure, and only hunt occasionally, when their absence does not interfere with their farming operations, usually in the autumn. They all profess christianity, the majority are Wesleyan Methodists, and the others Roman Catholics. They have no place of worship of their own. The Methodist minister, however, who is stationed in the town of Amherstburg, visits those of his persuasion every Sunday, and the Roman Catholics attend chapel at Amherstburg, which is about three miles from their settlement. There is at present no school among them, but they have expressed their desire to establish one.

The Chippewas are in very different and inferior condition. They chiefly depend upon hunting and fishing About ten families commenced to till the ground within the last twelve years. They have only about three or four acres each under cultivation, they raise only Indian corn, and use no implement but the hoe The women perform almost all the field work They are all heathens, and it does not appear that any efforts have been made for their conversion. Their number is on the decrease, occasioned by exposure, intemperance, and insufficiency of food.

In 1842, the number belonging to each tribe was as follows:
Chippewas 258
Hurons 88
Munsees 22
Shawnees 6
                                                                        ———
                                                                        374

Formerly Amherstburg was the chief post for the distribution of presents to the Indians residing west of Toronto, and to those of the United States Since the formation of the establishment at Manitoulin Island, the distributions at Amherstburg and Drummond Island have been discontinued, except to the Indians in the immediate neighbourhood of the former place, and have since been made at Manitoulin.

DICKENSON'S LANDING.

A Village in the township of Osnabruck, situated at the head of the Cornwall Canal, eleven miles west from Cornwall It contains about 200 inhabitants, a Catholic church, six stores, and five taverns.

DORCHESTER. NORTH.

A Township in the London District, is bounded on the east by the township of Oxford, on the north by Nissouri; on the west by London and Westminster; and on the south by South Dorchester In North Dorchester 15,837 acres of land are taken up, 4,326 of which are under cultivation This is a small township, with land of variable quality, some part being good, with hardwood timber, and a considerable portion light soil, with pine timber. There are one grist and seven saw mills in the township

Population in 1842, 1,018
Ratable property in the township, £15,714.

DORCHESTER, SOUTH.

A Township in the London District, is bounded on the east by the township of Dereham, on the north by North Dorchester, on the west by Westminster and Yarmouth; and on the south by Malahide and a small portion of Yarmouth. In South Dorchester 8,505 acres are taken up, 1,098 of which are under cultivation. There are three large swamps on the east side of the township, from the centre one of which Kettle Creek takes its rise, it then follows a westerly course, across the centre of the township, into Yarmouth South Dorchester is at present but little settled One hundred and fifty acres of Crown lands are open for sale in South Dorchester, at 8s. currency per acre. There are two grist and three saw mills in the township.

Population in 1842, 418.
Ratable property in the township, £5,106.

DOURO.

A Township in the Colborne District, is bounded on the east by the township of Dummer; on the north-west by Smith, and on the south by Otonabee. In Douro 23,971 acres are taken up, 4,241 of which are under cultivation. This is a triangular-shaped township, and is separated from Smith by the

Otonabee River. There is some good land in Douro. Timber—hardwood, intermixed with pine There are two saw mills in the township. Douro is settled principally by Irish Catholics. Two thousand two hundred and fifteen acres of Crown lands are open for sale in the township, at 8s currency per acre.
Population —
Ratable property in the township, £11,732.

DOVER, EAST & WEST.

A Township in the County of Kent, in shape a triangle, is bounded on the west by Lake St Clair, on the north-east by the township of Chatham, and on the south by the River Thames Dover contains 13,237 acres, of which 2,432 are under cultivation about one-third of the whole is open prairie, well adapted for grazing; the remainder covered with good timber—the soil is rich and fertile That part of Dover East bordering on the Thames is well settled. The township contains a mixed population, in number 1,242 A small stream runs through the upper portion of this township.

The Canada Company possess 7500 acres in Dover; and 5,200 acres of Crown lands are open for sale in the township, at 8s currency per acre There is a tannery in the township, and the registry office for the county is kept about two miles below Chatham. Along the banks of the river are several wood wharves, for supplying steamboats with fuel

Amount of ratable property in the township, 10,011.

DOWNIE.

A Township in the Huron District, is bounded on the north-east by Ellice; on the north-west by Fullarton, on the south-west by Blanshard, and on the south-east by South Easthope In Downie 32,082 acres are leased or sold, 2,777 of which are under cultivation The River Avon runs across the township from east to west, and two creeks pass, one through the north, and the other through the south corner of the township. The land is much the same as that of the adjoining townships.

Population of Downie, 1,370.
Ratable property in the township, £12,134.

DRESDEN.

A Settlement in the township of Dawn, just laid out at the head of the navigation of the east branch of Bear Creek. It is a good situation for a village, but at present it contains only one store, and three or four houses. Vessels of 300 tons can load here.

DRUMMOND

A Township in the Bathurst District, is bounded on the north-east by the township of Beckwith, on the north-west by Lanark, on the south-west by Bathurst, and on the south-east by Elmsley. In Drummond 33,795 acres are taken up, 9541 of which are under cultivation The north and south branches of the Mississippi unite in the west corner of the township, where they are also joined by the River Clyde, the whole forming one stream, which takes a north course till near the north corner of the township, where it makes a bend, and runs to the east, when near the eastern border of the township it expands into the Mississippi Lake, which stretches away into the township of Beckwith. Several small streams stretch across the township. The town of Perth is situated near the south corner of the township The base of the south of the township is granite, but excellent white freestone is found in great abundance through the centre of the township There are many good farms in the township. In Drummond 3500 acres of Crown lands are open for sale at 8s. c'y

per acre. There are two grist, three saw mills, and three distilleries in the township.
Population in 1842, 3451.
Ratable property in the township, £38,084.

DRUMMOND ISLAND

An Island in the north-west of Lake Huron, between Cockburn Island and Isle St. Joseph, formerly belonging to Great Britain, but given up by the British Government to the United States It was formerly fortified; but is now entirely deserted.

DRUMMONDVILLE

A small Village in the township of Stamford. situated about a quarter of a mile back from the Falls of Niagara. It contains about 130 inhabitants, two stores, two taverns, two tailors, two shoemakers, one blacksmith.

DUFFIN'S CREEK, or CANTON.

A Village in the township of Pickering, situated on Duffin's Creek, about three miles from Lake Ontario and twenty-three miles from Toronto. Contains about 130 inhabitants Churches and chapels, 4, viz, Presbyterian, Catholic, British Wesleyan, and Quaker. The eastern road runs through the village.

Post Office, post every day

Professions and Trades.—One grist mill, one brewery, one tannery, three stores, two taverns, three shoemakers, two tailors, one blacksmith, one waggon maker.

DUMFRIES

A Township in the Gore District, is bounded on the north by the township of Waterloo, on the west by Blenheim, on the south by Brantford; and on the east by Beverley and a small portion of Puslinch. Dumfries contains 92,364 acres, of which 49,238 are under cultivation The Grand River enters the township four miles from the north-east boundary, runs south-west about half the length of the township, then makes a bend and runs west for about three miles, then south-west to within three miles of the south-west boundary, at which point it is joined by Smith's Creek A creek having three small lakes in its course, takes its rise about the centre of the west of the township, runs a south-west course, and enters Smith's Creek a mile and a half from the west boundary A small lake about fifteen acres in extent, called "Blue Lake," is situated on the east side of the river, about three miles from the south boundary. The settlement of Dumfries was commenced in the year 1816, by Mr W. Dickson, and nearly every lot is now taken up There are in the township the villages of Galt, Paris, St George, Ayr, and Jedburgh The soil is generally stoney—the land hilly Large quantities of plaster are obtained from beds on the banks of the river in the neighbourhood of Paris. There are in the township seven grist and sixteen saw mills

No census of the township has been taken since 1841, when the population amounted to 6129

Ratable property in the township, £145,584.

DUMMER.

A Township in the Colborne District, is bounded on the east by the township of Belmont, on the north by Burleigh; on the west by Douro; and on the south by Asphodel. In Dummer 21,317 acres are taken up, 5040 of which are under cultivation. Dummer is separated from Burleigh by a chain of lakes, and several small lakes are scattered over the township. Dummer is well settled, and contains some good farms. The settlers are principally Scotch.

There are two mills (grist and saw) in the township; and the village of Warsaw is situated in the south-west of the township. In Dummer 16,000 acres of Crown Lands are open for sale, at 8s. currency per acre.

Ratable property in the township, £12,390.

DUNDAS

A manufacturing Village in the township of Flamborough West, five miles from Hamilton; situated at the western extremity of the valley which borders the south-western portion of Lake Ontario. An extensive marsh reaches from the village to Burlington Bay. A canal, five miles in length, called the Desjardins Canal, after a Frenchman who first commenced the work, has been cut to connect the village with the bay, through which all articles manufactured in the place, and farming produce, can be sent to Lake Ontario.

Dundas is surrounded on three sides by high table land, commonly called "the mountain," from whence large quantities of excellent freestone and limestone are obtained; much of which is exported to Toronto, and other places on Lake Ontario. Through the influence of its extensive water power, the village has been gradually rising into prosperity during the last fifteen or twenty years.

Dundas possesses six churches and chapels, viz., Episcopal, Presbyterian, Catholic, Baptist, Methodist, and one free to all denominations. There are also a fire and hook and ladder company, who possess an engine house and one engine; and a mechanics' institute.

Population, about 1700.

Professions and Trades.—Three physicians and surgeons, two lawyers two grist mills (one with five run of stones), one oatmeal mill, one manufactory (for making furniture, edge-tools, pumps, and turnery-ware), one carding machine, fulling mill, and cloth factory, two foundries (for making steam engines and all kinds of machinery, one of which employs nearly 100 hands), one bur millstone factory, one planing machine, one axe factory, one comb factory, one soap and candle factory, one tannery, nine stores, three breweries, six taverns, one druggist and bookseller, two saddlers, three bakers, two watchmakers, four butchers, six blacksmiths, two waggon makers, one hatter, six groceries, six shoemakers, two chair makers, four painters and glaziers, four schools. One bank agency, "British North America."

Post Office, post every day.

Principal Tavern.—"Bamberger's"

The office of the Registrar for the county of Halton is kept in Dundas.

Forwarders, Warehousemen, and Commission Merchants, { M. W. & E. Browne, Land & Routh, Parsons & Blaine.

Exports through the Desjardins Canal, for the year 1845.

Description	Quantity.
Flour	62,153 barrels.
Biscuit	93 do.
Oatmeal	90 do
Whiskey	1,101 do.
Pork	115 do.
Ashes	120 do
Lard	4 do
Grass Seed	180 do.
Butter	63 firkins.
Potatoes	230 bushels.
Staves, puncheon	230,510 pieces
Do. pipe	7,779 do.
Free Stone	785 tons.

F

DUNDAS.

A County in the Eastern District, comprises the townships of Mountain, Matilda, Winchester, and Williamsburg It returns a member to the House of Assembly.

DUNN.

A Township in the Niagara District, is bounded on the east and north by the grand river, on the west by the township of Cayuga, and on the south by Lake Erie. In Dunn, 6,912 acres are taken up, 1,534 of which are under cultivation. This township is, as yet, but little settled The settlements of Port Maitland, and Haldimand, opposite Dunnville, are situated in it, on the Grand River. The banks of the river, in the lower portion of the township, are rather low. There is one grist mill in Dunn.

Population in 1841, 345.

Ratable property in the township, £6,380.

DUNNVILLE.

A Village in the township of Moulton, situated on the Grand River, at its junction with the feeder of the Welland Canal, four miles and three quarters from Lake Erie It commenced settling in 1829, and now contains about 400 inhabitants. A steam boat plies here regularly during the season, and a smaller boat continues the route to Brantford Considerable quanties of lumber are shipped here. Dunnville contains an Episcopal church, and a Presbyterian church is in progress

Post Office, post three times a week.

Professions and Trades —One physician and surgeon, two grist mills, three saw mills, one distillery, one Tannery, one carding machine and cloth factory, six stores, four taverns, four groceries, two waggon makers, four blacksmiths, one saddler, two tinsmiths, four shoemakers, three tailors, two cabinet makers, one baker, one turner.

DUNWICH

A Township in the London District, is bounded on the north east by the township of Southwold; on the north west by the River Thames; on the south west by Aldborough, and on the south east by Lake Erie. In Dunwich 28,563 acres are taken up, 3,193 of which are under cultivation. There are some good farms, with tolerable clearings, in the south of the township, but the houses and farm buildings are generally poor, settlers principally Irish. A large swamp is situated on the west side of the township A foot path has been cut out through the township from the Talbot road to the River Thames There are two grist and two saw-mills in the township.

Population in 1842, 712

Ratable property in the township, £13,957.

DURHAM

A County in the Newcastle District comprises the townships of Clarke, Cavan, Cartwright, Darlington, Hope, and Manvers It returns a member to the House of Assembly.

EASTERN DISTRICT.

Consists of the Counties of Stormont, Dundas and Glengarry. This is an old settled district, which returns four members to the House of Assembly— three for the counties and one for the town of Cornwall, rather more than its share, considering its relative importance, compared with some of the more western districts The Eastern District is bounded on the south by the River St Lawrence, and the west of the district is watered by the Petite Nation River and its tributaries: it is pretty well settled; and Cornwall, the district town, is pleasantly situated; but much of the land is poor and cold. The district advances but slowly. Two thousand one hundred and fifty acres of Crown lands are open for sale in the district, at 8s. currency per acre; to purchase any of which application must be made to the Crown Lands Agent at Cornwall.

Population in 1842, 29,893; since when it has probably increased one-tenth. The following abstract from the assessment rolls will show the rate of increase and improvement in the district.

Date.	No. of Acres Cultivated.	MILLS. Grist.	MILLS. Saw.	Milch Cows.	Oxen, 4 years old, and upwards.	Horned Cattle, from 2 to 4 years old.	Amount of Ratable Property.
1842	89,237	20	46	12,291	642	3,519	£366,956
1843	89,240	21	53	13,241	662	3,268	366,404
1845	90,872	17	50	13,269	710	2,871	372,604

Government and District Officers in the Eastern District:

Judge of District Court	G. S. Jarvis	Cornwall.
Sheriff	A. McMartin	"
Treasurer	A. McLean	"
Clerk of Peace and District Clerk	James Pringle	"
Judge of Surrogate Court	Robert Cline	
Registrar of County of Stormont	John McLean	Kingston.
" " Dundas	A. McDonell	Mariatown.
" " Glengarry	A. Fraser	
Inspector of Licenses	P. VanKoughnet	Cornwall.
Crown Lands Agent	Samuel Hart	"
Collector of Customs	G. C. Wood	"
" "	A. McDonell	Mariatown.
" "	John Cameron	Charlottenburg.
Clerk of District Court, and Deputy Clerk of Crown	George Anderson	Cornwall.
Warden	Hon. A. Fraser	

No. of Common Schools in operation in the Eastern District.—Matilda, eighteen; Mountain, twelve; Cornwall (town), six; Cornwall (township), twenty-one; Charlottenburg, twenty-two; Finch, six; Kenyon, ten; Lancaster, fourteen; Lochiel, fourteen; Osnabruck, twenty-one; Roxborough, three; Williamsburg, fourteen; Winchester, six. Total, 167.

EASTHOPE, SOUTH.

A Township in the Huron District; is bounded on the north-east by North Easthope; on the north-west by Downie; and on the south by Missouri and Zorra. In South Easthope 15,076 acres are leased or sold, 3,069 of which are under cultivation. A branch of the Thames runs through the township. There are three saw-mills in the township.

Population 820.

Ratable property in the township, £8,453.

EASTWOOD.

A Settlement in the township of East Oxford; contains about sixty inhabitants and an Episcopal church, two stores, one tavern, one saddler, one waggon-maker, and two blacksmiths.

EASTHOPE, NORTH.

A Township in the Huron District; is bounded on the north-east by the townships of Wellesley and Wilmot, on the north-west by Ellice, and on the south by South Easthope. In North Easthope 28,216 acres are leased or sold, 4,172 of which are under cultivation. The Avon, a branch of the Thames, runs through the south of the township, making its egress at the village of Stratford. The Big Swamp encroaches on the north of this township.

Population in 1844, 1,151
Ratable property in the township, 12,501.

EDWARDSBURGH.

A Township in the Johnstown District, is bounded on the east by the township of Matilda, on the north by South Gower and Oxford, on the west by Augusta, and on the south by the River St Lawrence. In Edwardsburgh 31,557 acres are taken up, 7,748 of which are under cultivation. The land on the river is generally good, but back, for about seventeen miles, it is mostly poor, and much of it swampy, the farmers raising scarcely sufficient produce for their own consumption. In Edwardsburgh 950 acres of Crown lands are open for sale, at 8s. c'y per acre. There are three grist and six saw mills in the township.

Population 2.837
Ratable property in the township £31,174.

EGREMONT.

A Township in the Wellington District, is bounded on the east by the township of Proton, on the north by Glenelg, on the west by Normanby, and on the south by Arthur. This township has only lately been surveyed and laid out, and no return has yet been made from it.

EKFRID

A Township in the London District, is bounded on the north-east by the township of Cariadoc, on the north-west by Adelaide, on the south-west by Mosa, and on the south-east by the River Thames. In Ekfrid 30,072 acres are taken up, 5,655 of which are under cultivation. A large swamp occupies about a fourth of the township, and there is a considerable quantity of wet land, particularly in the north of the township. There is one saw-mill in Ekfrid.

Population in 1842, 1,174
Ratable property in the township, £13,989.

ELDON

A Township in the Colborne District, is bounded on the east by the township of Fenelon, on the north by unsurveyed lands, on the west by Thorah; and on the south by Mariposa. In Eldon 19,699 acres are taken up, 2,875 of which are under cultivation. This township is well watered, and contains some good land. In Eldon 2,100 acres of Crown lands are open for sale, at 8s. c'y per acre.

Population —
Ratable property in the township £9,029

ELIZABETHTOWN

A Township in the Johnstown District, is bounded on the east by the township of Augusta, on the north by Kitley and Wolford; on the west by Yonge; and on the south by the River St Lawrence. In Elizabethtown 48,187 acres are taken up, 21,834 of which are under cultivation. There are four small lakes in the township, each containing about 600 acres, viz:—Jones' Pond, Lamb's Pond, Mud Lake, and Atkin's Lake. The Petitè Nation River takes its rise in this township, nearly in the rear of Brockville, and the south branch of the

River Rideau takes its rise in Mud Lake. Limestone is to be obtained in abundance throughout the whole township. The soil varies in quality, some parts being excellent, and others hilly and broken. Timber, principally hardwood, intermixed occasionally with pine and hemlock. The town of Brockville is situated in the south-east corner of the township. In Elizabethtown 250 acres of Crown lands are for sale, at 8s c'y per acre. There are five grist and nine saw mills in the township.

Population 6,437.

Ratable property in the township, £97,297, which includes the town of Brockville.

ELLICE.

A Township in the Huron District, is bounded on the north east by Crown lands, on the north west by the township of Logan, on the south west by Fullarton and Downie, and on the south east by North Easthope. In Ellice 8,245 acres are leased or sold, 1,511 of which are under cultivation. The land bordering upon the Goderich road is rather poor, and the big swamp takes a considerable slice out of the north east of the township. The rest of the township is mostly good land. A creek, a branch of the Thames, runs through the west of the township. There are in Ellice one grist and two saw mills.

Population, 528.

Ratable property in the township, £4,810.

ELMSLEY, SOUTH

A Township in the Johnstown District, is bounded on the east by the township of Montague; on the north by the Rideau Canal and Otter Lake; on the west by Burgess, and on the south by Kitley and Bastard. In South Elmsley 10,275 acres are taken up, 3,566 of which are under cultivation. The River Tay passes through this township from north west to south east, and enters the Rideau Lake two miles east from Oliver's Ferry. It has been made navigable to Perth, for small vessels. The soil of the south of the township is of fair average quality. Timber, a mixture of pine, cedar, and hardwood. That portion of it, however, bordering on the canal, is mostly poor and stony, and much of it overflowed by the waters of the Lake. A small settlement called Pike Falls, is situated in the township. In South Elmsley, 330 acres of Crown lands are open for sale at 8s currency per acre. There are one grist and two saw mills in the township.

Population, 815, who are principally Irish and Scotch, with some few English and Canadians.

Ratable Property in the township, £9,789.

ELMSLEY, NORTH

A Township in the Bathurst District, is bounded on the north east by the township of Montague, on the north west by Drummond and Bathurst, on the south west by Burgess, and on the south east by the Rideau Lake and Canal. In North Elmsley, 18,603 acres are taken up, 3,891 of which are under cultivation. A fair proportion of the land in this township is of good quality, and there are some tolerable farms in it. Timber, pine intermixed with hardwood. The flourishing village of Smith's Falls is situated in the east of the township, on the Rideau Canal; and Oliver's Ferry, the place where the road from Perth to Brockville crosses the Rideau Lake, is also in North Elmsley, seven miles from Perth. There are one grist and two saw mills in the township.

Population in 1842, 1154.

Ratable property in the township, 15,416.

ELORA.

A Village in the township of Nichol, beautifully and romantically situated on the Grand River, about thirteen miles from Guelph, was first settled in 1832 by Mr. W. Gilkison   The "Falls" of Elora are very beautiful, and are much visited, the river having worn a channel thirty-five or forty feet deep through the solid lime stone rock. A large rock stands in the centre of the stream, just above the Falls, bearing trees; the base of which is nearly worn away by the constant friction of the water. Just below the village, the river is joined by a branch called the Irvine. The situation of Elora is hilly. The village contains about 100 inhabitants, and has an Episcopal church, and a Methodist chapel.

Post Office, Post three times a week

Professions and Trades—One physician and surgeon, one grist and oatmeal mill, one saw mill, carding machine and cloth factory, one store, one tavern, one chemist and druggist, two blacksmiths, three shoemakers, two waggon makers, two tailors

Crown Lands Agent, A. Geddes.

ELZEVIR

A Township in the Victoria District is bounded on the east by the township of Kaladar; on the north by Grimsthorpe, on the west by Madoc, and on the south by Hungerford   This township has only lately been opened for sale, and no return has yet been made from it   Thirty-eight thousand four hundred and seventy-five acres of Crown lands are open for sale in Elzevir, at 8s. c'y. per acre.

EMBRO

A Village in the west of the township of Zorra, situated on the road leading from Governor's road to Stratford   There is a Presbyterian church in the village

Population about 150, who are principally Highland Scotch.

Professions and Trades.—One grist and saw-mill, carding machine and cloth factory, one distillery, one tannery, three stores, two taverns, one waggon maker, two blacksmiths, three shoemakers, one tailor

Post Office, post three times a-week

EMILY

A Township in the Colborne District, is bounded on the east by the townships of Ennismore and Smith, on the north by Verulam, on the west by Ops, and on the south by Cavan   In Emily, 35,357 acres are taken up, 5399 of which are under cultivation. This is a good township, and is well settled by a mixed population, principally Irish Protestants. It has a good mill stream running through it, and a small settlement, called Metcalfe, is situated in its south-west corner   There are two grist and two saw-mills, and one distillery in the township   Four thousand one hundred acres of Crown lands are open for sale in Emily, at 8s c'y per acre

Population, —

Ratable property in the township, £18,015.

ENNISMORE.

A Township in the Colborne District, is bounded on the north-east and south by part of the great chain of lakes situated in the district, and on the west by the township of Emily   This is a small township, of nearly a triangular shape. In Ennismore 8321 acres are taken up, 935 of which are under cultivation. Inhabitants principally Irish Catholics   One thousand four hundred acres of Crown lands are open for sale in the township, at 8s c'y per acre.

Population, —

Ratable property in the township, £3494.

ENNISKILLEN.

A Township in the Western District; is bounded on the east by the township of Brooke; on the north by Plympton; on the west by Moore, and on the south by Dawn. In Enniskillen, 2450 acres are taken up, 347 of which are under cultivation. The north branch of Bear Creek runs across the township, entering it at its north-east corner, and making its exit at its south-west corner. This township possesses a large portion of excellent land, but it is as yet but little settled Seven thousand five hundred acres of Crown lands are open for sale in Enniskillen, at 8s. c'y per acre. There is a grist and saw-mill, and tannery in the township.

Population taken with that of the township of Moore.

Ratable property in the township, £1,212.

ERAMOSA.

A Township in the Wellington District; is bounded on the north-east by the township of Erin, on the north-west by Garafraxa, on the south-west by Nichol and Guelph; and on the south-east by Nassagaweya. In Eramosa 28,701 acres are taken up, 7,285 of which are under cultivation. A branch of the Grand River passes through the township. The upper portion of the township, to the bank of the river, is excellent land, below, it is broken and stony. Eramosa is thickly settled, principally by Scotch and Irish, many of whom have fine farms. In the south-east of the township, on a branch of the Speed, there are "Strange's Mills" and shingle machine, and at the same place a last factory, blacksmith, and Quaker meeting-house. At "Murphy's Mills," or "Little Falls," there are a saw mill, carding machine, fulling mill, and store. At "Cripp's Mills," on the town line between Eramosa and Nassagaweya, a grist and saw mill, and store. Altogether there are six saw mills in the township

No census has been taken since 1841, when the population amounted to 935.

Ratable property in the township, 20,839

ERIE, LAKE

The most southerly of the Canadian lakes, and also the most shallow. It forms the southern boundary of the Niagara, Talbot, London and Western Districts It is 231 miles in length, and, in its widest part, about 70 miles in breadth. It receives the waters of the upper lakes from the Detroit River, and discharges itself into the Niagara River It is 564 feet above the level of the sea, and thirty feet below Lake Huron Several small islands are scattered over the western extremity of the lake, only one of which, "Point Pele Island," is inhabited This is the most dangerous of all the lakes to navigate in stormy weather, in consequence of the ground swell, from the shallowness of the lake, being very heavy. The banks vary in height, no portion of them, however, is above a hundred feet in height There are considerable quantities of red cedar on particular portions of the coast The principal harbours on the Canadian side of Lake Erie are Port Dover, Port Stanley, and the Rond 'Eau.

ERIEUS

The name of a post office, in the township of Raleigh, on Talbot Road—ten miles from Blenheim. There is a tavern two miles farther west.

ERIN

A Township in the Wellington District; is bounded on the north-east by the township of Caledon, on the north-west by Garafraxa, on the south-west by Eramosa; and on the south-east by Esquesing In Erin 32,447 acres are taken up, 7,945 of which are under cultivation. Much of the land in the township is hilly and stony There is a small settlement in the south-west of the township called "McMullen's Mills," where are a grist and saw mill, tavern and blacksmith's shop, and between forty and fifty inhabitants. There are one grist and four

saw mills in the township. In Erin, 1,527 acres of Crown lands are open for sale, at 8s. currency per acre.
Population in 1841, 1,368.
Ratable property in the township, 23,797.

ERNESTOWN.

A Township in the Midland District, is bounded on the east by the townships of Portland and Kingston, on the north by Camden, on the west by Fredericksburgh, and on the south by Lake Ontario. In Ernestown, 59,447 acres are taken up, 22,507 of which are under cultivation. The village of Bath is situated in the east of the township, on the lake; and a settlement called "Wilton," is in the north-east of the township, where is a Presbyterian church, and a Methodist chapel, a mill and post office. There is also a Methodist chapel in the north-west corner of the township. There are four grist and fourteen saw mills in the township.

Ernestown is well settled, and contains 4,317 inhabitants.
Ratable property in the township, £64,031

ERROL

A Village in the township of Plympton, laid out in 1838 by government. It is thirteen miles from Port Sarnia, contains a post office, post twice a week, a water saw mill on the lake shore; and a church, free for all denominations. It also possesses a school. Town lots sold at $20.
Professions and Trades.—One school, one saw mill, and three carpenters.

ESQUESING.

A Township in the Gore District, is bounded on the north-east by the township of Chinguacousy, on the north-east by Erin, on the south-west by Nassagaweya, and on the south-east by Trafalgar. In Esquesing, 57,347 acres are taken up, 19,622 of which are under cultivation. This is a fine township, containing excellent land, and many good farms, which are generally well cultivated. Wheat of superior quality is grown in this and the adjoining townships. The land is mostly rolling. The River Credit runs through the north-east of the township. Nine hundred acres of Crown lands are open for sale in Esquesing, at 8s. currency per acre. The villages of Norval and Hornby are situated in Esquesing, and there are four grist and eleven saw mills in the township.

Population —, who are principally English, Irish and Scotch.
Ratable property in the township, £78,101

ESSA

A Township in the Simcoe District, is bounded on the north by the townships of Vespra and Sunnidale, on the west by Tossorontio, on the south by Tecumseth, and on the east by Innisfil. In Essa 13,987 acres are taken up, 2,906 of which are under cultivation. The Nottawasaga River runs directly through the township, from south to north. A large portion of the township is excellent land. In the north-east, however, it is hilly and broken. There is a swamp in the south of the township, on the town-line between Essa and Innisfil. There are in Essa 8,500 acres of Crown lands for sale, at 8s. currency per acre. There are in the township one grist and one saw mill.

Population in 1842, 534.
Ratable property in the township, £7,334.

ESSEX

A County in the Western District, comprises the townships of Anderdon, Colchester, Gosfield, Maidstone, Mersea, Malden, Rochester, and Sandwich. It returns a member to the House of Assembly.

ETOBICOKE

A Township in the Home District; is bounded on the east by the township of York; on the north by Vaughan; on the west by the Gore of Toronto, and the township of Toronto; and on the south by Lake Ontario. In Etobicoke, 24,934 acres are taken up, 12,516 of which are under cultivation. This is a well settled township, containing good land; although that portion bordering on the lake is generally poor and sandy. Timber near the lake, mostly pine, but farther back it is principally hardwood. The River Humber, which is an excellent mill stream, forms the dividing line between Etobicoke and the township of York. The village of Weston is situated on the Humber, in the north-east of the township; and the settlement called "Mimico" on the Mimico river, on Dundas Street. There are five grist and nine saw mills in the township.

Population in 1842, 2,467.
Ratable property in the Township, £38,339.

ETOBICOKE RIVER

Takes its rise in the township of Chinguacousy, runs through the east of the township, and the north and east of the township of Toronto, and enters Lake Ontario close to the town-line between Toronto and Etobicoke townships.

EUPHRASIA

A Township in the Simcoe District, is bounded on the north by the township of St Vincent, on the west by Holland, on the south by Artemisia, and on the east by Collingwood. In Euphrasia, 1,200 acres are taken up, only twenty-five of which are under cultivation. This township was added to the Simcoe District in the year 1844, previous to which time it formed part of the Home District. In Euphrasia there are 49,600 acres of Crown lands for disposal, at 8s currency per acre; to purchase which, application must be made to the Crown lands agent at Barrie. No return has been made of the population of this township, but it must be very small indeed.

Ratable property in the township, £311

FARMERSVILLE

A Village in the centre of the north of the township of Yonge. It contains about 200 inhabitants, who have a Methodist meeting-house, one physician and surgeon, grist and saw mill, carding machine and cloth factory, three stores, two taverns, one saddler, two blacksmiths

FAWN ISLAND

A small Island in the River St. Clair, 18 miles below Port Sarnia It contains about fifty acres

FENELON, or CAMERON'S FALLS

A Village in the township of Fenelon, situated in the north-east of the township, about forty miles from Peterboro', and twenty-five miles north from Lindsay It contains about 130 inhabitants, who have an Episcopal Church. The village also contains one grist and saw mill, one store, one tavern, one blacksmith, one shoemaker, one tailor, one boatbuilder.

Post Office, post once a-week

FENELON AND BEXLEY.

These Townships are united for district purposes, being yet but little settled. Bexley lies north, and Fenelon south Fenelon is bounded on the north by Bexley; on the east by Verulam, on the west by Eldon and Mariposa, and on the south by Ops Bexley is bounded on the east by Somerville; on the north by unsurveyed lands, on the west by unsurveyed lands and the township of

Eldon; and on the south by Fenelon. In Fenelon and Bexley 7279 acres are taken up, 862 of which are under cultivation A large lake, called "Balsam Lake," fills up a considerable portion of the south and east of Bexley, and of the north of Fenelon; and a portion of Sturgeon Lake stretches along the coast of Fenelon. The land bordering these lakes is mostly pine. A small settlement, called "Fenelon Falls," is situated in the north-east of the township. The settlers are principally English. There are one grist and two saw mills in these townships. In Bexley 11,592, and in Fenelon 9065 acres of Crown lands are open for sale, at 8s. currency, per acre.

Ratable property in the townships £3713.

FERGUS.

A Village in the township of Nichol, situated on the Grand River, thirteen miles from Guelph, was laid out in 1833, by the Hon. A. Fergusson and Mr. Webster, on the road to the government settlement at Owen Sound. The situation is hilly and cold, and the soil in the neighbourhood of the village is poor and stoney. Population, 184, who are principally Scotch. Fergus contains a Presbyterian church.

Post Office, post three times a-week.

Professions and Trades.—One physician and surgeon, one grist and saw mill, one distillery, one tannery, three stores, one baker, one watchmaker, three shoemakers, one brewery, two blacksmiths, two carpenters, one cabinet maker and turner, one tailor.

FIGHTING ISLAND.

An Island in the Detroit River, three miles below Sandwich, contains about 1800 acres, of which 300 are fit for cultivation; the remainder being marsh, which is used for grazing cattle. It possesses a good fishery.

FINCH.

A Township in the Eastern District; is bounded on the north-east by the township of Roxborough; on the north-west by Cambridge and Russell; on the south-west by Winchester; and on the south-east by Osnabruck. In Finch 15,410 acres are taken up, 2305 of which are under cultivation. The Petit Nation River runs through the north of the township, from south to north. There is considerable pine on its banks, much of which is floated down the Ottawa. There are one grist and three saw-mills in the township. One hundred and fifty acres of crown lands are open for sale in Finch, at 8s. c'y per acre.

Population, 756; who are principally Scotch, and have a Presbyterian church. Ratable property in the township, £9504.

FINGAL.

A Village in the township of Southwold; six miles from Port Stanley. It contains about 150 inhabitants, who have a church, free to all denominations.

Professions and Trades.—One physician and surgeon, three stores, two taverns, two groceries, three waggon makers, one saddler, two blacksmiths, two tailors, four shoemakers.

FITZROY.

A Township in the Dalhousie District; is bounded on the north-east by the township of Tarbolton; on the north-west by McNab; on the south-west by Pakenham; and on the south-east by Huntly. In Fitzroy 29,392 acres are taken up, 5,304 of which are under cultivation. The Mississippi River runs through the west of the township, from south to north; on the banks of which there is considerable pine. Two thousand seven hundred and fifty-one acres of Crown lands are open for sale in Fitzroy, at 8s. c'y per acre. The village of

Fitzroy Harbour is situated in the north corner of the township, on the Ottawa River; and there are two grist and four saw-mills in the township.
Population in 1842, 1746.
Ratable property in the township, £18,268.

FITZROY HARBOUR.

A Village in the township of Fitzroy; situated on a bay of the Ottawa River. There are some very beautiful falls a short distance above the village. During the season, a steamboat runs from Aylmer, a village on the Lower Canadian side of the Ottawa, six miles above Bytown, to Fitzroy Harbour, three times a week, (fare 7s. 6d. c'y) Another steamboat starts from Mississippi Island (an island in the Ottawa, containing about 1000 acres, two miles and a half above Fitzroy Harbour), and runs to the Snows, a lumbering establishment on the Ottawa, twenty-eight miles above the harbour, the space between Fitzroy Harbour and Mississippi Island being unnavigable, on account of the falls and rapids in the river. Fitzroy Harbour contains about 500 inhabitants; and a Catholic church.
Post Office, post three times a-week
Professions and Trades—One Physician and Surgeon, one grist and three saw-mills, one brewery, one ashery, four stores, two taverns, two blacksmiths, one waggon maker, one fanning mill maker, one cabinet maker, four shoemakers, two tailors.

FIVE STAKES

A small Village in the township of Southwold, three miles from St Thomas. It contains about 100 inhabitants, one store, ashery, three taverns, two blacksmiths, one tailor, one waggon maker, one shoe maker.

FLAMBOROUGH.

A Village in the township of Flamborough West, on the Hamilton road, seven miles from Hamilton, contains about 150 inhabitants
Post Office, post every day.
Professions and Trades.—Four stores, one tavern, one foundry, four blacksmiths, one waggon maker, one tailor, one saddler, two shoe makers

FLAMBOROUGH, EAST.

A Township in the Gore District, is bounded on the north east by the township of Nelson, on the north by Nassagaweya, on the south west by Flamboro' West, and on the south by Burlington Bay. In East Flamborough 25,537 acres are taken up, 8,750 of which are under cultivation This s a fine township, containing excellent land and good farms, timber, a mixture of hardwood and pine There are two grist and nine saw mills in the township
Population in 1841, 1341
Ratable property in the township, £38,393.

FLAMBOROUGH WEST.

A Township in the county of Wentworth, is bounded on the north east by the township of Flamborough East, on the west by Beverly, on the north west by Puslinch, and on the south by Burlington Bay and Ancaster In Flamborough West 24,224 acres are taken up. 9551 of which are under cultivation. There are some good farms in this township, which contains the villages of Dundas and Flamborough, and there are also, on a creek running through the township, four grist mills, seven saw mills, carding machine and fulling mill, oil mill, cloth factory, pump, fanning mill, and chair factory, paper

mill, two tanneries, and two distilleries. There are also in the township one Presbyterian church, and one Methodist chapel.
Population in 1841 (since when no census has been taken), 2,428.
Ratable property in the township, £54,272.

FLOS.

A Township in the Simcoe District; is bounded on the north by the township of Tiny; on the west by Sunnidale; on the south by Vespra; and on the east by Medonte. In Flos, 5,749 acres are taken up, 685 of which are under cultivation. The Nottawasaga river runs through the south west corner of the township, and its north west corner is cut off by the Nottawasaga Bay. A small lake containing about 500 acres is situated in the north west of the township about two miles from the bay; and another lake of the same extent in the north of the township, on the town line between Flos and Medonte. The township is well watered by numerous small streams. That portion of the township bordering on the Penetanguishine Road, is light and sandy, and the timber principally pine and hemlock. A short distance back from the road, the land becomes heavy, and the timber good. The lower portion and the centre of the township are level, the upper portion rolling. In Flos 24,000 acres of Crown lands are open for sale at 8s. currency per acre.
Population in 1842, about 200.
Ratable property in the township, £2,536.

FORT ERIE.

A Fort situated in the south east corner of the township of Bertie, on the Niagara River, noted as being the scene of several severe engagements between the British troops, and the invading Americans, during the last American war; The principal of which took place, on the 28th October, 1812, when the fort was captured by a large force of the enemy, and retaken by the British troops, at the point of the bayonet; and again in August 1814, when, the fort having previously fallen again into the hands of the enemy, General Drummond, at the head of a party of British troops, advanced upon the fort for the purpose of investing it. On the 13th August, having completed his batteries, he commenced a brisk cannonade on the position of the enemy, which, with a few intermissions, was continued for two days, after which it was determined to carry the fort and outworks of the enemy by a nocturnal assault; about two o'clock on the morning of the 15th the attack commenced; and after a desperate conflict, the fort was carried, the enemy driven from the ramparts at the point of the bayonet, and the guns of the fort turned upon the garrison; but at the very moment of victory, a large quantity of ammunition accidentally took fire and exploded, by which the greater portion of the British forces, who had entered the fort, were blown into the air; the few British troops who survived the explosion, were insufficient to maintain their position, and they were consequently obliged to retire under shelter of their own works. On the 17th September following, a large American force attacked the British batteries, and succeeded in destroying the works; but before they could make good their retreat, a reinforcement of British troops arrived, and they were soon obliged to make a precipitate flight before the British bayonets, after losing nearly 600 men. The American general soon after evacuated Fort Erie, and retreated across the river to the United States, which ended the campaign.

FRANKVILLE.

A Settlement in the township of Kitley, situated on the Perth road, twenty-two miles from Brockville. It contains about fifty inhabitants, one store, two taverns, one saddler, and one blacksmith.

FREDERICKSBURGH.

A Township in the Midland District; is bounded on the north-east by the township of Ernestown; on the north-west by Richmond and a portion of the Bay of Quinté; on the south-east by the Bay of Quinté, and on the south-west by Adolphustown In Fredericksburgh 41,098 acres are taken up, 18,916 of which are under cultivation. A large bay, a portion of the Bay of Quinté, runs for some distance into the township, and about its centre expands to a considerable size, forming a large basin. A settlement called Clarkville is situated in the north-east corner of the township Fredericksburgh is well settled and contains some good farms. There are three grist and five saw-mills in the township.

Population 2,949.
Ratable property in the township, £47,243.

FREDERICKSBURGH, or MIDDLETON

A Village situated on the town line between Windham and Middleton, twelve miles from Simcoe, and twelve miles from the lake It contains about 100 inhabitants, one store, two taverns, one blacksmith, one waggon-maker, one tailor, and two shoemakers

FRENCH RIVER.—(See LAKE NIPISSING.)

FROOMEFIELD, or TALFOURD'S,

As it is more commonly called, a Village in the township of Moore, situated on the River St. Clair, four miles and a half from Port Sarnia It was laid out in 1836 by F Talfourd, Esq The situation is one of the most beautiful on the river. Steamboats stop here to take in wood A small stream, formerly called "Commodore's Creek," on which is a grist and saw-mill (not now in operation), enters the River St. Clair at this point Here is a neat Episcopal Church, and an excellent windmill. Number of inhabitants about forty Village lots of one-third of an acre are selling here at £10 currency.

Trades.—Two waggon makers, one tailor, one shoemaker, one blacksmith, two joiners.

FRONTENAC

A County in the Midland District, comprises the townships of Bedford, Barrie, Clarendon, Hinchinbrooke, Kingston, Kennebec, Loughborough, Olden, Oso, Portland, and Pittsburgh, which includes Howe Island, Palmerston, Storrington, and Wolfe Island; and, except for the purpose of representation in the Legislative Assembly, the town of Kingston.

FULLARTON

A Township in the Huron District is bounded on the north-east by Logan and Ellice, on the north-west by Hibbert, on the south-west by Usborne and Blanshard, and on the south-east by Downie Soil mostly good A branch of the Thames runs through the township Fullarton contains 42,108 acres; 8,063 of which are leased or sold, of which 393 acres are under cultivation.

Population 419
Ratable property in the township, 2,339.

GAINSBOROUGH.

A Township in the Niagara District, is bounded on the east by the township of Pelham, on the north by Clinton and Grimsby, on the west by Caistor; and on the south by Moulton and Wainfleet In Gainsborough 28,848 acres are taken up, 8448 of which are under cultivation. Gainsborough is well settled, and contains good farms. There is considerable pine in the township. There are one grist and six saw mills in the township.

Population in 1841, 1598, who are principally Canadians, with some few emigrants from Europe.

Ratable property in the township, £24,207.

GALT.

A Village in the township of Dumfries, prettily situated on the Grand River, in a valley surrounded by high hills; twenty-five miles from Hamilton, and eighteen from Brantford. It has very valuable water-power, by the employment of which, in milling and manufacturing, the place is fast rising into prosperity; and already begins to assume the appearance of a town. The streets are neatly laid out, and the employment of stone in building (which is procurable in any required quantity from the banks of the river), gives the houses and other buildings, a very substantial appearance. Galt contains about 1000 inhabitants, who are principally Scotch. They have a curling club, mechanics' institute, circulating library, and fire engine company. Stages run every day to Hamilton and Guelph, and three times a-week to Goderich. A newspaper is published here every Saturday—the "Dumfries Courier." There are in Galt five churches and chapels, viz., one Episcopal, three Presbyterian, one Methodist.

Post Office, post every day.

Professions and Trades.—Three physicians and surgeons, two lawyers, one apothecary, two grist mills (each containing four run of stones), two saw mills, two foundries, two carding machines and cloth factories, one brewery, two distilleries, one tannery, eight stores, one pail factory, one last factory, one chemist and druggist, nine taverns, two groceries, one veterinary surgeon, one printer, seven blacksmiths, one saddler, one watchmaker, five waggon makers, eight tailors, one cabinet maker, four shoemakers, three bakers, two chair factories, three tinsmiths, three butchers, two livery stables, four coopers, one gunsmith, one edge-tool maker, ten carpenters, one painter, one tallow chandler, one school. One bank agency, "Gore."

Stage Fare from Galt to Hamilton		$1
Do.	Galt to Guelph	0¾
Do.	Galt to Goderich	4
Quantity of Flour ground in Galt for exportation, from Sept. 1844, to July, 1845		15,755 barrels.

GANANOQUE.

A Village in the township of Leeds, situated on the River St. Lawrence, at the mouth of the Gananoque River, sixteen miles east of Kingston; the eastern road passes through it. It contains about 300 inhabitants, who have a church (Presbyterian).

Post Office, post every day.

Professions and Trades.—Grist mill (four run of stones), saw mill, nail works, carding machine and cloth factory, pail factory, three stores, two taverns, one physician and surgeon, one tailor, two shoemakers.

GARAFRAXA.

A Township in the Wellington District; is bounded on the south-east by Caledon, Erin, and Eramosa; on the south-west by Nichol and Peel; and on the north by Luther and Amaranth. In Garafraxa 13,318 acres are taken up, 1638 of which are under cultivation. This is a triangular shaped township, much of the land in which is of excellent quality. The Grand River runs through the west corner of the township. Three thousand seven hundred and

fifty-five acres of Crown lands are open for sale in Garafraxa, at 8s currency per acre. There are one grist and two saw mills in the township.
Population in 1841, 322.
Ratable property in the township, £6207.

GARDEN ISLAND.

A small Island in Lake Ontario, opposite Kingston, containing about thirty acres. It is occupied by a firm who are largely engaged in the rafting business, it being conveniently situated for the purpose. A large number of vessels are employed in bringing staves from all parts of the western country to the island, where they are unloaded, and the staves made into rafts for the voyage to Quebec.

GEORGETOWN.

A flourishing Village in Esquesing, situated on a branch of the River Credit, 17½ miles north from Dundas Street. It contains about 700 inhabitants.
Professions and Trades.—One grist mill, one saw do, cloth factory, two tanneries, two stores, one foundry, one ashery, one tavern, one chair maker, three waggon makers, one cabinet maker, four blacksmiths, two tailors, three shoemakers.

GEORGINA.

A Township in the Home District, is bounded on the north by Lake Simcoe; on the west by the township of Gwillimbury North, on the south by Scott, and on the east by Brock. In Georgina 11,827 acres are taken up, 2653 of which are under cultivation. Much of the land in this township is hilly and broken; some of it, however, is of excellent quality, and is heavily timbered. The banks of the lake in Georgina are generally rather high. A stream, called Black River, runs through the east of the township, from south to north, on which is a village, called Bouchers', or Sutton Mills, situated about two miles south of the lake. On the lake shore, about three miles from the village, is an Episcopal church. The steamboat "Beaver" stops at Jackson's Point in the township. 2900 acres of Crown lands are open for sale in Georgina at 8s currency per acre. There are two grist and three saw mills, and one distillery in the township.
Population in 1842, 586.
Ratable property in the township, £8419.

GERMANY, LITTLE.

A German Settlement in the township of Waterloo, about nine miles south-west from Preston, within half a mile of the township of Guelph, contains a catholic church, two taverns, two blacksmiths, and about sixty inhabitants.

GIBBS' MILLS

A Settlement in the township of Whitby, about one mile south from Oshawa. It contains about 150 inhabitants, grist mill, oatmeal do, pot barley do, distillery, tannery, and cloth factory (the machinery of which is worked by water), where excellent coarse cloths and blankets are made.

GLANFORD.

A Township in the Gore District, is bounded on the east by the township of Caistor; on the north by Barton, on the west by Ancaster, and on the south by Seneca. In Glanford, 18,805 acres are taken up, 7,342 of which are under cultivation. This is a small, well settled township, containing good farms, and a mixed population. There is one saw mill in the township.
Population in 1841, 996.
Ratable property in the township, £26,794

GLASGOW, or "SHOEMAKER'S MILLS."

A Village in the township of Waterloo, fourteen miles from Galt, situated on a branch of the Grand River, contains about 160 inhabitants. There is a large establishment here, consisting of grist and saw mills, distillery, fulling mill and carding machine, and oil mill for making linseed oil; and one cigar manufacturer.

GLENELG.

A Township in the Wellington District; is bounded on the east by the township of Artemisia, on the north by Holland; on the west by Bentinck; and on the south by Egremont. This township has only lately been surveyed and laid out, and no return has yet been made from it.

GLENGARY.

A County in the Eastern District, comprises the townships of Charlottenburg, Kenyon, Lochiel, Lancaster, and the Indian reserve. It returns a member to the House of Assembly

GODERICH

The District Town of the Huron District, situated on Lake Huron, at the entrance of the Maitland River It was laid out in 1827 by Mr. Galt, then secretary of the Canada Company. The town is handsomely situated, the greater part being built on a rising ground, more than 100 feet above the level of the lake, and it is consequently dry and healthy The scenery in the neighbourhood is beautiful, but the town is rather exposed to north and north west winds from the lake, in consequence of which the weather is occasionally wintry, even in the middle of summer, on the whole however, it is a very pleasant summer residence Owing to its remote situation, and partly from its being inaccessible by land from any part of the Province west of London, Goderich has not increased as fast as many other places of the same age A harbour has been constructed at an expense of £16,000, but the piers are now getting out of repair This is the only harbour between Port Sarnia and the Saugeen Islands A light house is just about being erected by the government. In 1827 a road was opened to the township of Wilmot, at a cost of £1900; a road has also been made to the town of London. A steamboat and several schooners have been built here Stages run twice a week from Goderich to London and Galt, and during the last season the steamboat "Goderich" (late "Gore") called here on her weekly trips from Windsor to Owen's Sound. A fishing company was established here, some years since, but from some mismanagement did not succeed very well, and is now broken up A fine pelican was shot here during the spring of 1845, while feeding in the harbour.

Goderich contains five churches and chapels, viz, Episcopal, Presbyterian, Catholic, Secession and Methodist, there is also a stone jail and court house, and the Canada Company's offices are kept here

Post Office, post four times a week
Population, 659.

The following government and district offices are kept in Goderich Clerk of Peace, Treasurer of District, Sheriff, Registrar of the County, Collector of Customs, Inspector of Licenses, Inspector of Fish, District Clerk, Clerk of District Court

Professions and Trades—Three physicians and surgeons, two lawyers, one surveyor, two breweries, three distilleries, two tanneries, nine stores, one druggist, five taverns, one tinsmith, five tailors, two grocers, one foundry, two watchmakers, two waggon makers, three blacksmiths, ten shoemakers, one gunsmith, two bakers two schools, one bank agency, "Upper Canada."

Principal tavern, "Rattenbury's."

Goderich is fifty-nine miles from London, and eighty-two from Galt; for stage fares, see London, Galt, and Hamilton. The exports for 1844 were small, but during the spring of 1845, about 12,000 bushels of wheat were shipped.

GODERICH.

A Township in the Huron District, is bounded on the north by the River Maitland; on the west by Lake Huron; on the south by the River Bayfield; and on the east by Hullett. The soil on the banks of the lake, and the Rivers Maitland and Bayfield, is poor and stony; the rest of the township is good land. The township contains 56,066 acres, 35,118 of which are leased or sold, of which 5,156 acres are under cultivation. Goderich contains one grist and two saw mills, fulling-mill, and carding machine. There is a tavern on the Bayfield road, four miles south of Goderich.

Population, 1,673.

Ratable property in the township, £16,189 8s.

GORE DISTRICT.

Consists of the Counties of Wentworth and Halton, and contains some of the richest, best settled, and most highly cultivated townships in Canada West. The rapid growth of Hamilton, the district town, seems to have given an impetus to the rest of the district, and it has increased in wealth faster, during the last few years, than any other portion of the province. Between January 1842, and January 1844, 44,000 acres of land have been brought into cultivation, a very great increase. There are many large farms in the district, one of which in particular deserves mention; that of Mr. Colman, near Paris, in the township of Dumfries, who last year had 375 acres of land in wheat. There are many scientific English and Scotch farmers in the District, who possess stock that would be a credit to any country. Large numbers of the farms have flourishing orchards attached to them. The Grand River runs through the district, on which, and its tributaries, are numerous grist and saw mills. Hamilton, the district town, being the key to the west, is becoming the great depot for merchandize intended for the west, and western produce; and the villages of Dundas and Galt are fast becoming manufacturing towns, through the agency of their extensive water power. A profitable trade is carried on in freestone and limestone, much of which is exported. A large portion of the inhabitants of the district are English, Scotch and Irish, and the remainder, Canadians, Americans and their descendants, and a few Germans. 2,400 acres, only, of crown lands are open for sale in the Gore District, to purchase any of which, application must be made to the Crown lands' agent at Hamilton.

The population of the Gore District in 1841, amounted to 31,507, since when the number has probably increased one third; the town of Hamilton alone, has doubled its population in the period.

The following abstract from the assessment rolls will show the rate of increase and improvement in the district.

Date.	No. of Acres Cultivated.	MILLS. Grist.	MILLS. Saw.	Milch Cows.	Oxen 4 years old, and upwards.	Horned Cattle from 2 to 4 years old.	Amount of Ratable Property.
1842	222,098	37	115	16,087	5899	7873	986,499.
1843	....	......	......	......	......	......	......
1844	266,842	38	130	16,577	6099	8097	1,041,713

Government and District Officers in the Gore District.

Sheriff	Edward Cartwright Thomas	Hamilton.
Registrar.	Alexander Stewart	Wentworth.
Clerk of the Peace..	S. B. Freeman	Hamilton.
Treasurer	Henry Beasley	"
Judge of District Court..	Miles O'Reilly	"
Clerk of do	Andrew Stuart	"
District Clerk	H N. Jackson	"
Inspector of Licenses	John Wilson	"
Collector of Customs.	John Davidson	"
Warden.	John Wetenhall	"
Crown Lands Agent	Peter Carroll	"
Judge of Surrogate Court.	John Wilson	"
Registrar of do	George Rolph	"
Emigrant Agent	John H Palmer.	"
District Superintendent of Schools.	Patrick Thornton	"
Coroner.	John Ryckman	"

Number of Common Schools in operation in each township in the Gore District.— Barton, six; Glanford, five; Saltfleet, ten; Binbrook, four, Brantford, twenty-three, Onondaga, four, Ancaster, fifteen, Dumfries, twenty-nine, Beverly, eighteen, Esquesing, fifteen, Nassagaweya, six, Nelson, fifteen, Trafalgar, eighteen, East Flamboro', seven, West Flamboro', nine, Oneida, four; Seneca, seven.—Total, 195.

GOSFIELD.

A Township in the county of Essex, is bounded on the north by the townships of Rochester and Maidstone, on the west by Colchester, on the south by Lake Erie; and on the east by Mersea. In Gosfield 24,803 acres of land are taken up, of which 5,030 are under cultivation About half the land in this township is wet, and requires considerable draining; the remainder is mostly excellent land. Timber—maple, ash, oak, beech, black walnut, butternut, chestnut, &c, with a small quantity of cedar on the lake, at the mouth of Cedar Creek. Belle River, and the River Ruscom, take their rise in this township. In the south-east of the township, about four miles from the lake, are found large quantities of iron ore, which produces iron of excellent quality. A furnace and foundry have been in operation here since 1834, and large quantities of iron have been made. In Gosfield there are two steam grist and saw mills, and one water grist-mill, situated on the lake shore; and two tanneries, one store and ashery, and a tavern, on Cedar Creek, in the south-west of the township. There are also one Methodist and one Baptist chapel. Gosfield is well settled. Population 1338. The Canada Company possess about 6,000 acres in the township. And 200 acres of Crown lands are open for sale in the township, at 8s. c'y per acre.

Ratable property in the township, 17,006

GOULBOURN.

A township in the Dalhousie District, is bounded on the north-east by the township of Nepean; on the north-west by Huntley and March; on the south-west by Beckwith, and on the south-east by Marlborough In Goulbourn 44,714 acres are taken up, 9,319 of which are under cultivation This is the best settled township in the Dalhousie District, and contains some good farms. The village of Richmond is situated in the east corner of the township, and there is one grist-mill and one saw-mill in the township. Ten thousand five hundred and forty acres of Crown lands are open for sale in Goulbourn, at 8s c'y per acre.

Population in 1842, 2,606.

Ratable property in the township £26,755.

GOUGICHIN LAKE.

A continuation of Lake Simcoe, north of the Narrows It is about twelve miles long, and from three to five miles broad. The scenery of this small lake is very romantic, the shores being indented with many beautiful bays, and the lake itself studded with almost innumerable islands, varying in size from a few square yards to many acres. The village of Orillia is situated on its western shore, and that of Rama on the east At the northern extremity of the lake, its waters enter the Severn River, and from thence make their way to Lake Huron.

GOWER, SOUTH

A Township in the Johnstown District, is bounded on the north-east by the township of Mountain, on the north-west by North Gower, on the south-west by Oxford; and on the south-east by Edwardsburgh. In South Gower 14,307 acres are taken up, 4,311 of which are under cultivation This is a long narrow township, is pretty well settled, and contains some good farms Six hundred and fifty acres of Crown lands are open for sale in South Gower, at 8s. c'y per acre. There are two saw-mills in the township

Population in 1842, 687

Ratable property in the township, £10,466.

GOWER, NORTH.

A Township in the Dalhousie District, is bounded on the east and south-east by the Rideau Canal, on the north-west by Nepean, and on the south-west by Marlborough In North Gower 17,474 acres are taken up, 3,400 of which are under cultivation. Much of the land in this township, bordering on the Rideau Canal, is poor and stony. Four hundred and thirty acres of Crown lands are open for sale in North Gower, at 8s c'y per acre.

Population in 1842, 855.

Ratable property in the township, £9,549.

GRAFTON

A Village in the township of Haldimand, situated on the eastern road, eight miles east from Cobourg. Population about 200 Grafton contains three churches and chapels, viz—Episcopal, Free Church and Methodist.

Post-office, post every day.

Professions and Trades —Two physicians and surgeons, one conveyancer, three stores, one druggist, one distillery, one tannery, two taverns, four blacksmiths, two waggon makers, and five shoemakers

GRAFTON HARBOUR

A small cove on Lake Ontario, three miles from the village of Grafton

GRAND RIVER, or OUSE

Takes its rise in the township of Amaranth, about thirty miles above Fergus, runs south and a little west through Garafraxa, south west through Nichol, south through Woolwich, at the south-east border of which it is joined by the Canastoga, a branch from the west; it then runs south through Waterloo, in the south-east of which it is joined by the River Speed, a branch from the townships of Guelph and Dumfries, when it enters Brantford, and runs south-east to Lake Erie, forming the dividing line between the townships of Onondaga and Tuscarora, Seneca and Oneida, passes through Cayuga, and forms the boundary of Canboro', Moulton, and Sherbrooke, on the north and east, and Dunn on the south and west In its course it is very tortuous, sometimes making sudden bends to the east or west, and as suddenly curving back again in the opposite direction.

The Grand River is navigable for large vessels as far as Dunnville, where the feeder of the Welland Canal enters it; and for smaller boats to within a short distance of the town of Brantford (sixty miles above Dunnville), where a canal, three miles in length, and with three locks, to overcome an ascent in the river of thirty-three feet, has been constructed to enable vessels to reach the town. In order to render the river navigable above Dunnville, five locks have been built, to overcome an ascent of forty-three feet. There are several grist and saw mills, and other machinery on the river, both above and below Brantford. The damming of the river in order to supply the Welland Canal, has caused it to overflow much of the low land near its mouth.

At the termination of the war of Independence, the Six Nations Indians of the Mohawk valley, who had taken part with the British against the Americans, became apprehensive that consequences injurious to themselves might result from their hunting grounds being within the territory belonging to the United States. They accordingly deputed their chief, Joseph Brant, (Tyendenaga) to represent their fears to General, afterwards Sir F. Haldimand, who was then Governor of the Province of Quebec, and who, in the following year, by a proclamation, dated October 25, 1784, granted to the Six Nations and their heirs for ever, a tract of land on the Ouse, or Grand River, six miles in depth on each side of the river, beginning at Lake Erie, and extending to the head of the river. This grant was confirmed, and its conditions defined, by a patent under the Great Seal, issued by Lieutenant Governor Simcoe, and bearing date January 14, 1793.

The original extent of the tract was 694,910 acres, but the greater part of this has been since surrendered to the Crown, in trust to be sold for the benefit of these tribes. And some smaller portions have been either granted in *fee simple* to purchasers, with the assent of the Indians, or have been alienated by the chiefs upon leases, which, although legally invalid, the government did not at the time consider it equitable or expedient to cancel. The following is a list of the principal surrenders.

January 15, and February 6, 1798.—The lands now forming the townships of Dumfries, Waterloo, Woolwich, and Nichol, extending downwards on both sides of the river from the northern extremity of the reserve; and the greater part of the townships of Canboro' and Moulton, on the eastern side of the entrance of the Grand River—352,707 acres.

April 19, 1830.—The site of the town of Brantford, on the Grand River—807 acres.

April 19, 1831.—The northern part of the present township of Cayuga, on the lower part of the river—20,670 acres.

February 8, 1834.—The residue of Cayuga, the present township of Dunn, (which adjoins that of Cayuga), and part of Canboro' and Moulton—50,212 acres.

March 26, 1835.—A confirmation of all the preceding surrenders.

January 18, 1841.—The residue of the land, with the exception of a reserve of 20,000 acres, and the lands actually in the occupation of Indians, amounting to upwards of 220,000 acres.

Of the earlier surrenders, the greater portion has been already sold, and the proceeds have been invested either in consols in England, or in the Grand River navigation stock. The survey of the portion last surrendered is not complete, but a considerable part is already occupied by settlers or squatters, and the whole will probably be soon settled.

The Six Nations consist properly of the Mohawks, Oneidas, Senecas, Onondagas, and Cayugas, which formed the original confederacy of the "Five Nations," called Iroquois, by the French, with the Tuscaroras, who were adopted into the confederacy. But the community on the Grand River includes also a few Delawares, Tutulies, Muntures, Nanticokes, and some other Indians, together with a few families of Negroes, adopted into the nation. The number of the whole, according to a census taken in 1843, is 2223. They are settled in small bands, divided according to their tribes, or collected under separate chiefs, on both sides of the river, from the Cayuga township line to the south side of the Hamilton Road; but are at present about to retire altogether to the south side The greater part live in log houses, scattered over this tract, very few comparatively live in villages. Of these there are properly but three, the Mohawk, Tuscarora, and Cayuga. The first, which is between one and two miles from Brantford, was established in 1785, the year after the emigration of the Six Nations. It contains about twenty-four houses, and extends in a very irregular form, for above a quarter of a mile. Its church, which is said to be the oldest in Canada West, is a very neat building, in excellent repair, and contains the family vault of the celebrated Chief of the Mohawks, Joseph Brant. All the Indian inhabitants of this village, with the exception of four or five families, have sold their improvements to white settlers, and have removed to other parts of the reserve, chiefly for the convenience of procuring fuel, which they had great difficulty in obtaining at the village. The Tuscarora village is a mile and a half from the site of the Six Nations' Council House, which is eleven miles from Brantford. It was established ten or fifteen years later than the Mohawk village, and is of nearly the same extent, but the houses, of which there are about thirty, are less scattered. It contains few or no white settlers; and there is a neat little church at one end of the village The Upper Cayuga village is now deserted by the Indians, the houses are all of logs, and in each settlement there are several barns None of the Six Nations Indians reside in wigwams.

According to an account taken in 1843, it appears that the 2223 individuals, forming about 500 families, occupy 397 houses, having 55 barns attached to them They possess 85 waggons, 127 sleighs, 153 ploughs, and 97 harrows, Their stock consists of 350 horses, 561 oxen, 790 cows, 2070 swine, and 83 sheep. The extent of improved land among them is, 6908 acres, or on an average, about fourteen acres to a family Some, however, hold extensive farms, as will be seen by the following abstract —

No. of Indians holding no improved land	50
do. do. under 5 acres	96
do. do. from 5 to 10 acres	85
do. do. do. 10 to 20 "	67
do. do. do 20 to 50 "	68
do do do 50 to 100 "	28
do. do. do 100 to 150 "	9
do. do do 150 to 200 "	1

In those cases in which the family has no improved land, the men generally work out in the winter. In the spring and summer, and in the early part of the autumn, they engage as labourers, for which they receive high wages The females remain with their relations, and are supported by the earnings of the men. Many of the Indians work on the farms of the white settlers during harvest time.

The land is not subdivided into regular plots, but each Indian selects his own locality, and takes as much land as he can cultivate, or wishes to reserve to himself, without the interference of the chiefs. They are generally secure from the intrusions of other Indians, and they can transmit their land to their heirs, or convey their interest in it to any other Indian If any disputes arise, they are submitted to the chiefs in council, who decide upon the matter. They depend almost entirely upon agriculture for subsistence, and seldom resort to hunting and fishing for a supply of food, although many of them indulge in these sports for various periods, extending from a fortnight to three months, towards the close of the year Their chief hunting-grounds are in the townships of Norwich, Zorra, Dereham, Windham, and Blenheim, and at the Chippawa Creek; but when unsuccessful at these places, they resort to more distant localities. At least one-third do not hunt at all, and it is probable, that by the time the game becomes exhausted in the surrounding townships, the inclination of the remainder for the chase will have altogether ceased. They are much improved in their habits of industry and mode of agriculture, and they raise a greater variety of grain and vegetables than formerly.

As regards religion, the Mohawks had been Christians for many years before the American revolution. The church at the Mohawk village was built by the government for their use, the year after the settlement. For many years, however, they had no resident missionary among them, the nearest clergyman lived at Niagara, seventy miles distant. About 16 years ago, a clergyman was first settled here for the benefit of the Indians, by the "Company for the Propagation of the gospel in New England, and the parts adjacent in America," commonly called the "New England Company." Some attention had been previously paid to the inhabitants of this neighbourhood, by one of the missionaries of the Society for the Propagation of the Gospel in Foreign Parts; but by an arrangement with the New England Company, the care of this station was entirely resigned to that company, who have ever since maintained a missionary at the Mohawk village, kept the church in repair, and have established several schools, and a mechanics' institute, for the Indians in and about the station. More recently they have established an assistant missionary in the Tuscarora village, where they have built a church and a parsonage house. There is also a Methodist church at the Salt Springs.

A large majority of the Indians on the Grand River are Christians, and belong mostly to the Church of England. A few years ago, some of the Lower Mohawks left that church and attached themselves to the Episcopalian Methodists, but lately, part of these have returned to the Church. During the last year, about forty of the Tuscarora tribe joined the Baptists; there are also some Wesleyan Methodists. A considerable number, however, of the Upper and Lower Cayugas, the Onondagas, Senecas, and some of the Delawares are still heathens.

A boarding School has been established by the New England Company in the Mohawk village. The instruction is carried on altogether in English. Fifteen boys are being instructed in the several trades of waggon making, blacksmith, carpentering, and shoemaking. The girls, twelve in number, are taught house-keeping, needlework, spinning and knitting. The total number of children under instruction in the settlement is 160. These tribes have increased by about 100, during the last ten years. The number of half-breeds among them is small, not above three in a hundred.

The Six Nations Indians are under the superintendence of an officer of the Indian Department, who resides at Brantford, and they receive medical attendance from practitioners in the same town, who are remunerated out of the funds of the tribe.

A large portion of the land on the banks of the Grand River is well settled and cultivated. The township of Dumfries, which has been settled about forty years, is the best settled township in the Province, and the townships of Waterloo, Guelph and Brantford, are also in a high state of cultivation. Most of the land on the Grand River is rolling, the timber varying according to locality, but being generally a mixture of hardwood and pine. Splendid white oak is found in great quantities, within a convenient distance from the river, and a considerable business is carried on in square timber, sawed lumber and staves. Gypsum of excellent quality has been found in large beds in the neighbourhood of Paris, in the township of Oneida, and in Cayuga; it is much used in agriculture, many of the farmers coming several miles to procure it. The flourishing towns and villages of Dunnville, Cayuga, Indiana, York, Seneca, Caledonia, Brantford, Paris, Galt, Preston, Elora (where is a beautiful fall), and Fergus, are situated on the Grand River.

The following produce passed through the Grand River during the season of 1844.—

Sawed Lumber	6,485,997 feet.
Square Timber	362,224 do
Round do.	7,279 do.
Pipe Staves	4,494 pieces.
W. I do	31,760 do
Flour Barrel do.	16,600 do.
Saw Logs	1,102 do
Whiskey	15 barrels.
Ashes	3 do.
Flour	13,124 do
Wheat	25,655 bushels.
Oats	18 do.
Plaster, ground and unground	1,333 tons.
Sheep Skins	1½ do.
Shingles	96¼ m

GRANTHAM.

A Township in the Niagara District; is bounded on the east by the township of Niagara, on the north by Lake Ontario; on the west by Louth, and on the south by Thorold. In Grantham, 20,565 acres are taken up, 11,049 of which are under cultivation. This is an old settled township, containing some good farms. The town of St Catharines is situated in Grantham, on the Welland Canal, which enters the township at its north-west corner, and, after bending to the south-east until it reaches the centre of the township, runs directly south till it emerges from it into the township of Thorold. Much of the land in Grantham is hilly. There are five grist and two saw mills in the township, of which four grist mills are in the town of St Catharines. Much of the population of the townships bordering on the canal is floating, large numbers of labourers being employed on the canal, who, when their work is completed, remove to another locality; and many stores are temporarily opened to supply them with necessaries, which on their removal are closed.

Population in 1842, 3832; who are a mixture of Canadians, Americans, Irish, Scotch and English.

Ratable property in the township, £57,605

GRAPE ISLAND

An Island in the Bay of Quinte, to the north of Big Island, where formerly was a missionary station for the Indians. It is now deserted.

GRENVILLE.

A County in the Johnstown District, it comprises the townships of Augusta, Edwardsburgh, South Gower, Oxford and Wolford. It returns a member to the House of Assembly.

GRIMSBY

A Township in the Niagara District, is bounded on the east by the township of Clinton, on the north by Lake Ontario, on the west by Saltfleet, and on the south by Caistor and Gainsboro'. In Grimsby, 27,758 acres are taken up, 9,745 of which are under cultivation. This is a well settled township, containing some excellent farms. much of the land is rolling. Timber—a mixture of hardwood and pine. There are five grist and four saw mills in the township; and the village of Grimsby is also in the township.

Population in 1841, 1,784; who are a mixture of Canadians, Americans and Europeans

Ratable property in the township, £35,498.

GRIMSBY, OR FORTY-MILE CREEK, *as it was originally called.*

A Village in the township of Grimsby, beautifully situated on the St. Catharines road, seventeen miles from Hamilton, in the midst of some very fine scenery. A good mill stream flows through the village. During the summer season Grimsby is a favourite resort for pleasure parties from Hamilton. There are two churches in the village—one episcopal and one free to all denominations.

Population about 200.

Post office, post every day.

Professions and Trades.—Two physicians and surgeons, two grist mills, two saw mills, one brewery, one distillery, one foundry, two waggon makers, three blacksmiths, two shoemakers, one cabinet maker, three tailors, one saddler, three stores, two taverns.

GUELPH.

The District Town of the Wellington District, in the county of Waterloo, forty-two miles from Hamilton; was laid out by the late Mr. Galt, on a block of land belonging to the Canada Company, in the year 1828. The situation was well chosen, being in the midst of a finely undulating country, and is high, dry and healthy. The neighbourhood of the town is well settled by respectable families from the old country, principally English, many of whom came from Suffolk and Norfolk, and who have some very fine farms. The River Speed, a branch of the Grand River, runs past the town. The gaol and court house are built of stone, and are handsome structures; but are placed in a bad situation, being almost out of sight. A newspaper is published here every Friday, the "Guelph and Galt Advertiser." Stages run every day to Preston and Galt. Guelph contains five churches and chapels, viz., Episcopal, Presbyterian, Catholic, British Wesleyan and Congregational.

Number of inhabitants, 1,240; who are principally English and Scotch, with some few Irish. They have a literary club, cricket club and fire company.

The following government and District offices are kept in Guelph:—Judge of District Court, Sheriff, Clerk of Peace, Treasurer, Inspector of Licenses, District Clerk, Clerk of District Court, Deputy Clerk of Crown.

Professions and Trades.—Four physicians and surgeons, two lawyers, three grist mills, one saw mill, one carding machine, three tanneries, fifteen stores, seven taverns, one bookseller, one druggist, one printing office, two breweries, two distilleries, one starch factory, one nursery, six blacksmiths, six waggon makers, eight cabinet makers and house carpenters, three coopers, four butchers, two bakers, one confectioner, ten tailors, thirteen shoemakers, three saddlers, one tinsmith, one sieve maker, one gunsmith, two painters, one watchmaker, three chair makers, three stone masons, three bricklayers, two undertakers, one fanning-mill maker, two schools, two bank agencies, "Gore" and "Montreal."

Post office, post every day.

There are three good taverns in Guelph—the "British Hotel" (the principal), "Farmers' Arms," and "Ratcliffe's."

GUELPH.

A Township in the Wellington District; is bounded on the north-east by the township of Eramosa; on the north-west and west by the townships of Nichol, Woolwich and Waterloo; and on the south-east by Puslinch. In Guelph 24,473 acres are taken up, of which 12,840 are under cultivation. This is one of the best settled townships in Western Canada. The land having been taken up generally by respectable English families, most of whom brought some capital with them. The land is mostly rolling, and, when the country is well cleared up, will present as fine and picturesque an appearance as any township in the province. Excellent wheat is raised in this and the adjoining townships. The River Speed, a branch of the Grand River, runs nearly through the centre of

the township, from north to south. There are in Guelph, three grist mills, two of which are in the town of Guelph, and two saw mills.
Population of the township in 1845, 3,400.
Ratable property in the township, £44,285.

GWILLIMBURY, EAST.

A Township in the Home District; is bounded on the north by the township of North Gwillimbury; on the west by West Gwillimbury; on the south by Whitchurch; and on the east by Scott In East Gwillimbury, 28,380 acres are taken up, 9,215 of which are under cultivation. This township has been settled about forty-five years; and contains a mixed population consisting principally of Pennsylvanian Dutch and their descendants, Canadians and Irish, with a few English and Scotch. There are many very excellent farms in the township. The quality of the soil varies, some part being hilly and poor; but a large portion of the township consists of rolling land, with good timber. An extensive swamp runs through the north of the township The villages of Sharon and Queensville, and part of Holland Landing, are in the township. Three thousand one hundred acres of Crown lands are open for sale in East Gwillimbury, at 8s. currency per acre There are two grist and five saw mills in the township
Population in 1842, 1,796
Ratable property in the township, £30.526.

GWILLIMBURY, WEST.

A Township in the Simcoe District, is bounded on the north by the township of Innisfil, on the west by Tecumseth, on the south by King, and on the east by East Gwillimbury. In West Gwillimbury, 40,224 acres are taken up, 14,269 of which are under cultivation A small portion of the north-east corner of the township is cut off by Cook's Bay, a portion of Lake Simcoe An extensive marsh, varying in breadth from a quarter of a mile to a mile, and bordered by a tamarac swamp, extends from the bay to the south-west corner of the township. The west branch of the Holland River runs through the centre of this marsh. The east branch enters the township at the Holland Landing, and runs nearly a north course till it joins the east branch about three miles from the lake. Like the west branch, it is bordered by a broad marsh on the greatest part of its course. Above the "Forks" the navigation of the east branch is difficult, from the numerous bends and shallowness of the water The steamboat "Beaver," however, manages to ascend within four miles of Holland Landing. The west branch is said to be navigable for seven or eight miles above Bradford At the Bradford Bridge it is about ten feet deep The soil of the township varies in quality: some of it is very good, other parts again are poor The soil of the north-east of the township is light, but of tolerable quality Timber —pine, intermixed with oak, poplar, &c. The west of the township is well settled, and contains very good farms The villages of Bradford, Bond Head, and Middletown, are situated in the township Two thousand eight hundred acres of Crown lands are open for sale in the township, at 8s currency per acre. The township is principally settled by Irish, Scotch, Canadians and Americans.
Population of the township in 1842, 2,702
Ratable property in the township, £35,294.

GWILLIMBURY, NORTH

A Township in the Home District; is bounded on the east by the township of Georgina; on the north and west by Lake Simcoe and Cook's Bay; and on the south by East Gwillimbury In North Gwillimbury 13,080 acres are taken up, 3,424 of which are under cultivation A large portion of the north and west of the township is light soil, with pine timber. There are some good farms in the township. In some parts of the township the banks of the lake are high, in others there is a considerable quantity of marsh. Eight hundred acres of Crown lands are open for sale in North Gwillimbury, at 8s. c'y per acre

Population in 1842, 697.

Ratable property in the township, £9,588.

HALDIMAND

A County in the Niagara District, it comprises the townships of Canboro, Cayuga, Dunn, Moulton, Sherbrooke, and for the purposes of representation in the Legislative Assembly, and of registration of titles only, the townships of Seneca, Oneida, Rainham and Walpole. It returns a member to the House of Assembly.

HALDIMAND.

A Township in the Newcastle District, is bounded on the east by the townships of Cramahe and Percy, on the north by Alnwick, on the west by Hamilton, and on the south by Lake Ontario. In Haldimand 44,157 acres are taken up, 17,744 of which are under cultivation. The village of Grafton is situated in the south of the township, on the eastern road. The north of the township consists of oak plains, the centre and south are good land, timber principally hardwood, intermixed with large pine. There are three grist and eleven saw-mills in the township. In Haldimand 300 acres of Crown lands are open for sale, at 8s. currency per acre.

Population in 1842, 2826.

Ratable property in the township, £44,725.

HALDIMAND.

A settlement in the township of Dunn, situated on the Grand River, about one quarter of a mile from Dunnville. It contains about sixty inhabitants one grist-mill, two saw mills, two taverns.

HALL'S MILLS (See WESTMINSTER.)

HALLOWELL.

A Township in the Prince Edward District, is bounded on the north by Sophiasburgh and the Bay of Quinté, on the east by Marysburgh on the south by Athol, and on the west by Lake Ontario and the township of Hillier. Hallowell, contains 38,625 acres, 18,746 of which are under cultivation. A large bay called "West Lake," having several small islands in it, penetrates into this township, it is connected with Lake Ontario by a very short narrow channel. The east portion of "West Lake" is marshy. The town of Picton is in this township. There are four grist and ten saw-mills in the township.

Population in 1842 (not including the town of Picton), 2322.

Ratable property in the township, £63,889.

HALTON

A County in the Gore District, comprises the townships of Beverly, Esquesing, East Flamboro', West Flamboro', Nassagaweya, Nelson, and Trafalgar, and for all purposes, except that of representation in the Legislative Assembly, the township of Dumfries, and for the purpose of representation in the Legislative Assembly only, the township of Erin. It returns a member to the House of Assembly.

HAMBURG.

A Village in the township of Wilmot, two miles from Haysville, and twenty-two miles from Galt, situated on Smith's Creek. It was laid out in 1837, and contains about 300 inhabitants: two churches, Methodist.

Professions and Trades.—One grist-mill, carding machine and fulling-mill, distillery, four stores, one tavern, one waggon maker, one blacksmith, one tailor, two shoe makers.

HAMILTON.

The District Town of the Gore District, in the township of Barton and county of Wentworth; is situated in an extensive valley on the south side of Burlington Bay, at its western extremity. The town was laid out in the year 1813, by a Mr. Hamilton, from whom it derived its name. On account of the swamp in the vicinity of the bay, the principal part of the town has been placed about a mile back from the bay, on a gently rising ground. Immediately behind the town rises the mountain (to the height of at least 150 feet), or more correctly speaking, the high table land, which stretches away to the Niagara River. Previous to the completion of the Burlington Canal, vessels could not approach nearer than Burlington Beach, about ten miles from the town, where a customhouse and warehouses were established. Since the opening of the canal, the trade of the town has increased rapidly, and it is now the principal market for the western merchants. An immense amount of goods is annually imported.

Excellent freestone and limestone are procured from the mountain, which are of great advantage to the town, as the merchants are beginning to build almost exclusively of stone, and the town promises in a few years to become one of the handsomest on the continent of America. Many buildings are already erected with cut stone fronts among the handsomest of these, are the Gore Bank and the Bank of British North America. The streets are well laid out. Some years since, a person offered to supply the town with water, conveyed from a spring on the mountain above the town; the height of which would have allowed of the water being carried to the very top of every house, provided the monopoly was secured to him for a certain number of years. His offer, however, was declined, had it been acceded to, it would have been of immense benefit to the town.

The first district court was held in Hamilton in the year 1822. The town was incorporated in 1833, and in the same year sent a representative to the House of Assembly. The population of Hamilton, according to a census taken in the summer of 1845, is 6475.

Excellent roads now stretch away in every direction, and stages leave Hamilton every day for London, Port Stanley, Chatham, Detroit, Port Dover, Galt and Guelph, Niagara and St Catharines, and Toronto, and three times a-week for Goderich. The British steamboats "Eclipse" and "Queen," leave daily, during the season, for Toronto, and the American steamboat "Express," for Queenston and Niagara. Eleven schooners, whose collective tonnage amounts to 970 tons, and one barque of 230 tons, are owned here.

The public buildings and institutions consist of a stone jail and court-house, two market-houses (one of which is of brick, over which is the town hall, containing a room ninety by fifty feet, and fifteen feet high) custom house, post office, police office, engine house (with two engines), and theatre. There are eleven churches and chapels, viz., Episcopal, Presbyterian, Catholic, Free Church, Secession, Congregational, Wesleyan Methodist, Ryerson Methodist, Canadian Wesleyan, and two for coloured people, Baptist and Methodist.

There are two societies established for charitable purposes, "St George's" and "St. Andrew's". There are two news and reading rooms in the town—the "Commercial News Room," established and supported by means of a subscription amongst some of the merchants of the place, and "Bull's News Room," attached to the Gazette Office, where the following newspapers and periodicals may be seen —

Montreal Times, Courier, Transcript, Canada Gazette, Gazette, and Herald; Toronto British Canadian, Herald, British Colonist, Globe and Banner. Kingston Chronicle, British Whig, News; London (C.W.) Times; Woodstock Herald;

Guelph Herald; Peterboro' Chronicle; Brockville Recorder; Dumfries Courier; Brockville Statesman, Niagara Chronicle, and Argus; Ottawa Advocate; The Church; Cobourg Star; Woodstock Monarch; Chatham Journal; St. Catharine's Journal; Brantford Courier; St. Thomas Standard; Belleville Intelligencer; Life at the Springs; Deutsch Canadian; Hamilton Gazette.

British Papers.—European Times and News Letter, Dublin Warder, Downpatrick Recorder, Leinster Express, Dublin Monitor, Edinburgh Weekly Journal, Army List, Navy do., Blackwood's, Dublin University Magazine.

New York.—Anglo American, Evening Express, Albion, Sun, Spirit of the Times, Commercial Advertiser, Utica Gospel Messenger.

The Journals of the House of Assembly are also kept here.

There is also a Mechanics' Institute. Three newspapers are published here, " the " Hamilton Gazette," " Journal and Express," and " Herald." Sir Allan McNab has a handsome mansion, called " Dundurn," a short distance out of the town.

Amount of ratable property in the town of Hamilton, £109,998.

List of Government and District Offices kept in Hamilton.—Sheriff, Clerk of Peace, Treasurer, Judge of District Court, Inspector of Licenses, Collector of Customs, Warden, Judge of Surrogate Court, Registrar of do., Crown Lands Agent, Emigrant Agent, Superintendent of Schools, District Clerk, Clerk of District Court, Coroner, Registrar of county of Wentworth.

Professions and Trades.—Nine physicians and surgeons, sixteen lawyers, three breweries, ten wholesale importers of dry goods and groceries, five importers of hardware, forty-nine stores, two foundries, four printing offices, three booksellers, three chemists, sixty-five taverns, two tanneries, three coachmakers, two soap and candle factories, four auctioneers, five saddlers, eleven cabinet makers, three watchmakers, six bakers, ten shoemakers, three gunsmiths, three confectioners, fourteen groceries, eleven beer shops, six builders, five stone masons, five tinsmiths, four hatters, fourteen tailors, eight painters, one marble and stone works, thirteen blacksmiths, three ladies' seminaries, two schools for boys. Four banks—" Gore," " Commercial," " Montreal," and " Bank of British North America."

Principal Taverns and Stage Houses.—" Week's (late Press's) Royal Exchange," and the " Commercial." The former contains above sixty rooms.

Land Agents.—J. T. Gilkison, King Street; Alex. Glen, King Street; and —— Wedd, —— Street.

Commission Merchants and Shipping Agents.—M. W. & E. Browne, Land & Routh.

Stage and Steamboat Fares from Hamilton to the following places:—

Place.	Conveyance.	Time of Starting.	Distance.	Fare.
				s. d.
Toronto	Per Stage	6 P. M.	45 miles	10 0
Port Dover	Do.	8 A. M.	38 do.	7 6
London	Do.	8 P. M.	90 do.	20 3
Galt	Do.	8 A. M.	25 do.	5 0
Guelph	Do.	8 A. M.	39 do.	7 6
St. Catharines	Do.	8 P. M.	32 do.	12 6
Toronto	Per steamer Eclipse	8 A. M.	45 do.	7 6
Do.	Do. Queen	2 P. M.	45 do.	7 6
Queenston and Niagara	Do. Express	7 A. M.	......	10 0

Exports from the Port of Hamilton, for the years 1843 *and* 1844:—

DESCRIPTION.	1843.	1844.
Flour, barrels	52463	81597
Pork, do.	246	1172
Whiskey, do.	1167	1252
Butter, kegs	220	430
Lard do.	89	—
Do. barrels	3	—
Wheat, bushels	10351¾	18430
Lumber (boards), feet	20000	329647
West India Staves, pieces	153208	196245
Pipe do. do.	29405	3012
Beer, barrels	42	26
Apples, bushels	181	56
Ashes, barrels	267	430
Pot Barley, do.	270	—
Oats, bushels	60	530
Stone, toises	15	33
Barley, bushels	......	52
Potatoes, do.	......	1007
Merchandise, cwts.	2643½	—
Domestic Manufactures, cwts.	......	6121
Other Merchandise, do.	......	2255

Tolls collected at Burlington Bay, in the years 1843 *and* 1844:—

In 1843 ....£1986 9 4
In 1844 .... 2933 0 2

Increase £946 10 10

HAMILTON.

A Township in the Newcastle District; is bounded on the east by the township of Haldimand; on the north by Rice Lake, and a portion of South Lake; on the west by Hope; and on the south by Lake Ontario. In Hamilton 49,599 acres are taken up, 21,527 of which are under cultivation. Rice Lake occupies a large portion of the north of the township. The town of Cobourg is situated on the lake shore, near the centre of the south of the township. Hamilton is well settled, and possesses excellent farms. There are six grist and seventeen saw-mills in the township.

Population in 1842, 4774.

Ratable property in the township, 84,274.

HARVEY.

A Township in the Colborne District; is bounded on the east by the township of Burleigh; on the north by unsurveyed lands; on the west by Verulam; and on the south by Smith and Ennismore. Harvey was originally well settled, by emigrants from the old country, but finding the greater part of the township unfit for cultivation, they left it, and it is now almost deserted. Two hundred acres only are taken up, forty of which are under cultivation. It is separated from Smith and Ennismore by a chain of Lakes, a large portion of which stretch across the centre of the township. There is a grist and saw-mill in the

township. In Harvey 37,277 acres of Crown lands are open for sale, at 8s. c'y per acre.
Population ——
Ratable property in the township, £380.

HARWICH.

A Township in the county of Kent, in the Western District ; bounded on the north-west by the River Thames , on the south-west by the township of Raleigh , on the south by Lake Erie; and on the north-east by the township of Howard. In Harwich 32,845 acres are taken up, of which 4,942 are under cultivation. Soil extremely fertile, consisting of reddish loam, with intervening ridges of sandy or gravelly loam Timber—white oak, black walnut, maple, beech, hickory, bass-wood, &c &c , and on the lake shore may be found cedar, both white and red McGregor's creek runs across the township to its north-western corner, where it enters the Thames. This township is well settled, containing 1898 inhabitants. Harwich contains a mixed population. The Canada Company possess 2,600 acres in Harwich At the southern extremity of this township is the Rond Eau, to which harbour an excellent road has lately been formed from Chatham Amount of ratable property in the township £25,208. The town of Chatham is partly situated in Harwich.

HASTINGS

A County forming the Victoria District ; it comprises the following townships—Elzevir, Grimsthorp, Hungerford Huntingdon, Lake, Marmora, Madoc, Rawdon, Sydney, Tudor, Thurlow, and Tyendenaga. It returns a member to the House of Assembly.

HATSFIELD

A village in the township of Plantagenet four miles south of the Ottawa ; contains about eighty inhabitants , grist and saw mill, one store, two taverns.

HAWKESBURY EAST.

A Township in the Ottawa District, is bounded on the east by Lower Canada; on the north by the Ottawa River; on the west by Hawkesbury West, and on the south by Lochiel In East Hawkesbury 24,037 acres are taken up. Four thousand seven hundred and forty-six of which are under cultivation. The land in this township, particularly that bordering on the Ottawa, is mostly poor and cold, and much of it is wet. There is a settlement in the south of the township, called "East Hawkesbury Mills," containing grist, saw and oatmeal mills. There are four grist and seven saw mills in the township. One thousand two hundred and ninety-six acres of Crown lands in Hawkesbury East are open for sale, at 8s. currency per acre.
Population, 1,751.
Ratable property in the township, £18,946.

HAWKESBURY, WEST.

A township in the Ottawa District; is bounded on the east by East Hawkesbury, on the north by the Ottawa, on the west by Longueil and Caledonia; and on the south by Lochiel. In West Hawkesbury, 23,459 acres are taken up, 7,201 of which are under cultivation. The land of this township is similar to that of East Hawkesbury Hawkesbury village is situated in the north of the township, and Hawkesbury Mills, the largest sawing establishment in Canada West, is a short distance from the village Two hundred and fifty acres of Crown lands are open for sale in West Hawkesbury, at 8s. per acre. There are two grist and eight saw mills, and one distillery in the township
Population, 1,976.
Ratable property in the township, £27,138.

HAWKESBURY VILLAGE, or HEADPORT.

A Village in the township of Hawkesbury West, situated near the Ottawa, four miles east of L'Orignal. It contains about 250 inhabitants. Churches and chapels two; viz., Episcopal and Congregational.

Professions and Trades.—One grist and saw mill, distillery, carding machine and cloth factory, four stores, two taverns, one blacksmith.

About one mile west of the village are Hawkesbury Mills, one of the largest establishments for sawing lumber in Canada, giving employment to between two and three hundred hands. Here are a grist and three saw mills, store, and various mechanics supported by the establishment.

HAY.

A Township in the Huron District; is bounded on the north by the township of Stanley; on the west by Lake Huron; on the south by Stephen; and on the east by Tuckersmith and Usborne. The soil is good, with the exception of the land bordering on the lake. There is a post office in the south-east corner of the township, on the London road. Hay contains 33,684 acres, 3,301 of which are leased or sold; of which 397 are under cultivation.

Population, 113.

Ratable property in the township, £1,720 16s.

HAYSVILLE.

A small Village in the township of Wilmot, situated on the Huron road, twenty-two miles from Galt. It contains about seventy inhabitants, grist and saw mill, one store, two taverns, one blacksmith.

HEADPORT.—(*See* HAWKESBURY.)

HELMSPORT, or "THE JUNCTION."

A small Settlement in the township of Crowland, situated at the junction of the main channel of the Welland Canal with the feeder from the Grand River, fifteen miles from St. Catharines. It contains about sixty inhabitants, two stores, two taverns, one blacksmith, one tailor, one shoemaker.

HEN AND CHICKENS.

A group of Islands, four in number, situated in the west of Lake Erie, about nine miles west from Point Pele Island. The largest island, called "The Hen," contains about five acres of good land, the other three are mere rocks.

HEYWOOD'S BAY,—(*See* GREAT MANITOULIN.)

HIBBERT.

A Township in the Huron District; is bounded on the north-east by the townships of McKillop and Logan; on the north-west by Tuckersmith; on the south-west by Usborne; and on the south-east by Fullarton. Most of the land in this township is good. A branch of the Bayfield river runs through the north of the township. Hibbert contains 42,306 acres; 2100 of which are leased or sold, of which 172 are under cultivation.

Population, 95.

Ratable property in the township, £751 12s.

HILLIER.

A Township in the Prince Edward District; is bounded on the north by the township of Ameliasburgh, Weller's Bay, Consecon Creek and Lake Consecon; on the east by Sophiasburgh and Hallowell; and on the south and west by Lake

Ontario Hillier contains 30,717 acres, 16,460 of which are under cultivation. Three small bays, called Young's Lake, Pleasant Bay, and Hugh's Bay, run into the township on its west side. The township is well watered by several creeks running into these bays. The village of Wellington is situated at the south-east corner of the township There are four grist and twelve saw mills in the township

From the loose manner in which the census was last taken in this township, it was impossible to ascertain the population with any accuracy.

Ratable property in the township, £41,657.

HINCHINBROOKE.

A township in the Midland District, is bounded on the east by the township of Bedford; on the north by Kennebec and Olden; on the west by Storrington, and on the south by Portland A large lake, having an island in its centre, is situated a little west of the centre of the township; and several small lakes are scattered over it Fifty thousand acres of Crown lands are open for sale in the township, at 8s currency per acre.

Hinchinbrooke has only lately been opened for sale, and no return has yet been made from it.

HOLLAND.

A Township in the Wellington District, is bounded on the east by the township of Euphrasia, on the north by Sydenham, on the west by Sullivan, and on the south by Glenelg This township has only lately been surveyed and laid out, and no return has yet been made from it.

HOLLAND LANDING, ST. ALBANS, or BEVERLY.

A Village on Yonge Street Road, thirty-two miles north from Toronto; situated partly in the township of East, and partly in West Gwillimbury. It is three miles from the steamboat landing on the Holland River, and ten miles from Lake Simcoe The place had been partially settled for some years, but was not laid out as a village till the year 1835 It is situated in the midst of hills, and the east branch of the Holland River runs through it. During the season, the steamboat "Beaver" leaves the Holland River for Barrie and Orillia every Monday, Wednesday and Friday, returning on the alternate days, and a stage leaves Holland Landing every morning at six o'clock, for Toronto. There are two churches—Episcopal and Methodist.

Population, about 260

Post office, post three times a week

Professions and Trades—One physician and surgeon, one lawyer, one grist and saw mill, one brewery, one distillery, carding machine and fulling mill, one tannery, one foundry, four stores, four taverns, one druggist, one saddler, one waggon maker, one baker, one cabinet maker, one watchmaker, one fanning-mill maker, one tinsmith, one blacksmith, two tailors, two shoemakers, one ladies' seminary, one bank agency—"Commercial"

Quantity of wheat purchased at Holland Landing, from September, 1844, to May, 1845, about 55,000 bushels

HOME DISTRICT.

Consists of the County of York and the City of Toronto. The county of York is divided into four ridings, each returning one member to the Legislative Assembly The north riding comprises the townships of Brock, North Gwillimbury, East Gwillimbury, Georgina, Mara, Reach, Rama, Scott, Thorah, Uxbridge and Whitchurch. The south riding comprises the townships of Etobicoke, King, Vaughan, and York, and for the purposes of registration of titles only, the city of Toronto. The east riding comprises the townships of

Markham, Pickering, Scarborough, and Whitby; and the west riding comprises the townships of Albion, Caledon, Chinguacousy, Toronto Gore, and Toronto township. The Home District is situated nearly in the centre of the Province, and is bounded on the east by the Newcastle and Colborne Districts, on the north by the Simcoe District, Lake Simcoe, and Lake Gougichin, on the west by the Simcoe, Wellington, and Gore Districts, and on the south by Lake Ontario. The Home District has been settled about fifty years, and in 1799 it contained only 224 inhabitants.

This district comprises a great variety of soil, and also a considerable difference in point of climate, the townships bordering on Lake Simcoe being about 530 feet above Lake Ontario. The land for from two to three miles back from the margin of Lake Ontario, is generally rather poor and sandy, with the exception of the cedar swamps, the soil of which is very rich. As you recede from the lake, the land improves in quality, and at from four to five miles from the lake you frequently come upon splendid wheat land. A succession of pine ridges traverses the district, running through the north of Whitby, and south of Reach, the centre of Uxbridge and Whitchurch, the centre of King and Albion, and the north of Caledon, and from thence into the Simcoe and Wellington Districts. The district is watered by the Credit, Humber, Don, Rouge, and the Holland Rivers, and the Etobicoke and Duffin's Creek, besides numerous other small streams, many of which are excellent mill streams, and are well studded with both grist and saw mills. The Nottawasaga River also takes its rise in this district. The northern townships in the district, although enjoying a fine climate, and containing excellent land, have hitherto been kept very much in the back-ground for want of good roads, some parts being altogether impassable for vehicles except during the time when the (so called) roads were covered with snow, and others almost so during a large portion of the year. Even the principal road in the district, the great northern thoroughfare, with the exception of the sixteen miles (to Richmond Hill) which is macadamised, has generally been for some time during every spring, in such a state that no farmer having any regard for his horses would allow them to travel on it. It is now, however, under contract, and there is a prospect that in the course of two or three years, when the newly made road shall have settled down, the farmers in the townships about Lake Simcoe may be able to bring their produce to Toronto market. Good roads into the interior of the northern back townships are still however very much wanted.

Next to the Gore District, the Home is the best settled district in the Province. The road for eighteen miles along the Kingston road from Toronto is planked, and the Yonge Street road is macadamised to Richmond Hill (sixteen miles), and the Dundas Street to Cooksville (sixteen miles). The former is now to be macadamised as far as the Holland Landing, and the latter for some distance farther westward.

The principal town in the district is Toronto, the district town, and formerly the capital of the Upper Province, and there are besides in the district the villages of Oshawa and Windsor in Whitby, Markham, Richmond Hill, and Thornhill, in Markham, Newmarket, in Whitchurch, Holland Landing, partly in East and partly in West Gwillimbury, Lloydtown, in King, Mimico and Weston, in Etobicoke, Cooksville, Springfield, Port Credit, Streetsville, and Churchville, in Toronto; besides numerous others of less note. In the Home District 24,410 acres of Crown lands are open for sale, at 8s. currency per acre, to purchase any of which, application must be made to the Crown Lands Agent, at Toronto. These lands are situated principally in the townships of Mara, Georgina, East and North Gwillimbury, Brock, Thorah, and Rama. Nearly 30,000 acres of land have been brought into cultivation between January, 1842, and January, 1844.

Population of the district in 1842, 58,853, since when it has probably increased one-fifth.

H

The following abstract from the Assessment Rolls will show the rate of increase and improvement in the district:—

Date.	No. of Acres Cultivated.	MILLS. Grist.	MILLS. Saw.	Milch Cows.	Oxen, 4 years old, and upwards.	Horned Cattle, from 2 to 4 years old.	Amount of Ratable Property.
1842	270,512	65	209	22,499	6448	10,331	£789,789
1843	283,600	72	218	23,345	6791	9,826	831,433
1844	300,301	76	237	23,735	6173	10,130	878,732

Government and District Officers in the Home District:

Judge of District Court	Robert Easton Burns	Toronto.
Sheriff	Wm. Botsford Jarvis	Do.
Clerk of Peace	George Gurnett	Do.
Treasurer	James S. Howard	Do.
Registrar	Samuel G. Ridout	Do.
Judge of Surrogate Court	Hon. S. B. Harrison	Do.
Registrar of do.	William Chewett	Do.
Inspector of Licenses	James McDonell	Do.
Crown Lands Agent	Thomas Baines	Do.
District Clerk	John Elliot	Do.
Clerk of District Court	Walter McKenzie	Do.
Deputy Clerk of Crown	None	
Warden	Edward W. Thomson	Do.
Auditors	Thomas Bell	Do.
	Robert Beekman	Do.
District Superintendent of Schools	Hamilton Hunter	Do.
Coroners	A. Smalley	N. Gwillimbury.
	Geo. Duggan	Toronto city.
	D. Bridgford	Vaughan.
	Geo. Walton	Toronto city.
	W. B. Crew	Do.
	F. Osborne	Thorah.
	M. Macdonagh	Mara.
	Jas. Adamson	Toronto township.
	J. Clarke	Whitby.

Number of Common Schools in operation in the District.—Whitby, twenty-one; Markham, twenty-three; Pickering, twenty-one; Whitchurch, sixteen; Vaughan, eighteen; Toronto, twenty-two; Chinguacousy, twenty-three; York, twenty-three; Etobicoke, six; Scarborough, nine; Gore of Toronto, four; North Gwillimbury, three; East Gwillimbury eleven; Georgina, five; Reach, nine; Uxbridge, four; Scott, one; Thorah, four; King, twenty; Brock, eleven; Albion, thirteen; Caledon, thirteen; Mara and Rama, four. Total, 284.

HOPE.

A Township in the Newcastle District; is bounded on the east by the township of Hamilton; on the north by Cavan; on the west by Clarke; and on the south by Lake Ontario. In Hope 42,058 acres are taken up, 16,409 of which are under cultivation. A considerable stream, possessing valuable mill privileges, runs through the township, and enters the lake at its south-east corner. The town of Port Hope is situated on the Lake, at the mouth of this creek, which forms the harbour. This township is well settled, and possesses excellent land.

Timber principally hardwood, with some pine There are five grist and fourteen saw-mills in the township.

*Population in 1842, 4,432
*Ratable property in the township, £58,468
* These include the town of Port Hope.

HORNBY

A small settlement, situated partly in Esquesing, and partly in Trafalgar, eight miles from Dundas Street It contains about sixty inhabitants, two stores, one tavern

Post-office, post three times a week

HORSE ISLAND.

An Island in Lake Huron (also called Fourth Manitoulin) 141 miles from Goderich, and about one mile south-east of the Great Manitoulin, so named from the circumstance of a horse, supposed to have escaped from a wreck, having existed upon the island for about eight years, where it became so wild that it was impossible to capture it. It was at length destroyed. The island is uninhabited

HORTON

A Township in the Bathurst District, is bounded on the north-east by the Ottawa River, on the north-west by the township of Ross, on the south-west by Admaston, and on the south-east by McNab In Horton 15,807 acres are taken up, 2,181 of which are under cultivation. This is a small township, having some large lakes in it There is some good land in the township Nineteen thousand six hundred acres of Crown lands are open for sale in Horton, at 8s c'y per acre. There are one grist and two saw-mills in the township
Population in 1842, 544.
Ratable property in the township, £7,989

HOUGHTON

A township in the Talbot District, is bounded on the north-east by the township of Walsingham, on the west by Bayham, and on the south by Lake Erie In Houghton 9,830 acres are taken up, 1,803 of which are under cultivation This is a small wedge-shaped township, the timber of which is principally pine There are six saw-mills in the township
Population in 1841, 277
Ratable property in the township, £6,491

HOWARD

A Township in the county of Kent, in the Western District, is bounded on the north by the River Thames; on the south-west by the township of Harwich, on the north-east by the township of Orford, and on the south by Lake Erie In Howard 35,501 acres are taken up, 6,545 of which are under cultivation The soil of the greater part of this township is a fine light loam, intermixed with gravel, being very easy of cultivation. McGregor's Creek runs across the township One hundred acres of Crown lands are open for sale in Howard at 8s c'y per acre, and the Canada Company possess about 4,500 acres in the township There are in the township three grist and six saw mills, of which number one grist and three-saw mills are on Big Creek, a stream running into Lake Erie There is an Episcopal Church in Howard

Howard is well settled, and contains a mixed population, consisting of English, Irish, Scotch, Canadians, Germans, and Americans From this and the two adjoining townships there were exported last year—

10,500 Bushels of Wheat, valued at	....	£1,968	15 0
114,000 Pipe Staves	" "	1,282	10 0
169 Barrels Pork,	" "	338	0 0

Some seasons, as much as 100 hogsheads of Tobacco have been shipped from this township, but latterly, from the diminished duty imposed upon tobacco from the United States, the crop has become unprofitable, and the farmers have consequently discontinued the cultivation.

Population in 1845, 1,896

Ratable property in the township, £22,122

HULLETT.

A township in the Huron District, is bounded on the north-east by Crown lands; on the west by the townships of Colborne and Goderich; on the south-west by Tuckersmith, and on the south-east by McKillop. A branch of the Maitland River runs through this township. The soil is generally good. Hullett contains 35,941 acres, 3,960 of which are leased or sold, of which 324 acres are under cultivation.

Population 195.

Ratable property in the township, £1,470 4s.

HUMBER RIVER

Takes its rise in the township of Vaughan, and follows nearly a south course to Lake Ontario, forming the boundary between the townships of Etobicoke and York. The village of Weston is situated on the Humber, in the township of Etobicoke, and there are several grist and saw mills on it.

HUMBERSTONE

A Township in the Niagara District, is bounded on the east by the township of Bertie, on the north by Crowland, on the west by Wainfleet, and on the south by Lake Erie. In Humberstone 20,484 acres are taken up, 6,596 of which are under cultivation. Humberstone contains good land, but many of the farms are not well cultivated. There are one grist and two saw mills in the township.

Population in 1841, 1,376, who are principally Pennsylvanian Dutch and their descendants, with a small mixture of Canadians, Americans and Germans.

Ratable property in the township, £23,704

HUNGERFORD.

A Township in the Victoria District, is bounded on the east by the township of Sheffield, on the north by Elzevir, on the west by Huntingdon, and on the south by Tyendenaga and Richmond. In Hungerford 19,472 acres are taken up, 3,933 of which are under cultivation. A small lake is situated near the centre of the township, having several small streams running into it. The Moira River takes its rise in this lake, and leaves the township at its south-west corner. There are four grist mills and one saw mill in the township. Five thousand four hundred and fifteen acres of Crown lands are open for sale in Hungerford, at 8s currency per acre.

Population in 1842, 880, who are principally protestant Irish.

Ratable property in the township, £10,715.

HUNTINGFORD

A Settlement in the east of the township of Zorra. It contains about fifty inhabitants, an Episcopal church, a tavern, and a blacksmith's shop.

HUNTINGDON

A Township in the Victoria District, is bounded on the east by the township of Hungerford, on the north by Madoc, on the west by Rawdon; and on the south by Thurlow. In Huntingdon 20,299 acres are taken up, 5,509 of which are under cultivation. There is a small lake in the north-east corner of the township. Huntingdon is well settled, and contains some good farms. There are three saw mills in the township One thousand one hundred acres of Crown lands are open for sale in Huntingdon, at 8s currency per acre

Population in 1842, 1,099, who are principally protestant Irish.

Ratable property in the township, £14,590.

HUNTLEY.

A Township in the Dalhousie District, is bounded on the north-east by the township of March, on the north-west by Fitzroy, on the south-west by Ramsay; and on the south-east by Beckwith In Huntley 30,626 acres are taken up, 5,727 of which are under cultivation This township is getting well settled there is some good land in it, but a considerable portion of the timber is pine. A branch of the Mississippi River and Carp River run through the township Fourteen thousand and seventy-nine acres of Crown lands are open for sale in Huntley, at 8s currency per acre There is one saw mill in the township.

Population in 1842, 1771.

Ratable property in the township, £16,686

HURON DISTRICT.

Consists of the County of Huron, which returns a member to the House of Assembly, and comprises the following townships — Ashfield, Biddulph, Blanshard, Colborne, Downie, Ellice, South Easthope, North Easthope, Fullarton, Goderich, Hibbert, Hay, Hullett, Logan, McKillop, McGillivray, Stephen, Stanley, Tuckersmith, Usborne, and Wawanosh. All the townships, except the first and the last, which belong to the Crown, are the property of the Canada Company, and were formed out of the Huron Tract, which was purchased from the Crown by the Canada Company in the year 1827 The Huron Tract was declared a district in 1842, previous to which time it formed a part of the London District A large portion of the land in the district is good, although some parts are rather hilly and broken, and the land generally on the borders of the lake, and also on the Maitland River, is rather poor There is but little pine in the district The district is watered by the Maitland and Bayfield Rivers, and also by the River Aux Sables and the Thames, the former of which is an excellent mill stream, and the mouth of it forms the Goderich Harbour The Great Swamp, as it is called, which is situated to the north of the Huron Tract, encroaches on the townships of McKillop, Logan and Ellice In this swamp the rivers Maitland, Saugeen, Bayfield, Thames, and it is believed also the Grand River, take their rise The Canada Company were allowed by the government 100,000 acres of land as compensation for any loss that might arise to them from the swamp forming any part of their purchase. The Huron District is settled almost exclusively by emigrants from England, Ireland, and Scotland, and a few Germans Goderich, the district town, is handsomely and healthily situated on Lake Huron There are no Crown lands for sale in the district, except in the townships of Ashfield and Wawanosh; in which 86,500 acres are open for sale, at 8s currency per acre (a town has been laid out by the Crown in the township of Ashfield, on the lake shore, in which town lots are sold at £5 currency each), to purchase any of which application must be made to the Crown lands agent at Goderich.

Population in 1843, 13,500.

The following abstract from the assessment rolls, will show the rate of increase and improvement in the district:

Date.	No. of Acres Cultivated.	MILLS. Grist.	MILLS. Saw.	Milch Cows.	Oxen 4 years old, and upwards.	Horned Cattle, from 2 to 4 years old.	Amount of Ratable Property.
1842	20,355	7	17	2,519	1,709	1,713	£ 91,120
1843	24,844	7	20	2,967	1,943	2,035	106,862
1844	30,816	8	21	3,304	2,465	2,046	127,290

Government and District Officers in the Huron District:

Judge of District Court	A. Acland	Goderich.
Sheriff	John McDonald	Do.
Treasurer	Henry Ransford	Do.
Clerk of Peace	Daniel Lizars	Do.
Registrar	John Galt	Do.
Collector of Customs	Do.	Do.
Inspector of Fish	Do.	Do.
Inspector of Licenses	Charles Widder	Do.
Superintendent of Schools	John Bignall	Do.
District Clerk	D. Don	Do.
Clerk of District Court	John Colville	Do.
Warden	W. Dunlop	Do.
Coroner	Geo. Fraser	Do.

No. of Common Schools in operation in the Huron District.—Ashfield, one; Biddulph, three; Blarshard, none; Colborne, one; Downie, two; Ellice, one; North Easthope, two; South Easthope, two; Fullarton, none; Hibbert, none; Hullett, one; Hay and Stephen two; Stanley, one; McGillivray, two; Usborne, seven; Goderich, seven; Wawanosh, none; McKillop, one; Tuckersmith, three; Williams, three. Total, thirty-nine.

HURON LAKE.

The second lake in point of size in Canada. It is 218 miles in length, and 180 broad at its widest part, and 594 feet above the level of the sea. On the east it is bordered by Indian reserves, the Huron District, and the northern portion of the Western District; on the north, altogether by wild and unoccupied lands; and on the west by the United States. It receives the waters of Lake Superior and Lake Michigan, and discharges itself into the River St. Clair. A large wing of the lake, called the "Georgian Bay," extends itself in a south-easterly direction for about a hundred miles, including within its bounds the harbours of Owen Sound, Nottawasaga Bay, Penetanguishene Bay, and Gloster Bay; and it is connected by means of the Severn River (which, however, is not navigable) with Lake Simcoe.

The Georgian Bay is studded with islands, several thousands in number, and varying in size, from a few square feet to many acres. The scenery of the bay is very beautiful.

A large island, called the Great Manitoulin, about 100 miles in length, and from four to twenty-five miles wide, is situated in the north of Lake Huron; and several smaller islands are scattered around it. The Great Manitoulin, however, is the only one inhabited. The waters of the lake are remarkably pure and clear: they have been gradually rising during the last few years; and many parts along the south-east shore, where three or four years ago there were several yards of sandy and gravelly beach, between the base of the cliffs and the water's edge, are now under water. The banks of the lake vary in height, in some parts being low and sandy, and in others high clay banks, at least 120 feet in height. Lake Huron is rather subject to sudden storms, and the south of the lake is deficient in good harbours, the principal of which are Goderich and Saugeen. Vessels, however, if caught in a storm on the lake, if not too far to the north, generally run down for shelter to the bay in the River St Clair, above Port Sarnia, formed by the projection of Point Edward, and sometimes in bad weather, a dozen vessels may be seen at anchor here at one time.

There are as yet but few British steamboats on Lake Huron, but, as the country bordering on the lake and the Georgian Bay becomes settled up, these will gradually increase in number.

HURD, CAPE.

The north-western extremity of the land between Lake Huron and the Georgian Bay. It is 121 miles from Goderich.

INDIANA.

A small Village in the township of Seneca, pleasantly situated on the Grand River, twelve miles from Caledonia. It contains about 120 inhabitants and a Catholic Church.

Post Office, post three times a week.

Professions and Trades.—One grist mill, two saw do, distillery, two stores, two taverns, one pail factory, one blacksmith, two shoemakers, one cabinet maker, one tailor, one waggon maker.

INGERSOLL.

A Village in the township of West Oxford, situated on the plank road, twenty-two miles east from London, and ten miles west from Woodstock. The east branch of the River Thames runs through it. Ingersoll was laid out in 1831, and now contains nearly 400 inhabitants. There is an Episcopal Church in the village, and a Free Church and a Methodist do in course of erection. The registry office for the county of Oxford, is kept in Ingersoll.

Post Office, post every day.

Professions and Trades.—One grist and two saw mills, one carding machine and fulling mill, foundry, one brewery, one distillery, one tannery, one ashery, one physician and surgeon, one cabinet maker, two chair factories, one carriage maker, two waggon makers, seven stores, two taverns, two groceries, one baker, one tinsmith, one saddler, one fanning-mill maker, five blacksmiths, three tailors, three shoemakers

Land Agent.—Edward Merigold

INNISFIL.

A Township in the Simcoe District, is bounded on the north by Kempenfeldt Bay and part of the township of Vespra, on the west by Essa, on the south by West Gwillimbury, and on the east by Lake Simcoe and Cook's Bay. In Innisfil 23,591 acres are taken up, 4609 of which are under cultivation. This is rather a rough township; that portion of it bordering on Lake Simcoe and its bays, is mostly wild land; the cause of which is said to be its being in the hands of absentees. In the centre of the township are some pretty good farms. A large swamp extends for some distance along the town line between Innisfil and Essa, and reaches into Tecumseth and West Gwillimbury. The surveyor who originally surveyed the township states, that although there are a large number of cedar swamps in it, still that every lot possesses sufficient good land to make a farm. 2200 acres of Crown Lands are open for sale in Innisfil at 8s currency per acre. There are in the township one grist and two saw mills, carding machine and fulling mill, and brewery.

Population in 1842, 762, who are principally Irish and Scotch.

Ratable property in the township, £12,603.

IRVINE SETTLEMENT

A Scotch settlement in the township of Nichol, a short distance west from Elora. Inhabitants principally from Aberdeen

ISLE AUX CERFS.—(See Stag Island.)

ISTHMUS, THE, or NEWBORO'.

A small Settlement in the township of North Crosby, on the Rideau Canal, twenty miles from Oliver's ferry, and forty-two from Kingston It contains about eighty inhabitants, four stores, one tavern, two shoemakers, one blacksmith.

JAMESTOWN.

A small Settlement near the south-east corner of the township of Yarmouth, on Catfish Creek, about one mile from Lake Erie, contains a grist and saw mill, distillery, and about ten houses

JAMESVILLE —(See Morpeth.)

JEDBURGH.

A small Settlement in the township of Dumfries, situated on Cedar Creek, a branch of the Nith, about a quarter of a mile from Ayr. It contains about thirty inhabitants, one grist and saw mill, one distillery, one blacksmith

JOHNSTOWN DISTRICT.

Consists of the Counties of Leeds and Grenville, it is bounded on the south-east by the River St Lawrence, and is watered besides by the Rideau River and lakes, and several other lakes, some of which are very large, are scattered over the district The Rideau Canal runs through the north and west of the district There is a considerable quantity of good land in the district, although a large portion of that bordering on the canal and lakes is poor and rocky. Altogether the District is well settled, and contains some good farms The inhabitants are principally Scotch and Irish Brockville, the district town, is handsomely situated, and contains some good stone buildings Thirteen thousand three hundred and fifty-five acres of Crown lands are open for sale in the Johnstown District, at 8s c'y, per acre, to purchase any of which application must be made to the Crown Lands Agent at Prescott

Population in 1842, 36,768, since when it has probably increased one-fifth

The following abstract from the assessment rolls will show the rate of increase and improvement in the district

Date	No of Acres Cultivated	MILLS Grist	MILLS Saw	Milch Cows	Oxen, 4 years old and upwards	Horned Cattle, from 2 to 4 years old	Amount of Ratable Property.
1842	111734	26	46	11915	2921	4997	£402,922
1843	120168	26	56	12719	3142	5785	428,105
1844	125095	25	62	13251	3363	5362	442,992

Government and District Officers in the Johnstown District:

Judge of District Court	George Malloch	Brockville.
Sheriff	A. Sherwood	do
Treasurer	A. N Buell	do
Inspector of Licenses	J Weatherhead	do.
Clerk of Peace and District Clerk	James Jessup	do.
Registrar of County of Leeds	David Jones	do
Do of County of Grenville	John Patton	Prescott.
Clerk of District Court	J D Campbell	Brockville
Warden	R F Steele	do
Crown Lands Agent	W J. Scott	Prescott.

JORDAN

A village in the township of Louth, situated on the Hamilton road, eight miles from St Catherines. It contains four churches and chapels, viz.—Episcopal, British Wesleyan, Canadian do and Presbyterian.
Population about 200
Post-office, post every day.
Professions and Trades —Three stores, carding machine and cloth factory, one tannery, two taverns, one saddler, one cabinet-maker, two waggon-makers, four blacksmiths, two shoemakers, one tailor

JUNCTION, THE.

A settlement in the township of Westminster, six miles from London, situated at the junction of the plank road to St Thomas, with the Delaware road It contains about sixty inhabitants, one store, three taverns Distillery and steam grist mill erecting

KALADAR

A Township in the Midland District, is bounded on the east by the township of Kennebec, on the north by Anglesea, on the west by Elzevir, and on the south by Sheffield and a small portion of Hungerford This township is well watered by numerous small streams it has only lately been opened for sale, and no return has yet been made from it Sixty-five thousand acres of Crown lands are open for sale in Kaladar, at 8s ey per acre

KATLSVILLE

A small settlement in the township of Adelaide, situated on Bear Creek It contains about thirty inhabitants and one store

KLENE

A village in the township of Otonabee, situated on the Indian River near Rice Lake, thirteen miles south-east from Peterborough It contains about 140 inhabitants, who have two churches, Presbyterian and Wesleyan Methodist
Professions and Trades —One grist mill, one saw ditto, distillery, tannery, carding machine four stores. three taverns, one waggon maker, one blacksmith.
Post-office, post three times a week

KEMPENFELDT.

A small settlement on Kempenfeldt Bay, about two miles from Barrie ; it contains about forty inhabitants.

KEMPENFELDT BAY.—(*See* LAKE SIMCOE)

KENNEBEC.

A Township in the Midland District: is bounded on the east by the township of Olden; on the north by Barrie; on the west by Kaladar; and on the south by Sheffield and Hinchinbrooke. Two long lakes, one of which is called "Long Lake," stretch across the centre of the township; these are the principal sources of Salmon River. This township has only lately been opened for sale, and no return has yet been made from it. Sixty-five thousand acres of Crown lands are open for sale in Kennebec, at eight shillings currency per acre.

KENT.

A County in the Western District. It comprises the townships of Bosanquet, Brooke, Camden, Chatham, Dawn, East Dover, West Dover, Enniskillen, Harwich, Howard, Moore, Orford, Plympton, Raleigh, Romney, Sarnia, Sombra, East Tilbury, Warwick and Zone. It returns a member to the House of Assembly.

KENYON.

A Township in the Eastern District; is bounded on the north-east by the township of Lochiel; on the north-west by Caledonia; on the south-west by the reserve of the St. Regis Indians; and on the south-east by Charlottenburgh. In Kenyon, 43,166 acres are taken up, 3,837 of which are under cultivation. The land in Kenyon varies in quality. Timber, pine, intermixed with hardwood. There are two grist mills in the township.

Population in 1842, 2,536, who are principally Irish Catholics and Scotch. The latter have a Presbyterian Church in the township.

Ratable property in the township, £20,812.

KILWORTH.

A Village in the township of Delaware, situated on the River Thames, about five miles from Delaware. It contains about 150 inhabitants. There is a stone school-house in the village, which is used for religious services. About one mile from the village, in the township of Lobo, Lord Mountcashel has a house, finely situated, being erected on an eminence commanding a fine view of the Thames.

Professions and Trades.—Two grist mills, one saw ditto, carding machine and fulling mill, one distillery, two tanneries, four stores, two taverns, one saddler, two tailors, two shoemakers, one waggon-maker, and one blacksmith.

KING.

A Township in the Home District; is bounded on the north by the townships of Gwillimbury West and Tecumseth; on the west by Albion; on the south by Vaughan; and on the east by Whitchurch. In King, 53,240 acres are taken up, 13,818 of which are under cultivation. This is an old settled township, and possesses some fine farms; but a portion of the township is hilly and broken, the timber being hemlock intermingled with hardwood. The west branch of the Holland River runs through the centre of the north of the township, and is bordered by a considerable extent of swamp. The village of Lloydtown is situated in the north-west corner of the township, and one mile and a half to the north-east is the village of Brownsville. There are also in King, Bogarttown in the north-east of the township about two miles from Yonge Street, containing about ten dwellings, grist and saw mill, waggon maker and blacksmith; and Tyrwhit's Mills, eight miles east from Lloydtown, between that village and Yonge Street, containing grist and saw mill, tavern, store, cooper, and blacksmith. King is settled by a mixed population, consisting principally of Irish, with a few English, Scotch, Canadians, and Americans. One hundred

acres of Crown lands are open for sale in King, at 8s currency per acre There are eight grist and twelve saw mills in the township.
Population in 1842, 2625.
Ratable property in the township, £42,064.

KINGSTON.

The District Town of the Midland District, in the township of Kingston, situated on Lake Ontario, 199 miles from Montreal and 177 from Toronto It was incorporated in the year 1838. It is a fine healthy situation, but having a barren back country, its principal dependance for support was upon the carrying trade, until the removal of the Seat of Government from Toronto, by Lord Sydenham in June, 1841, when the town began rapidly to improve. Handsome stone buildings were erected, and the inhabitants, supposing that Kingston would continue to be the capital of the Province, went to considerable expense in improving, not merely the public buildings, but also their places of business and private dwellings. However, the Seat of Government being again removed (to Montreal) they have been thrown back upon their old resources, burdened with the expenses of their improvements This, for a time, was a great shock to the town; but it is beginning gradually to recover its prosperity. What effect the opening of the St Lawrence Canals, and the enlarging the locks of the Welland Canal, will have upon it, remains to be seen Hitherto, all the up and down freight has been transhipped at Kingston, to either larger or smaller vessels, according as it has been going up or down, in carrying which a fleet of about 200 barges and schooners, of from 60 to 250 tons burthen, has been employed. As soon as the improvements in the canals are completed, large vessels will be enabled to run direct up from Montreal to Toronto and Hamilton, thus avoiding Kingston altogether There are ten daily steamboats running to and from Kingston

The principal public building in Kingston, is the market house, as it is called, although the market occupies but a small portion of it This is the finest and most substantial building in Canada, being built entirely of hewn stone and cost about $90,000 In the front portion of the building are the Post Office, Offices of the Corporation Officers, News and Reading Room, above is the Town Hall a large and handsome room, used occasionally as a ball and assembly room and arranged for six quadrille parties Another room opposite, on the same floor, and the same size, but more handsomely finished, is let to the Free Church congregation for religious services it will comfortably accommodate 500 persons The dome at the top of the building is surrounded in the interior by a gallery, from whence a fine view may be obtained of the town of Kingston and the surrounding country, including Lake Ontario, with the islands in the vicinity.

The Presbyterians have a collegiate institution, called "Queen's College and University of Kingston" The court house is a square stone building There are ten churches and chapels, v z, three Episcopal, two Catholic, one Presbyterian, two Methodist (British Wesleyan and Canadian Wesleyan), Baptist and Livingite. The hospital is supported partly by government and partly by voluntary contributions. The "Hotel Dieu," is attended by sisters of charity There is a news and reading room, and a Mechanics' Institute

Five newspapers are published weekly —the "Chronicle & Gazette," "Herald,' "British Whig," "News," and "Argus"

A marine railway was established here in 1827, for the purpose of hauling out and repairing vessels The railway is 572 feet in length, worked by four horses, with machinery giving a multiplying power of 215 times, thus producing 860 horse power, and a capacity for hauling out a vessel of 300 tons. The

also a small railway for hauling out river boats and barges. A shipyard is connected with the railway.

There is a mineral spring, "Boyle's," at the corner of King and Arthur streets, the water of which was obtained by boring 75 feet. The following analysis of the water was by Professor Croft, of King's College, Toronto:—

Specific gravity at 68 Fahrenheit 1.018

One pint contains of solid matter—

	GRAINS.
Chloride of Sodium	108.193
Chloride of Calcium	74.959
Chloride of Magnesium	9.463
Sulphate of Soda	3.954
	196.569

A bridge a third of a mile in length has been constructed across the Cataraqui Bay, on the opposite side of which, on an eminence commanding the entrance to the bay and the town of Kingston, is situated Fort Henry; and below the hill, on the bay, are the marine barracks. A large portion of the town, called "Lot Twenty-four," and the village of Portland, are not included within the limits of the corporation.

At Portsmouth Harbour, about two miles west from the market house, is the Penitentiary, a large stone building, surrounded by a substantial stone wall, having towers at the outer corners; at present containing about 400 convicts. (This is the only Penitentiary in the Province, consequently this number includes the convicts of both the Upper and Lower Provinces.) Here are workshops for carpenters, blacksmiths, shoemakers, tailors, and a rope walk. The cells are so arranged that the keepers, without being perceived, can at all times ascertain what is going on within. The establishment appears to be well regulated.

A short distance from the Penitentiary, are baths and mineral springs, which have been much frequented by health and pleasure seekers. There are two wells; the first was discovered in the year 1843, in boring for water for the use of the neighbouring distillery: it is near the edge of the lake, and the water was obtained by boring through the rock, to the depth of 145 feet. The other well is higher up the bank, and the water was found at about eighty-five feet from the surface. The following is an analysis of the water of the two wells, by Professor Williamson, of Queen's College:—

Analysis of the Upper Well.

Specific gravity 1.0432

In an Imperial Pint.

	GRAINS.
Carbonate of Lime	3.2631
Carbonate of Magnesia	11.2653
Sulphate of Lime	3.4716
Chloride of Sodium	261.3108
Sulphate of Magnesia	4.3092
Chloride of Calcium	112.8025
Chloride of Magnesium	60.8475
Iodine and Bromine, (traces.)	
	457.2700

Gas, Carbonic Acid Gas.

Analysis of the Lower Well.

Specific gravity.................................. 10.10

In an Imperial Pint.

	GRAINS.
Chloride of Sodium	45.64
Sulphate of Soda	21.36
Chloride of Calcium	35.09
Chloride of Magnesium	15.43
	117.52

Gases, Carbonic Acid Gas and a trace of Sulphuretted Hydrogen.

A saloon and bath house have been erected

There is also in the neighbourhood a marine railway and shipyard, and an extensive establishment consisting of brewery, distillery, and saleratus factory The brewery and saleratus factory are connected together, and the saleratus is very ingeniously and economically made, by exposing pearlash to the action of the carbonic acid gas, which is generated during the fermentation of the beer, and which is conveyed to the room containing the pearlash The proprietor offers to supply 2000 lbs per day

The population of the town of Kingston, within the limits of the corporation, is 6123 (being 1700 less than before the removal of the Seat of Government), including "Lot Twenty-four" and the village of Portland, it amounts to between 11,000 and 12,000

Ratable property in the town, £146,766

Post Office, post every day

The following government and district offices are kept in Kingston Judge of District Court, Sheriff, Clerk of Peace, Inspector of Licenses, Emigration Agent, Collector of Customs, Treasurer, Registrar of County of Frontenac, District Clerk, Clerk of District Court, Deputy Clerk of Crown

Professions and Trades.—One steam grist mill, four breweries, three tanneries, ten physicians and surgeons, fourteen lawyers, three foundries, steam planing machine, thirty-six dry goods and hardware stores, thirty-seven groceries, three booksellers, five druggists, two shipbuilders, one surveyor, five printers, one engraver, one dentist, ninety-four taverns, three bookbinders, one marble factory. eight boarding houses, six tallow chandlers, two coach makers, five waggon makers, eight saddlers, one veterinary surgeon, four watchmakers, one boat builder, two sail makers, ten cabinet makers, seven livery stables, five painters, ten tinsmiths, nine bakers, seven blacksmiths, five confectioners, four coopers, five stone masons, thirty-six shoemakers, twenty-nine tailors, two chair makers, four hatters, two barbers, seven butchers, two sausage makers, five ladies' schools, two do for boys Bank agencies, 4—"Commercial," "British North America,' "Upper Canada," and "Montreal"

Principal Taverns—"Daley's," "Lambton House," "St Lawrence Hotel," "Exchange Hotel," and "National Hotel."

Principal Boarding Houses—Mrs. Olcott's, Princess Street, S. Bourne's, do, Mrs. Hilton's, Wellington Street

Forwarders—H & S Jones, Quebec Forwarding Company, People's Line, J. S McCuaig & Co., Hooker, Henderson, & Co, Macpherson & Crane, Sanderson & Murray, Pioneer Steamboat Company.

The following Steam and Sailing Vessels are owned at Kingston:—

Name of Vessel.	Tonnage.	Horse Power.
Canada	330	50
Gilderslieve	255	50
Hunter	197	28
Prince Albert	150	30
Beaver	197	28
Otter	197	28
Prince Edward	188	45
Prince of Wales	130	40
Bytown	100	20
Juno	100	25
Mercury	100	25
Meteor	100	25
Charlotte	50	18
Britannia	100	30
Caledonia	100	25
Lily	100	25
Grenville	75	25
Ontario	100	32
Frontenac	138	45
Total	2707	594
Schooner Eleonora (formerly "Great Britain" steamer)	562	
Thirty-one schooners, whose total tonnage amounts to	3352	
Total	6621	

Exclusive of many barges and other small craft.

KINGSTON.

A Township in the Midland District; is bounded on the east by the township of Pittsburgh; on the north by Portland and Loughborough; on the west by Ernesttown; and on the south by Lake Ontario. In Kingston 47,649 acres are taken up, 16,218 of which are under cultivation. The Cataraqui River, or Rideau Canal, runs through the east of the township, and enters Lake Ontario on the east side of Kingston, forming at its mouth a kind of bay, across which an excellent bridge has been constructed, leading to the village of Barryfield, which is situated on the east side of the bay, opposite Kingston; near which, on an eminence commanding the town of Kingston, is Fort Henry.

The village of Waterloo is situated on the western road, about three miles from the town of Kingston; and on the Rideau Canal, about six miles north from Kingston, is Kingston Mills, a spot the scenery of which is very picturesque. There are two grist and three saw mills in the township.

Kingston is well settled, and contains 6,289 inhabitants: this number, however, includes portions of the outskirts of the town of Kingston, known as "Lot 24," and the village of Portland, which are not included in the corporation.

Ratable property in the township, £71,151.

KITLEY.

A Township in the Johnstown District; is bounded on the north-east by the township of Wolford; on the north-west by South Elmsley; on the south-west by Bastard; and on the south-east by Yonge and Elizabethtown. In Kitley

40,497 acres are taken up, 11,589 of which are under cultivation. This is a well settled township, containing good land, and well cultivated farms One hundred acres of Crown lands are open for sale in Kitley, at 8s. currency per acre. There are one grist and two saw mills in the township

Population in 1842, 2,964; who are principally English, Irish and Scotch.
Ratable property in the township, £30,185.

LAKE.

A Township in the Victoria District, is bounded on the east by the township of Tudor, on the north by unsurveyed lands, on the west by Methuen, and on the south by Marmora This township has only lately been opened for sale, and no return has yet been made from it. Fifty thousand acres of Crown lands are open for sale in the township, at 8s currency per acre

LAKE ONTARIO

Is about 181 miles in length, and, in its widest part, about 60 in breadth It receives the waters of the upper lakes from the Niagara River, and discharges them into the St Lawrence It is the safest of the three lakes to navigate, having several excellent harbours, the principal of which are Toronto, Presqu' Isle (opposite the village of Brighton), Kingston and Port Hope, besides almost innumerable bays about the Prince Edward District, the Bay of Quinté, and the Islands. By cutting a canal of about a mile in length, between the lake and the Bay of Quinté, the Prince Edward District would become an island in Lake Ontario There are several considerable islands scattered over the eastern extremity of the lake, the principal of which are Wolfe Island, Amherst Island, Garden Island, Gage Island &c At the western extremity of the lake is a large bay, called "Burlington Bay," on which is situated the town of Hamilton. The Niagara River enters the lake about forty-five miles from its western extremity. Lake Ontario is 234 feet above the level of the sea it is never frozen over; and steamboats frequently run across from Toronto to Niagara throughout the winter, when the weather is fine The principal towns situated on the lake are Toronto, Kingston, Hamilton (on Burlington Bay), Port Hope, and Belleville (on the Bay of Quinté)

LAMBTON, or MILTON

A Village on Dundas Street, situated partly in the township of Toronto and partly in the township of York (the River Humber dividing the townships and the village), eight miles from Toronto

Population about 250, who have a Methodist church

Professions and Trades.—Two grist mills (one with five run of stones), one saw mill, one planing machine, distillery, carding machine and cloth factory, two stores, three taverns, four coopers, two blacksmiths, two waggon makers, one saddler, three shoemakers, one tailor.

Post Office, post every day.

About one mile south of the village, on the Humber, is situated "Milton Mills," a large establishment, containing a grist mill with six run of stones th re are also a saw mill, tavern and blacksmith's shop.

LANARK

A County in the Bathurst District, comprises the townships of Bathurst, Beckwith, Dalhousie, Darling, Drummond, North Elmsley, North Burgess, Levant, Lanark, Montague, Ramsay, North Sherbrooke and South Sherbrooke For the purpose of representation in the House of Assembly, it is united to the County of Renfrew; and the two return one member to the House of Assembly.

LANARK.

A Village in the township of Lanark, situated on the River Clyde, twelve miles from Perth, contains about 250 inhabitants. Churches and chapels, three; viz, Episcopal, Methodist, and Presbyterian

Post Office, post three times a week.

Professions and Trades—Four stores, one tannery, one ashery, two taverns, one cabinet maker, one blacksmith

LANARK.

A Township in the Bathurst District, is bounded on the north-east by the township of Ramsay, on the north-west by Darling, on the south-west by Dalhousie, and on the south-east by Drummond. In Lanark 40,901 acres are taken up, 10,430 of which are under cultivation. The township is well watered by branches of the Mississippi River, which are scattered over it. It contains some excellent land, and the timber is a mixture of pine and hardwood. Lanark is well settled, principally by Scotch emigrants, and contains many good farms. Seven thousand six hundred acres of Crown lands are open for sale in Lanark, at 8s currency per acre. The village of Lanark is situated in the south of the township; and there are also two grist and three saw mills in the township.

Population in 1842, 2,129

Ratable property in the township, £25,521.

LANCASTER

A township in the Eastern District, the most south-easterly township in Canada West, is bounded on the north-east by Canada East or Lower Canada; on the north-west by the township of Lochiel, on the south-west by Charlottenburgh, and on the south-east by Lake St Francis, a portion of the River St Lawrence. In Lancaster 49,273 acres are taken up, 10,094 of which are under cultivation. This is an old and well-settled township, containing some good farms. It is well watered by numerous streams running across it from west to east, and all of which flow into the St Lawrence. Timber—a mixture of pine and hardwood. The village of Dalhousie is situated in the north-east corner of the township, and the village of Lancaster in the south-west corner. There are two grist and seven saw mills in the township.

Population in 1842, 3,171

Ratable property in the township, £38,627

LANSDOWNE.

A Township in the Johnstown District, is bounded on the east by the township of Yonge, on the north by Bastard, on the west by Leeds, and on the south by the St Lawrence. The assessments for Lansdowne and the adjoining township of Leeds have been made together, and the townships are divided into Leeds and Lansdowne in front, and Leeds and Lansdowne in rear. In Leeds and Lansdowne in front 27,496 acres are taken up, 5,821 of which are under cultivation. In Leeds and Lansdowne in rear 18,212 acres are taken up, 4,978 of which are under cultivation. The principal part of the great Gananoque Lake is situated in the east of the township—it empties itself into the Gananoque River, which enters the St Lawrence in the township of Leeds. There are two small lakes in the north-west of the township. In Lansdowne 2,100 acres of Crown lands are open for sale, at 8s currency per acre. There are in the two townships three grist and six saw mills. These townships are well settled, and contain good farms. In Lansdowne is a settlement called "Furnace Falls," or "Lyndhurst."

Population of Leeds and Lansdowne in front, 2,260; ditto, in rear, 952.

Ratable property in Leeds and Lansdowne in front, £25,767, ditto, in rear, £15,876.

LATIMER'S CORNER.

A small Settlement on the town line between West Gwillimbury and Tecumseth, nine miles from Bradford, contains a store and tavern, and about eighty inhabitants.

LEEDS.

A county in the Johnstown District, comprises the townships of Bastard, South Burgess, North Crosby, South Crosby, South Elmsley, Elizabethtown, Kitley, Lansdowne, Leeds, and Yonge. It returns a member to the House of Assembly.

LEEDS

A Township in the Johnstown District, is bounded on the east by the township of Lansdowne, on the north by Crosby, on the west by Pittsburgh; and on the south by the St Lawrence. There are three lakes in this township, viz, Grippen Lake, in the north, South Lake, west of the centre, and Oven Lake, east of the centre, the whole of which are connected together by means of small streams, and discharge themselves into the Gananoque River, which falls into the St. Lawrence, in this township. The Rideau Canal passes through the north-west corner of Leeds, and the village of Gananoque is in the township, at the mouth of the Gananoque River. In Leeds 3700 acres of Crown lands are open for sale at 8s currency per acre.

For number of acres cultivated and uncultivated, grist and saw mills, population, and amount of ratable property, see LANSDOWNE.

LENNOX

A County in the Midland District, comprises the townships of Adolphustown, Fredericksburgh, and Richmond. For the purpose of representation in the Legislative Assembly, it is united to the county of Addington, and the two return one member to the House of Assembly.

LEVANT

A Township in the Bathurst District, is bounded on the north-west by the township of Madawaska, on the south-west by Palmerston, on the south east by Sherbrooke and Dalhousie, and on the north-east by Darling. The River Clyde runs across the centre of the township from west to east. A number of small lakes are scattered over the township, many of which are connected by means of small streams with the River Clyde. This township is as yet but little settled, and no separate assessment has been made in it, it having been included in Dalhousie. In Levant, 32,200 acres of Crown Lands are open for sale, at 8s currency per acre.

Population in 1842, 40

LINCOLN

A County in the Niagara District, comprises the townships of Caistor, Clinton, Gainsborough, Grantham, Grimsby, Louth. Niagara, and, except for the purpose of representation in the House of Assembly, the town of Niagara. The county of Lincoln returns a member to the House of Assembly.

LINDSAY.

A Village in the township of Ops prettily situated on the Scugog River, which runs through the village. It was laid out by government about thirteen years since, and contains about 200 inhabitants. Churches and chapels, 2, viz, Catholic and Presbyterian

Professions and Trades.—One grist mill (six run of stones), one saw mill, carding machine, one distillery, six stores, three taverns, four blacksmiths

LITTLE RIVER OR PETIT RIVIERE

A small Stream, on which is a saw mill, in the north-east corner of the township of Sandwich. It runs into the Detroit River.

I

LLOYDTOWN.

A Village in the north-east of the township of King; prettily situated in rather a hilly country; it was settled about sixteen years since by Mr. Jesse Lloyd; and is chiefly noted as being the place from whence the first party of rebels started at the commencement of the rebellion. It is fourteen miles from Newmarket, nearly due west. It contains 160 inhabitants. There are two churches and chapels, viz., Episcopal and Canadian Wesleyan.

Post Office, post twice a-week.

Professions and Trades.—One physician and surgeon, one surveyor, one grist and saw mill, carding machine, ashery, distillery, two tanneries, three stores, two taverns, two saddlers, two blacksmiths, two chairmakers, one cabinet maker, three wheelwrights, two carpenters, two tailors, four shoemakers, one cooper.

LOBO.

A Township in the London District; is bounded on the east by the township of London; on the north-west by Williams; on the south-west by Adelaide and Carradoc; and on the south by the River Thames. In Lobo, 33,293 acres are taken up, 4671 of which are under cultivation. The east branch of Bear Creek runs across the north of the township, and a branch of the Thames through the south-east. There is a considerable quantity of good land in the township. Timber—hardwood, intermixed with pine. There are three grist and six saw mills in the township.

Population in 1842, 1299.

Ratable property in the township, £18,595.

LOCHIEL.

A Township in the Eastern District; is bounded on the north-east by the township of Hawkesbury East; on the north-west by Hawkesbury West; on the south-west by Kenyon; and on the south-east by Lancaster, and a portion of Lower Canada. In Lochiel 53,886 acres are taken up, 8366 of which are under cultivation. The settlement of Alexandria, or Priest's Mills, is situated in the south-west corner of the township, on the River de L'Isle. It contains a Catholic church: there are also Presbyterian and Baptist churches in the township, in a settlement called Breadalbane. Six hundred acres of Crown lands are open for sale in Lochiel, at 8s. currency per acre. There are two grist and three saw mills in the township.

Population in 1842, 2,047.

Ratable property in the township, £32,445.

LOGAN.

A Township in the Huron District; is bounded on the north-east by Crown lands; on the north-west by the township of McKillop; on the south-west by Hibbert and Fullarton; and on the south-east by Ellice. The soil of Logan is mostly good. A branch of the River Thames runs through the township. Logan contains 55,551 acres, 2101 of which are leased or sold, of which 49 are under cultivation.

Population, 134.

Ratable property in the township, £715.

LONDON DISTRICT.

Consists of the County of Middlesex, which comprises the townships of Adelaide, Aldborough, Bayham, Carradoc, Delaware, Dorchester, Dunwich, Ekfrid, Lobo, London, Metcalfe, Mosa, Malahide, Southwold, Westminster, Williams, Yarmouth, and, except for the purpose of representation in the Legislative Assembly, the town of London. The London District, which formerly included the present district of Huron, is bounded on the east by the Talbot and Brock Districts; on the north by the Huron District; on the west by the Western District; and on the south by Lake Erie.

The district is watered by the River Thames, the north or principal branch of which enters the district in the east of the township of London; in the south of the township it receives the east branch; it then flows south, and afterwards south-west, forming the dividing boundary between the townships of Lobo, Caradoc, Ekfrid, and Mosa, on the north; and Westminster, Delaware, Southwold, Dunwich, and Aldborough, on the south. The district is also watered by Otter Creek, Kettle Creek, Bear Creek, Catfish Creek, and the River Aux Sables.

This is a district containing a large portion of very excellent land; there is some poor land in it, but the quantity is comparatively small. The land in the district is mostly rolling, and on the banks of all the rivers and creeks there are many beautiful situations for farms. Some parts of the district have been settled about forty years, and are now in a high state of cultivation. The oldest settled town in the district is St. Thomas, which was laid out about thirty years since. The town of London, the present district town, was laid out in the year 1826, at which time the "London" was declared a separate district. Previous to the building of London the village of Vittoria, in the township of Charlotteville, now in the Talbot District, was the district town. The best settled townships in the district, are Yarmouth, London, Westminster, Southwold, and Malahide. Yarmouth, London, Delaware, Malahide, Carradoc, Adelaide, Dunwich, Aldborough, and Lobo, are settled principally by emigrants from Great Britain and Ireland. Westminster is settled principally by Americans and Pennsylvanian Dutch. Most of the settlers in the London District are in comfortable circumstances, and many of them have become independent. Many of the farms have large clearings, and are in a good state of cultivation, with flourishing orchards. Excellent roads are made through the district, leading from the town of London to Brantford and Hamilton, Galt and Guelph, and Goderich, Chatham, Port Sarnia, and Stanley; the latter of which is planked, and passes through the flourishing village of St. Thomas.

Large quantities of fine wheat and other grain are grown in this district and exported; and a considerable business is carried on, on the different mill streams, in sawed lumber, much of which is exported. Eighteen thousand acres of land were brought into cultivation between January, 1842, and January, 1844.

The principal towns and villages in the district are London, in the township of London; St. Thomas and Port Stanley, in Yarmouth; Delaware in Delaware; and Richmond and Vienna, in Bayham.

In the London District 600 acres only of Crown lands are open for sale, at 8s. currency per acre, to purchase any of which application must be made to the Crown lands agent at London.

Population in 1842, 31,350, since when it has probably increased one-fifth.

The following abstract from the assessment rolls will show the rate of increase and improvement in the district.

Date.	No. of Acres Cultivated.	MILLS. Grist.	MILLS. Saw.	Milch Cows.	Oxen, 4 years old, and upwards.	Horned Cattle, from 2 to 4 years old.	Amount of Ratable Property.
1842	112,633	35	79	11,440	5299	6378	£408,330
1843	119,803	34	80	11,995	5717	7049	427,216
1844	130,329	35	93	12,102	6096	6636	455,373

Government and District Officers in the London District

Judge of District Court	Henry Allen	London.
Sheriff	James Hamilton	Do.
Clerk of Peace	John B Askin	Do.
Treasurer	John Harris	Do.
Inspector of Licenses	Joseph B. Clench	Delaware.
Crown Lands Agent	John B. Askin	London.
Registrar	Vacant.	
Judge of Surrogate Court	Henry Allen	Do.
District Clerk	James B Strathy	Do.
Deputy Clerk of Crown	John Harris	Do.
Clerk of District Court	John B Askin	Do
District Superintendent of Schools	Wm. Elliott	Adelaide.
Warden	John S Buchanan	
Auditors of District Council	W. W. Street	
	Daniel Hanvey	
Coroners	Dr D J Bowman	St Thomas.
	Dr Thomas Phillips	London.
	Dr Ed Mills	Carradoc.
	Dr C. B Hall	Westminster.

Through the absence of the Superintendent, I was unable to obtain any statement respecting the number of common schools in the district.

LONDON

The District Town of the London District, situated in the township of London, on the River Thames, eighty-five miles from Hamilton, twenty-six from Port Stanley, and seventeen from St Thomas. The town was laid out in 1826 by the Crown, on land reserved by Governor Simcoe, it returned a member in 1836, and was incorporated in 1840. It is finely situated, being in the midst of a beautiful country, and at the point of junction of the two branches of the River Thames.

London possesses a handsome jail and court house, built of brick in the form of a castle, the building of the two cost above £10,000. Large barracks, capable of accommodating a regiment, and Artillery barracks in addition, both of which are occupied. A fire company with one engine, a theatre, and two market buildings. Within the last two years London has been twice nearly destroyed by fire. The Episcopal Church was burnt down in February, 1844; a large subscription was raised to rebuild it, and London can now boast of possessing the handsomest gothic church in Canada West. It was designed by Mr Thomas, Architect, of Toronto (late of Leamington, England). Its erection cost nearly £5000. A fire took place on the 8th October, 1844, when a large portion of the town was burnt; a second fire occurred on the 12th April, 1845, when about 150 buildings were consumed. Building, however, has been proceeded with rapidly, and in place of the old frame buildings, handsome streets have been erected, composed of brick buildings three and four stories high.

Excellent roads stretch away in every direction. A plank road has been formed to Port Stanley, and a plank and macadamized road to Brantford. New roads have also been completed to Chatham and Port Sarnia. Stages leave London daily for Hamilton, Chatham, and Detroit, and all intermediate places; three times a-week for Port Sarnia and Port Stanley, and twice a-week for Goderich.

A weekly newspaper, the "Times," is published here.

Churches and chapels, 10; viz, Episcopal two Presbyterian, Catholic, British Wesleyan, Canadian Wesleyan, Episcopal Methodist, Congregational, Baptist (for coloured people), and Universalist.

Post Office, post every day.

Population about 3500.

The following Government and District offices are kept in London:—Judge of District Court, Sheriff, Clerk of Peace, Treasurer, Crown Lands Agent, Judge of Surrogate Court, District Clerk, Clerk of District Court, Deputy Clerk of Crown.

Professions and Trades.—Seven physicians and surgeons, seven lawyers, one grist mill, one saw do., twenty-six stores, four breweries, two distilleries, carding machine and cloth factory, eighteen taverns, three hardware stores, one carriage maker, one fanning-mill maker, one smut machine maker, two foundries, one printer, three machine shops, five notaries public, four druggists, two auctioneers, four tallow chandlers, one bookseller and stationer, three tanneries, twelve groceries, ten cabinet makers, five saddlers, fifteen tailors, two hatters, two livery stables, nine butchers, one builder, four tinsmiths, two chair makers, five waggon makers, fifteen blacksmiths, eight bakers, four coopers, one gunsmith, two nursery gardens, one dyer, one tobacconist, six painters and glaziers, three confectioners, one well-sinker, two stone cutters, three watchmakers, four barbers, seventeen shoemakers, one ladies' school. Four bank agencies—" Upper Canada," " Montreal," " Commercial," and " Gore."

Principal Taverns.—The " Hope Hotel," " Western Hotel," and " London Coffee House." Lee's and Scott's are also comfortable houses. A large hotel is now in course of erection.

Land Agent.—John H. Caddy.

Stage Fares from London to the following Places:

Place.	Days.	Time of Starting.	Fares.
			s. d.
Hamilton	Daily	From 10, A.M. till 1, P.M.	22 6
Woodstock	Do.	Do.	8 9
Ingersol	Do.	Do.	6 3
Brantford	Do.	Do.	15 0
Port Sarnia	Mondays, Wednesdays & Fridays,	7, A.M.	15 0
Port Stanley	Do.	10, A.M.	5 0
Chatham	Daily	Do.	17 6
Detroit	Do.	Do.	30 0

LONDON.

A Township in the London District; is bounded on the east by the township of Nissouri; on the north by Blanshard, Biddulph and McGillivray; on the west by Lobo and a small portion of Williams; and on the south by Westminster. In London 87,681 acres are taken up, 19.210 of which are under cultivation. The River Thames divides the township from Westminster; and the township is also watered by the north branch of the Thames (which joins the east branch in the south of the township, at the town of London), and by the River Medway and Springer's Creek, both branches of the Thames—the Medway enters the Thames near the town of London. This is a well settled township, containing many good farms, with flourishing orchards. There are numerous wet places in the township, but a large proportion of the land is rolling; and there are many beautiful situations on the Thames. Timber—pine, intermixed with hardwood. There are three grist and six saw mills in the township.

Population in 1842, 3,955; who are principally emigrants from Great Britain, with a few Canadians and Americans.

Ratable property in the township, £56,007.

LONG POINT, or NORTH FORELAND.

A long strip of land in Lake Erie. It is nearly twenty miles long, and from one to two broad it was formerly a peninsula, running out from the land in an easterly direction, nearly half way across the lake, but the sea having made a wide breach across its western extremity, has converted it into an island. There is a light-house upon the eastern extremity of the island; and the anchorage about it is said to be good.

LONGUEIL.

A Township in the Ottawa District, is bounded on the east by the township of Hawkesbury West; on the north by the Ottawa River, on the west by Alfred, and on the south by Caledonia. In Longueil 16,949 acres are taken up, 4,546 of which are under cultivation. The land in this township is generally rather cold and wet, and much of it is unfit for profitable cultivation. The village of L'Orignal, the district town of the Ottawa District, is situated in the north-east of the township, on the Ottawa; and there is also a grist mill and a saw mill in the township.
Population in 1842, 1,122.
Ratable property in the township, £17,922.

LOUGHBOROUGH.

A Township in the Midland District, is bounded on the east by the township of Pittsburgh, on the north by Bedford, on the west by Portland; and on the south by Kingston. In Loughborough 20,745 acres are taken up, 6,972 of which are under cultivation. A great number of lakes are scattered over the township. Loughborough contains some good, but a large portion of poor land. There is a Methodist church in the south-west of the township, and a Catholic church in the south-west corner. Thirteen thousand five hundred acres of Crown lands are open for sale in Loughborough, at 8s. currency per acre. There are one grist and six saw mills in the township.
Population in 1842, 1,483.
Ratable property in the township, £19,252.

L'ORIGNAL.

The district town of the Ottawa District, in the township of Longueil, situated on the Ottawa River. This is a poor little place, and is merely supported by the district offices being kept here, and the travel through it, the land in the neighbourhood being mostly poor and wet. The situation must be pleasant in summer. A stage runs daily to Point Fortune, to meet the steamboat from Montreal, and is met again at L'Orignal by the boat to Bytown. Population about 200. Churches and chapels, three, viz, Episcopal, Catholic, and Presbyterian.

The following government and district offices are kept in L Orignal:—Judge of District Court, Clerk of Peace, Sheriff, Inspector of Licenses, Treasurer, Registrar of County of Prescott, Registrar of County of Russell, District Clerk, Deputy Clerk of Crown, District Superintendent of Schools.

Professions and Trades.—One physician and surgeon, one lawyer, one grist mill, one saw mill, four stores, two taverns, one cabinet maker, one blacksmith.
Land Agent, G D Reed.

LOUISVILLE.

A Village in the township of Chatham, in the County of Kent, is situated on the great western road—six miles from Chatham, and sixty from London; at the head of the steam navigation of the River Thames. Number of inhabitants 70.
Post Office, post every day.

List of Professions and Trades.—One physician and surgeon, one store, one grocery, one druggist, one waggon maker, one tannery, two blacksmiths, one tavern, one carpenter, one school.

Here is a ferry across the Thames.

LOUTH.

A Township in the Niagara District, is bounded on the east by the township of Grantham; on the north by Lake Ontario; on the west by Clinton; and on the south by Pelham. In Louth 16,591 acres are taken up, 7,318 of which are under cultivation. This is an old-settled township, containing well-cleared farms and good orchards The Welland Canal enters Lake Ontario close to the town line between Louth and Grantham, at the north-east corner of the township, where is situated the village of Port Dalhousie; and a good mill stream, called "Twenty-mile Creek," enters the lake near the north-west corner of the township There are one grist and six saw mills in the township.

Population in 1841, 1,392, who are principally Canadians, Americans, and Pennsylvanian Dutch and their descendants.

Ratable property in the township, £22,464.

LUTHER.

A Township in the Wellington District; is bounded on the east by the township of Amaranth; on the north by Proton, on the west by Arthur; and on the south by Garafraxa. Luther has only lately been opened for sale; and no return has yet been made from it. Seventy-three thousand six hundred acres of Crown lands are open for sale in the township, at 8s. currency per acre.

MACNAB

A Township in the Bathurst District; is bounded on the north and north-east by the Ottawa River, on the north-west by the township of Horton, on the south-west by Madawaska, and on the south-east by Pakenham In Macnab 19,814 acres are taken up, 3,195 of which are under cultivation. The Madawaska River runs across the south of the township, from west to east; at the east corner of the township it enters the township of Pakenham, makes a short bend, re-enters Macnab, and runs north to Lake Chat, making many curves in its course There are one grist and one saw-mill in the township.

Population in 1842, 782, who are principally engaged in the lumber trade.

Ratable property in the township, £10,534.

MADAWASKA RIVER.

A Tributary of the Ottawa, takes its rise in the unsettled country to the north of the Victoria District, it follows nearly a west course, and after passing through the townships of Admaston, Bagot, Blythefield and McNab, it enters Lake Chat, an expansion of the Ottawa In its course it flows through, and receives accessions from, several lakes, some of them of considerable size. Large quantities of lumber are cut on its banks, and slides and dams have been constructed in the river, in order to facilitate the passage of lumber down it. It was estimated that of

  Red Pine . . . . .1,099,000 feet, and of
  White Pine . . . . 354,000 feet,

would pass down the Madawaska during the spring of 1845. This of course would be included in the return from Bytown.

MADOC.

A Township in the Victoria District, is bounded on the east by the township of Elzevir; on the north by Tudor, on the west by Marmora, and on the south by Huntingdon. In Madoc 18,375 acres are taken up, 3,800 of which are under cultivation This township is said to possess iron ore of as good quality as the adjoining township of Marmora, but it has not yet been worked, it possesses more land fit for cultivation, and is better settled There is a small settlement in the south of the township, containing a grist and saw-mill, and foundry, and a few houses. There is also another saw-mill in the township. One thousand

three hundred and seventeen acres of Crown lands are open for sale in Madoc, at 8s c'y per acre
Population in 1842, 926, who are principally Scotch and Irish.
Ratable property in the township, £10,363.

MAIDSTONE.

A Township in the county of Essex; is bounded on the north by Lake St. Clair; on the east by the township of Sandwich; on the west by Belle River; and on the south by the townships of Colchester and Gosfield. In Maidstone 16,184 acres are taken up, of which 1524 are under cultivation. The soil in this township is good, and the whole of the land fit for cultivation. Timber,—maple, elm, beech, oak, &c &c. The River *Aux Puces* enters Lake St Clair about the centre of this township, after running through its entire length, and the River Aux Peeches enters the lake about three miles below. Two thousand six hundred acres of Crown lands are open for sale in Maidstone, at 8s. c'y per acre. The Canada Company possess 2,500 acres in Maidstone
Population, 783.
Ratable property in the township, £7,255.

MAITLAND RIVER

Takes its rise in the Indian territory north of the Huron Tract, passes through Wawanosh, into Colborne, where it is joined by the east branch (which takes its rise in the great Swamp), and enters Lake Huron at the town of Goderich. There is some beautiful scenery on its banks, and its bed for great part of its course is composed of limestone rock. About eight miles from its mouth are some pretty falls. There are many good mill sites on the Maitland, and its water-power is by some considered equal to that at Rochester.

MAITLAND.

A Village in the township of Augusta, situated on the St Lawrence, five miles east of Brockville, the eastern road passing through it It was built on the site of an old French fortification. The Kingston and Montreal steamboats touch here Maitland contains about 100 inhabitants, who have an Episcopal church
Post Office, post every day.
Professions and Trades—One steam grist-mill, two stores, two taverns, one blacksmith, one hatter, one shoemaker.

MALAHIDE.

A Township in the London District, is bounded on the east by the township of Bayham, on the north by Dorchester, on the west by Yarmouth, and on the south by Lake Erie. In Malahide 46,717 acres are taken up, 11,806 of which are under cultivation. Catfish Creek, an excellent mill-stream, runs along the western border of the township to Lake Erie, and the township is also well watered by numerous small streams. The timber of the south of the township is principally pine, and that of the north is pine, intermixed with hard wood Malahide is well settled, and forms part of the Talbot settlement The land is generally rolling, and there are many beautiful situations on Catfish Creek Large quantities of lumber are annually exported from the township. There are three grist and seventeen saw-mills in Malahide.
Population in 1842, 2372
Ratable property in the township, £39,303.

MALDEN.

A Township in the Western District; is bounded on the east by the township of Colchester, on the north by Anderdon; on the west by the Detroit River;

and on the south by Lake Erie. In Malden 17,432 acres are taken up, 3,775 of which are under cultivation. This is a very old-settled township, some of the farms having been under cultivation since the time when Canada was in the possession of the French; and nearly every lot is taken up. The land generally is of the richest quality, and capable of producing large crops of Indian corn, tobacco, &c. Tobacco has been grown in this township, which has sold for 1s. 10½d. c'y per pound, on the premises The timber consists of the best kind of hard wood maple, oak, beech, hickory, elm, black walnut, butternut, &c The town of Amherstburg is situated near the south-west corner of the township, on the Detroit River. About a mile below the town, close to the river, and a little above the entrance of Lake Erie, is a chalybeate spring, the water of which is said to resemble that of Cheltenham, in England. There are two grist-mills in the township, one of which is a windmill, and the other is worked by horse-power

Population in 1845, 1934, about half of whom are French Canadians, and the remainder a mixture of English, Irish, Scotch, English Canadians and Americans.

Ratable property in the township, £26,356.

MALDEN, FORT (See AMHERSTBURG)

MANITOULIN ISLAND GREAT, OR THIRD

The principal island in Lake Huron, it is about one hundred miles in length, and in breadth varies from four to twenty-five miles, it is indented by an almost innumerable number of bays, and the scenery is in many parts magnificent. Manitoulin Gulf, (which is in reality a long narrow lake connected with Lake Huron), and Heywood's bay, which run into the island at its widest part, one from the south, the other from the north, approach each other to within three miles, thus almost dividing the island into two In summer, the sun is very hot on these islands, and vegetation exceedingly rapid. The Great Manitoulin is settled exclusively by Indians, the only whites on the island being those attached to the government station at Manitowawning, (Hudson's Sound) and two or three at the Roman Catholic village at Wequemikong, (Smith's Bay) The island is frequently visited by Indian traders Manitowawning is about 190 miles from Penetanguishine, and 176 from Goderich

Previously to the year 1829, the distribution of presents to a large portion of the Indians, included under the term "western tribes," consisting of the visiting Indians, north of Penetanguishine, of those at Sault St Marie, and on the shores of Lake Superior, of those from the south-west, and Lake Michigan, Green Bay, the Fox River, Wisconsin, even from the distant Mississippi, was made at Drummond's island, the old military post on Lake Huron

In that year the island having been finally ceded to the Americans, and the government being desirous of ascertaining the disposition of the Indians to embrace civilization, the distribution was made at the island of St. Joseph's, about nine miles north-west from Drummond's island

The proposition of settling at Manitou appears to have been founded on a report from Major Winnett, in the early part of the same year, in which, in reference to the civilization of the Indians he stated that the Great Manitoulin island offered greater advantages for the formation of a settlement for the Indians than St Joseph's could present, with respect to soil, climate, and lake fishing; the last a great object in the estimation of old Indians It is distant one hundred miles and upwards from any American military post, and between sixty and seventy from any part of the American territory

In 1830 and the following five years, the distribution of presents was made at Penetanguishine, and thus, the western tribes were brought within the influence of the efforts of the government to civilize them. Their visits to the prosperous settlements at Coldwater and the Narrows were frequent; they witnessed the advantages enjoyed by their brethren who were settled there and applications were consequently numerous for a participation in the same benefits. In 1835, after Mr. Superintendent Anderson had visited the island, a scheme was matured and authorised by Sir John Colborne, for forming an extensive establishment upon it, and for making it the future place of distribution, instead of Penetanguishine, and Amherstburg, where the remainder of the western tribes had previously been supplied.

In the spring of that year, Mr. Anderson found, on his visit, five or six families of the Ottawa tribe, Roman Catholics, from Lake Michigan, settled in Wequamekong Bay (Smith's sound), where they had cultivated two or three acres of land, and were living in temporary bark huts; these, and a few wandering Chippewas, were all the Indians he met with on the island, amounting to perhaps seventy or eighty persons.

In 1836 the present settlement at Manitowawning, (Hudson's Sound), about eight miles distant from Wequamekong, was commenced, some land was cleared and houses built. It does not appear how many Indians were settled on the island this year. The first issue of presents at this post was made in the autumn, and was attended by 2697 individuals. On this occasion the Lieut. Governor, Sir F. B. Head, was present, and formed the view of collecting at Manitoulin, not the wild Indians from the north of Lake Huron, as had been at first proposed, but all those who had settled, or were wandering among the white population, in various parts of Upper Canada. With this intention he induced the chiefs of the Ottawa and Chippewa nations then present, to resign their exclusive rights to the occupancy of the Great Manitoulin, and all the other islands, estimated at above 23,000, on the north shore of Lake Huron.

He also obtained from the Saugeen Indians the surrender of the greater proportion of their territory, and proposed their removal to Manitoulin. To other Indians whom he visited in the western parts of Canada, he likewise made the same proposals; offering them the assistance and encouragement of the government at this island. These offers, however, do not appear to have been generally acceptable to the settled Indians, as few or none availed themselves of them. The settlers at the island have, for the most part, come from the United States, or from the shores of Lake Huron and Lake Superior.

In 1837, further progress was made in clearing land and building houses; the number of settlers on the island was reckoned at 268.

In the autumn of 1838, the officers appointed to form the future establishment of this settlement, including the superintendent, Mr. Anderson, a clergyman of the church of England, and a surgeon, with several artisans and labourers, arrived at Manitowawning, and took up their residence there, being the first white men who had wintered in the island. This year the number of Indian settlers was 307.

In the following year the clearings were extended; a saw mill was built; and the number of settlers increased to 655. A school was commenced at Manitowawning, but it was ill attended; the Roman Catholics at the other settlement would not allow their children to frequent it.

In 1840, 732 Indians reported themselves as settlers, of whom only 437 were christians.

In 1841, many Pottawatamies from the River St. Clair, who had promised to settle, and some Ottawas and Chippewas from Lake Michigan, returned to their homes; but the actual number thus reduced was not recorded Some Indian houses, a carpenter's shop, and a smith's, were erected. The school was better attended, and eight Indian boys were in the course of instruction in different branches of handicraft. A School was also opened by a Roman Catholic schoolmaster in the other settlement.

In 1842, twenty-five Indian houses were built by contract, and a large store, cooper's shop, and barn, were erected by the mechanics attached to the establishment. A saw mill was also nearly finished at Wequemakong Bay. The attendance at the Roman Catholic school had fluctuated greatly; at one time as many as seventy pupils were present, but more frequently from five to twenty, and at some seasons not one. The number at the Manitowawning school had not exceeded forty-five, but it had never fallen below twelve.

On the 15th November, there were resident at Wequemakong, ninety-four families, and at Manitowawning forty-four families, making together 138 families, which on an average of four members to a family, would form a population of 552. The number settled, or wandering in other parts of the island, and living in wigwams, or temporary bark huts, was estimated at 150 at least, making a total population of 702.

The following is the present size and extent of the two settlements, each occupies about 200 acres of land. The several houses are surrounded with gardens, and the farms are for the most part at a distance. This arrangement was resorted to, with a view of preserving their crops from the cattle, without the trouble of making enclosures; but it has not answered the intention, as the cattle roam much farther than was expected, and it has been found necessary to commence fencing.

The Wequemakong village, which has been longest established, contains in all seventy-eight buildings, viz, seventy-three Indian houses, one for the missionary, and another for the schoolmaster, a church, a school-house, and a saw-mill.

The Manitowawning village contains fifty-five buildings, viz, thirty-seven Indian houses, six of the same description occupied by the mechanics and labourers, four larger houses, occupied by the superintendent, missionary, surgeon, and schoolmaster, three shops (blacksmiths', carpenters', and coopers'), an excellent frame store, of sixty by thirty feet, and two stories in height, one log barn, a school-house, a saw-mill (built by contract in 1839), and a sawyer's house, and a church has since been erected. Besides these there are, in both villages, a number of outhouses for cattle, small storehouses, &c.

All the buildings are of wood, those of the latter village have been erected either by the resident artisans in the employment of the government, or by contract. Those at Wequemakong having been chiefly built by the Indians themselves, with the assistance of nails and glass, axes, &c afforded by the government, are neither so neat nor substantial as the others.

Soon after the commencement of the settlement of the Manitoulin, doubts were entertained as to the climate and fertility of the island, and its fitness for the residence of the Indians, which increased the reluctance of the Indians settled in the more southern portions of the province, to resort to the island, and has continued to prove an obstacle to the increase of the settlement. These objections having been represented to the Secretary of State, his Lordship suggested that an enquiry should be made on the spot by Major Bonnycastle, of the Royal Engineers. The result has not come under the notice of the commissioners, but the reports of the resident Agent leave no reason to doubt that the island is in every way suited for habitation. The climate is very healthy, the temperature is moderate, the winter sets in about the beginning of November, the cold is not unusually severe, the snow seldom lies more than two feet deep, and the spring opens about the middle of April. The formation of the islands is limestone. The soil is generally a mixture of clay and sand, with limestone pebbles. Some parts of the island are stony, but there is abundance of land favourable for cultivation. The cedar swamps on the high land, of which perhaps one-third of the island consists, though at present wet in the fall and spring, appear to be land of the finest quality, being of a deep black loam, and free from stone. When these are opened and exposed to the sun, they will become dry, and fit for any kind of cultivation. The timber of the uplands is of the usual kinds of hard wood met with in other parts of the province, viz, maple, basswood, elm, red and white oak, pine, &c &c. Both the soil and climate are favourable to cultivation, abundant crops of all kinds of grain raised by the Indians in other parts of the province, have been annually produced. Cattle thrive well, during the winter they are allowed to roam about and find their own food in the bush. In 1842, a few sheep were added to the stock. There is not much game on the island, but fish is in abundance on its shores.

The Indians collected here, belong chiefly to the Ottawa and Chippewa tribes; the former, who immigrated from the United States, have all their lives been *Indian* farmers; some of them brought horses and stock to the island. On their arrival they sought no other means of subsistence than the produce of the soil, and the fish they caught in the immediate neighbourhood of their own village; and in the autumn, each family cured a sufficiency to supply them through the winter; consequently it was not necessary for them to leave their homes in search of food, nor to trust, like the Chippewas, to the precarious resource of spearing fish through the ice.

The Chippewas, on the other hand, who had never, until collected at Manitoulin, cultivated the soil, were slow in adopting a new mode of life. For some time they were reluctant to settle in a fixed place of residence; they frequently shifted their camps, and although many of them lived within a day's journey from the new settlement, and admitted the benefits arising from a change of life, still it required much persuasion and perseverance to induce them to make a commencement.

The Ottawas, moreover, had long been converted from heathenism, and were members of the Roman Catholic church. In 1838, they were joined by a priest of that persuasion, who has since resided with them at Wequemakong. The Chippewas, on the contrary, were all heathens, and the work of conversion only commenced among them in the same year, when a missionary of the Church of England, attached to the establishment, arrived at the island.

These differences will account for the greater increase of the settlement at Wequemakong, and its more rapid progress in the cultivation of the land, and the acquisition of stock, which are exhibited in the following table:—

Extent of Land cleared, and of Stock owned at the two Settlements in Feb. 1843:

	WEQUEMAKONG.	MANITOWAWNING.
Acres of Land cleared	200	140
Horses	19	2
Horned Cattle	58	24
Pigs	161	17
Sheep	8	11
Barn-door Fowls	157	62
Geese	—	8

Some families have perhaps ten acres or more cleared, whilst others have only a patch under cultivation. Their principal support at both villages is now derived from farming and fishing; they sometimes kill hares, partridges, and even deer and bears. They also manufacture considerable quantities of maple sugar of very excellent quality; for which they find a ready market at Penetanguishene, Goderich, and sometimes in the towns on the American frontier.

The land in the village is laid out in half acre lots, and a few farms of fifty acres were in the commencement surveyed and staked out; but the labour and expense were found too great, and each Indian now selects such place as he pleases, and takes possession of it, in most cases, without consulting the superintendent or chiefs. As long as he continues to cultivate his piece of land, he enjoys quiet possession of it; but if he happens to leave it for a season, some other Indian will most likely enter upon it; and in such cases, there is frequently a difficulty in arranging the matter amicably.

With regard to their mode of agriculture, they are improving but slowly. They are now beginning to plough their old fields, to make more substantial fences, to cultivate garden vegetables, &c. Each individual cultivates his farm separately.

Formerly the Ottawas were pretty well supplied with hoes, and an inferior kind of small axe. The Chippewas had a smaller quantity of the same implements. Both tribes, in planting, supplied the deficiency with a crooked stick conveniently shaped for the purpose. At present the government has supplied them with a sufficiency of these articles, and with a few spades, shovels, ploughs, harrows, pick-axes, &c.

The men, of all ages, do most of the chopping, but after that, men, women, and children take share in the labour, from the burning of the timber to the reaping of the crop.

The fondness of the converted Indians for hunting and fishing is decidedly diminished. They seldom leave the island for either purpose. They occasionally go out spearing fish at night, or set their nets in the evening, and take them up early in the morning; they also spend from six to fifteen days in the autumn to lay in a stock of fish for the winter. A large proportion of the Chippewas are still heathens; there were received into the Church of England in

1836–7	5, all adults
1839	38 "
1840	84 "
1841	45 "

Making a total of 172, together with 30 converts from the Roman Catholic Church.

Since August, 1841, the superintendent reports, that he is not aware that even one adult heathen has been brought into the church since that time. The principal obstacles to the conversion of the heathens are stated to be their superstition—their fear that the "great spirit" they worship should visit them with his vengeance, were they to become Christians—their fear of not being allowed to drink whiskey—the bad advice of traders, who erroneously suppose it will destroy their trade—and among those who have a plurality of wives, an objection to turn them away.

The Ottawa tribes, who subsist by agriculture, are supposed to be rapidly on the increase; and the Chippewas, who live chiefly on fish, to be on the decrease. Among the former, it is not unusual to meet with families having six or seven, and sometimes even ten or twelve children all living; although in many instances, they do not rear one-half of the number born. The Chippewas are neither so prolific, nor so successful in rearing their children. In both tribes, the adults seldom reach an advanced age. The proportion of half-breeds among them is not above one in twenty.

The establishment at Manatowawning is under the local superintendent. There is a resident surgeon, a clergyman of the Church of England, a schoolmaster, a master carpenter, a blacksmith, a millwright, a mason, a cooper, a shoemaker, a sawyer, and six labourers, supported by the Parliamentary grant. The schoolmaster at Wequemakong is paid out of the same fund, but the priest is maintained by the church to which he belongs.

Owing to the infrequency and difficulty of communication with the main land, it has hitherto been deemed necessary to engage a certain number of mechanics and labourers by the year. Part of the buildings, however, have been erected by contract, during the summer months; and in this manner, as many as twenty-five were built in 1842. The Roman Catholic village appears to be entirely under the charge of the priest.

The remaining bands, which are widely scattered over the island, have no local superintendents, but are under the general care of the chief superintendent. The settlements are altogether twelve in number. Four schooner loads of maple sugar were shipped from Wequemakong, during the spring of 1845; much of which was equal in appearance to any Brazil or West India sugar.

MANVERS.

A Township in the Newcastle District: is bounded on the east by the township of Cavan; on the north by Ops; on the west by Cartwright; and on the south by Clarke. In Manvers, 21,281 acres are taken up, 3,800 of which are under cultivation. Scugog Lake cuts off a small portion of the north-west corner of the township The land of this township is of mixed qualities, some parts being very good, and others rather indifferent Timber—hardwood, intermixed with pine. Four hundred acres of Crown lands are open for sale in Manvers, at 8s currency per acre.

Population in 1842, 697.

Ratable property in the township, £9,650.

MARA.

A Township in the Home District, is bounded on the north by the township of Rama, on the west by Lake Simcoe, on the south by the Talbot River; and on the east by unsurveyed lands In Mara 9,514 acres are taken up, 799 of which are under cultivation This is a new township not long settled, but it contains some very good land, and on the lake shore there are some good clearings A village, called "Atherly," was laid out here (close to the Narrows) in 1843, by Captain Creighton, a gentleman who possesses a considerable quantity of land in the township, bordering on Lake Simcoe

A road is in course of formation from the Narrows (where an excellent bridge has been constructed) to Scugog, whence a plank road is formed to Windsor Bay on Lake Ontario, which, when completed, will be a great benefit to the neighbouring townships, admitting of easy transportation for all farm produce to the lake.

The steamboat "Beaver" stops at Atherly to take in wood

Population in 1842, 278, which includes the township of Rama, no separate census having been taken

Ratable property in the township, £3,466

MARCH.

A Township in the Dalhousie District, is bounded on the north-east by the Ottawa River; on the north-west by the township of Tarbolton, on the south-west by Huntley; and on the south-east by Goulbourn In March 19,323 acres are taken up, 3,092 of which are under cultivation A lake, called "Constance Lake," containing about 500 acres, is situated in the centre of the north of the township The land in the south of the township is of excellent quality, that in the north is not so good The timber in the south is principally hardwood; that in the north is mostly pine. One thousand three hundred and seventy-two acres of Crown lands are open for sale in March, at 8s. currency per acre. There are one grist and two saw mills in the township.

Population in 1842, 831.

Ratable property in the township, £9,772.

MARIPOSA.

A Township in the Colborne District, is bounded on the east by the townships of Ops and Fenelon, on the north by Eldon, on the west by Brock, and on the south by Cartwright In Mariposa 35,543 acres are taken up, 6,417 of which are under cultivation This is a fine township, well settled, and containing good land There is a grist and saw mill in the township. In Mariposa 900 acres of Crown lands are open for sale, at 8s. currency per acre

Ratable property in the township, £18,116.

MARIATOWN.

A Village in the township of Williamsburgh, situated on the St Lawrence, contains about 100 inhabitants, one store, one tavern, and post office, post every day

MARKHAM VILLAGE, or REESORVILLE

A Village prettily situated near the south-east corner of the township of Markham, close to the River Rouge, twenty miles from Toronto. It has been settled about twenty-five years, by Canadians, Pennsylvanian Dutch, Germans, Americans, Irish, and a few English and Scotch. There are two churches in the village—Presbyterian and Methodist, and an Episcopal church is erecting. A circulating library is kept up, supported by subscriptions.

Population about 300

Post Office, post three times a week

Professions and Trades.—One physician and surgeon, grist and oatmeal mill, woollen factory, five stores, one distillery, one brewery, one tannery, one pump and fanning mill maker, one cabinet and threshing machine maker, two taverns, four blacksmiths, five waggon makers, four tailors, four shoemakers, one foundry, one tinsmith.

MARKHAM.

A Township in the Home District, is bounded on the east by the townships of Pickering and Uxbridge; on the north by Whitchurch, on the west by Vaughan, and on the south by Scarborough. In Markham 66,259 are taken up, 29,005 of which are under cultivation. The River Don runs through the west of the township, the River Rouge through the east, and Duffin's Creek through the north-east corner, all of which flow into Lake Ontario.

This is the second township in the province, in point of cultivation and amount of ratable property (Dumfries being the first). It is well settled, and contains many excellent and well cultivated farms. The land is generally rolling, and the timber a mixture of hardwood and pine. The village of Markham is situated in the south-east of the township, and the villages of Richmond Hill and Thornhill are partly in the township, being situated on the Yonge Street Road. There are eleven grist and twenty-four saw mills in the township.

Population in 1842, 5,698.

Ratable property in the township, £86,577.

MARLBOROUGH.

A Township in the Dalhousie District, is bounded on the north-east by the township of North Gower, on the north-west by Goulbourn; on the south-west by Montague, and on the south-east by Oxford. In Marlborough 18,114 acres are taken up, 2,993 of which are under cultivation. The Rideau River and Canal borders the township on the south-east. There is a considerable portion of good land in the township, but some of that on the Rideau Canal is poor and stoney, and much of the timber is pine. In Marlborough 8,254 acres of Crown lands are open for sale, at 8s currency per acre. There are two saw mills in the township.

Population in 1842, 893.

Ratable property in the township, £10,157.

MARMORA.

A Township in the Victoria District, is bounded on the east by the township of Madoc, on the north by Lake, on the west by Belmont, and on the south by Rawdon. In Marmora 8,629 acres are taken up, 1,762 of which are under cultivation. The Marmora River runs through the centre of the township, from north to south. Marmora has been long noted for the excellence and richness of its iron ore, which is said to yield seventy-five per cent of iron of the best quality. There is no doubt that this township alone, under proper management, would be capable of furnishing sufficient iron for the consumption of the whole of British North America. Some years since a large sum was expended in erecting works for the purpose of smelting, but the speculation unfortunately fell through, for want of sufficient capital. There is one grist and one saw mill in the township. Marmora is but little settled, much of the land being unfit for cultivation. Sixteen thousand three hundred and forty-three acres of Crown lands are open for sale in this township, at 8s. currency per acre.

Population in 1842, 317.

Ratable property in the township, £5,368.

MARSHVILLE

A small Village in the township of Wainfleet, situated on the Grand River feeder of the Welland Canal, ten miles from Port Colborne. It contains about sixty inhabitants, grist mill, two stores, one tavern, one blacksmith.

Post Office, post three times a week

MARTINTOWN.

A Village in the west of the township of Charlottenburgh, situated on the River aux Raisins, thirteen miles from Cornwall. It contains about 200 inhabitants, and one Presbyterian Church

Professions and Trades.—One grist and saw mill, seven stores, one tavern, four asheries, one saddler, one waggon maker, three blacksmiths, three tailors, three shoemakers.

MARYBOROUGH.

A Township in the Wellington District, is bounded on the north-east by the township of Arthur; on the north-west by unsurveyed lands, on the south west by Mornington, and on the south-east by Peel. This township has only lately been surveyed and laid out, and no return has yet been made from it. It formerly formed part of what was called the "Queen's Bush."

MARYSBURGH

A Township in the Prince Edward District, is bounded on the north, east and south by the Bay of Quinte and Lake Ontario, and on the west by the townships of Hallowell and Athol. In Marysburgh 38,202 acres are taken up, 12,684 of which are under cultivation. A river, called "Black River," runs through the west of the township, from west to east, and enters Lake Ontario. In the north-west of the township is a small lake, called the "Lake of the Mountain," situated on the summit of a hill, at a considerable height above the level of Lake Ontario. A range of hills runs nearly across the north-east portion of the township. A large proportion of the land in the north-east of Marysburgh is good, but in the south-east it is generally poor, and is covered with cedar, a considerable quantity of which is exported. The village of Milford is situated in the west corner of the township, and there are three grist and ten saw mills in the township

Population in 1842, 2,207; who are principally U. E. Loyalists and their descendants

Ratable property in the township, £37,299.

MATCHADASH

A Township in the Simcoe District, is bounded on the north and east by the River Severn, on the west by the township of Tay, and on the south by Orillia. Very little is known of this township, and in 1845 there was only one settler in it. There are 40,000 acres of Crown lands open for sale in the township, at 8s currency per acre, to purchase which application must be made to the Crown lands agent at Barrie.

MATCHADASH BAY.

A Bay at the south-eastern extremity of the Georgian Bay. On an island in the Bay, called Beausoleil Island, is a settlement of Chippewa Indians who removed, under their chief "Ahsance," from the village of Coldwater. Their present village was only commenced in 1844. it contains fourteen houses and a barn The number of the band is 232, they have about 100 acres under cultivation. The majority of these Indians are Roman Catholics; they have not as yet any place of worship or school In the former settlement they were occasionally visited by the Roman Catholic priest resident at Penetanguishene.

MATILDA.

A Township in the Eastern District, is bounded on the north-east by the township of Williamsburgh, on the north-west by Mountain; on the south-west by Edwardsburgh, and on the south-east by the St. Lawrence. In Matilda 37,763 acres are taken up, 6,518 of which are under cultivation. There is a small village in the township, called Matilda, situated on the St Lawrence. Two hundred acres of Crown lands are open for sale in Matilda, at 8s currency per acre. There is a Methodist church in the township, and three saw mills.
Population in 1842, 2,535
Ratable property in the township, £29,064.

MACHEL'S CORNERS.

A Settlement on Yonge Street, twenty-six miles from Toronto. It contains about 100 inhabitants. There are in the settlement a grist and saw mill, called "Hollinshed Mills," three stores, one tavern, one blacksmith, one saddler, one shoemaker, one tailor.

MEDONTE.

A Township in the Simcoe District, is bounded on the north by the township of Tay; on the west by Flos, on the south by Oro, and on the east by Orillia. In Medonte 17,516 acres are taken up, 2,465 of which are under cultivation There is some good land in the township, but a large portion of it is hilly and broken, particularly in the centre and north. Nearly in the centre of the township there is some very high land, from whence both the lakes Huron and Simcoe may be seen In Medonte there are 2,100 acres of Crown lands for disposal, at 8s. currency per acre. There are in the township one grist and three saw mills.
Population in 1842, 548.
Ratable property in the township, £8,584.

MELANCTHON

A Township in the Wellington District, is bounded on the east by the township of Mulmur; on the north by Ospry, on the west by Proton, and on the south by Amaranth Melancthon has only lately been surveyed and laid out, and no return has yet been made from it Seven thousand nine hundred acres of Crown lands are open for sale in the township, at 8s. currency per acre.

MERRITTSVILLE.

A small Settlement in the township of Crowland, one mile and a half from the junction At this place an aqueduct has been constructed to convey the Welland Canal over the Welland or Chippewa River, the level of the canal being here forty feet above the surface of the river Merrittsville contains about 100 inhabitants, five stores, three taverns, two tailors, two shoemakers

MERSEA.

A Township in the County of Essex, is bounded on the north by the township of Tilbury West, on the West by Gosfield, on the south by Lake Erie; and on the east by Romney In Mersea 20,574 acres are taken up, of which 2,593 are under cultivation. An extensive, triangular-shaped point of land, embracing about one-third of the township, called "Point Pelé," runs out into the lake This is principally sand and marsh, and incapable of being cultivated A small

K

stream, called "Sturgeon Creek," on which is a grist mill, runs from about the centre of the township into Lake Erie. The Talbot Road runs through the township. Five thousand eight hundred acres of Crown lands are open for sale in Mersea, and the Canada Company possess about 7,500 acres in the township.
Population of Mersea, 798
Ratable property in the township, £9,723.

METHUEN.

A Township in the Colborne District; is bounded on the east by the township of Lake; on the north by unsurveyed lands, on the west by Burleigh and Dummer, and on the south by Belmont There is a large, irregularly shaped lake situated in the north-west corner, and several smaller ones are scattered over the centre and south of the township. This township is but little settled, and no return has yet been made from it In Methuen 45,878 acres of Crown lands are open for sale, at 8s currency per acre.

McGILLIVRAY

A Township in the Huron District, is bounded on the north by the township of Stephen; on the west by the Sable River, on the south by Williams; and on the east by Biddulph Most of the land in the township is good. McGillivray contains 20,323 acres, 11,832 of which are leased or sold, of which 808 acres are under cultivation.
Population 448
Ratable property in the township, £3,912.

McKILLOP.

A Township in the Huron District, is bounded on the north-east by Crown lands; on the north-west by the township of Hullett, on the south-west by Tuckersmith and Hibbert; and on the south-east by Logan The soil of this township is principally good A branch of the Maitland River runs through its southern portion, on which is a saw mill. There is a post office in the western corner of the township, on the Huron Road McKillop contains 53,422 acres, 6,790 of which are leased or sold, of which 789 are under cultivation.
Population 321.
Ratable property in the township, £3,025 4s.

McMULLEN'S MILLS (See ERIN).

MIDLAND DISTRICT.

Consists of the counties of Frontenac, Lennox, and Addington, it is bounded on the east by the Johnstown and Bathurst Districts, on the north by unsurveyed lands, on the west by the Victoria District, and on the south by Lake Ontario and part of the Bay of Quinté The islands of Amherst and Wolfe are included in the district The district is watered by the Napanee, Salmon, and Cataraqui rivers, besides branches of the Mississippi, and numerous other small streams, and lakes of various sizes are scattered over it. The townships in the south-west and south of the district, comprising Kingston, Ernestown, Fredericksburgh, Camden, and Richmond, contain excellent land. The northern townships are some of them but little settled, and Kennebec and Kaladar, Olden and Oso, are altogether vacant The foundation of the district is limestone, and in places fine marble is to be found, in the north of the district there are beds which are a continuation of those in the Bathurst District, and a bed of marble has lately been discovered in the township of Camden, twenty-two miles north-west from Kingston Much of the land in the north and east is poor and rocky and unfit for cultivation, but land of excellent quality is said to have been lately discovered to the north of Kingston.

The principal towns and villages in the district are Kingston, the district town, and lately the seat of government for the province, in the township of Kingston; Napanee, in Richmond; and Bath, in Ernestown. Three hundred and ninety-nine thousand five hundred acres of Crown lands are open for sale in the Midland District, at 8s. c'y per acre; to purchase any of which, application must be made to the Crown Lands Agent, at Napanee.

Population of the district in 1842, 38,770; since when it has probably increased one-sixth.

The following abstract from the assessment rolls, will show the rate of increase and improvement in the district:

Date.	No. of Acres Cultivated.	MILLS.		Milch Cows.	Oxen 4 years old, and upwards.	Horned Cattle from 2 to 4 years old.	Amount of Ratable Property.
		Grist.	Saw.				
1842	......	......	......	......	......	......	526,201.
1843	119,594	19	71	11,732	2022	4229	562,143.
1844	131,928	19	69	11,194	2390	4053	582,556.

Government and District Officers in the Midland District:

Judge of District Court	S. F. Kirkpatrick	Kingston.
Sheriff	Thos. A. Corbett	"
Clerk of Peace	Jas. Nickalls	"
Treasurer of District	D. S. Smith	"
Inspector of Licenses	James Sampson	"
Registrar of County of Frontenac	Chas. Stuart	"
" " Lennox & Addington	J. Fraser, Dy	"
Collector of Customs	Thos. Kirkpatrick	"
District Clerk	Saml. McGowan	"
Clerk of District Court	A. Pringle	"
Deputy Clerk of Crown	Jno. S. Smyth	"
Crown Lands Agent	Allan McPherson	Napanee.
Emigrant Agent	A. B. Hawke	Kingston.

Coroners... { Thos. W. Robison, H. W. Benson, Geo. A. Detlor, Jno. W. Ferguson, Chas. A. Booth, Jas. Chamberlain, Henry Davis, Lewis Daley, Geo. Baxter, Geo. W. Yarker.

The following is the number of *School Districts* in the district, each of which is *supposed* to have a school in it, but I could not ascertain the actual number of schools in operation: Kingston (town) eighteen, Kingston (township) twenty-six, Pittsburgh eleven, Ernestown twenty-one, Fredericksburg nineteen, Adolphustown four, Richmond twelve, Sheffield nine, Camden thirty-one, Loughborough seven, Storrington seven, Bedford two, Amherst Island five, Wolfe Island seven.

MIDDLETON.

A Township in the Talbot District, is bounded on the east by the township of Windham, on the north by Norwich and Dereham, on the west by Bayham, and on the south by Walsingham. In Middleton 13,249 acres are taken up, 1976 of which are under cultivation. Otter creek runs through the north-west corner of the township, and a branch of Big Creek through the east of the township. The land in Middleton is generally light, and the timber mostly pine; large quantities of which are sawn up, and exported. The village of

Middleton is situated in the township, on the Talbot street. There are seven saw mills in the township.

Population in 1841, 555.

Ratable property in the township, £7673.

MIDDLETOWN.

A Village in the township of West Gwillimbury, two miles west of Bradford, on the Bond Head road, contains about fifty inhabitants There is a good, and comfortable tavern, one blacksmith, one wheelwright, one shoemaker, one carpenter.

MILFORD.

A small Village in the south-west corner of the township of Marysburgh. It contains about 100 inhabitants, grist and saw mill, one blacksmith, one shoe maker, one tailor.

MILL CREEK.

A Village in the township of Ernestown, situated on the eastern road thirteen miles west from Kingston, contains about 150 inhabitants, who have a Catholic church.

Post Office, post every day.

Professions and Trades.—One grist and saw mill, carding machine and fulling mill, planing machine, two stores, three taverns, two tailors, two shoemakers.

MILLBROOK

A Village in the township of Cavan, situated a little south of the centre of the township. It contains about 250 inhabitants, who have a Methodist chapel.

Professions and Trades.—Two physicians and surgeons, one grist and saw mill, one distillery, one tannery, four stores, two taverns, two waggon makers, four blacksmiths

Post Office, post twice a week

MILLE ROCHES.

A Village in the township of Cornwall, five miles from the town of Cornwall. It is situated between the River St Lawrence and the Cornwall canal It was once flourishing, but the formation of the Cornwall Canal has cut it off from the surrounding country A quarry of splendid black lime stone, resembling black marble, and which takes a beautiful polish, is situated close to the village.

Mille Roches contains a grist and saw mill, carding machine and fulling mill, and two stores

Post Office, post every day

MILTON MILLS—(See LAMBTON.)

MILLVILLE, OR ELLOTT'S MILLS.

A small Village in the township of Darlington, six miles north of Bowmanville. It contains about 150 inhabitants, grist and saw mill, two stores, one tavern, one blacksmith, one tailor, one shoemaker

MIMICO

A Village in the township of Etobicoke, situated on Dundas Street, on the Etobicoke Creek, nine miles and a half from Toronto It contains about 150 inhabitants A neat Wesleyan chapel is erected, and an Episcopal church is in course of erection.

Mimico contains two saw-mills, one store, one physician and surgeon, two taverns, one blacksmith, one butcher, one baker, two shoemakers, two wheelwrights and waggon makers, two carpenters and joiners, one tailor.

MINTO.

A Township in the Wellington District; is bounded on the east by Arthur; on the north by Normanby; and on the west and south by unsurveyed lands. Minto has only lately been surveyed and laid out, and no return has yet been made from it.

MISSISSIPPI RIVER.

A Tributary of the Ottawa, two branches of which take their rise in the north of the Midland District, the south branch flows through the townships of Olden, Oso, South Sherbrooke, Bathurst, and into the west corner of Drummond, where it is joined by the north branch, which takes its rise in a chain of lakes in the townships of Bairie, Clarendon, and Palmerston, and flows through North Sherbrooke and Dalhousie. The two branches unite in Drummond, and soon afterwards the river expands into the Mississippi Lake, which extends through the north-east of Drummond and the west of Beckwith, near the north-west corner of which township it terminates The river then passes through the north-east of Ramsay, the east of Pakenham, and the west of Fitzroy, and enters the Ottawa a little below Lake Chats The river is joined in its course by several smaller branches. Large quantities of timber are cut on its banks, which are carried down the Ottawa.

MISSISSIPPI ISLAND.—(See FITZROY HARBOUR.)

MOIRA RIVER.

A River, numerous branches of which take their rise in, and are spread over the several townships of Marmora, Madoc, Tudor, Elzevir, Grimsthorpe, Kalador, and Sheffield. They unite in a small lake which is situated a little north-west of the centre of Hungerford, and the river then flows on to the Bay of Quinte, passing through the north-west corner of Tyendenaga, and across the township of Thurlow, in which township, at the town of Belleville, it enters the bay.

MONAGHAN, SOUTH.

A Township in the Newcastle District; is bounded on the east and north by the Otonabee River and North Monaghan, on the west by Cavan, and on the south by Hamilton and Rice Lake. In South Monaghan 14,896 acres are taken up, 6233 of which are under cultivation. A considerable swamp extends through the north of this township The land is of mixed qualities—good, bad, and indifferent Timber—hardwood, intermixed with pine. In South Monaghan 100 acres of Crown lands are open for sale, at 8s currency per acre.

Population in 1842, 719

Ratable property in the township, 13,085.

MONAGHAN, NORTH.

A Township in the Colborne District, is bounded on the east by the Otonabee River; on the north by the township of Smith, on the west by Cavan, and on the south by Hamilton and Rice Lake. In Monaghan 10,138 acres are taken up, 3205 of which are under cultivation. This township is well settled by a mixed population. The town of Peterborough is situated at its north-east corner, on the Otonabee River. There are three grist-mills, two saw-mills, and three distilleries in the township In Monaghan only 180 acres of Crown lands are open for sale at 8s c'y per acre.

Ratable property in the township, £20,416.

MONO.

A Township in the Simcoe District, is bounded on the north by the township of Mulmer, on the west by Amaranth, on the south by Garafraxa and Caledon; and on the east by Adjala. In Mono 28,229 acres are taken up, 3108 of which are under cultivation. There are some well cultivated farms in the township, some of which have good orchards, but a large portion of the township is hilly and sandy. In some parts the land is so high, as to give a view of the township of Essa. On about the centre of the town line between Mono and Adjala there are some good limestone quarries, but they are not as yet much worked. Four thousand nine hundred acres of Crown Lands are open for sale in Mono, at 8s. c'y per acre. There are two grist mills and one tannery in the township.
Population in 1842, 1020
Ratable property in the township, £11,829.

MONTAGUE

A Township in the Bathurst District, is bounded on the north-east by the township of Marlborough, on the north-west by Beckwith, on the south-west by North and South Elmsley, and on the south-east by Wolford. In Montague 39,303 acres are taken up, 7498 of which are under cultivation. There is a fair proportion of good land in the township, and many well-cultivated farms; timber, a mixture of pine and hard wood. In Montague 1000 acres of Crown lands are open for sale, at 8s c'y per acre. There are three saw-mills in the township.
Population in 1842, 2097, who are principally Scotch.
Ratable property in the township, £22,330.

MOORE

A Township in the county of Kent, bounded on the north by the township of Sarnia, on the west by the river St. Clair, on the south by Sombra, and on the east by Enniskillen. In Moore 19,192 acres are taken up, of which 1901 are under cultivation. The soil is, generally, of excellent quality. There is a tamarac swamp in the south-east corner of the township, two miles long, and one mile broad. In the township are the villages of Froomefield, Sutherlands, and Corunna. There is also a store and wood-wharf on the river, seven miles and a-half below Port Sarnia. The front of the township, along the river, is well settled. Two thousand nine hundred acres of Crown lands are open for sale in Moore, at 8s c y per acre.
Population, about 780
Ratable property in the township, £9,523.

MORNINGTON

A Township in the Wellington District, formerly a portion of what was called "Queen's Bush", is bounded on the north-east by the township of Maryborough, on the north-west by unsurveyed lands, on the south-west by Ellice, and on the south-east by Wellesley. Mornington has only lately been surveyed and laid out, and no return has yet been made from it.

MORPETH, or JAMESVILLE

A Village in the township of Howard, pleasantly situated on Talbot road, in the midst of a beautifully undulating country, one mile and a-half from Lake Erie. Contains a post-office, post three times a-week, three stores, two taverns, two blacksmiths, one distillery, one cabinet maker, one tailor, two carpenters.

MOSA

A Township in the London District, is bounded on the north-east by Ekfrid and Brooke, on the west by Brooke and Zone, and on the south-east by the River Thames. In Mosa 25,243 acres are taken up, 5,099 of which are under cultivation. This is a triangular-shaped township, with its base towards the River Thames There is a considerable portion of good land in it, although there are some wet spots scattered over it. Timber—principally hardwood. The east branch of Bear Creek runs through the north-west of the township. On the bank of the Thames, about thirty-eight miles from Chatham, is a spring containing sulphuretted hydrogen gas, and about half a mile from it is a naphtha spring. The village of Wardsville is situated in the township, on the western road There are two grist and two saw mills in the township

Population in 1842, 1,154.

Ratable property in the township, £15,557.

MOUNT PLEASANT.

A small Village in the township of Brantford, five miles from Brantford, on the road to Simcoe It contains about 130 inhabitants. Churches and chapels, three, viz, Episcopal, Presbyterian and Methodist.

Post Office, post three times a week

Professions and Trades—Four stores, two taverns, one waggon maker, two blacksmiths, two tailors, two shoemakers.

MOULINETTE.

A Village in the township of Cornwall, situated on the St Lawrence, seven miles from Cornwall. It contains about one hundred inhabitants Churches and chapels, two; viz, Episcopal and Methodist

Professions and Trades.—One grist and saw mill, one brewery, carding machine, foundry, one store, one tavern, one cabinet maker, one blacksmith.

MOULTON

A Township in the Niagara District, is bounded on the north-east by the townships of Wainfleet and Gainsborough, on the north-west by Canboro', and on the south by the Grand River, Sherbrooke and Lake Erie In Moulton 8,985 acres are taken up, 1,716 of which are under cultivation A large swamp is situated in the south-east corner of the township, and extends into the township of Wainfleet. The feeder of the Welland Canal is formed through the south of the township, and enters the Grand River at the village of Dunnville, which is situated near the south-west corner of the township. There are two grist and two saw mills in the township.

Population in 1841, 628.

Ratable property in the township, £10,915.

MOUNTAIN.

A Township in the Eastern District, is bounded on the north-east by the township of Winchester, on the north-west by Osgoode, on the south-west by South Gower; and on the south-east by Matilda In Mountain 25,362 acres are taken up, 6,269 of which are under cultivation The Petite Nation River runs through the west and south of the township, leaving it at its eastern corner Mountain is pretty well settled, and contains some good land. Timber—a mixture of pine and hardwood Two hundred acres of Crown lands are open for sale in the township, at 8s currency per acre There is an Episcopal church in the township, and one grist and four saw mills.

Population in 1842, 1,316

Ratable property in the township, £18,275.

MULMUR.

A Township in the Simcoe District, is bounded on the north by the township of Nottawasaga, on the west by Melancthon, on the south by Mono, and on the east by Tossorontio. In Mulmur 6,988 acres are taken up, 681 of which are under cultivation. The quality of the land varies in this township; some parts being good, and others poor and hilly. The township is well watered by numerous small streams; but it is as yet but little settled In Mulmur there are 22,000 acres of Crown lands for disposal, at 8s. currency per acre.

Population in 1842, 218.

Ratable property in the township, £2,878.

MURRAY.

A Township in the Newcastle District, is bounded on the east by the township of Sidney, on the north by Seymour, on the west by Cramahe, and on the south by Lake Ontario and the Bay of Quinté. In Murray 41,907 acres are taken up, 13,029 of which are under cultivation. A considerable portion of the north of the township consists of "Oak Plains." The River Trent runs along the north border of the township, from west to east, enters Sidney, and re-enters Murray at its south-east corner, where it enters the Bay of Quinté. The village of Trent is situated at its mouth. The village of Brighton is situated on the west line of the township, and Presqu' Isle Harbour is also partly in this township, and partly in Cramahe. There are two grist and fourteen saw mills, and one distillery in the township. In Murray 1,700 acres of Crown lands are open for sale, at 8s. currency per acre.

Population in 1842, 2,765.

Ratable property in the township, £41,226.

MURPHY'S MILLS. (*See* ERAMOSA.)

NANTICOKE.

A small Village situated near the west corner of the township of Walpole, about three quarters of a mile from the lake, and seven miles from Port Dover. It contains about 100 inhabitants, and an Episcopal church, one grist mill, one saw mill, one store, one tannery, one tavern, one tailor, one shoemaker.

Post Office, post twice a week.

NAPANEE. (*Corrupted from the original Indian name Appanee.*)

A Village in the township of Richmond, on the eastern road, twenty-five miles west from Kingston, and twenty-five from Belleville, situated on the Napanee River, which is navigable to the village for schooners drawing six feet water. Napanee is situated in the midst of a hilly country, on a limestone foundation, with some good farming country in its rear. A canal, cut through the solid limestone, is in course of formation, in the village, for hydraulic purposes. The road from here to Kingston is macadamized. The stage from Kingston to Toronto, passes through the village daily. Napanee contains about 500 inhabitants. Churches and chapels, three, viz, Episcopal, (stone) two Methodist, (one of which is of brick.)

Post Office, post every day.

Professions and Trades.—Two physicians and surgeons, two lawyers, two grist mills, attached to one of which is an oatmeal mill, two saw mills, one ashery, carding machine, fulling mill and cloth factory, one tannery, one foundry, two saddlers, four taverns, three blacksmiths, two waggon makers, six tailors, eight stores, two druggists, one painter, one cabinet maker, one hatter, one tinsmith, two bakers, one watchmaker, one cooper, one chair maker.

Principal Tavern.—" Storeys "

Land Agent.—John Low.

Exports from Napanee for the year 1844.

Description.	Quantity
Lumber	1,265,000 feet.
Ashes	1,152 bushels.
Flour	1,205 barrels.
Wheat	13,170 bushels.
Pipe Staves	4,000
West Indian do.	15,000.

NAPANEE RIVER.

A River, different branches of which take their rise in the north of the Midland District, in the townships of Sheffield, Hinchinbrooke, and Loughborough; they unite close to the west line of the township of Camden East, and the river enters the Bay of Quinté, in the township of Richmond. The village of Napanee is situated on the river, which is an excellent mill stream.

NASSAGAWEYA.

A Township in the Gore District, is bounded on the north-east by the township of Esquesing; on the north-west by Eramosa, on the south-west by Puslinch and Flamborough, and on the south-east by Nelson. In Nassagaweya 25,121 acres are taken up, 7314 of which are under cultivation. The township is well watered by numerous small streams running through it, and it contains some excellent land. Timber principally hardwood. There are one grist and three saw mills in the township.

Population in 1841, 1182.

Ratable property in the township, £30,759.

NELSON.

A Township in the Gore District, is bounded on the north-east by the township of Trafalgar, on the north-west by Nassagaweya, on the south-west by Flamborough, and on the south-east by Lake Ontario. In Nelson 43,433 acres are taken up, 18,354 of which are under cultivation. This is an old and well settled township, containing good land, excellent farms, and fine flourishing orchards. It is well watered by Twelve Mile Creek, and numerous small streams running through it. Most of the land is rolling. Timber, hardwood intermixed with pine. The village of Nelson is situated in the township, on Dundas Street; and there are two grist and seventeen saw mills in the township.

Population in 1841, 3059.

Ratable property in the township, £70,740.

NELSON

A small Village on Dundas Street in the township of Nelson, it contains about fifty inhabitants; tavern, store and post office.

NEPEAN

A Township in the Dalhousie District, is bounded on the east by the township of Gloucester; on the north by the Ottawa River, on the west by March and Goulborne, and on the south-east by North Gower. In Nepean 37,481 acres are taken up, 7454 of which are under cultivation. The Rideau river and canal form the eastern border of the township. The town of Bytown is situated in the north-east corner, on the Ottawa River and a small settlement, called Britannia, in the north of the township. Nepean is well settled, and contains some good farms, the great demand for provisions at Bytown, occasioned by the extensive business carried on in lumber in the District, always ensuring the farmer a good price for his produce, Seven hundred and eighty-

six acres of crown lands are open for sale in Nepean, at 8s. currency per acre. There are two saw mills in the township, exclusive of three in Bytown.
Population in 1842, 7,294, which included the town of Bytown.
Ratable property in the township, (not including Bytown), £21,275.

NEWBURGH.

A Village in the township of Camden, situated on the Napanee River, seven miles above Napanee—contains about 300 inhabitants, who have a Methodist chapel

Professions and Trades.—Two grist mills, two saw do., one carding machine and fulling mill, axe factory and trip hammer, four stores, one tavern, two groceries, three blacksmiths, one pot and pearl ashery.

NEW EDINBURGH

A Village in the north-west corner of the township of Gloucester, situated on the Ottawa, at the mouth of the river Rideau, about one mile east from Bytown. The river, a short distance above the village, divides into two branches, which fall into the Ottawa, forming two perpendicular falls of about thirty-four feet in height. The scenery about the village is very picturesque. New Edinburgh contains about 150 inhabitants, one grist mill, one saw do., brewery, carding machine and cloth factory, two stores, one shoemaker.

NEW HOPE.

A small Village in the township of Waterloo, four miles from Preston, on the Guelph road, situated on the River Speed. It contains about 100 inhabitants, one grist and saw mill, one tannery, one tavern, one store, one pail factory, two blacksmiths, two tailors, two shoemakers

NEWCASTLE DISTRICT

Consists of the counties of Northumberland and Durham. This district formerly comprised the townships to the north, which have since been separated from it, and formed into the Colborne district, which bounds it on the north, on the east it is bounded by the Victoria District, on the west by the Home District, and on the south by Lake Ontario. Rice Lake commences in the north-west of the township of Hamilton, and, with its continuation, the River Trent, separates the district from that of Colborne, as far as the township of Seymour, through which it runs from north to south, it then follows a west course through the north of Murray, into the township of Sidney, makes a bend and runs south and a little west till it re-enters Murray, in which township it emerges into the Bay of Quinte. The Skugog Lake is situated in the north and centre of the township of Cartwright, and the district is watered besides by numerous excellent mill streams, one of the best of which is, that which enters Lake Ontario at Port Hope.

The land in this district varies in quality, most of it, however, is sufficiently good for agricultural purposes. A range of Oak Plains, called "Rice Lake Plains," extends through the townships of Murray, the north of Cramahe, and Haldimand, the centre of Hamilton and Hope, and a small portion of Clarke. These plains were formerly difficult of sale, and would not command more than 4s currency per acre, till they were discovered by some settlers from the neighbourhood of Brantford, who had been accustomed to farming the oak plains, and knew their value, and who made some purchases of part of them. These soon astonished their neighbours by the facility with which they cleared the land, and the excellence of their wheat crops, the latter having supposed, from the light and sandy nature of the soil, that it was valueless. The consequence was, that the oak plains became in demand, and instead of four shillings per acre, they now fetch four dollars! The land in the Newcastle District is generally rolling

The townships in front of the district are all very well settled, the farms are well cleared and in a good state of cultivation, and most of the houses have orchards attached to them. The district is peopled principally by emigrants from Great Britain and Ireland, most of whom are in good circumstances. Large quantities of wheat and other grain, all of excellent quality, are raised in the district. A new gravelled road has lately been made from Port Hope to Rice Lake.

Cobourg, the district town, is well laid out, and is a place of considerable business. Port Hope, Bowmanville, Newcastle, Colborne, Grafton, Brighton, and Trent, are also thriving villages.

Four thousand five hundred and fifty acres of Crown lands are open for sale in the district, at 8s. currency per acre, to purchase any of which application must be made to the Crown lands agent at Port Hope.

Population in 1842, 32,033; since when it has probably increased one-fifth.

The following abstract from the Assessment Rolls will show the rate of increase and improvement in the district:—

Date.	No. of Acres Cultivated.	MILLS. Grist.	MILLS. Saw.	Milch Cows.	Oxen, 4 years old, and upwards.	Horned Cattle, from 2 to 4 years old.	Amount of Ratable Property.
1842	167,463	37	82	10,638	3844	4944	£424,122
1843	149,777	36	99	11,657	4205	5664	446,408
1844	160,193	34	113	10,327	4126	4718	474,052

Government and District Officers in the Newcastle District:

Judge of District Court	George M. Boswell	Cobourg.
Sheriff	Henry Ruttan	Do.
Treasurer	Zaccheus Burnham	Do.
Clerk of Peace	Thomas Ward	Port Hope.
Inspector of Licenses	George S. Daintry	Cobourg.
District Clerk	Morgan Jellett	Do.
Registrar of county Durham	Thomas Ward	Port Hope.
Do. Northumberland	George Boulton	Cobourg.
Judge of Surrogate Court	Thomas Ward	Port Hope.
Registrar of do.	M. F. Whitehead	Do.
Deputy Clerk of Crown	Henry Jones	Hamilton.
Clerk of District Court	Henry Covert	Cobourg.
Crown Lands Agent	Elias P. Smith	Port Hope.
District Superintendent of Schools	John Steele	Grafton.
Collectors of Customs	Wm. H. Kitson	Cobourg.
	M. F. Whitehead	Port Hope.
	Henry S. Reid	Darlington.
	John Short	Brighton.
Coroners	Benjamin Ewing	Haldimand.
	Thomas V. Tupper	Cavan.
	David Brodie	Cobourg.
	Donald Campbell	Colborne.
	William Lawson	Cavan.
	R. D. Chatterton	Cobourg.
	John Scott	Darlington.
	Henry Mead	Brighton.
	Jacob Ford	Trent Port.
	Benjamin Bird	Port Hope.

Number of Common Schools in operation in the Newcastle District.—Darlington, sixteen; Clarke, eight, Hope, thirteen: Hamilton, nine; Haldimand, sixteen; Cramahe, seventeen; Murray, twenty-four; Seymour, three; Percy, one; Alnwick, one, South Monaghan, five; Cavan, seventeen; Manvers, one, Cartwright, two. Total, 133.

NEWCASTLE.

A pretty little Village in the township of Clark, five miles east from Bowmanville, and seventeen from Port Hope, it contains about 300 inhabitants. Churches and chapels two, viz, Methodist and Congregational. There is an Episcopal church a mile and a-half from the village.

Post Office, post every day.

Professions and Trades.—Eight stores, one druggist, two tanneries, two taverns, one axe factory, two saddlers, four blacksmiths two waggon makers, four tailors, two shoe makers.

NEWMARKET.

A Village in the township of Whitchurch, three miles and a-half from Holland Landing, and about thirty miles from Toronto. It is situated on the east branch of the Holland River, in the midst of a finely undulating, old settled. and well cultivated country, and is surrounded by very fine farms. The village was commenced about thirty years since, and was originally settled by Pennsylvanian Quakers. The principal part of it is built on the south side of a gently sloping hill, forming one long narrow street, the remainder of the village is built on the side of a hill, a little to the east. Newmarket contains about 600 inhabitants. There are six churches and chapels, viz, Episcopalian, Presbyterian, Catholic, Congregational, Methodist, and Christian.

Post Office, post every day in summer, and three times a week in winter.

Professions and Trades.—Three physicians and surgeons, two grist-mills, two breweries one distillery, one tannery, one foundry, one carding machine and cloth factory, five stores. three taverns, one druggist, one painter, two ladies seminaries, one gunsmith, two cabinet makers, three blacksmiths, one watch maker, one tinsmith, six shoemakers, three waggon makers, two saddlers, three tailors, four carpenters, one hatter.

NEWPORT, or BIRCH'S LANDING.

A Settlement lately started in the south-east of the township of Brantford, on the Grand River, four miles from the town of Brantford. It contains at present about sixty inhabitants, one store, one tavern, and two storehouses for storing grain.

NEWTON, or CLARKE.

A Village in the township of Clarke, twelve miles from Port Hope, laid out in the year 1834, contains about 130 inhabitants, who have a Presbyterian church.

Post Office, post every day.

Professions and Trades.—Three stores, one tannery, three taverns, one waggon maker, one wheelwright and chair maker, two blacksmiths, one cooper, four shoemakers.

NIAGARA DISTRICT.

Consists of the counties of Lincoln and Welland, and the county of Haldimand, except the townships of Seneca, Oneida, Rainham, and Walpole. The district is bounded on the north by Lake Ontario; on the east by the Niagara River, on the south by Lake Erie, and on the west by the Gore and Talbot districts. The principal part of the district consists of a high table land, about

150 feet above the level of the lake, which approaches at Stony Creek to within about a mile and a half of the lake, it then gradually recedes till it crosses the Niagara River above Queenston, seven miles from Lake Ontario. This is a very old settled district, a large part of it having been peopled soon after the American war of independence. The foundation of the table land consists of limestone and freestone, which are worked at different places, water-lime and gypsum are also found in considerable quantities in the townships of Oneida, Cayuga, and Thorold. The land of the district is mostly rolling, it is generally of very good quality, consisting for the most part of a mixture of clay and loam, in those portions timbered with hardwood, and light sandy soil where the timber consists of pine. In some parts of the district, as in the neighbourhood of the town of Niagara, are extensive oak plains; the most easily cleared, and cultivated of any kind of land, and under proper cultivation producing wheat of excellent quality.

A large portion of the district is settled by Americans and their descendants, and native Canadians, and there are also a considerable number of Pensylvanian Dutch, neither of whom make first-rate farmers, so that, although the farms in the district are as well situated, and cleared, as any one could desire, they are generally badly cultivated, and many of them are becoming what the proprietors call *worn-out*, which means in reality, that they have been taking too much wheat off the ground, and putting too little manure on it. I was informed that many of the farmers had been in the habit of growing lately not more than ten or twelve bushels of wheat to the acre. Some of them, however, are beginning to improve, and to follow the example of the English and Scotch farmers settled amongst them, and are beginning to alter their mode of farming; most of them have fine orchards.

The best settled townships in the district, are those of Bertie, Pelham, Stamford, Thorold, Grantham, Niagara and Clinton Grimsby and Gainsborough are also well settled

The district is watered by the Grand River, which enters Lake Erie between the townships of Dunn and Sherbrooke, the Welland river, which flows through nearly the centre of the district, and enters the Niagara River between the townships of Stamford and Willoughby, and numerous small streams, which are scattered over it. The Welland Canal enters the district at the north-west corner of the township of Grantham, and strikes the Welland River in the township of Thorold, after leaving the Welland River, it divides into two branches in the township of Crowland, one of which runs straight on to Lake Erie, and the other passes through the township of Wainfleet, and enters the Grand River in Moulton. The land in the district has greatly increased in value since the formation of the Welland Canal. In the neighbourhood of Port Colborne is a high hill or mound, of a conical form, called "Sugar-loaf Hill," from the top of which an extensive view may be obtained of Lake Erie and the surrounding country.

Near the same neighbourhood one of the early settlers, about fifty years since, in excavating the ground for a cellar, discovered an immense quantity of human bones, which were supposed by the Indians to be part of the remains of the extinct tribe of the Erie Indians, deposited there after one of their last battles. On the spot under which the bones were discovered stood a tree the trunk of which was about eighteen inches through, which had grown there since the bodies were interred; thus bearing evidence of the antiquity of the remains. Although they had been so long underground, the bones when discovered were in a very perfect state of preservation, and many of them remain so to the present day.

The principal towns and villages in the district are Niagara, the district town, St. Catharines, the principal place on the canal, Queenston, Dunnville, Grimsby, Stoney Creek, Jordan, and Beamsville There are no Crown lands for sale in the Niagara District.

Population in 1841, 31,549; since when it has probably increased one-fifth

The following abstract from the assessment rolls will show the rate of increase and improvement in the district:

Date.	No. of Acres Cultivated.	MILLS. Grist.	MILLS. Saw.	Milch Cows.	Oxen, 4 years old and upwards.	Horned Cattle, from 2 to 4 years old.	Amount of Ratable Property.
1842	156,954	52	94	12,987	3,214	5,574	£578,179
1843	159,410	41	98	13,729	3,500	6,058	596,737
1844	161,334	46	83	14,220	3,504	5,298	617,085

Government and District Officers in the Niagara District.

Judge of District Court	Edward C. Campbell	Niagara.
Sheriff	William Kingsmill	Do.
Clerk of Peace	Charles Richardson	Do.
Treasurer	Daniel McDougall	Do.
Judge of Surrogate Court	W. Claus	Do.
Registrar of do.	C. B. Secord	Queenston.
Registrar of County of Lincoln	John Powell	Niagara.
Inspector of Licenses	Wm. D. Miller	Do.
Collector of Customs	Thomas McCormic	Do.
Crown Lands Agent	Jas. H. Cummings	Chippewa.
Deputy Clerk of Crown	W. D. Miller	Niagara.
Warden	D. Thorburn	Queenston.
District Clerk	Charles Richardson	Niagara.
Clerk of District Court	J. Clench	Do.
Coroners	W. D. Miller	Do.
	J. Wynn	Queenston.
	T. Raymond	St. Catharine's.
	Z. Fell	Jordan.
	John Jarron	Dunn.
	Richard Graham	Bertie.
	P. B. Nelles	Grimsby.
	John Mewburn	Stamford.
	G. McMichie	Chippewa.
	Samuel Wood	Grantham.
	H. W. Timms	Port Robinson.
	J. A. Wilford	Do.
	James Thompson	Wainfleet.
District Superintendent of Schools	Jacob Keefer	Thorold.

In consequence of the absence of the superintendent, I was unable to obtain any statement respecting the number of common schools in operation in the district.

NIAGARA RIVER AND FALLS.

The Niagara River receives the waters of Lake Erie, and conveys them to Lake Ontario: it is thirty-four miles in length. At its entrance stand the remains of Fort Erie, which was destroyed during the American war; and about a mile below is the village of "Waterloo," opposite which is the American village "Black Rock." The river is here about one mile in width; and a steam ferry-boat plies constantly between the two places. About three miles and a half below Waterloo, Grand Island commences, which is about nine miles in length, and about seven broad at its widest part. This island belongs to the

Americans. A little to the north-west of Grand Island is situated Navy Island, noted for having been taken possession of during the late rebellion by a party of rebels and American vagabonds (who styled themselves "*sympathizers*"); and opposite whence the American steamboat "Caroline" (which was used to assist them by carrying ammunition and stores from the American side to the island), was cut out, set on fire, and sent over the Falls.

The rapids commence about the lower portion of Navy Island; and from thence to the verge of the Horse-shoe Fall there is a descent of fifty-seven feet— to the verge of the American Fall the descent is fifty-two feet. The Horse-shoe, which is the principal Fall, is on the Canadian side; from a portion of the rock in the centre of the Fall having been carried away a few years since, it has no longer the form of a horse-shoe, but more resembles two sides of a triangle. it is about 1900 feet across, and the fall is 158 feet. The American Fall is about 920 feet across, and the fall is 164 feet. The whole width of the river at the Falls is about three-quarters of a mile. A large island, called Goat, or Iris Island, divides the American from the Horse-shoe Fall. On the Canadian side, almost on the verge of the Horse-shoe Fall, and just below it, is the "Table Rock," a large flat ledge of rock which projects over the torrent portions of this rock have fallen from time to time, and there is a large fissure in the rock, which should warn visitors to be careful how they venture upon it. It *may* stand for many years, but no doubt the time will come when the whole rock will give way, and it is more than probable that some curious personage will go with it. As there is nothing to be gained by venturing upon it, it is better to remain on the safe side. A little above the Horse-shoe Fall are two small islands, called "Long Island," which is near the shore, and "Gull Island," situated opposite the centre of the Horse-shoe Fall, and which is supposed never to have been trodden by the foot of human being both these islands are covered with cedar. On the American side there are also several islands, three of which, situated opposite the south-east of Goat Island, are called "The Sisters."

On the American side a small portion of the stream has been diverted from its course to turn the machinery of a paper mill, and, what is truly characteristic of the people, the Americans have converted every portion of their side of the Falls into a source of money making. Goat Island is laid out as a pleasure ground (to enter which you pay a quarter of a dollar), and a building is erected on it, where you are informed by a painted notice that you may obtain soda water, ices, strawberries and cream, &c. On the rocks, a little to the west of Goat Island, a tower has been erected, from whence a view may be obtained over the Horse-shoe Fall, and a bridge has been formed to it from the island. There is some pretty scenery about the Falls on the American side, but by far the finest view of the whole is to be obtained from the Canadian side. The best view of the Falls, taking in the Horse-shoe Fall, the American Fall, and the surrounding scenery, is to be obtained from the Clifton House, a large hotel, which is situated a little below the American Fall, on the Canadian side, and close to the ferry landing.

Those who feel any curiosity on the subject, may obtain oil-skin dresses and a guide from Mr. Barnett of the Museum. to enable them to proceed behind the sheet of water composing the Horse-shoe Fall, an undertaking which, to those who attend to the instructions of the guide, is said to be neither difficult nor dangerous. All persons visiting the Falls should also pay a visit to the museum of Mr. Barnett, which is really worth seeing, comprising a great variety of native and foreign birds and animals, both living and stuffed—amongst others, a very fine pair of Buffaloes. Here also may be purchased a variety of Indian curiosities.

A pamphlet is offered for sale here, called "Every Man his own Guide to the Falls of Niagara," which, with a little information, contains a great deal of trash. It is the production of an American on the opposite side, and, while professing to point out all objects of interest about the Falls, it is evident the only object of the author, who keeps a shop on the American side, is to draw all travellers to that side, by painting everything to be seen there in the brightest colours, and throwing all points of interest on the Canadian side into the shade. One-and-twenty pages of this precious production are taken up with what the compiler calls a "chronological table, containing the principal events of the late war between the United States and Great Britain," the whole of which might be summed up in four words—"*we licked the British.*" To sell this pamphlet on the other side, in order to gratify the inordinate vanity of his countrymen, might answer the purpose of the author very well, and prove a profitable adjunct to his trade in walking sticks; but to send it over to Canada to be sold, is a piece of impudence almost unparalleled, even among the *free and independent citizens*

The principal hotels on the Canadian side are the Clifton House and the Pavilion Hotel, both of which are at present under the same management. There are several other houses in the immediate neighbourhood; and parties wishing to stay for a few weeks, for the purpose of enjoying the scenery of the Falls and the surrounding neighbourhood (probably the most magnificent in the world), will have no difficulty in procuring accommodation in private boarding houses. The "Cataract House," on the American side, is a large building, kept by an *American general*, therefore, those who have any ambition to visit a house kept by an *American general*, may have an opportunity of doing so.

The Falls are two miles from Chippewa, and seven from Queenston, between which places a railroad has been constructed, and during the summer cars run daily, conveying passengers to the Falls. The Falls, however are very magnificent in the winter, and equally well worth seeing, the rocks at the sides being encrusted with icicles, some of them measuring perhaps fifty or sixty feet in length. During the winter stages run daily from St Catharines to Chippewa, whence private conveyances may be obtained to the Falls. Occasionally, from the immense quantity of ice carried over the Falls, the channel becomes completely choked and blocked up a short distance below the Falls, so as to become passable for foot passengers. This was the case during the winter of 1845-6, when a path was marked out across the ice opposite the Clifton House, and some enterprising *Yankee*, intent on money-making, erected a shanty on the ice in the centre of the river for the sale of refreshments.

Three miles below the Falls is a whirlpool, which is caused by a sudden bend in the river, and which is also well worth visiting, and four miles below the whirlpool is the village of Queenston. Here the river becomes navigable for steamboats, the current is still rapid, but not sufficiently so to impose any obstacles in the way of steamboats, and seven miles lower down, at the mouth of the river, where it discharges itself into Lake Ontario, is the town of Niagara. From Lake Erie to the rapids, a distance of sixteen miles, the fall of the river is not more than twenty feet, in the rapids, in a quarter of a mile, the fall is forty feet, at the Falls, one hundred and sixty-four feet; and between the Falls and Queenston, a distance of seven miles, one hundred and one feet. The Falls of Niagara are supposed at one time to have been situated at the Queenston Heights, and to have gradually receded, from the wearing away of the rocks.

NIAGARA. (*Formerly called* NEWARK.)

The District Town of the Niagara District, in the township of Niagara, situated at the entrance of the Niagara River, forty-eight miles by land from Hamilton, and thirty-six by water from Toronto. Niagara is a very old town, and was for five or six years the capital of the country. It was settled by Colonel Simcoe, when Lieutenant Governor of the province, and was incorporated in the year 1845. It has been a place of considerable trade, before the opening of the Welland Canal. On the east side of the town is a large military reserve. About half a mile up the river are the ruins of Fort George, where the remains of General Brock were originally interred, they were removed in

1824 to Queenston heights, and a monument erected over them. At Fort Mississaga, which is a little below the entrance of the river, a company of rifles, and a few artillerymen are stationed. The jail and court-house are situated about one mile south-west from the town, and the barracks are about midway between the town and jail. A new town-hall and court-house are intended to be erected by the Corporation during the present season. There are in the town a fire company, with two engines, and a hook and ladder company. Churches and chapels five, viz., Episcopal (stone), Presbyterian (brick), Catholic, Methodist, and Baptist. Two newspapers are published weekly, the "Niagara Chronicle," and "Argus."

Steamboats run daily, as long as the weather will allow of it, from Toronto to Niagara and Queenston, and during the summer, boats run also from Hamilton to Niagara. The Niagara River, from the swiftness of its current, being generally free from ice up to Queenston, except at the breaking up of the frost in the spring, when it occasionally becomes blocked up with ice carried down the stream from above.

The Niagara Harbour and Dock Company were incorporated in the year 1830, and have ship-yards at Niagara and Chippewa. The machinery belonging to the establishment is of a very perfect description, worked by a steam-engine, and adapted for work of a superior kind, as the vessels turned out by the Company sufficiently prove, one of which, the steamboat "London," which commenced running in the spring of 1845, is the fastest boat on the upper lakes, and a very beautiful model. The Company usually employ about 150 hands, and, when particularly busy, have employed as many as 350. There is also on the premises a marine railway, large enough for hauling up vessels of the first class. The following vessels and engines were built by the Niagara Harbour and Dock Company between the years 1832 and 1839.—*Steamboats* Traveller, 400 tons, Experiment, 200 tons and 25 horse power engine, Queen, 250 tons and 25 horse power, and Gore, 200 tons and 45 horse power, *Schooners* Jesse Woods, Princess, Fanny, Toronto, Sovereign, 150 tons each, *Land engines* one of 12, one of 14, and one of 20 horse power. Vessels and engines built by the Niagara Harbour and Dock Company, between the years 1839 and 1845.—*Steamboats*. Sovereign, 400 tons and 75 horse power, City of Toronto 400 tons and two engines of 45 horse power each, Princess Royal, 444 tons and 80 horse power, America, 320 tons and 60 horse power, Chief Justice Robinson, 400 tons and 75 horse power, Admiral, 400 tons and 68 horse power, Eclipse, 350 tons and 55 horse power, Minos, 450 tons, Emerald, 250 tons and 50 horse power, London, 450 tons and 75 horse power, Dart, 75 tons and 25 horse power, Oak, 75 tons and 16 horse power, Gem, 75 tons and 32 horse power, Shamrock, 75 tons and 32 horse power, Ann, 75 tons and 32 horse power, *Propellers* Adventure, Beagle, and Traveller, each 90 tons and 25 horse power, *Schooners* William Cayley, Shannon, Clyde, and Shamrock, 150 tons each, *Barges* eighteen, of 40 tons each, *Engines* two of 50 horse power for steamboat Ontario, one of 45 horse power for the Porcupine, one of 25 horse power for the Burlington, one of 15 horse power for the propeller Precursor, and one of 15 horse power for the propellor St. Thomas, *Land engines* one of 5, one of 8, four of 12, and one of 20 horse power. Now building,—one steamboat of 800 tons and 150 horse power.

Niagara is a pleasant place to reside in, particularly during the summer months.

Post Office, post every day.

The following Government and District Offices are kept in Niagara Judge of District Court, Sheriff, Clerk of Peace, Registrar, Judge of Surrogate Court, Inspector of Licenses, Collector of Customs, Crown Lands Agent, Treasurer, District Clerk, Clerk of District Court, Deputy Clerk of Crown

Professions and Trades.—Three physicians and surgeons, nine lawyers, one foundry, twelve stores, — taverns, two chemists and druggists, three booksellers and stationers, two saddlers, four waggon makers, two watchmakers, one gun-

L

smith, two tallow-chandlers, marble works, two printers, two cabinet makers, one hatter, four bakers, two livery stables, two tinsmiths, three blacksmiths, six tailors, seven shoemakers, one tobacconist, one bank agency, "Upper Canada."

Principal Taverns—"Howard's," and "Moffatt's."

The quantity of wheat shipped from Niagara is small, amounting in 1844 to only 6000 bushels, but large quantities of apples, peaches, and cider are shipped annually.

NIAGARA.

A Township in the Niagara District, is bounded on the east by the Niagara River; on the north by Lake Ontario, on the west by Grantham; and on the south by Stamford. In Niagara 20,323 acres are taken up, 10,555 of which are under cultivation. This is an old and well settled Township, containing good farms, and flourishing orchards. The town of Niagara is situated in the north-east corner of the township, and the villages of Queenston and St David's in the south-east of the township, the two former on the Niagara River. The timber of the township is a mixture of hard wood and pine, and there is a considerable extent of oak plains in the east of the township. A mill stream, called "Four Mile Creek," waters the north of the township, and flows into Lake Ontario. There are three grist and two saw-mills in the township.

Population in 1841, 2109, a large portion of whom are emigrants from Great Britain.

Ratable property in the township, £36,172.

NICHOL.

A Township in the Wellington District, is bounded on the north-east by the townships of Eramosa and Garafraxa, on the north-west by Peel, on the south-west by Woolwich, and on the south-east by Guelph. In Nichol 20,482 acres are taken up, 5,392 of which are under cultivation. This is a long narrow township, it is well settled, and contains excellent land, the greater part of which is rolling, and timbered with hard wood. The Grand River runs across the north of the township, on which are situated the villages of Fergus and Elora; and a short distance west from the latter village is a Scotch settlement, called "Irvine Settlement." There are two grist and four saw-mills in the township.

Population in 1842, 1019, who are principally from Scotland.

Ratable property in the township, £16,479.

NIPISSING LAKE

A large Lake to the north-west of Lake Huron, about ninety-five miles north from Penetanguishine. It is connected with the Georgian Bay by French River, and with the Ottawa by the south-west branch. The passage, however, from the Georgian Bay to the Ottawa, can only be made in canoes, on account of the obstructions caused by portages in the south-west branch, and by rapids in French River. There are several islands in the lake, some of which are inhabited by Indians, who number somewhere about 200. Lake Nipissing is noted for its immense flocks of wild geese. French River has four portages, it is a considerable stream, and is in some places a mile in width, being studded with islands. It has three mouths or entrances into the Georgian Bay.

NISSOURI.

A Township in the Brock District, is bounded on the east by the township of Zorra; on the north by Downie and Blanshard, on the west by London, and on the south by North Dorchester and North Oxford. In Nissouri 29,784 acres are taken up, 5,918 of which are under cultivation. The north branch of the Thames runs through the north-west of the township, and there are several smaller branches spread over it. There is a swamp in the south-west corner of the township. The village of St. Andrews is situated near the south-east corner, on the town-line, partly in Nissouri and partly in North Dorchester. The land in Nissouri is generally of excellent quality, and the timber the best kinds of hard wood. There are two grist and two saw-mills in the township. Nissouri contains a mixed population, which in 1842 amounted to 1460.

Ratable property in the township, £17,298.

NORFOLK.—(See TALBOT DISTRICT.)

NORMANBY.

A Township in the Wellington District; is bounded on the east by Egremont; on the north by Bentinck, on the west by unsurveyed lands; and on the south by Minto. This township has only lately been surveyed and laid out, and no return has yet been made from it.

NORMANDALE.

A Village near the centre of the south of the township of Charlotteville, situated on Lake Erie, has been settled about twenty-five years. A blast furnace, for smelting iron ore, has been in operation since 1823. It is supplied with ore, of the description called "bog ore," from this and the adjoining townships. As much as three or four thousand tons of ore have been found within the space of a few acres. The ore yields from twenty to thirty-five per cent. of iron; but averages twenty-seven per cent, and is worth at the furnace from $2¼ to $2½ per ton. The furnace is kept in operation about ten months in the year, and when in blast produces about four tons of iron per day. There is also in the establishment, a cupola furnace, and castings of all descriptions are made. There are in the village, a machine shop, blacksmith, one store, one tavern, one tailor, two shoemakers.

Population about 300.

Post Office, post twice a-week.

NORVAL.

A Village in the township of Esquesing, situated on the Credit River, twelve miles north-west from Dundas Street. It contains about 200 inhabitants. There are two churches in the village—Episcopal and Presbyterian.

Professions and Trades.—One grist mill, one oatmeal do, one saw do, one distillery, one tannery, two blacksmiths, one saddler, two stores, one tavern, one waggon maker, two tailors, three shoemakers.

NORWICH.

A Township in the Brock District, is bounded on the east by the townships of Burford and Windham, on the north by East Oxford, and a small portion of West Oxford, on the west by Dereham, and on the south by Middletown. In Norwich, 48,463 acres are taken up, 14,243 of which are under cultivation. Several branches of Big Creek are distributed over the township. The land in the north of the township is of excellent quality, and timbered with hardwood: in the south, the land is generally light, and the timber principally pine, large quantities of which are exported. The village of Norwichville is situated in the north-east of the township, and the village of Otterville in the south, on Otter Creek. There are four grist and seven saw mills in the township.

Population in 1842, 2747, who are principally of American descent, with a few English and Irish.

Ratable property in the township, £42,962.

NORWICHVILLE.

A Village in the east of the township of Norwich, pleasantly situated on Otter Creek—contains about 180 inhabitants.

Post Office, post three times a week.

Professions and Trades.—One physician and surgeon, one grist mill, carding machine and fulling mill, one distillery, one tannery, four stores, two taverns, one chair maker, one waggon maker, one blacksmith, one tailor, one shoemaker.

NORWOOD, or KEELER'S MILLS

A Village in the east of the township of Asphodel, ten miles south-east from Warsaw, and six miles north from the Trent River. It contains about 120 inhabitants. There are some fine lime-stone quarries in the neighbourhood. In Norwood is a Congregational chapel, also a grist and saw mill, tannery, three stores, one tavern, two blacksmiths.

Post Office, post three times a-week.

NORTHUMBERLAND.

A County in the Newcastle District—comprises the townships of Alnwick, Cramahe, Hamilton, Haldimand, South Monaghan, Murray, Percy and Seymour. It returns a member to the House of Assembly.

NOTTAWASAGA.

A Township in the Simcoe District, is bounded on the north by Nottawasaga Bay on the west by the townships of Collingwood and Ospry; on the south by Mulmur and a small portion of Melancthon, and on the east by Sunnidale. In Nottawasaga 18,850 acres are taken up, 1539 of which are under cultivation. The township is well watered by numerous small streams, and a large portion of the township is good land. A village, called Hurontario, has been lately started on the bay, where there are a grist and saw mill, and store. There are large quantities of fine cedar on the bay. There is a quarry in the township, of the stone of which excellent grind-stones are manufactured, lime-stone also is abundant. In Nottawasaga, there are 7900 acres of Crown lands open for sale at 8s. currency per acre. There are three grist and three saw mills in the township.

Population in 1842, 420, who are principally Scotch.

Ratable property in the township, £7877.

NOTTAWASAGA BAY.

A large Bay, situated in the south of the Georgian Bay. It receives the Nottawasaga River.

NOTTAWASAGA RIVER

A River, different branches of which take their rise in the high lands in the townships of Albion, Tecumseth, Mono, Melancthon, Mulmur, and Innisfil; and are spread besides over the townships of Adjala, West Gwillimbury, Essa, Tossorontio, Vespra, Flos, and Sunnidale, in which latter township the river enters the Nottawasaga Bay. The Nottawasaga River is not navigable for large vessels. There is a great deal of excellent land, and fine timber on its banks.

OAKLAND

A Township in the Brock District, is bounded on the north-east by the township of Brantford, on the west by Burford, and on the south by Townsend. In Oakland 9,182 acres are taken up, 5,850 of which are under cultivation. This is a small township, the greater part of it is under cultivation. A large cedar swamp extends from the township of Brantford into the north-west of Oakland, and reaches nearly to the centre of the township. The village of Scotland is situated in the west of the township, close to the town-line between Oakland and Burford, and the village of Oakland a little south of the centre of the township. There are one grist and two saw mills in the township.

Population in 1842, 464, who are principally of Scotch descent.

Ratable property in the township, £12,831.

OAKLAND.

A Village in the south of the township of Oakland, situated on the road leading from Brantford to Simcoe. It contains about 160 inhabitants.

Post Office, post daily.

Professions and Trades.—One grist and saw mill, carding machine and fulling mill, one store, two taverns, one hatter, one waggon maker, one blacksmith, one tailor, one shoemaker.

OAKVILLE.

A Village in the township of Trafalgar, situated on Lake Ontario, at the mouth of Sixteen-mile Creek, sixteen miles west from Toronto. It contains about 550 inhabitants. This is a place of considerable business for its size; about 150,000 bushels of wheat, besides large quantities of lumber, being annually shipped here. Twelve schooners are owned in Oakville; and there are three extensive warehouses for storing grain. Churches and chapels, three; viz., Episcopal, Catholic and Congregational.

Professions and Trades.—One steam grist mill, one water do., one saw mill, one distillery, one physician and surgeon, six stores, one druggist, one threshing-machine maker, three taverns, two waggon makers, five blacksmiths, one watch and clock maker, three cabinet makers, two saddlers, two butchers, two bakers, one tinsmith, four tailors, twelve shoemakers.

OLDEN.

A Township in the Midland District; is bounded on the east by the township of Oso; on the north by Clarendon; on the west by Kennebec; and on the south by Hinchinbrooke. Several lakes are scattered over the township. Olden has only lately been opened for sale, and no return has yet been made from it. Sixty-five thousand acres of Crown lands are open for sale in Olden, at 8s. currency per acre.

OLIVER'S FERRY.

A Ferry across a narrow portion of the Rideau Lake, seven miles from Perth. The road from Brockville to Perth crosses the lake at this point. Here is a small tavern, wharf and storehouse.

ONEIDA.

A Township in the Gore District; is bounded on the north-east by the Grand River; on the north-west by the township of Tuscarora; on the south-west by Walpole; and on the south-east by Cayuga. In Oneida 3,548 acres are taken up, 1,734 of which are under cultivation. The plank road from Hamilton to Port Dover passes through the township; and a portion of the village of Caledonia is situated near the north corner, on the plank road. Most of the timber in the township is pine. There is a bed of excellent gypsum in Oneida, close to the Grand River; it is worked, and a plaster mill is erected close to the bed. The plaster, when ground, is worth about four dollars per ton at the mill. Large quantities are exported for agricultural purposes. This township formerly formed part of the Niagara District; but was separated from it in 1845, and added to the Gore District. When the last census was taken, there was no return from Oneida.

Ratable property in the township, £5,716.

ONONDAGA.

A Township in the Gore District; is bounded on the north-east by the township of Ancaster; on the north-west and west by Brantford; on the south by the Grand River; and on the south-east by Seneca. In Onondaga 2,332 acres are under cultivation (there is no return of the quantity taken up). Onondaga contains good land Timber—a mixture of hardwood and pine. There is one saw mill in the township. This township has been added to the Gore District since the last census was taken, consequently there is no return of the population.

Ratable property in the township, £5,664.

OPS.

A Township in the Colborne District; is bounded on the east by the township of Emily; on the north by Fenelon; on the west by Mariposa, and on the south by Manvers. In Ops 32,024 acres are taken up, 4,379 of which are under cultivation. The Scugog River enters the township about the centre of its northern boundary, and emerges again at its south-west corner, where it enters the Scugog Lake The village of Lindsay is situated on the river, a little north of the centre of the township There are some good farms in the township and one grist and one saw mill. In Ops 6,971 acres of Crown lands are open for sale, at 8s currency per acre.

Ratable property in the township, £14,705

ORFORD

A Township in the Western District, is bounded on the north-east by the township of Aldborough, on the north-west by the River Thames; on the south-west by Howard, and on the south-east by Lake Erie In Orford 16,625 acres are taken up, 3,231 of which are under cultivation The soil of this township is generally of very excellent quality, and the timber consists of the best kinds of hardwood—maple, oak, beech, elm, &c Large quantities of staves are annually exported from the township, the principal part of which is included in the exports from Howard Formerly tobacco was much grown in the township: but the diminution of the duty on tobacco imported from the United States has caused the farmers to discontinue its cultivation, it being a very uncertain crop, and not worth cultivating unless with the certainty of its commanding a good price. In the north of the township, near the Thames, is an Indian settlement, called "Moravian Town," for a description of which see "River Thames" Five hundred and fifty acres of Crown lands are open for sale in Orford, at 8s. currency per acre

Population in 1845, 910, who are a mixture of Canadians, English, Irish, Scotch, and Americans

Ratable property in the township. £9,959

ORILLIA.

A Village in the township of Orillia, situated on Lake Gougichin, nineteen miles from Sturgeon Bay, and twenty-eight from Barrie This was originally an Indian village, and stores were erected by merchants in the immediate vicinity for the convenience of trading with the Indians About six years back the lands were purchased by the government, and the village of Orillia was laid out A road has been cut out by the government from the village to Sturgeon Bay, on Lake Huron, which passes through the village of Coldwater; and during the season of 1845 a regular line of communication was kept up between Toronto and Buffalo, through Lakes Simcoe, Huron, St Clair and Erie The steamboat "Goderich," leaving Windsor and Detroit immediately on the arrival of the "London" from Buffalo, conveyed the passengers to Sturgeon Bay, touching at various places on the River St Clair Goderich, Owen Sound, and Penetanguishene, from thence they took the stage to Orillia, where the steamboat "Beaver" awaited them, and conveyed them to the Holland Landing, whence they took stage to Toronto The "Beaver" remains at Orillia three nights in the week, during her circuit round the lake There is some fine scenery in the neighbourhood, the lake being studded with islands, most of them of small size, and some of them mere rocks, and its shores are much indented with beautiful bays. The neighbourhood of the village is settled principally by emigrants from the old country. There is an Episcopal church in the village, and a comfortable tavern.

Population about 200.

Post Office, post three times a week.

Professions and Trades.—Two physicians and surgeons, four stores, three taverns, one tannery, two blacksmiths, four shoemakers, one tailor, one chair maker, one cabinet maker. There is a grist and saw mill about a mile from the village.

ORILLIA, NORTH AND SOUTH.

Townships in the Simcoe District (which, being but little settled, are at present united for district purposes), are bounded on the north-west by the township of Matchedash, on the south-west by Medonte and Oro, and on the east and south-east by the River Severn, Lake Gougichin and Lake Simcoe. In Orillia 8,081 acres are taken up, 994 of which are under cultivation. These townships are but newly settled, and have hitherto, in common with other townships in the neighbourhood, been kept back for want of good roads. The opening of the government road from Scugog (by the Narrows) to Sturgeon Bay—which road passes through these townships—will have the effect of making them known, and promoting their settlement. The village of Orillia is situated on the lake shore in South Orillia. In North Orillia 26,400 acres of Crown lands are open for sale, at 8s currency per acre. In South Orillia there are none. There are one grist and three saw mills and a tannery in South Orillia.

Population in 1842, 440.

Ratable property in the townships, £5,971.

ORO.

A Township in the Simcoe District; is bounded on the north by the township of Medonte, on the west by Vespra, on the south by Kempenfeldt Bay and Lake Simcoe, and on the east by the township of Orillia. In Oro 31,358 acres are taken up, 4,911 of which are under cultivation. A small lake, called Bass Lake, containing about 1,000 acres, is situated in the north corner of the township, on the town-line between Oro and Orillia. The land bordering on the lake and bay is generally poor and stony, and the timber principally pine. In the interior of the township the land is mostly good, and the timber principally hard wood, still there is a portion of swamp. In Oro 500 acres of Crown Lands are open for sale, at 8s c'y per acre.

Population in 1842, 1190.

Ratable property in the township, £15,306.

ORONO.

A Settlement in the township of Clarke, about five miles north from the village of Newcastle, contains about 100 inhabitants, saw-mill, carding machine, and one store.

OSGOODE.

A Township in the Dalhousie District, is bounded on the north-east by the township of Russell, on the north-west by Gloucester, on the west by North Gower; and on the south-east by Mountain and Winchester. In Osgoode 46,035 acres are taken up, 5,486 of which are under cultivation. The Rideau Canal and River border the township on the west for the greater portion of its depth. At the north-west corner of the township is an island containing about 1,000 acres, formed by two branches of the Rideau River. There is some good, but a large portion of poor land in the township, particularly that bordering on the Rideau Canal. In Osgoode 7,459 acres of Crown lands are open for sale at 8s c'y per acre. There is one saw-mill in the township.

Population in 1842, 1440.

Ratable property in the township, £16,748.

OSHAWA.

A Village in the township of Whitby, situated on the eastern road, thirty-three miles east from Toronto, and three miles from Port Oshawa, on Lake Ontario Oshawa is a place of considerable business, having a good farming country behind it; it contains about 1000 inhabitants. Churches and chapels three, viz., Catholic, Methodist and Christian.

Post Office, post every day.

Professions and Trades—Three physicians and surgeons, two lawyers, two grist-mills (one containing five run of stones), one foundry, one brewery, one carding machine and fulling mill, two distilleries, one ashery, eleven stores, one machine shop, one trip hammer driven by water, one bookseller, one chemist and druggist, one auctioneer, three hatters, seven blacksmiths, four taverns, two watchmakers, five tailors, five shoemakers, one grocery and bakery, one chair factory, four cabinet makers, three waggon makers, one bank agency, "Commercial."

Principal Tavern—"Oshawa House."

Exports from the Port of Oshawa for the year 1844—

Flour	18,690 barrels.
Pork	599 do.
Ashes	544 do.
Oatmeal	819 do.
Whiskey	377 do
Wheat	11,314 bushels.
Oats	2,715 do.
Grass Seed	148 do.
Potatoes	521 do
Lumber	145,000 feet.

OSHAWA HARBOUR

A small shipping-place on Lake Ontario, three miles from the village of Oshawa. There are store-houses for storing produce, one tavern, and houses for the wharfinger and deputy custom-house officer.

OSNABRUCK.

A Township in the Eastern District, is bounded on the north-east by the township of Cornwall, on the north-west by Finch, on the south-west by Williamsburgh, and on the south-east by the St Lawrence. In Osnabruck 45,163 acres are taken up, 12,116 of which are under cultivation. This township is well watered by numerous small streams running through it. It is well settled, and contains good farms. There is a large quantity of pine in the township. The villages of Charlesville, Santa Cruz, and Dickenson's Landing are in the township, and all situated on the St Lawrence, the latter at the head of the Cornwall Canal. One hundred and fifty acres of Crown lands are open for sale in Osnabruck, at 8s currency, per acre. There are two grist and ten saw mills in the township.

Population in 1842, 3623

Ratable property in the township, £45,235

OSO

A Township in the Midland District; is bounded on the east by the townships of North and South Sherbrooke, on the north by Palmerston; on the west by Olden, and on the south by Hinchinbrooke and Bedford. This township has only lately been opened for sale, and no return has yet been made from it. Sixty-five thousand acres of Crown lands are open for sale in the township, at 8s. currency per acre.

OSPRY.

A Township in the Simcoe District, is bounded on the north by the township of Collingwood, on the west by Artemisia, on the south by Melancthon; and on the east by Nottawasaga. This township has been added to the Simcoe District since 1844. It is only just surveyed, and is not yet opened for sale.

OTONABEE.

A Township in the Colborne District, is bounded on the east by the township of Asphodel, on the North by Douro, on the west by the Otonabee River, and on the south by Rice Lake. In Otonabee 42,667 acres are taken up, 10,863 of which are under cultivation. This township is well settled, principally by Scotch emigrants, and contains good farms. Timber—hardwood, intermixed with pine. The village of Keene is situated in the south-east of the township, near Rice Lake, and there is a settlement of Indians in the township, called "Rice Lake Settlement," situated on Rice Lake, about twelve miles from Peterboro'. It is composed of Mississagas, or Chippawas who in the year 1818, surrendered the greater part of the tract now forming the Newcastle District, for an annuity of £740. They have all been reclaimed from their primitive wandering life, and settled in their present location within the last ten or twelve years. The Indians in the settlement, number 114. They possess about 1550 acres of land, which is subdivided into 50 acre lots, of this, 1120 acres were granted in April, 1834, to trustees, "in trust, to hold the same for the benefit of the Indian tribes in the Province, and with a view to their conversion and civilization," and the remaining 430 have been since purchased with their own funds. They have about 400 acres cleared and under cultivation. The village contains thirty houses, three barns, a school-house, and a chapel with a bell. The head chief of the tribe resides here. For some time, these Indians were under the charge of an officer appointed by the Indian Department, who assisted in their settlement, but at present they have no special superintendent. These Indians are Methodists. They have a school, and a schoolmaster is supported by the Methodist Missionary Society.

Six hundred and sixty acres of Crown lands are open for sale in Otonabee, at 8s. currency per acre.

There are in the township, one grist and two saw mills.

Ratable property in the township, £29,154.

OTONABEE RIVER.—(See Rice Lake.)

OTTAWA DISTRICT.

Consists of the Counties of Prescott and Russell. It is the most north-easterly district in the Province, and is bounded on the north by the Ottawa River, on the south by the Eastern District, on the east by a portion of Lower Canada, and on the west by the Dalhousie District. The Petite Nation River runs through the west and centre of the district, and enters the Ottawa in the northwest of the township of Plantagenet, and there are besides several good mill streams in the district.

Much of the land in the front of the Ottawa District is cold and wet; in the rear it is better, but the people of the district are much more extensively engaged in getting out lumber for the Quebec market, than in improving the soil; consequently agricultural operations go on very slowly.

The district is settled by a mixed population, consisting of French Canadians, English Canadians, Scotch, Irish, English, and Americans.

There is no large town in the district, and the principal villages are Hawkesbury and Vankleek Hill, in the township of Hawkesbury, Caledonia, in Caledonia, L'Orignal, the district town, in Longueil, and Hattsfield, in Plantagenet.

In Hawkesbury West is an establishment for sawing lumber, which is the most extensive in Canada West, giving employment to above two hundred hands.

In the Ottawa District, 121,355 acres of Crown lands are open for sale, at 8s. currency per acre; to purchase any of which, application must be made to the Crown lands agent, at Vankleek Hill.

Population of the district in 1842, 7944; since when it has probably increased one-fifth

The following abstract from the assessment rolls, will show the rate of increase and improvement in the district

Date	No of Acres Cultivated	MILLS. Grist.	MILLS. Saw.	Milch Cows	Oxen 4 years old, and upwards	Horned Cattle, from 2 to 4 years old	Amount of Ratable Property
1842	20,659	8	18	2,430	419	943	£ 86,387
1843	21,366	9	21	2,754	431	1,002	178,571
1844	24,141	10	25	2,905	401	.	96,528

Government and District Officers in the Ottawa District

Judge of District Court .... Peter Freel .... . L'Orignal.
Clerk of Peace . ... D McDonald ... . Do.
Inspector of Licenses . .. .. Do
District Clerk .. . .. . Do
Sheriff .... Charles P Treadwell Do
Registrar of County of Prescott. . Geo D Reed ... . Do
Do do Russell Do
Judge of Surrogate Court ... David Pattee . Hawkesbury.
Superintendent of Schools . . Rev C Gregor L Orignal.
Treasurer and Deputy Clerk of Crown Thos H Johnson . Do
Warden .. . . Arch Petrie .. . Cumberland.
{ D McDonald .... Plantagenet.
Coroners .. .. { O Gates ... . Longueil.
{ H Hughes .. Alfred.

Number of Common Schools in operation in the District—East Hawkesbury, nine, West Hawkesbury, eight, Longueil, five, Caledonia, four, Alfred, two; Plantagenet, five, Clarence, one, Russell, one, Cambridge and Cumberland, three. Total, thirty-eight.

OTTAWA RIVER

The second River in point of size and importance in Canada It takes its rise in the unsettled regions to the north, flows to the south and south-east, dividing Upper from Lower Canada and forming the northern boundary of the Bathurst, Dalhousie and Ottawa Districts, and enters the St Lawrence just above the island of Montreal. There are two large islands in the river, the one being called "Back River Island" or "Point Allumet Island," and the other "Grand Calumet Island," both of which are situated in the north of the Bathurst District. Two expansions of the river are called "Lac des Chats," and "Lake Chaudière." The Ottawa has several rapids in it, the descent of which is too great to allow of steamboats or other vessels ascending them. Passengers ascending the river from Montreal are therefore obliged to take stage from Montreal to Lachine, from thence the steamer runs to Point Fortune, where the stage again conveys the passengers to L'Orignal, whence the steamboat takes them to Bytown The steamboats on the Ottawa are of an inferior class to those on the St Lawrence and the lakes, their accommodation is neither equal, nor are they so well found. Much of the scenery on the Ottawa is magnificent, particularly that in the neighbourhood of Bytown The country on the banks of the Ottawa is not generally well adapted for farming; much of the land being of poor quality, and the winter of rather too great length The principal importance of the Ottawa arises from the immense quantity of fine timber cut on its banks, and the banks of its tributaries The principal portion of the timber carried to Great Britain from Canada is conveyed down the Ottawa—the preparing of which gives employment to a great number of hands.

Great improvements have been made in the Ottawa within the last year or two, slides and dams have been constructed at various places to facilitate the passage of lumber down the river, and many obstructions in the course of the stream, such as rocks, &c, have been removed

Previous to making the improvements, goods and supplies for the use of the lumberers, &c, were landed from the steamboat at Portage du Fort (nearly five miles below the foot of the Calumet), and stored there until the canoes, with orders for them, arrived from above The articles were then carted over the Portage du Fort one mile, at a cost of 6d per cwt, and were canoed thence to Miller's Bay. from Miller's Bay they were carted to the Dargee Bay, three miles, at 6d. per cwt, they were again canoed to the foot of the Calumet, less than a mile, and from thence were partly carted, and partly carried by men, to the head of the Calumet, at the rate of 7½d per cwt Canoes are manned at an average in the proportion of one man to every four hundred weight of lading, and a canoe coming down for a load, almost invariably took three days from the time of landing at the head of the Calumet, until it was again loaded and ready to leave on its way upward Each canoe-man, with finding, costs his employer at least 5s per diem, therefore canoe-men forwarding made a cost of 3s 9d per cwt, and, allowing the damage to the bark canoe, which is always subject to much injury from loading and unloading, not to exceed 3d. per cwt, the whole cost of cartage, &c, is 5s 7½d per cwt, whereas, in consequence of the improvement effected last year, supplies, &c, were forwarded over the same portion of the Ottawa at 1s 6d per cwt, being a saving of 4s. 1½d. per cwt, and in this charge of 1s 6d per cwt is included an allowance for a month's storage at the Calumet, when required The difference in transport is therefore 4s 1½d per cwt, and, as the quantity of pork, flour, goods, &c, forwarded during the past season amounted to nearly 364 tons, the saving to the lumber trade at this point, in the matter of forwarding alone, amounts to £1,501 10s.

Amount of expenditure on the Ottawa River for Slides, and a Bridge at Bytown, up to 1st January, 1845

	£	s	d.
Madawaska Slide ..	6,835	15	8
Mountain do	3,282	13	6
Calumet do. ..	8,202	19	1
Joachim do .	3,662	10	9
General expenditure .	2,953	17	3
Travelling expenses	244	15	3
Bridge over the Ottawa, at Bytown	17,143	17	5
	£41,816	14	11

The principal branches of the Ottawa are the Mississippi, the Rideau, Petite Nation, and Madawaska, on the Upper Canadian side, and the River du Moine, River aux Lievres, and Lac des Deux, on the Lower Canadian side

There is no town of any importance on the Ottawa, with the exception of Bytown, which is the head quarters of the lumberers, and just above which are the beautiful Chaudière Falls.

OTTERVILLE.

A Quaker Settlement in the south-east of the township of Norwich, prettily situated on Otter Creek. It contains about 150 inhabitants, one physician and surgeon, two grist mills, one saw mill, one store, one tavern

Post Office, post three times a week

OWEN SOUND

A long narrow Bay jutting into the land from the south-west extremity of the Georgian Bay. The land bordering on it has only lately been laid out and surveyed, but it is settling up fast. On the shores of the Big Bay, a bay of the Sound, is a settlement of Chippewa Indians.

These Indians were formerly either wanderers in the Saugeen tract, surrendered to Sir F. B. Head, or lived in scattered wigwams, on the shores of Big Bay. According to the agreement then made with them, it was proposed that they should either repair to Manitoulin, or to that part of their former territory which lies to the north of Owen's Sound, upon which it was promised that houses should be built for them, and proper assistance given, to enable them to become civilized, and to cultivate land.

In 1842, their present settlement was permanently formed by the erection of fourteen log houses, and a barn, out of the proceeds of their annuity, under the direction of the Indian Department. Their number is 130, and they have about 120 acres of land under cultivation, but from the short time they have settled, and the little experience which they can have yet acquired, it is not probable that they have made much progress in agriculture. In 1842, they were supplied with two yoke of oxen, paid for out of their annuity, and are anticipating an extension of their present plantations. They are Christians, and a Wesleyan Methodist missionary, resident at St. Vincent, twenty-five miles distant, has visited them regularly since October, 1841. A resident missionary was appointed to this settlement last year, by the Canadian Wesleyan Methodist Conference. They have also had a school, conducted by an Indian, and maintained by the same body, since the close of 1842. They share the same annuity as the Chippewas of Saugeen.

OXFORD

A Township in the Johnstown District, is bounded on the north-east by the township of South Gower, on the north-west by Marlborough; on the south-west by Wolford, and on the south-east by Edwardsburg. In Oxford, 42,031 acres are taken up, 9298 of which are under cultivation. The Rideau Canal and River forms the north-western boundary. The land in the south of the township is generally good, and there are some well cultivated farms in it; in the north the land is of inferior quality. Timber—in the south, a mixture of hardwood and pine, in the north, principally pine. In Oxford 800 acres of Crown lands are open for sale, at 8s. currency per acre. There are two grist and seven saw mills in the township.

Population in 1842, 2960.

Ratable property in the township, £31,225.

OXFORD WEST.

A Township in the Brock District, is bounded on the east by the township of East Oxford; on the north-west by North Oxford, and on the south by Dereham. In West Oxford 19,345 acres are taken up, 6410 of which are under cultivation. The east branch of the River Thames separates the township from North Oxford. This is a small township, but it is well settled; the land is generally rolling, and there are some handsome farms in it; the timber is principally pine, intermixed with hardwood. The village of Ingersol is situated in the north-west of the township, and the village of Beachville in the north-east; both near the River Thames. There are three grist and ten saw mills in the township, and large quantities of lumber are exported from it.

Population in 1842, 1321, who are principally Canadians, with a few English, Irish, and Scotch.

Ratable property in the township, £25,396.

OXFORD EAST.

A Township in the Brock District; is bounded on the east by the township of Burford, on the north by Blandford, on the west by West Oxford, and on the south by Norwich. In East Oxford, 21,936 acres are taken up, 5836 of which are under cultivation. This is a small township, but it is pretty well settled. The soil of the north and west of the township is mostly light, and the land is timbered with pine, in the south-east, the timber consists of pine, intermixed with hardwood. There are one grist and three saw mills in the township.

Population in 1842, 1280; who are principally Canadians, with a few English, Irish and Scotch

Ratable property in the township, £19,050

OXFORD, NORTH

A Township in the Brock District, is bounded on the south-east by the township of West Oxford, on the north by Zorra and Nissouri, and on the west by North Dorchester. In North Oxford 9,207 acres are taken up, 1,950 of which are under cultivation. This is a small township, containing excellent land, which is timbered generally with hardwood. There is a large lime-stone quarry in the east corner of the township, which extends into the township of West Oxford. There is one saw mill in the township.

Population in 1842, 444, who are principally European emigrants.

Ratable property in the township, £6,148

PAISLEY BLOCK.

A Scotch Settlement in the township of Guelph. It commences about six miles north-east from the town of Guelph, and extends about four miles in length. The settlement was commenced about seventeen years ago, and it now contains good farms, which are generally well cultivated

PAKENHAM.

A Township in the Bathurst District, is bounded on the north-east by the township of Fitzroy, on the north-west by Macnab, on the south-west by Darling, and on the south-east by Ramsay. In Pakenham 14,014 acres are taken up, 4060 of which are under cultivation. The Mississippi River runs through the east of the township from south to north. The village of Pakenham is situated in the township. Pakenham is well settled, principally by emigrants from Scotland, and contains some good farms. Twenty-four thousand four hundred acres of Crown lands are open for sale in the township, at 8s currency per acre.

Population in 1842, 1142

Ratable property in the township, £12,257.

PAKENHAM

A Village in the township of Pakenham, about forty miles from Bytown, forty from Perth, and ten from Fitzroy Harbour. It contains about 250 inhabitants. Churches and chapels, three, viz, Episcopal, Presbyterian, and Methodist. Post Office, post six times a-week.

Professions and Trades.—One physician and surgeon, one grist and saw mill, carding machine and cloth factory, four stores, one tannery, two taverns, three waggon makers, two cabinet makers, one tinsmith, three tailors, two coopers, four blacksmiths.

PALERMO.

A Village in the township of Trafalgar, situated on Dundas street, thirty miles from Toronto, and eighteen from Hamilton. There is an Episcopal church in the village

Population about 200.

Post Office, post every day.

Professions and Trades—Three stores, one foundry, two taverns, two waggon makers, three blacksmiths, two tailors, two shoemakers.

PARIS

A considerable Village in the south of the township of Dumfries, and partly in Brantford, situated on the Grand River, at the entrance of Smith's Creek. It is twenty-two miles west from Dundas, and twenty-one east from Woodstock, six miles above Brantford, and thirteen miles below Galt Before the formation of the plank road, Paris was on the high road from London to Hamilton, but it is now left a little to the north, and most of the travel passes it. It was laid out in 1830, and was called Paris from the large quantities of gypsum or plaster of Paris found in the immediate neighbourhood It is divided into the upper town and the lower town, the lower town being within the forks of the river, and the upper town a little to the south, on the opposite side of Smith's Creek, in the township of Brantford. The village is beautifully situated, in the midst of a rolling country, most of which was what is called "Oak Plains," and is surrounded by fine, flourishing, well cultivated farms. It is a thriving settlement, and promises to become a place of considerable manufacturing importance, having the advantage of very extensive water power There were exported from the mills at the village, last year, about 1200 tons of plaster (at the price of $4½ per ton), about 1,500,000 feet of lumber, and 120,000 bushels of wheat have been purchased from the crop of 1845 There are five churches and chapels, viz., Episcopal (of stone), Presbyterian, Roman Catholic, Methodist and Baptist.

Paris contains about 1000 inhabitants, who are a mixture of Americans, Scotch, English, and Irish.

Post Office, post three times a-week.

Professions and Trades—Two grist mills (with eight run of stones), one mill for grinding gypsum or plaster of Paris, three physicians and surgeons, three distilleries, one brewery, one woollen factory, one tannery, fulling mill, one saw mill (with two saws), one foundry and plough factory, fourteen dry goods and grocery stores, one druggist, one civil engineer and surveyor, five taverns, one conveyancer, five waggon makers, four cabinet makers, one machine shop, one fanning-mill maker, two chair makers, six blacksmiths, one whitesmith, one gunsmith, one tinsmith, seven joiners, five cooperages (in one of which the staves are cut and dressed by machinery, which is worked by a steam engine), five tailors, seven shoemakers, two schools for young ladies.

Principal Tavern.—"Gross's"

PEACH ISLAND.

An Island situated at the entrance of Lake St Clair, near the Canadian shore—contains about 150 acres, of which about 50 are fit for cultivation. It is used principally as a fishing station

PECHES, RIVIERE AUX.

A small Stream which takes its rise in the township of Sandwich, and enters Lake St. Clair, after running through the north-west corner of Maidstone.

PEEL.

A Township in the Wellington District; is bounded on the north-east by the township of Garafraxa; on the north-west by Maryborough, on the south-west by Wellesley; and on the south-east by Woolwich and Nichol. This township forms part of what was formerly called "Queen's Bush," it has not long been open for settlement, and no return has yet been made from it. It is said to contain about 1000 inhabitants.

PELHAM.

A Township in the Niagara District, is bounded on the east by the township of Thorold; on the north by Louth; on the west by Gainsborough and a small portion of Clinton, and on the south by Wainfleet. In Pelham 26,896 acres are taken up, 11,424 of which are under cultivation. The Chippewa or Welland River, forms the south boundary of the township; and a good mill stream flows through the north-east of the township. Pelham is an old-settled township, and contains good farms and excellent orchards. Timber—pine, intermixed with hardwood. There are three grist and ten saw mills in the township.

Population in 1842, 1,522, who are principally Canadians and Americans.

Ratable property in the township, £34,060.

PELE, POINT.

A Point of Land, part of the township of Mersea, which runs out into Lake Erie.

PEMBROKE.

A Township in the Bathurst District; is bounded on the north and north-west by the Ottawa River; on the west by unsurveyed lands, and on the south by Westmeath and Stafford. This township and Stafford, being as yet but little settled, are assessed together. In the two townships 11,205 acres are taken up, 1,658 of which are under cultivation. Farming produce in these northern townships usually commands a high price, in consequence of the expense of carriage so far up the Ottawa; there being a great demand for produce of all kinds, particularly for hay and oats, for the use of the lumberers on the river. On the whole, however, where the winter is so long, and stock of all kinds must necessarily require so much feeding, farming cannot be very profitable, even with the high prices the produce brings. In Pembroke 1,900 acres of Crown lands are open for sale, at 8s currency per acre. There are one grist and two saw mills in the township.

Population in 1842, 193.

Ratable property in the township, £3,992.

PEMBROKE.

A Village in the north-west of the township of Pembroke, situated on the Ottawa River, at the mouth of the Muskrat River. It is supported entirely by the lumber trade. There is as yet no road to the settlement passable for waggons, but one has been lately surveyed. All goods intended for the settlement are conveyed up the Ottawa. Pembroke contains about 250 inhabitants, one Methodist church, one physician and surgeon, one grist and saw mill, one waggon maker, five stores, six taverns, and two blacksmiths.

Post Office, post once a week.

PENETANGUISHENE.

A Village in the township of Tiny, beautifully situated on Penetanguishene Bay, forty miles from Barrie. Penetanguishene was commenced in the year 1818, in consequence of the government having formed a naval and military establishment on the bay, in the township of Tay, two and a half miles off, at which station the war steamer *Midas* is laid up in ordinary. There are also large barracks, but a very small military establishment is kept up. There is a collector of customs at Penetanguishene, but it is *eleven years* since he had an entry, so I was informed on *good authority*. The inhabitants of the surrounding neighbourhood are nearly all half-French, half-Indian. The principal trade of the place is derived from the government establishment, and the fur trade with the Indians. There is a Catholic church in the village. and an Episcopalian one, half-way between the village and the establishment.

Penetanguishene contains about 120 inhabitants

There are four stores, one grist and two saw mills, one tavern, one blacksmith, one tinsmith, two tailors, two shoemakers. There is also a tavern at the establishment.

PERCH, THE—(*See* RIVIERE AUX PERCHES)

PERCHES, RIVIERE AUX, *or the* PERCH, *as it is generally called.*

Takes its rise in the township of Enniskillen, enters Sarnia at its south-east corner, runs a north-west course till it reaches the west corner of Lake Waywanosh, it emerges from the east corner of the lake, and enters Lake Huron at the north corner of the township of Sarnia.

PERCY.

A Township in the Newcastle District, is bounded on the east by the townships of Seymour and Murray, on the north by the River Trent, on the west by Alnwick and Haldimand, and on the south by Cramahe. In Percy 21,264 acres are taken up, 4,303 of which are under cultivation. A small settlement, called "Percy Mills," is situated in the south-east of the township. The timber in Percy consists of hardwood, intermixed with pine. There are one grist and five saw mills in the township

Population in 1842, 920

Ratable property in the township, £13,813.

PERTH.

The District Town of the Bathurst District situated in the south of the township of Drummond seven miles from the Rideau Canal, forty from Brockville, and by water seventy from Kingston ('There is at present no road to Kingston fit to be travelled by vehicles) Perth is built on a rising ground, on a sandy soil, with a granite foundation, and is consequently dry and healthy. The town occupies a space of 400 acres It was laid out by the government in the year 1816, the streets are wide, and are built at right angles The River Tay runs through the town and is made navigable from Perth to the Rideau Canal, by means of five locks, each ninety-five feet by twenty The canal is eleven miles in length, and enters the Rideau Canal two miles below Oliver's Ferry Barges carrying eighty tons can pass through it. This work was formed by a private company, who received a grant from the government of a portion of the centre of the town of Perth, (an island formed by two branches of the River Tay), towards the expenses of the work This was undertaken about thirteen years since, and cost about £7000

Churches and chapels, seven, viz, Episcopal, two Presbyterian, one Free Church, Catholic, Methodist, and Baptist

The jail and court house is a handsome building of white freestone; and the town contains several good buildings of stone and brick; and one or two ornamented with white marble, which may be procured in any quantity within a few miles of the town

A weekly newspaper is published here—the "Bathurst Courier."

A stage runs three time a-week to Brockville

Population, about 1800

Post Office, post three times a-week.

The following Government and District Offices are kept at Perth:—Judge of District Court, Sheriff, Treasurer, Clerk of Peace, Inspector of Licenses, Crown Lands Agent, Judge of Surrogate Court, Registrar, District Clerk, Clerk of District Court, Superintendent of Schools, Deputy Clerk of Crown.

Professions and Trades.—Three physicians and surgeons, five lawyers, one grist mill, one saw mill, eleven stores, seven taverns, three foundries, four tanneries, three distilleries, one printer, two breweries, two druggists, four saddlers, seven blacksmiths, three tinsmiths, four waggon makers, two watchmakers, seven coopers, one cabinet maker, twelve tailors, fifteen shoemakers, three weavers, one bank agency—"City Bank of Montreal."

Principal Tavern—"Matheson's."

Stage fare to Brockville, 10s. currency.

PETERBOROUGH.

The District Town of the Colborne District, beautifully situated in the north-west of the township of North Monaghan, on the Otonabee River, thirty miles north from Port Hope, and about thirty-four from Cobourg. The town was laid out by government in the year 1826; and property has greatly increased in value within the last few years; so much so, that the few town lots now remaining in the hands of the Crown are valued at from £12 10s. to £300; and £350 was lately paid for a portion of a lot, containing not more than about a tenth of an acre. The town is well laid out, and has a handsome appearance, and is at present very flourishing. A portion of the town, on the east side of the river, is called Peterborough East. There is some fine scenery in the neighbourhood of the town; the land being a succession of hill and dale. During the season, the steamboat "Forester" leaves the town every day for Rice Lake, where it is met by the stage for Port Hope and Cobourg; and during the winter, a stage runs every day from Peterborough to the same places. A gravelled road is in course of construction from Rice Lake to Port Hope.

The jail and court-house is a handsome stone building, erected on a rising ground in the rear of the town. Churches and chapels, seven; viz., Episcopal (stone), Presbyterian (stone), Catholic (stone), Baptist (brick), British Wesleyan, Canadian Wesleyan, and Christian.

There is in Peterborough a fire company, with one engine. Two newspapers are published here weekly—the *Peterborough Gazette* and *Peterborough Chronicle*.

Population about 2,000.

Post Office. post every day.

The following Government and District Offices are kept in Peterborough:—Judge of District Court, Sheriff, Clerk of Peace, Inspector of Licenses, Crown Lands Agent, District Clerk, Clerk of District Court, Deputy Clerk of Crown, Treasurer, Registrar.

Professions and Trades.—Four physicians and surgeons, five lawyers, two grist mills, two saw mills, one brewery, one ashery, two distilleries, three foundries, three tanneries, thirty stores, two druggists, five taverns, one woollen factory, one carding machine and fulling mill, two surveyors, four chair factories, one fanning-mill maker, five saddlers, two tinsmiths, one pearl ashery, two watchmakers, six waggon makers, five bakers, four cabinet makers, three coopers, thirteen blacksmiths, four butchers, two millwrights, eighteen shoemakers, twelve tailors, one weaver, one gunsmith, one school, one veterinary surgeon, one bank agency—"Montreal."

Principal Taverns.—"Albert House," and "Union Hotel."

PETITE NATION RIVER.

Takes its rise in the township of Osgoode; flows south to near the south border of Mountain, where it makes a bend to the north-east, and passes through the south of that township, the south-east of Winchester, and the west of Finch;

in the south of Cambridge it receives a branch which takes its rise in the north of Osgoode, and flows through the centre of Russell After receiving this branch, the Petite Nation River passes through the centre of Cambridge, running nearly north; at the north corner of the township it receives a branch from Gloucester, Cumberland, and Clarence, and flows north-east to near the south-east corner of Plantagenet, where it makes a bend, and runs north-west to the Ottawa River, which it enters near the north-west corner of Plantagenet. Large quantities of lumber are cut on its banks, which is mostly carried down the Ottawa.

PHILLIPSVILLE.

A small Village situated in the south-west of the centre of the township of Bastard It contains about forty inhabitants, one store, one tavern, and one blacksmith.

PIGEON LAKE. (*See* RICE LAKE).

PICKERING.

A Township in the Home District; is bounded on the north by the township of Uxbridge, on the west by Markham and Scarborough, on the east by Whitby, and on the south by Lake Ontario In Pickering 63,061 acres are taken up, 24,551 of which are under cultivation. The land in the interior of the township is rather hilly, and the timber of a large proportion of it is pine At the entrance of Duffin's Creek, which runs through the township, is a bay called Big Bay (also called Frenchman's Bay, from a battle said to have been fought on its banks between the old French settlers and the Indians), about three miles in circumference, with a depth of from two to three fathoms it is separated from the lake by a narrow sand bar, through which a channel is sometimes formed having a depth of six feet of water. In Pickering are four grist and twenty-one saw mills, from which latter were exported last year about 3,000,000 feet of lumber.

Population in 1842, 3752.
Ratable property in the township, £62,894.

PICTON.

The District Town of the Prince Edward District, in the township of Hallowell, pleasantly situated on the banks of the Bay of Quinte. The principal part of the town is built about half a mile back from the bay, on gently rising ground A narrow arm of the bay divides the town into two portions; and, being marshy, makes that part of the town bordering on it rather unhealthy at seasons, which might easily be remedied by dredging and deepening the channel. Picton is an old-settled town, and is a place of considerable business it possesses many excellent houses, several of which are built of stone. The jail and court-house is a handsome cut-stone building, enclosed with a stone wall, surmounted by iron railings, with iron gate, the appearance of which is light and elegant. During the season of navigation, two steamboats call at Picton daily, on their passages to and from Kingston and Trent There are four churches and chapels, viz., Episcopal, Presbyterian, Catholic and Methodist There is also a fire and hook and ladder company, with one engine, and a circulating library.

Two newspapers are published here weekly—the "Prince Edward Gazette," and "Picton Sun"

Post Office, post every day.
Population about 1,200.

The following Government and District Offices are kept in Picton —Judge of District Court, Sheriff, Clerk of Peace, Treasurer, Inspector of Licenses, Collector of Customs, Crown Lands Agent, District Clerk, Clerk of District Court, Deputy Clerk of Crown, and Superintendent of Schools.

Professions and Trades.—Three physicians and surgeons, four lawyers, one apothecary, thirteen stores, one brewery, one distillery, three tanneries, two saw mills, two printers, two booksellers, two foundries, two asheries, six taverns, four saddlers, six blacksmiths, three waggon makers, two bakers, one hatter, two watchmakers, five shoemakers, seven tailors, three cabinet makers, two tinsmiths, two butchers, one school, two bank agencies—"Commercial," and "Montreal"

Principal Taverns—"Ketchum's" and "Church's"

Exports from Picton during the year 1844.

Description.	Quantity
Wheat	25,169 bushels
Flour	5,649 barrels
Pork	423 do.
Ashes	138 do.
Peas	1,703 bushels
Barley	2,946 do.
Rye	1,302 do.
Buckwheat	2,960 do.
Indian Corn	760 do.
Coarse Grain	11,053 do.
Fish	250 barrels.
Leather	3,000 sides
Butter	5,000 lbs.

PITTSBURGH.

A Township in the Midland District, is bounded on the east by the township of Leeds; on the north by Bedford and South Crosby, on the west by Loughborough and Kingston; and on the south by Lake Ontario. In Pittsburgh 37,433 acres are taken up, 6,231 of which are under cultivation. The Rideau Canal runs across the township, from north-east to south-west, a navigable channel having been made through the Cataraqui River and a chain of lakes in the north of the township. Most of the land through which the canal passes is unfit for cultivation, the high ground being composed principally of granite rocks, and the low ground being generally flooded. There are three saw mills in the township. Two thousand four hundred acres of Crown lands are open for sale in Pittsburgh, at 8s. currency per acre.

Population, 2,132.

Ratable property in the township, £24,160.

PLANTAGENET.

A Township in the Ottawa District, is bounded on the east by the township of Alfred, on the north by the Ottawa River, on the west by Clarence and Cambridge; and on the south and south-east by Roxborough and Caledonia. In Plantagenet 18,075 acres are taken up, 2,356 of which are under cultivation. This is a large township, extending back the whole depth of the Ottawa District. It is divided into Plantagenet in front, and Plantagenet in rear. The Petite Nation River enters the township near its north-west corner, runs across the township, in a south-easterly direction, till it reaches the eastern border, where it makes a bend, and flows west, and a little south, to the north-east corner of Cambridge, which township it enters. Plantagenet is as yet but little settled—24,616 acres of Crown lands are open for sale in it, at 8s. currency per acre. There is one grist mill and one saw mill in the township.

Population in 1842, 934.

Ratable property in the township, £10,589.

PLYMPTON.

A Township in the County of Kent; is bounded on the north by Lake Huron; on the west by Sarnia, on the south by Warwick; and on the north-east by Bosanquet. In Plympton 19,484 acres are taken up, of which 2,516 are under cultivation The soil and timber of this township are of a very fine quality; the land being generally rich, and the timber the best kinds of hardwood. Large quantities of potash have been made in Plympton in the last two years, which is generally found to more than pay the expense of clearing the land. During 1845 a very large quantity will have been made. A water grist mill has recently been erected at the north-eastern extremity of the township, on the lake shore. There are several good mill sites in this township One thousand three hundred acres of Crown lands are open for sale in Plympton at 8s currency per acre; and of private individuals land is to be purchased at from two to three dollars per acre.

Population of Plympton, 639.
Ratable property in the township, 7,959.
There are in the township one blacksmith, one grist mill, two shoemakers.

POINT PELE ISLAND.

An Island in Lake Erie, opposite Point Pele, and about seven miles from it. It is about seven or eight miles in length, and averaging two in breadth. It has never been surveyed, consequently the number of acres it contains is not known About half the island is fit for cultivation, but at present only about 600 acres are under cultivation. Contains about fifty inhabitants The island is well supplied with red cedar, and possesses a fine lime-stone quarry. There is a grist-mill on the island, and a light-house on the north-east point.

POINT EDWARD —(*See* SARNIA.)

PORT BURWELL.

A Village in the township of Bayham, beautifully situated at the mouth of Otter Creek, on Lake Erie. It was settled about ten years since, and now contains about 200 inhabitants. A light-house has been erected on the high bank overlooking the lake, and a collector of customs is resident here. There is an Episcopal Church in the village.

Post office, post twice a week

Professions and Trades —Three stores, one tannery, two taverns, one waggon maker, one blacksmith, one painter, one tailor, one shoemaker, one cabinet-maker. About 3,000,000 feet of sawed lumber are annually exported from the different saw mills on the creek.

PORT COLBORNE.

A Village in the Township of Humberstone, situated on Lake Erie, at the mouth of the feeder of the Welland Canal; it is a port of entry, and has a resident collector of customs Population about 150.

Post office, post three times a week

Professions and Trades —Steam grist mill (not at present in operation), one store, three taverns, one baker, one grocery, one shoemaker.

PORT CREDIT

A Village on Lake Ontario, situated at the mouth of the Credit River, fourteen miles west of Toronto, and two and a half from Dundas Street. It was laid out in 1834 by government, and is the shipping port for the surrounding country It possesses a good harbour, which might be improved so as to be capable of affording refuge to almost any number of vessels. The harbour was made by a joint-stock company, at an expense of £2,500. Of the stock, the Indians at the adjacent village possess £1,350. They have also a warehouse at the port. This port would be of far more advantage to the surrounding neighbourhood, if the road from the village to Dundas Street was macadamised or planked, and the expense would be trifling. The quantity of farming produce and lumber shipped at the port is very great, and would be much greater if the road was in better condition. Several vessels have been built here; and five schooners of a good class are owned in the place. The steamers Eclipse and Queen call here on their passages to and from Hamilton and Toronto. The land in the neighbourhood of the village, extending for one mile on each side of the river, comprising 4,600 acres, is Indian reserve, belonging to the Nassisagua Indians. They have a village about two miles from Port Credit, which was built for them in 1825 by the Government. They have a Methodist chapel and a school attached. Port Credit contains about 150 inhabitants and a Methodist chapel.

Post office, post every day.

Professions and Trades.—Two stores, two taverns, one blacksmith, one shoemaker, one waggon maker, one tailor

Exports from Port Credit during the year 1844

Wheat	49,100 Bushels.
Flour	6,445 Barrels.
Pork	76 Do.
Ashes	32 Do.
Whiskey	12 Do.
Timothy Seed	43 Do.
Wool	59 Cwt.
Square Timber, Oak and Pine	278,800 Feet.
Lumber	1,433,369 Do.

PORT DALHOUSIE

The entrance of the Welland Canal from Lake Ontario. A harbour has been formed, having a basin of 500 acres in extent, with a depth of water of from twelve to sixteen feet. There is a small village on the east side of the canal, in the township of Grantham, five miles from St. Catharine's, where is a ship yard. Port Dalhousie contains about 200 inhabitants, two stores, one tavern, two blacksmiths.

PORT DOVER

A Village in the township of Woodhouse, situated on Lake Erie, at the mouth of the River Lynn. It was first laid out in the year 1835, but on account of the stagnation in the business of the province caused by the rebellion, it did not begin to increase till about 1842. About £9,000 have been expended in improving the harbour, erecting a light-house, and building a bridge across the river. Six or seven hundred pounds more are required to complete the works. A road has been formed from Port Dover to Hamilton (distance thirty-six and a half miles, four and a half of which are macadamized, and the remainder planked. Two daily stages run to Hamilton (fare 5s. currency), and during the season, steamboats call here regularly. There is a grammar school in the village, and a Presbyterian church in course of erection. Village lots sell at from £20. to £75. c'y.

Population nearly 400

Post office, post every day.

Professions and Trades.—One physician and surgeon, one brewery, five stores, two tanneries, one foundry, four taverns, two saddlers, four tailors, one baker, five shoemakers, two cabinet makers, three blacksmiths, two butchers, two waggon-makers.

Principal Taverns.—" North American," and " Royal Exchange "

There is a grist and saw mill on Paterson's Creek, about three quarters of a mile from the village.

PORT HOPE.

A Town in the south-east corner of the township of Hope, beautifully situated on Lake Ontario. The principal part of the town is built on the sides of a hill, having a fine view of the lake, and the surrounding country. The road from Toronto to Kingston passes through the town. A fine, rapid mill-stream runs through the town to the lake, at the mouth of which is a large basin, forming a natural harbour of considerable size, and well sheltered on the west and north. At present the greater portion of it is a mere marsh, having a branch of the stream passing on each side of it, but it might with ease be cleared out, when it would form a harbour capable of admitting and protecting any vessel on the lake. The town is incorporated, and is improving rapidly, and some very handsome buildings are in course of erection. The Toronto and Kingston stages pass through the town, and during the season of navigation, steamboats call daily on their passages to and from Toronto, Kingston and Rochester. A weekly newspaper the "Port Hope Gazette" was published here, but it has lately been discontinued. Churches and chapels four, viz Episcopal, Presbyterian, Catholic and Methodist.

Population about 1,200

The following Government and District Offices are kept in Port Hope:—Clerk of Peace, Registrar of County of Durham, Judge of Surrogate Court, Registrar of do, Crown Lands Agent.

Professions and Trades.—Four physicians and surgeons, three lawyers, one grist mill, (and a large stone grist mill in course of erection), one foundry, one brewery, four tanneries, five distilleries, one ashery, eighteen stores, six taverns, one surveyor, one druggist, one bookseller, four bakers, one livery stable, one printer, four waggon makers, two cabinet makers, one watchmaker, seven blacksmiths, three tinsmiths, eleven tailors, ten shoemakers, four saddlers, one school for boys, two ladies' seminaries, two bank agencies—"Upper Canada" and "Montreal."

Principal Taverns.—"Hastings' Hotel," and "North American."

Exports from Port Hope during the Year 1844.

Wheat	58,099	Bushels.
Potatoes	120	Do.
Flour	8,454	Barrels.
Potash	237	Do.
Pork	159	Do.
Beef	5	Do.
Timothy Seed	152	Do.
Whiskey	429	Casks.
Pipe Staves	5.130	
Shingles	78	Thousand.
Sawed Lumber	91,000	Feet.
Rags	10	Tons.
Butter	25	Kegs.
Do	22	Firkins.

PORTLAND.

A Township in the Midland District, is bounded on the east by the township of Loughborough; on the north by Hinchinbrooke, on the west by Camden and Ernestown, and on the south by Kingston. In Portland 23,030 acres are taken up, 6359 of which are under cultivation. A chain of lakes runs through the north of the township. The land in Portland is of mixed quality. Timber—pine, intermixed with hardwood.

Population in 1842, 1525

Ratable property in the township, £16,842.

PORTLAND.

A small Village in the north of the township of Bastard, situated on the south of Rideau Lake. It contains about 80 inhabitants, tannery, three stores, two taverns, one blacksmith.

Post Office, post twice a week.

PORT MAITLAND.

A Settlement and Shipping-place at the mouth of the Grand River, on Lake Erie. It contains about 50 inhabitants, and an Episcopal church, two stores, two taverns, one tailor, one blacksmith.

PORT NELSON.

A small Village in the township of Nelson, a mile and a half from Wellington Square. It contains about 60 inhabitants, one store, one tavern, one shoemaker.

PORT ROYAL.

A Settlement in the township of Walsingham, at the mouth of Big Creek, two miles and a half west from Port Rowan. It contains about 50 inhabitants, steam saw mill, one store, two taverns, one blacksmith, one waggon maker.

PORT RYERSE

A small Settlement and Shipping-place in the township of Woodhouse, at the mouth of Ryerse's Creek, six miles from Simcoe, and four miles from Port Dover. It contains a saw mill, one store, and about half a dozen houses.

PORT ROWAN.

A small Village in the township of Walsingham, situated on Lake Erie, four miles west of St Williams. It is a shipping-place, and has a resident collector of Customs. Population about 50. Post Office, post twice a week, one store, one tavern.

PORT ROBINSON.

A Village in the township of Thorold, situated on the Welland Canal, ten miles from St. Catharines. This place is the "head quarters" of the coloured company employed for the maintenance of order on the canal. There are two churches in the village, Episcopal and Presbyterian.

Population, about 300

Post Office, post three times a-week.

Professions and Trades.—One grist mill, three stores, three taverns, one saddler, one baker, three groceries, two waggon makers, one watchmaker, two blacksmiths, one tinsmith, three tailors, two shoemakers.

PORT STANLEY.

A Village on Lake Erie, at the mouth of Kettle Creek, situated partly in the township of Southwold, and partly in Yarmouth; the township being divided by Kettle Creek. It is nine miles from St. Thomas, and twenty-six from London, a plank road being formed between the two places. Port Stanley is beautifully situated, being in a valley surrounded by high and picturesque hills, and its harbour is well protected.

Churches and chapels, two, viz., Episcopal and Congregational

Population, about 500.

Post Office, post three times a week.

Professions and Trades.—One grist mill, one tannery, four stores, three groceries, two bakers, two waggon makers, three cabinet makers, three tailors, one blacksmith, three taverns, three shoemakers, three butchers. Two bank agencies—"Montreal" and "Commercial."

Forwarders and Commission Agents.—H B. Bostwick, G R. Williams, Alex. Hodge & Co.

Exports from Port Stanley, during the season of 1844.

Articles	Quantity.	Rate	Estimated Value.
			£ s d.
Wheat	23186	bushels,	4065 17 9
Flour	4984	barrels,	5147 11 3
Potatoes	60	bushels,	3 0 0
Ashes	74	kegs,	111 0 0
Do.	119	barrels,	523 0 0
Pork	504	do.	1008 0 0
Beef	200	do.	300 0 0
Lard	17	do.	42 10 0
Do	12	kegs	15 0 0
Butter	77	do.	120 10 0
Barley	1108	bushels.	110 16 0
Rags	......	barrel bulk,	58 0 0
Grass Seeds	52	barrels.	26 0 0
Skins	166	barrel bulk,	498 0 0
Peas	2	barrels,	0 7 6
Whiskey	17	do.	25 10 0
Cranberries	8	do.	5 0 0
Walnut lumber	63273	feet,	158 3 8
			12218 6 2

PRESCOTT.

The County Town of the county of Grenville, in the township of Augusta, situated on a rising ground on the banks of the St Lawrence, twelve miles east from Brockville, and opposite the American town, Ogdensburgh. The eastern road runs through it. This was a place of considerable trade previous to the opening of the Rideau Canal, since when it has increased very slowly. It was incorporated in the year 1834, and now contains about 2000 inhabitants. There are in Prescott four churches and chapels, viz, Episcopal, Free Church, Catholic, and Methodist. There is also a custom house. A company of Canadian Rifles and a few Artillerymen are stationed here, and a steam ferry boat plies between Prescott and Ogdensburgh. The St Lawrence is here about one mile and a quarter across. The office of the Registrar for the county of Grenville is kept here. A considerable quantity of pot and pearl ash is exported.

Post Office, post every day.

Professions and Trades.—Four physicians and surgeons, three lawyers, one notary public, one brewery, three distilleries, two tanneries, twelve stores (two of which also sell drugs), one ashery, one steam grist mill, eleven groceries, eight taverns, two saddlers, two watchmakers, one pottery, one axe factory, two livery stables, two bakers, two tinsmiths, four masons, three waggon makers, one hatter, one confectioner, two tallow chandlers, four coopers, two cabinet makers, six tailors, three butchers.

Principal Taverns.—" Commercial," and " North American "

Forwarders and Commission Merchants.—Hooke, Holter & Co.; Macpherson, Crane & Co., Pioneer Steamboat Company; S Fraser.

PRESCOTT.

A County in the Ottawa District, comprises the townships of Alfred, Caledonia, East Hawkesbury, West Hawkesbury, Longueil, and Plantagenet. It returns a member to the House of Assembly.

PRESTON.

A Village in the township of Waterloo, three miles from Galt and fourteen from Guelph—was laid out in 1834—contains about 600 inhabitants, who are principally Germans. There are two churches, viz,, one Lutheran and one Catholic.

Post Office, post every day.

Professions and Trades.—One steam grist mill and distillery, one tannery, two stores, four taverns, three breweries, one pottery, one grocery and drug store, three saddlers, two waggon makers, one baker, eight shoemakers, one watchmaker, one tinsmith, three cabinet makers, one cooper, five tailors

PRESQU' ISLE HARBOUR

A natural Harbour of Lake Ontario, formed by a large bay running into the land. It is capable of affording excellent shelter for vessels. It is situated nearly opposite the village of Brighton.

PRINCE ALBERT.

A Village in the township of Reach, situated a little east of the centre of the township, about fourteen miles north from Oshawa. The Post Office for the township of Reach is kept here, post every Thursday

Population, about 200

There is in the village a Methodist church, five stores, two taverns, two asheries, one blacksmith, one waggon maker, two shoemakers, two tailors

PRINCE EDWARD DISTRICT

Consists of the County of Prince Edward, which comprises the following townships—Athol, Ameliasburgh, Hallowell, Hillier, Marysburgh, and Sophiasburgh. This is the smallest district in the Province, and is nearly surrounded by the waters of Lake Ontario and the Bay of Quinté. It is very irregularly shaped, and its shores are indented by numerous bays. The land in the district is generally rolling, and much of it is of very good quality. The timber is for the most part hardwood, with occasionally a little pine, and here and there, on the shore of the lake, some very fine cedar is to be found

The Prince Edward District was originally settled by U E Loyalists, or persons who fought on the side of Great Britain during the American war, and is now held by them and their descendants. There is also a number of Pennsylvanian Dutch, and a few English, Irish, and Scotch. They are generally in comfortable circumstances, and many of them are wealthy. The greater part of the district is under cultivation, and many of the farms are very handsomely situated. There is no river of any magnitude in the district, but there are several good mill streams, which take their rise in the high land in the centre of the district. Lime stone of excellent quality is abundant. The land on the northern border of the district generally ascends with a gentle slope from the bay

Picton, the district town, is very handsomely situated on the Bay of Quinté, in the township of Hallowell. It is the only town of any size in the district; but there are also the villages of Wellington and Consecon, in Hillier, Milford, in Marysburgh, Bloomfield, in Athol, and Demorestville, in Sophiasburgh Besides which, there are numerous small shipping-places on the bay and lake.

There are no Crown lands for sale in the Prince Edward District, all the land in the district being in the hands of private individuals.

The population of the district probably amounts to about 16,000; but the census was so badly taken in some of the townships, that no dependence was to be placed on it.

The following abstract from the assessment rolls will show the rate of increase and improvement in the district.

Date.	No. of Acres Cultivated.	MILLS. Grist.	MILLS. Saw.	Milch Cows.	Oxen, 4 years old, and upwards	Horned Cattle, from 2 to 4 years old.	Amount of Ratable Property.
1842	86,767	22	42	6599	923	2383	£248,900
1843	90,310	20	47	6974	996	2715	258,888
1844	91,139	19	48	7014	981	1997	259,198

Government and District Officers in the Prince Edward District:

Judge of District Court	Arch. Gilkison	Picton.
Sheriff	Owen McMahon	Do.
Treasurer	D. Smith	Do.
Clerk of Peace	D. L. Fairfield	Do.
Clerk of District Court	Cecil Mortimer	Do.
Deputy Clerk of Crown		Do.
Registrar of Surrogate Court	Samuel Merrill	Do.
Inspector of Licenses	Adam Hubbs	Do.
Collector of Customs	Wm. Rorke	Do.
Coroners	Thomas Moore	Do.
	Paul E. Washburn	Do.
	Reuben Young	Do.
District Superintendent of Schools	Thomas Donelly	Do.
Crown Lands Agent	Wm. Rorke	Do.

In consequence of the absence of the superintendent, I was unable to obtain any statement respecting the number of common schools in operation in the district.

PRINCETON.

A Village on the road from Woodstock to Paris, situated on Homer's Creek, a branch of the Grand River, being partly in the township of Blenheim, and partly in Burford. It contains about 150 inhabitants, and an Episcopal church, a saw mill, one store, two taverns, one blacksmith, one tailor, two shoemakers.

Post Office, post three times a week.

PROTON.

A Township in the Wellington District; is bounded on the east by the township of Melancthon; on the north by Artemisia; on the west by Egremont; and on the south by Luther. This township has only lately been surveyed and laid out, and no return has yet been made from it.

PUCES, RIVIERE AUX.

Takes its rise in the south-west of Maidstone, and enters Lake St. Clair, about four miles west of Belle River.

PUSLINCH.

A Township in the Wellington District; is bounded on the north-east by Nassagaweya; on the north-west by the township of Guelph; on the west by

Waterloo; and on the south and south-east by Beverly and Flamborough. In Puslinch 50,653 acres are taken up, of which 13,140 are under cultivation. There are two lakes in the township, about nine miles from Guelph—one of which contains between 4 and 500 acres—the other at a distance of a quarter of a mile, contains about 50 acres. The land between the lakes is marshy. There are two small islands in the larger lake. There are five saw mills in the township.

Population in 1841, 1500; who are principally Highland Scotch.

Ratable property in the township, £59,806.

QUEENSTON.

A Village in the township of Niagara, seven miles from the town of Niagara, seven miles from the Falls, and forty-seven miles from Hamilton. It is pleasantly situated on the Niagara River, below the Heights, and opposite the American village "Lewiston." Before the opening of the Welland Canal, Queenston was a place of considerable business, being one of the principal depots for merchandise intended for the west, and also for storing grain: as much as forty or fifty thousand bushels of wheat have been shipped here in a season, which now finds its way by the Welland Canal. A rail-road from Queenston to Chippewa, nine miles in length, which cost about £19,000, was commenced in 1835 by a company of proprietors, and completed in 1841. A single line of rails was laid down, which passes close to, and above the Falls of Niagara; and during the summer the cars run daily, (fare to Chippewa, 2s. 6d. currency), and steamboats from Buffalo meet the cars at Chippewa. A telegraphic communication is about being established with Lewiston; and a macadamized road is being formed to St. Catharines. A horse ferry-boat plies across the river from Queenston to Lewiston. A handsome monument was erected on the Heights above the village, to the memory of the late General Brock, who was killed here on the 13th October, 1812, while repelling an invading army of Americans. This monument was blown up by some scoundrel during a night in the beginning of April, 1841. A subscription has since been raised for the purpose of rebuilding it; but the work is not yet commenced. The Niagara River at Queenston is only about 600 feet in width. The banks above the town are 230 feet in height; and, below the Heights, they are only about 70 feet. From the Heights above the town a very fine view may be obtained of the surrounding country. The Niagara River is supposed at one time to have been precipitated over these Heights, instead of where the Falls now are. During the season, boats ply here regularly from Toronto, and stages run from Hamilton to meet the boats. A party of Rifles are stationed at Queenston. Churches and chapels—Episcopal (gone to decay), Baptist, and Presbyterian (not completed); Methodists use the school room.

Post Office, post every day.

Population about 300.

Professions and Trades.—One lawyer, one tannery, three stores, eight taverns, one waggon maker, two blacksmiths, one baker, four shoemakers, one tailor.

Principal Tavern—" Queenston Hotel."

QUEENSVILLE.

A small Village two miles above Sharon, in the township of East Gwillimbury; contains about fifty inhabitants, two stores, one ashery, one blacksmith, one shoemaker, one pump maker.

QUINTE, BAY OF.

Is, properly speaking, an expansion of the River Trent; at the mouth of which River it commences. It is very irregularly shaped, and forms the northern boundary of the Prince Edward District; and enters Lake Ontario a little west of Amherst Island. In its course it receives the Moira, Salmon and Napanee

Rivers, and several smaller streams. There is a great deal of fine land on its banks, but some parts of its borders are rather marshy. The towns of Belleville and Picton are situated on the bay; the former in the Victoria, and the latter in the Prince Edward, District. There is also on the bay, in the township of Tyendenaga, a settlement of Mohawk Indians.

These Indians separated from the Mohawk nation and settled in their present locality about the year 1784. In 1793 they received from the Crown a grant of land, containing about 92,700 acres; but of this, in 1820, they surrendered 33,280 acres, in exchange for an annuity of £450. Their estate was then reduced to 59,400 acres. From this the surveyor general deducts 14,773 acres for crown and clergy reserves; viz., 6,858 for the former, and 7,915 for the latter. In December 1835 they made a further surrender of 27,857 acres, in trust, to be disposed of for their benefit; so that their present possessions do not exceed 16,800 acres.

The Indians live for the most part in detached farms, scattered over the reserve. Their present number is 383. They have 1,368 acres of land cleared, and about 500 acres under tillage. Some of them cultivate considerable quantities of land, so much as fifty acres; but in general the quantity is much less. There have been some instances of successful industry and thriftiness in this community. One of their chiefs, named Hill, who died a few years ago, was remarkable for his industrious habits, and for a desire to accumulate property. Besides his own homestead, to the cultivation and improvement of which he paid more than ordinary attention, he became possessed, by purchase, of some of the farms and improvements of other Indians; and at his death, left them, by will, to particular members of his family, who are at this day in full enjoyment of them.

One of his sons, who is catechist to the missionary at the settlement, recently applied for a loan to enable him to build a wharf and commence business as a general trader among his brethren, in partnership with a white man. They possess stock and agricultural implements corresponding to their progress in husbandry. Some of them grow a considerable surplus of grain for sale.

These Indians have long been Christians, probably before their arrival in Canada. A missionary was first appointed to the settlement in 1810, by the Society for the Propagation of the Gospel in Foreign Parts: their present missionary has been among them eleven years, and reports that, during that period, they have made a gradual advance in morals, piety, and industry.

Their church having become too small for the congregation, they are now engaged in the erection of a new and commodious stone edifice, the expense of which will be defrayed out of their own funds.

Some of the young men are employed in quarrying and carrying the materials for this building.

They support a schoolmaster out of the produce of certain small rents, which they receive and manage themselves.

RAINHAM.

A Township in the Talbot District; is bounded on the north-east by the township of Cayuga; on the west by Walpole; and on the south by Lake Erie. In Rainham 16,724 acres are taken up, 5,354 of which are under cultivation. This is a small township, containing good land and some well-cleared farms. Timber—mostly hardwood. It is well watered by numerous small streams running across it.

Population in 1841, 716.

Ratable property in the township, £13,838.

RALEIGH.

A Township in the County of Kent; is bounded on the north by the River Thames; on the west by Tilbury East; on the south by Lake Erie; and on the north-east by the township of Harwich. In Raleigh 33,151 acres are taken up, of which 5,569 are under cultivation. This township is improving fast. The portion of it lying along the bank of the Thames, as also the neighbourhood through which the Talbot Road passes, are well settled and cultivated. An extensive prairie, running parallel with the Thames, at a distance of from half a mile to a mile, and of an average width of from three to four miles, runs through nearly the whole length of this township, commencing about three miles below the town of Chatham, it requires considerable draining, and is at present used by the farmers in the neighbourhood principally for grazing cattle Near Erieus, on Talbot Road, is a steam mill   Soil and timber generally about the same as Harwich. In Raleigh 4,400 acres of Crown lands are open for sale, at 8s. currency per acre, and the Canada Company have about 6,500 acres.

Two branches of the River Thames run through this township, one of which enters the Thames about three miles below Chatham; the other joins it in Tilbury East, about a mile and a half below the town line

Number of inhabitants, 1,877.

Ratable property in the township, £20,427.

Exports from Raleigh (at Lake Erie), for the year 1844.

	£.	s.	d.
3,400 bushels Wheat, valued at	637	10	0
1,500 do. Indian Corn	140	12	6
32 hogsheads Tobacco	192	0	0
50,000 Standard Staves	562	10	0

Tobacco has been sold from this township at from 6d to 7d sterling per pound.

RAMA.

A Township in the Home District, is bounded on the east and north by unsurveyed lands; on the west by the Severn River and Lake Gougichin; and on the south by the township of Mara   In Rama 616 acres are taken up, 70 of which are under cultivation   In the west of the township, near the lake, is a bed of remarkably fine grey limestone, specimens of which have been sent to England for examination, it having the appearance of that kind of stone used for lithographic purposes, but it has not yet been sufficiently tested.

In the west of the township, on the lake, is a settlement of Chippewa Indians, who formerly occupied the lands about Lake Simcoe, Holland River, and the unsettled country in the rear of the Home District. In 1830 Sir John Colborne, then Lieutenant Governor, collected them on a tract of land on the north-west shore of Lake Simcoe, of 9,800 acres in extent, where they cleared a road between that lake and Lake Huron. They consisted of three tribes of Chippewas, under the chiefs Yellowhead, Aisance and Snake; and a band of Pottawotamies from Drummond Island. Their number was about 500, and they were placed under the care of Mr. Anderson (lately superintendent at Manitoulin Island), under whose superintendence they made rapid progress   The tribe under the chief Yellowhead, now settled at Rama, was located at the Narrows of Lake Simcoe (where the village of Orillia now stands)   Aisance's tribe, at present residing at Beausoleil, Matchadash Bay, was settled at Coldwater, at the other extremity of the reserve; the distance between them being fourteen miles.

"Prior to the year 1830," says Mr. Anderson in his report, "these tribes had become much demoralized from their long residence near the white settlements. They were in the constant habit of drinking spirituous liquors to excess: not one of them could read or write; and they scarcely knew anything of religion. Their hunting grounds were exhausted, the government presents were exchanged for whiskey. They were in debt to all the traders, and unable to obtain more credit: and thus were constantly in a state bordering on starvation. Their sufferings and misery were strongly marked in their personal appearance, and the condition of their wigwams, the latter imperfectly made, and very insufficiently supplied with fuel, could scarcely be said to afford shelter to the ragged and emaciated frames of the elder Indians, whilst the wretchedly diseased appearance of the children spoke still more forcibly of the intoxication and want of food of the parents. Miserable as was their state, it required considerable persuasion to prevail on them to accept the bounty of government. By studious attention to their habits and prejudices, they were at length brought to acquiesce, and the general result has been, that each Indian with a family has now a little farm under cultivation, on which he raises not only potatoes and Indian corn, but also wheat, oats, peas, &c.; his wigwam is exchanged for the log-house; hunting has in many cases been abandoned altogether, and in none appears, as formerly, to be resorted to as the only means of subsistence. Habitual intoxication is unknown; the Sabbath is carefully observed; their religious duties carefully attended to, and reading and writing, with a moderate knowledge of arithmetic, is almost universal among the young people.

"The log dwelling-houses for the Indians, were erected by government. Frame houses for the superintendent and the two chiefs, Aisance and Yellowhead, with school-houses at Coldwater and the Narrows, were also built at the commencement of the establishment. Since that time a grist mill and a saw mill have been added at Coldwater, and a saw mill is in progress at the Narrows. About 500 acres of the whole have been cleared and are under cultivation.

In 1836, a year after the date of the above account, they surrendered their reserve to the Government, and the tribe under Yellowhead removed, in 1838, from the Narrows to Rama, where there appeared a prospect of remaining for some years undisturbed by the white settlers. Here they purchased 1600 acres of land, at a cost of £800—paid out of their annuities—and applied themselves diligently to forming a new clearance, and cultivating the land, in which they have made considerable progress. Their number is now 184; their village contains twenty houses and four barns, and they have 300 acres of land under cultivation. During the last two years they have been very industrious, and have raised large quantities of produce. In 1841, their crop of potatoes was sufficiently abundant to enable them to dispose of four or five hundred bushels to the white settlers in Orillia and Medonte, without inconvenience to themselves.

These Indians are stated to be Wesleyan Methodists. They have a commodious school house, in which Divine service is performed by a missionary of that persuasion. A respectable teacher is in charge of the school.

But little of the township is as yet under cultivation, with the exception of that portion in the occupation of the Indians. Nine hundred acres of Crown lands are open for sale in the township, at 8s. currency per acre.

There has been no separate census yet taken of this township, it being included in the adjoining township of Mara.

Ratable property in the township, £223.

RAMSAY

A Township in the Bathurst District, is bounded on the north-east by the township of Huntley, on the north-west by Pakenham; on the south-west by Lanark; and on the south-east by Beckwith. In Ramsay 48,182 acres are taken up, 10,659 of which are under cultivation. The Mississippi River runs through the north-east of the township. This is the best settled township in the Bathurst District: much of the land is of excellent quality. The timber of the centre and west of the township is a mixture of hardwood and pine; in the east it is principally pine. Large quantities of timber are exported from the township, 4,100 acres of Crown lands are open for sale in Ramsay, at 8s. c'y per acre. There are five grist and five saw mills in the township.

Population in 1842, 2,461.

Ratable property in the township, £30,774.

RAWDON.

A Township in the Victoria District; is bounded on the east by the township of Huntingdon; on the north by Marmora; on the west by Seymour; and on the south by Sidney. In Rawdon 27,583 acres are taken up, 5,818 of which are under cultivation. The Marmora River passes through the north-west corner of the township. There is a considerable quantity of wet land in this township, but some of the land is of excellent quality. There is a grist and saw mill in the township. One thousand eight hundred and fifty acres of Crown lands are open for sale in Rawdon, at 8s. c'y per acre.

Population in 1842, 1,310, who are principally Canadian, with a few Irish.
Ratable property in the township, £17,102.

RAWDON.

A small Village in the township of Rawdon, sixteen miles from Belleville; contains about 125 inhabitants, one grist and saw mill, two stores, and four taverns.

REACH.

A Township in the Home District; is bounded on the east by the township of Cartwright, and a small portion of Mariposa; on the north by Brock; on the west by Scott and Uxbridge, and on the south by Whitby. In Reach 24,152 acres are taken up, 4,579 of which are under cultivation. The south-western extremity of Skugog Lake projects into the east of the township. The township of Reach contains some excellent land, particularly in its west and centre, where the timber is principally hardwood; in that portion of the township bordering on the lake, the timber is mostly pine. Five hundred acres of Crown lands are open for sale in Reach, at 8s. c'y per acre. A village, called "Prince Albert," is situated in the township, on the road leading from Windsor Bay to Skugog, and there are also five saw mills in the township.

Population in 1842, 1,052.
Ratable property in the township, £14,932.

RENFREW.

A County in the Bathurst District; comprises the townships of Admaston, Blithefield, Bagot, Bromley, Horton, Macnab, Pakenham, Pembroke, Ross, Stafford, and Westmeath.

RICE LAKE.

A Lake situated between the Otonabee River and the River Trent. It is one of a chain of lakes extending from the commencement of the River Trent to the north-east of the Colborne District. The principal of these lakes, are "Balsam Lake," which is situated in the township of Fenelon; Sturgeon Lake, in Fenelon and Verulam; Pigeon Lake, in Harvey; Shemong Lake, situated partly in Emily and partly between Ennismore and Smith; Shebauticon Lake, between Smith and Harvey; and Trout Lake between Burleigh and Dummer, and Smith and Douro. The latter lake discharges itself into the Otonabee River, which forms the dividing boundary between the townships of Monaghan and Otonabee, and then enters Rice Lake. Sturgeon Lake is also connected by means of the Skugog River with the Skugog Lake, which is situated in the townships of Cartwright and Reach. Rice Lake and the Otonabee River are navigable as far as the town of Peterborough, and during the season of navigation, a steamboat runs daily from a landing place at the south of the lake, to Peterborough. These lakes are noted for the superior quality of the fish in them, which is taken in large quantities, particularly Maskelonge, Bass, &c. Considerable business has been carried on within the last two or three years, on these waters, in the lumber trade—large quantities of pine and oak timber being carried down the Trent. In their course, these lakes receive many small streams which are scattered over the various townships.

RICEVILLE

A small Village in the township of Pelham, four miles west from Port Robinson. It contains about 50 inhabitants, two stores, and two taverns.

RICHMOND.

A Village in the south-east corner of the township of Goulbourn, twenty miles from Bytown, situated on the Goodwood River, which flows through the village. The houses are much scattered—the village extending over 200 acres of land, each lot containing one acre. The place was laid out, in 1818, by the Duke of Richmond, (who died shortly afterwards in the neighbourhood, of hydrophobia), and was originally settled by Highland Scotch. It contains about 1200 inhabitants. There are three churches in the village, viz., Episcopal, Presbyterian, and Catholic.

Post Office, post three times a-week.

Professions and Trades —Ten stores, four taverns, two waggon makers, one cabinet maker, two blacksmiths, three tailors, four shoemakers.

RICHMOND.

A small Village in the township of Bayham, situated on Talbot Street, twenty miles east from St Thomas. It contains about 80 inhabitants.

Post Office, post three times a week.

Professions and Trades —One store, one tannery, one tavern, one waggon maker, one tailor, two blacksmiths, two shoemakers, one cabinet maker.

RICHMOND.

A Township in the Midland District, is bounded on the east by the township of Camden, on the north by Hungerford; on the west by Tyendenaga; and on the south by Fredericksburgh, and the Bay of Quinté. In Richmond 40,434 acres are taken up, 10,301 of which are under cultivation. Two small lakes are situated in the north-west corner of the township, and the village of Napanee is in its south-east corner, on the Napanee River. Richmond is well settled, and contains some good farms. There is a considerable quantity of limestone in the township. Timber principally hardwood, with some pine. There are three grist and seven saw-mills in the township.

Population 2,630.

Ratable property in the township, 38,029.

RICHMOND HILL.

A small Village situated on Yonge Street, sixteen miles north from Toronto. It contains about 140 inhabitants. Churches two, Episcopal and Methodist. A stage runs daily from Richmond Hill to Toronto, and back again.

Post office, post every day.

Professions and Trades —Four stores, four taverns, one watchmaker, one baker, two tinsmiths, two tailors, three shoemakers, one blacksmith.

Principal Taverns —" Dalby's " (the stage house), and " Bingham's."

RIDEAU CANAL.

The line of water communication between the Ottawa River and Lake Ontario. It was constructed by the Government as a great military work. It commences at Bytown, where eight handsome locks have been constructed to overcome the fall in the river of thirty-four feet, and is formed through the bed of the Rideau River, with two or three deviations to avoid obstructions in its course, till it reaches the Great Rideau Lake, through which it is carried, and afterwards through Mud Lake. It is then carried into the bed of the Cataraqui River, and continues through its course till it reaches Kingston. It is 120 miles in length, and in some parts is very circuitous. The country through which it passes, bears in general a very different aspect to that traversed by the Welland Canal.

But little of the land bordering on the Rideau Canal is under cultivation, much of it is poor and rocky; and of that fit for cultivation, thousands of acres have been flooded by the damming of the rivers to form the canal, and immense quantities of timber have been consequently destroyed. Great numbers of trees are still standing, dead, and surrounded by water, and give those portions of the banks of the canal a decayed, deserted, miserable appearance. As their roots become decayed, however, they fall into the water, and are gradually carried off by the stream; and in the course a few years the canal will be free from them.

There are several handsome locks on the canal, the machinery of which is of a very perfect description There is much picturesque scenery on the canal, and some that may even be termed romantic. The finest spot on the canal, after leaving Bytown, is Kingston Mills, about six miles above Kingston.

The villages and settlements on the canal consist of Burritt's Rapids, forty-one miles from Bytown, Merricksville, forty-seven, Smith's Falls (a flourishing village in the Bathurst District), sixty; Oliver's Ferry (where the road from Perth to Brockville crosses the Rideau Lake, by means of a ferry-boat), seventy-two; the Isthmus, a small settlement, eighty-seven; Brewer's Upper Mills, 109, Kingston Mills, 120, Kingston, 126.

Hitherto the traffic on this canal has been very great, all merchandize intended for the country above Kingston having been sent through it, at a great expense; and the greater portion of the passenger traffic from Montreal to Kingston also passed through the canal; for the future, however, the opening of the St Lawrence canals will so much shorten the passage, and consequently lessen the expense, that no goods, except those intended for places along the canal, or the country above Bytown, will be forwarded by the Rideau; and of course passengers will choose the shorter route.

RIDEAU RIVER.—(*See* RIDEAU CANAL.)

ROCHESTER.

A Township in the county of Essex, bounded on the north by Lake St. Clair; on the west by Belle River; on the south by Gosfield; and on the east by Tilbury West In Rochester 12,124 acres are taken up, of which 922 are under cultivation Soil fertile, timber the same as Maidstone. The River Ruscom, which takes its rise in Gosfield, runs through this Township, and enters Lake St Clair, about four miles above Belle River. In Rochester, 1,100 acres of Crown lands are open for sale, at 8s. c'y per acre, and 2,500 acres of land belong to the Canada Company.

Population 174.

Ratable property in the township, £5,262

ROMNEY.

A township in the Western District, is bounded on the south-east by Lake Erie, on the north by the township of East Tilbury; and on the west by Mersea In Romney 7603 acres are taken up, 975 of which are under cultivation. This is a triangular-shaped township, with its base towards the lake; the land in it is of excellent quality, and the timber consists of the best kinds of hardwood—maple, oak, beech, elm, hickory, black walnut, &c, with a small quantity of cedar on the border of the lake. Romney is as yet but little settled, and in 1845 it only contained 257 inhabitants.

Ratable property in the township £3,532.

ROND' EAU, POINT AUX PINS, or LANDGUARD

A Harbour on Lake Erie, sixty-five miles below the head of the lake. A cape projects, which incloses a natural basin of about 6000 acres in extent, and with a depth of from ten to eleven feet. The communication between the basin and the lake is across a sand-bank of about forty yards in breadth, and only a few feet above the level of the water. The government has commenced improving the harbour, by cutting a channel through the bank, running out piers, &c. When completed, it will be a work of great importance to vessels navigating the lake, and also as a shipping-place to the surrounding country—it being fourteen miles from Chatham, in the County of Kent, and an excellent road having lately been completed between the two places.

ROSS

A Township in the Bathurst District, is bounded on the north-east by the Ottawa River; on the north-west by Westmeath; on the south-west by Bromley; and on the south-east by Horton. In Ross 6,468 acres are taken up, 615 of which are under cultivation. This township has lately been divided, and the township of Bromley separated from it. Ross is at present but little settled, and 29,200 acres of Crown lands are open for sale in it. There are two saw mills in the township.

Population in 1842, 168.
Ratable property in the township, £2,845

ROUGE RIVER.

A small River, which takes its rise in the township of Whitchurch, and flows through Markham and Scarborough, in which latter township it enters Lake Ontario. It is a good mill stream, and there is some excellent timber on its banks.

ROXBOROUGH.

A Township in the Eastern District, is bounded on the north-east by the reserve of the St Regis Indians, on the north-west, by Plantagenet and a small portion of Cambridge, on the south-west by Finch and on the south-east by Cornwall. In Roxborough 20,118 acres are taken up, 2,411 of which are under cultivation. This township is pretty well settled, and contains good land. Timber—a mixture of pine and hardwood. Three hundred and fifty acres of Crown lands are open for sale in Roxborough, at 8s currency per acre. There are one grist and two saw mills in the township.

Population in 1842, 1,107; who are principally Scotch and Irish.
Ratable property in the township, £9,992

RUSCOM RIVER.

Take its rise in the township of Gosfield, and runs through the township of Rochester, within from two to three miles of its eastern border, till it enters Lake St. Clair. It is several feet deep for some miles before it enters the lake.

RUSSELL

A Township in the Ottawa District, is bounded on the east by the township of Cambridge; on the north-west by Cumberland, on the south-west by Osgoode; and on the south-east by Winchester and Finch. In Russell 4,936 acres are taken up, 504 of which are under cultivation. Several branches of the Petite Nation River are spread over the township, on the banks of which there is a great deal of pine timber. Russell is as yet but little settled, and 19,335 acres of Crown lands are open for sale in it, at 8s currency per acre. There are one grist and three saw mills in the township.

Population in 1842, 196
Ratable property in the township, £2,390.

RUSSELL.

A County in the Ottawa District; comprises the townships of Clarence, Cumberland, Cambridge and Russell. It returns a member to the House of Assembly.

SABLES, RIVIERE AUX.

A River, different branches of which take their rise in the townships of Biddulph, Stephen, Usborne and London. It flows along the east and south border of the township of Williams, till it reaches its south-west corner, when it makes a bend and runs to the north, forming the western boundary of the townships of Williams and McGillivray, and separating them from Bosanquet; at the northern extremity of the latter township it makes a curve, and runs south, parallel with Lake Huron, and at an average distance of half a mile from it, for about ten miles, when it enters the lake, about five miles above Kettle Point. As its name imports, its bed and banks are very sandy. A ridge of sand hills separates it from Lake Huron. A saw mill was established at the north bend of the river soon after the first settlement of the Huron District, and has been in operation ever since.

SALTFLEET.

A Township in the Gore District, is bounded on the east by the township of Grimsby; on the north by Lake Ontario and Burlington Bay, on the west by Barton, and on the south by Binbrook and Caistor. In Saltfleet 23,734 acres are taken up, 11,112 of which are under cultivation. This township is watered by Stoney Creek, and two or three other small streams. It contains a large proportion of excellent land, and many old-settled and well-cultivated farms. The village of Stoney Creek is situated on the road from Hamilton to St Catharines, and Stoney Creek flows through it. There are one grist and six saw mills in the township.

Population in 1841, ———

Ratable property in the township, £42,341.

SANDWICH.

The District Town of the Western District, beautifully situated on the Detroit River, about two miles below Detroit, and nine miles below Lake St Clair. The town is neatly laid out, and, being an old settlement, with fine old orchards, and well kept flower gardens, has very much the appearance of an English country town. It is built on a gravelly soil, on a gently sloping bank, a short distance from the river, which is here about a mile wide. This is one of the oldest settlements in Canada. Colonel Prince, the member for the county, has a fine farm, in a highly improved state, a short distance out of town. There are in Sandwich an Episcopal church and a Methodist chapel. A newspaper is published here—the *Western Standard* Here are the jail and court house for the district. Sandwich has a cricket club.

The following Government and District Offices are kept in Sandwich. Clerk of Peace, Treasurer of District, Sheriff of do., Judge of Surrogate Court, Registrar of do., Registrar of County of Essex, Inspector of Licenses, Clerk of District Court, Clerk of Municipal Council, Auditors of Municipal Council.

Sandwich had barracks during the rebellion, but they have since been disposed of, and converted to private purposes.

Population about 450.

List of Professions and Trades.—Two physicians and surgeons, six lawyers, four surveyors, one steam grist mill and carding machine, two grist windmills, one brewery, one tannery, one ashery, six stores, one auctioneer, three tailors. two saddlers, six blacksmiths, one printing office, one gunsmith, two waggon makers, one hatter, one baker, one school, twelve taverns.

Principal Tavern—the "Western Hotel."

SANDWICH.

The north-western township of the County of Essex; bounded on the north and west by Lake St. Clair and the Detroit River; on the south by the townships of Anderdon and Colchester, and on the east by the township of Maidstone. In Sandwich 51,476 acres are taken up, of which 10,797 are under cultivation. It is well watered, having Little River at the north-east corner, on which is a saw mill, the Riviere aux Peches on the east, Turkey Creek running through the centre, on which is a grist mill; and the River Canard on the south. The soil is rich and fertile. This is one of the oldest settled portions of Canada; most of the inhabitants being French Canadians, and holding their lands under French grants. The orchards on the banks of the river are noted for their magnificent pear trees, some of which are of great size. A large portion of the inhabitants make their living by raising poultry, &c, for the supply of the city of Detroit. There are in the township of Sandwich a Catholic and an Episcopal church, and nine windmills.

The Canada Company possess 3,200 acres in the township.
Population in 1844, 3,624.
Ratable property in the township, £55,569.

SANTA CRUZ

A small Settlement in the township of Osnabruck, situated on the St Lawrence, fifteen miles from Cornwall It contains two churches—Episcopal and Presbyterian, and one tavern.

SARNIA, PORT.

A Village in the township of Sarnia, handsomely situated on the St. Clair River, opposite the American village Port Huron, near the entrance to Lake Huron. This is the last place on the Canadian side at which the American steamers touch, on their route to the upper lakes. The village was laid out by private individuals in the year 1833, and has increased rapidly, and must in time become a place of great importance An excellent road is formed from this place to the town of London, and stages run from Port Sarnia to London three times a week The American steamboats "Hercules," "Samson," "Princeton," and "St Louis," stop regularly on their passages to and from Buffalo and Chicago; and the "Huron" and "Red Jacket" leave here every morning alternately for Detroit. Several other American boats call occasionally. During the last season the British steamer "Gore," from Windsor to Goderich and Gloster Bay, also called here regularly. There is an excellent fishery just above the village, on the banks of Point Edward; and upwards of 1000 barrels of fish are generally exported annually.

Port Sarnia contains five churches and chapels; viz, Episcopal, Catholic, Presbyterian, Methodist and Congregational

Five schooners are owned here There is a saw mill on the river worked by means of a canal three miles and a half in length, fed by the Riviere aux Perches; and a steam grist mill and foundry have recently been erected Port Sarnia is a port of entry, and has a resident collector of customs.

Post Office, post three times a week
Population about 420

Professions and Trades—One physician and surgeon, one druggist, two tanneries, one foundry, one steam grist mill, one water saw mill, eight stores, one saddler, one tinsmith, three blacksmiths, one wheelwright, two taverns, two chair makers, one cabinet maker, three tailors, two bakers, one cooper, three shoemakers, three schools, one of which is for Indians.

Principal Tavern, the "Sarnia Exchange."
Agent for Steamboats—George Durand

Port Sarnia is sixty-one miles from London, seventy miles from Detroit, about sixty-five miles from Goderich, and sixty miles from Chatham. A new road is about being opened from Port Sarnia to the River Sydenham.

Stage fare to London, $3.   Steamboat fare to Detroit, $1¾.

List of Exports from Port Sarnia for the year 1844.

Quantity.	Description.	Value when shipped.		
		£.	s.	d.
400 barrels	Potash...	2000	0	0
10 do.	Beef...	17	10	0
1000 do.	Fish..	1250	0	0
12 do.	Sugar...	24	0	0
120,000 feet	Lumber...	180	0	0
2,800	Standard Staves	31	10	0
300 bushels	Wheat...	56	5	0
Total value of Exports from Port Sarnia..............£3559			5	0

SARNIA.

A Township in the County of Kent, is bounded on the north by Lake Huron; on the west by the River St. Clair, on the south by the township of Moore; and on the east by Plympton. In Sarnia 10,540 acres are taken up, of which 1,366 are under cultivation Ten thousand acres of the finest land in the township, reaching from Froomefield to Port Sarnia, are reserved for the Indians, who number about 700. They farm a little, but live principally by hunting and fishing They have a Methodist chapel and school. This township is well watered; the Riviere aux Perches, which takes its rise in Enniskillen, runs through the township till it reaches Lake Waywanosh, which it enters at its western side, about six miles from Port Sarnia, and emerges again at its southeast corner, and enters Lake Huron about eleven miles above Port Sarnia. Lake Waywanosh, the nearest point of which is half a mile from Lake Huron, contains about 2000 acres; average depth from six to eight feet; and is surrounded by prairie land Lake Chipican, a small lake about six acres in extent, is separated from Lake Huron by a ridge of high land it is two miles north from Port Sarnia. A ridge of sandy land, forming what are called "oak ridges," about a mile in width, extends from Port Sarnia, along the shore of Lake Huron, to nearly the extremity of the township the back of the township is good land. A point of land, called Point Edward, containing about 1000 acres, which is a military reserve, runs into the St Clair River just above Port Sarnia, at the entrance of Lake Huron. This is said by the old inhabitants to have been formerly an island; but the north portion of the channel on the east side of it has become filled up; thus connecting it with the main land, and forming a fine bay, sheltered on the north, east and west.

Population (exclusive of Indians) 610
Ratable property in the township, £8,472.

SAUGEEN.

A Settlement of Chippewa Indians, near the mouth of the Saugeen River, on Lake Huron It was from these Indians, and their brethren since settled at Owen's Sound, that Sir F Head, in 1836, obtained a surrender of that vast tract of land lying north of the London and Gore Districts, and between the Home District and Lake Huron, containing about 1,600,000 acres He reserved at the same time for the Indians, the extensive peninsula lying between Lake Huron and the Georgian Bay, north of Owen's Sound, and supposed to contain about 450,000 acres

Little was known of these Indians by the Government before that period, as their village was remote from any white settlement, but they appear to have been settled and converted about the year 1831. In 1837, their missionary gave the following description of their condition:—" This mission is beautifully situated; fine flats, containing from two hundred to three hundred acres, extend along the river, where the Indians cut sufficient hay for their oxen and cows, and grow excellent corn. There are some good log houses, and several comfortable bark shanties. On the hill, in rear of the flats, are several fine fields of corn and potatoes The Indians at this station have been remarkable for their stedfastness since they embraced Christianity. They appear to be a happy people much attached to their missionaries, teachable, and give solid proofs that they are progressing in civilization "

The chief superintendent, however, who visited them in the same year, reported that they appeared very poor and miserable, trusting very much to hunting and fishing for their support. The fishing is very productive, and has attracted the notice of the white people, who annoy the Indians by encroaching n what they consider their exclusive right, and on which they rely much for provisions They hunt in the tract belonging to the Canada Company, and on phe unoccupied lands to the south and east of Saugeen river.

This settlement does not appear to have been visited by any officer of the tGovernment since 1837, and so little is it known, that it is supposed to have been incorrectly laid down on the map by the extent of half a degree. The chief superintendent reports, that he cannot give an accurate account of it. He states that the greater number of Indians lived for a long while in very small log houses, and in houses made of elm bark. The present missionary states that there are only six log houses, and that the rest are bark huts or wigwams. The village is situated about two miles up the Saugeen River From the report of the chief superintendent it appears that the Indians contemplated abandoning this situation for one nearer the mouth of the river, but they have since determined to remain in their old locality, and have this year built by contract six excellent houses.

The mouth of the Saugeen River forms the best, and almost the only port of refuge on the eastern shore of Lake Huron, hence it is likely to become a place of considerable resort, and it is in contemplation to carry two roads in different directions through the Saugeen tract to this point. The rumour of this intention was lately a source of much inquietude among the Indians, as they became apprehensive of being obliged to quit their settlement, and surrender their improvements. This apprehension, however, has been removed, and they are now looking forward to the erection of a saw mill, and to the supplying the schooners, touching at the port, with lumber and fish.

A missionary of the Wesleyan Methodists has long resided among them. Their present missionary is an Indian, brought up at the Rice Lake Mission, and at a school in the United States. They have a chapel which serves as a school-house, and a mission house, which were built by the Wesleyan Methodist Society, about the year 1831. They have also had a schoolmaster for some time past Almost all the tribe have embraced Christianity.

These Indians are entitled to share in the annuity of £1250, recently granted in exchange for the Saugeen territory, surrendered to Sir F. Head in 1837.

SAUGEEN RIVER.

Takes its rise in the Indian territory, north of the Huron Tract, and after running nearly a west course, enters Lake Huron about sixty miles north of Goderich. At the mouth of the river is a pretty good harbour, allowing the entrance of vessels drawing eight feet of water, but the passage is difficult of entrance.

SAUGEEN, GEGETO, or FISHING ISLANDS.

A group of Islands, fifteen or twenty in number, lying about seventy-eight miles above Goderich, and eighteen above the Saugeen River. They are not inhabited, but a large quantity of fish is annually taken on their banks. About 1000 barrels are generally exported, but *any quantity* might be taken, there being no limit to the supply. As much as from two to three hundred barrels of fish have been taken at a single haul of the seine.

SCARBOROUGH

A Township in the Home District; is bounded on the east by the township of Pickering; on the north by Markham; on the west by York; and on the south by Lake Ontario. In Scarborough 38,709 acres are taken up, 16,083 of which are under cultivation. The River Don runs through the west of the township, and the River Rouge through the east. The land bordering on the lake is mostly poor, and the timber principally pine; in the rear of the township the land improves, and the timber is mostly hardwood. Scarborough is well settled, and contains many good farms. a large portion of which are let to the occupants, the average rent being $2 per acre. There are one grist and eighteen saw mills in the township, and large quantities of sawed lumber are exported.

Population in 1842, 2750; who are principally English, Irish, and Scotch emigrants.

Ratable property in the township, £42,181.

SCOTLAND.

A Village in the south-west of the township of Oakland. It contains about 150 inhabitants.

Professions and Trades.—Two stores, two taverns, one tannery, one saddler, one chair maker, one cabinet maker, one blacksmith. There is a carding machine and fulling mill near the village.

SCOTT.

A Township in the Home District; is bounded on the east by the townships of Reach and Brock; on the north by Georgina; on the west by East Gwillimbury; and on the south by Uxbridge. In Scott 5078 acres are taken up, 450 of which are under cultivation. The township is well watered by numerous small streams running through it. It is as yet but little settled. Six hundred acres of Crown lands are open for sale in Scott, at 8s. currency per acre.

For population of the township, *see* UXBRIDGE.

Ratable property in the township, £2063

SELBORNE, OR TALBOT MILLS.

A Village in the townships of Yarmouth and Southwold, situated on Kettle Creek, close to the plank road—one mile and half from Port Stanley.

Professions and Trades.—One grist mill, two distilleries, one foundry, two physicians and surgeons, one druggist, two stores, two taverns, two blacksmiths, one waggon maker, one shoemaker, one tailor.

SENECA.

A Township in the Gore District, is bounded on the east by the township of Canboro', on the north-east by Caistor, Binbrook, and Glanford, on the northwest by Onondaga, on the south-west by the Grand River; and on the southeast by the township of Cayuga. In Seneca 6182 acres are taken up, 3063 of which are under cultivation. There is a large proportion of good land in the township. it is mostly rolling; and the timber principally hardwood, with a small quantity of pine intermixed. There is abundance of fine large white-oak within convenient distances of the river. The villages of Caledonia, Seneca, York, and Indiana are in the township, all situated on the Grand River. There are four grist and eleven saw mills in the township, and large quantities of sawn lumber are exported from it.

Population in 1841, 831.

Ratable property in the township, £16,316.

SENECA.

A flourishing Village in the township of Seneca, situated on the Grand River, one mile below Caledonia. It contains about 140 inhabitants. There is a Methodist church in the village.

Professions and Trades.—One grist mill (four run of stones), one saw mill, carding machine and cloth factory, planing machine, chair factory, one physician and surgeon, two stores, three taverns, one turner, one cabinet maker, three shoemakers, three blacksmiths, one tailor.

SEVERN RIVER.

A River which receives the waters of Lake Simcoe and Lake Gougichin, and conveys them to the Georgian Bay. There is some beautiful scenery on the river; but it is not navigable on account of the falls and rapids in it. Between Lake Gougichin and Gloucester Bay, the falls are seven in number.

SEYMOUR.

A Township in the Newcastle District; is bounded on the east by the township of Rawdon, on the north by Belmont; on the west by Percy and Asphodel; and on the south by Murray. In Seymour 31,850 acres are taken up, 6323 of which are under cultivation. The River Trent enters the township at its north-west corner—runs northward for a short distance, then makes a curve and follows a south-east course till near the centre of the township, where it receives the Marmora River, it then runs south-west to near the south-west corner of the township, where it makes another bend, and runs along the town-line to the south-east corner of the township, where it enters Sydney. There is an island, called "Wilson's Island," in the river, part of which is in Seymour, part in Murray, and part in Sidney. There are also two smaller islands, one of which is in the south-east corner, and the other in the north of the township. There is much wet land in the township. The timber is a mixture of pine and hardwood. There are two grist and six saw mills in the township.

Population in 1842, 1899
Ratable property in the township, £18,669.

SHANNONVILLE.

A small Village in the township of Tyendenaga, situated on the Kingston road, about nine miles east from Belleville. The Salmon River runs through the village. It contains about 50 inhabitants, one store, two taverns, one blacksmith.

SHARON, or DAVIDTOWN.

A Village in the township of East Gwillimbury, three miles and a half from the Holland Landing, and about thirty-five from Toronto. It was first settled in the year 1800, by a Mr. David Wilson, from the state of New York, who, with a few followers, about six in number, seceded from the Society of Friends, and established a sect of his own. These have been since known as "Davidites." They have at great expense, and much labour, erected two large buildings of a most singular appearance, which strike the eye of the traveller at a considerable distance. The first of these, designed to be an imitation of the ancient Jewish temple, is a building, the ground floor of which is sixty feet square, and twenty-four feet high. Above this is a gallery, for musical performances, and above this again, a kind of tower or steeple. The whole height of the building is sixty-five feet. In the interior is a large space enclosed by twelve pillars, on each of which is inscribed in gold letters, the name of one of the Apostles. Within these again, are four others, inscribed in like manner with the words, "Hope," "Faith," "Charity," "Love." In the centre of the building, surrounded by these pillars, is a kind of cabinet, about five feet square, and seven feet high, made of oak, of elaborate workmanship; in shape, something resembling one story of a Chinese Pagoda; at the four corners and on the top of which are placed brass lamps. On each side of the cabinet are four windows The interior is lined with black cloth, trimmed with crimson. In the centre is a kind of table covered with black cloth, with crimson hangings, supporting a Bible. The temple was built by the congregation, who spent seven years about the work; working, of course, only at intervals It was completed in the year 1832. Every year, on the first Friday evening in September, the temple is brilliantly illuminated. A meeting is held here monthly for the purpose of making collections for the poor. The members subscribe altogether $8 per month. Since the completion of the temple, $1500 have been contributed, 600 of which have been expended

The second building is the meeting house; which measures 100 feet by 50. It is surrounded on the outside by rows of pillars. The ground floor is twenty feet high, the ceiling is arched, and is supported by three rows of pillars, on which are inscribed in letters of gold, the names—Daniel, Ezekiel, Jeremiah, Moses, Jacob, Abraham, Solomon, David (with a harp), Judah, Reuben, Samuel, Levi, Isaac, Benjamin, Aaron, Joseph, and "Our Lord is one God" There is also a tolerable organ. Above the meeting-house is a school-room, fifty by twenty-one feet. The building was completed in 1842 It was built by subscription, and cost about $2500. The members meet every Sunday for religious service; and twice a-year, viz, on the first Saturdays in June and September, for a feast or communion, at which time all comers are welcomed The congregation, including children, number about 200.

Population of Sharon, about 150

Post Office, post twice a-week

Professions and Trades—One tannery, two stores, one saddler, two blacksmiths, one tavern, one wheelwright, one tailor, one tinsmith, one weaver.

SHEFFIELD

A Township in the Midland District, is bounded on the east by Storrington; on the north by Kaladar and Kennebec, on the west by Hungerford, and on the south by Camden. In Sheffield 19,889 acres are taken up, 3869 of which are under cultivation. There are two lakes in the south-west of the township, called "Beaver Lake," and "White Lake," a lake in the north-east of the township, called "Long Lake," and several smaller lakes scattered over the township—the whole of which are connected together by small streams. The land in Sheffield varies in quality, some parts being good, and others of poor quality. Timber—a mixture of pine and hardwood There is one grist mill and one saw mill in the township.

Population in 1842, 1334

Ratable property in the township, £11,215.

SHEMONG LAKE—(*See* RICE LAKE.)

SHEBAUTICON LAKE. -(*See* RICE LAKE)

SHERBROOKE.

A Township in the Niagara District, is bounded on the north-east and north by the township of Moulton, on the west by the Grand River, and on the south and south-east by Lake Erie. In Sherbrooke 3,447 acres are taken up, 1,474 of which are under cultivation. This is a very small township, and it is but little settled, there is a marsh in the north-east of it, on the borders of the Grand River.

Population of Sherbrooke in 1841, 198.

Ratable property in the township, £3,841.

SHERBROOKE, SOUTH.

A Township in the Bathurst District; is bounded on the north-east by the township of Bathurst, on the north-west by North Sherbrooke; on the west by Oso, and on the south-east by North Crosby. In South Sherbrooke 5,119 acres are taken up, 467 of which are under cultivation. The north and middle branches of the Mississippi River run through the north of the township; and a chain of lakes, connected together by the River Tay, stretch along the south-east border of the township. South Sherbrooke is as yet but little settled. The base of the township is principally granite. In South Sherbrooke 19,800 acres of Crown lands are open for sale, at 8s. c'y per acre.

Population in 1842, 253
Ratable property in the township, £2,278.

SHERBROOKE, NORTH.

A Township in the Bathurst District; is bounded on the north-east by the township of Dalhousie; on the north-west by Levant; on the west by Palmerston and Oso, and on the south-east by South Sherbrooke. In North Sherbrooke 8,305 acres are taken up, 1,516 of which are under cultivation. A branch of the Mississippi River runs across the township, a little north of the centre. The base of the township is principally granite. North Sherbrooke is as yet but little settled, and 4,600 acres of Crown lands are open for sale in it, at 8s. c'y per acre.

Population in 1842, 350
Ratable property in the township, £3,985.

SIDNEY.

A Township in the Victoria District, is bounded on the east by the township of Thurlow; on the north by Rawdon, on the west by Murray; and on the south by the Bay of Quinté. In Sidney 52,604 acres are taken up, 19,837 of which are under cultivation. The River Trent passes through the north-west of the township. Sidney is well settled, principally by U. E. Loyalists and their descendants, who have very good farms. There are four grist, and eight saw mills in the township. One hundred and fifty acres of Crown lands are open for sale in Sidney, at 8s. c'y per acre.

Population in 1842, 3,363.
Ratable property in the township, 54,863.

SIMCOE.

The District Town of the Talbot District, situated in the north-west corner of the township of Woodhouse, twenty-four miles from Brantford. Simcoe is well situated, in the midst of a fine, old-settled country, but being away from any public road, and having no regular means of communication with any place except Brantford, it is kept rather in the back-ground. There is a stone jail and court-house. Churches and chapels three viz., Methodist, Baptist, and Congregationalist. A weekly newspaper is published here, the "Long Point Advocate."

Population about 1,400.
Post office, post every day.

The following Government and District Offices are kept in Simcoe: Judge of District Court, Sheriff, Clerk of Peace, Inspector of Licenses, Crown Lands Agent, District Clerk, Treasurer, Clerk of District Court, Deputy Clerk of Crown, Superintendent of Schools.

Professions and Trades.—Two grist-mills, two saw do, one brewery, two distilleries, one foundry, one ashery, one carding machine and fulling mill, three physicians and surgeons, two lawyers, one threshing machine maker, one surveyor, nine stores, six taverns, two druggists, six blacksmiths, one watchmaker, three cabinet-makers, two saddlers, six tailors, one chair-maker, one turner, one livery stable, one temperance house, two butchers, one cooper, one grocery, one gunsmith, four shoemakers, one bank agency—" Gore."

SIMCOE DISTRICT.

Consists of the county of Simcoe, which comprises the townships of Adjala, Artemisia, Collingwood, Essa, Flos, West Gwillimbury, Innisfil, Medonte, Matchadash, Mulmur, Mono, Nottawasaga, Ospry, Oro, Orillia, St. Vincent, Sunnidale, Tay, Tiny, Tecumseth, Tossorontio; Euphrasia and Vespra. It is bounded on the east by the Home District, Lake Simcoe, Lake Gougichin, and the Severn River; on the north by the Severn River and the various bays of the Georgian Bay; on the west by the Wellington District; and on the south by the Home District. It is watered by the Nottawasaga River, and the Holland and Coldwater Rivers, besides numerous small streams scattered over it. This district formed a portion of the Home District until the year 1843; when the county of Simcoe was declared a separate district. It contains a large portion of very excellent land, the settlement of which has been hitherto much retarded by the want of good roads; some of the farmers in the back townships finding it almost impossible to get out of the bush, except during sleighing time. Many of the townships are newly surveyed, and have not long been opened for sale. The townships of West Gwillimbury and Tecumseth are the best settled in the district; the inhabitants principally Irish and Scotch. Next to these are the townships or Oro, Innisfil, and Mono. There are many good farms above Barrie, on the road leading from Barrie to Penetanguishine; near the latter place the land is mostly stony and sandy, and the timber principally pine. There is excellent land in Orillia, which township is now beginning to settle up. Good roads into the interior of the district are much wanted to promote the settlement of the land.

Barrie, the district town, is beautifully situated on Kempenfeldt Bay, and there are besides in the district the villages of Bradford, Bond Head, and Middleton in West Gwillimbury; Penetanguishine in Tiny; Orillia in Orillia; and Coldwater in Medonte; besides a settlement called "Hurontario," in St. Vincent, on the Nottawasaga Bay. Two hundred and one thousand eight hundred and seventy-two acres of Crown lands are open for sale in the Simcoe District, at 8s. c'y per acre, to purchase any of which application must be made to the Crown Lands Agent at Barrie.

Population in 1842, 12,592, since when it has probably increased one-fifth.

The following abstract from the assessment rolls, will show the rate of increase and improvement in the district:

Date.	No. of Acres Cultivated.	MILLS. Grist.	MILLS. Saw.	Milch Cows.	Oxen 4 years old, and upwards.	Horned Cattle from 2 to 4 years old.	Amount of Ratable Property.
1842	44,639	10	23	4,126	2166	2424	143,046
1843	46,354	11	22	4,282	2120	2318	145,766
1844	51,681	12	29	4,588	2516	2516	157,791

Government and District Officers in the Simcoe District.

District Judge	James R. Gowan	Barrie.
Judge of Surrogate Court	Do.	Do.
Sheriff	B. W. Smith	Do.
Clerk of Peace	W. B. McVity	Do.
Treasurer	Edmund Lally	Do.

Registrar	George Lount	W. Gwillimbury
Inspector of Licenses	John Moberly	Barrie.
Crown Lands Agent	John Alexander	Do.
Superintendent of Schools	Rev S. B Ardagh.	Do.
District Clerk	John McWatt	Do.
Clerk of District Court	J. Lane	Do.
Deputy Clerk of Crown	H H. Gowan	Do.
Collector of Customs	W. Simpson	Penetanguishine.
Warden	None	
Coroner	None	

Number of Common Schools in operation in the District.—West Gwillimbury, seventeen; Medonte, seven; Tecumseth, seventeen; Mono, ten; Adjala, eight, Innisfil, eight, Essa, six; Vespra, two, Mulmur, two; Oro, ten; Tiny, one; Sunnidale one; Flos, 3, Orillia, one; Nottawasaga, three. Total, 96.

SIMCOE LAKE

A Lake situated partly in the Home and partly in the Simcoe Districts. It commences about thirty-five miles north from Toronto, and is in length nearly thirty miles, and in its widest part about eighteen. It is said to be about 170 feet above Lake Huron, into which it discharges itself, through Lake Gougichin, the Severn River, and the Georgian Bay. The scenery of Lake Simcoe is very picturesque, its shores being very much indented with bays, some of which are of considerable extent. A beautiful bay, called "Kempenfeldt Bay," runs into the land on the west side of the lake; it is about ten miles long, and from two to three miles wide. Barrie, the district town of the Simcoe District, is situated on its north-western extremity. Cook's Bay, the southern extremity of the lake, is about eight miles long, and from two and a half to four miles broad, it receives the Holland River. There are many islands in Lake Simcoe, and some of them are of large size, containing many acres, only one of them (Snake Island) is inhabited, and that by Indians.

The banks of the lake are generally clothed with wood down to the water's edge, consequently there is no beach. Some portions of the shores of the lake are marshy, a large marsh, bordered by tamarac swamp, borders Cook's Bay, and extends for some miles along the course of the Holland River. The land on the banks of the lake is mostly light, and the timber principally pine; in some parts, however the land is of excellent quality, and timbered with hard wood to the edge of the lake. The banks of the lake and the bays are generally rather low, few parts being more than from twenty to thirty feet high. On those portions of the banks in the township of North Gwillimbury, and also in a portion of the south of Georgina, there are some very prettily situated farms, which are well cultivated, the banks in Thorah are not so much settled, and those of Mara and Rama still less so; in the latter township is an Indian settlement on the banks of the lake. The banks in Oro and Vespra are partially settled, but not much, on the Innisfil side, they are clothed with wood to the water's edge.

At the "Narrows," which is a narrow channel connecting Lake Simcoe with Lake Gougichin, a handsome bridge has been constructed. The scenery at the Narrows would be very attractive were it not unfortunately a little disfigured by a small quantity of marsh. A steamboat has plied on this lake for about eleven or twelve years, the present one, the "Beaver," (which was launched in 1844), which is the third, is also the largest and best that has been built, she is a fine boat and has excellent accommodations. The Beaver makes regular trips round the lake, starting every second day from a landing place on the east branch of the Holland River, and running to Orillia, taking the east and west sides of the lake alternately, and returning by the opposite course. It lies over every night at Orillia, except Saturday, when it returns to the Holland River, and lies there till Monday morning.

The water in some parts of the lake is of considerable depth, and it is generally frozen completely over in the winter, so as to be passable with safety for sleighs; when the ice breaks up in the spring, it sinks at once to the bottom. Those accustomed to the ice generally know how long it is safe to venture on it, and accidents seldom happen.

About four years since, a settler on the lake was engaged to take a sleigh load of goods to the opposite side; the winter was breaking up, and the ice on the lake was becoming honey-combed underneath, a sure sign that it would not last much longer, and he knew that if he deferred his journey for a day or two there would be no chance of getting his load across till the steamboat commenced running. He therefore set off with his team in the night, took his load across in safety, and started on his return home just as the sun began to rise; he knew by the appearance of the ice, and from the direction of the wind, that the ice would not be safe many hours longer, he therefore put his horses to a gallop, and kept them at that pace the whole way home (12 miles), he crossed in safety, and *two hours* after he landed there was not a vestige of ice to be seen on the lake. Notwithstanding the temerity of those accustomed to the ice, it is very seldom that any serious accident, such as loss of life, occurs, horses, however, are lost every winter through the ice, but the drivers generally manage to save themselves. Very fine whitefish and maskelonge are taken in Lake Simcoe; and fine white cornelians are said to have been picked up on the shore of Kempenfeldt bay.

SISTERS, THE

Three Islands situated in the western extremity of Lake Erie, two of which belong to England, and the third to the United States. Of those belonging to England, the largest, or East Sister, contains about thirty-five acres, the Middle Sister contains about twelve or fourteen acres. They are not inhabited.

SCUGOG LAKE.—(*See* Rice Lake.)

SMITH.

A Township in the Colborne District, is bounded on the east by the Otonabee River, on the north and west by a chain of lakes, and a small portion of Emily, and on the south by Monaghan. In Smith 32,473 acres are taken up, 9653 of which are under cultivation. This is a fine township, and well settled, containing a mixed population. Timber—a mixture of hard wood and pine. There are two grist and three saw mills in the township. Two thousand eight hundred and nineteen acres of Crown lands are open for sale in Smith, at 8s. c'y per acre.

Ratable property in the township, £23,324.

SMITH'S FALLS.

A flourishing Village in the township of North Elmsley, pleasantly situated on the Rideau River, and also on the canal, fourteen miles from Perth. It contains about 700 inhabitants. Churches and chapels four, viz, Episcopal, Presbyterian, Catholic and Wesleyan Methodist.

Post Office, post three times a week.

Professions and Trades.—Three physicians and surgeons, two grist mills (one with four run of stones), two saw mills, one carding machine and fulling mill, seven stores, six groceries, one axe factory, six blacksmiths, two wheelwrights, one chair maker, one cabinet maker, one gunsmith, three carpenters, seven tailors, eleven shoemakers, one reed maker, one tinsmith, two taverns.

SMITH'S BAY.

A Bay of Lake Huron, six miles in length, running into the Great Manitoulin Island.

SMITH'S CREEK.

A branch of the Grand River, which takes its rise in the great swamp to the north of the Huron District; it passes through the townships of Mornington, Wellesley, Wilmot and Blenheim, and joins the Grand River in the south of the township of Dumfries, at the village of Paris. It is an excellent mill stream, and there are several mills, both grist and saw, situated on it.

SMITHVILLE.

A Village in the township of Grimsby, situated on the road leading from the village of Grimsby to Dunnville, eight miles south-east from the former village. It contains two churches, Episcopal Methodist, and British Wesleyan.

Population about 150.

Post Office, post twice a week.

Professions and Trades.—One grist mill, one saw mill, carding machine and cloth factory, four stores, one machine shop, one tannery, two blacksmiths, two tailors, two shoemakers.

SNAKE ISLAND.

An Island in the south of Lake Simcoe. It is occupied by a party of Chippewa Indians. This body of Indians was one of the three bands established at Coldwater and the Narrows, and separated from them on the abandonment of those settlements. They now occupy Snake Island, one of the three islands in Lake Simcoe, which were set apart for this tribe many years ago. They are 109 in number, and occupy twelve dwelling houses. They have also two barns, and a school house, in which their children are instructed by a respectable teacher, and Divine service is performed by a resident missionary of the Methodist persuasion, to which these Indians belong. They have about 150 acres under cultivation, and are improving in habits of industry and agricultural skill. Their missionary, who has been acquainted with them since July, 1839, states that the majority of them are strictly moral in their character, and that many of them for consistency of character, would not suffer by a comparison with white Christians of any denomination.

The superintendent, however, states that the soil of the island is stoney, and not well adapted for Indian modes of cultivation. The timber on the island is mostly hardwood, and includes a good proportion of maple; and, during the sugar-making season, many Indians come down from Penetanguishene and other places, to make a supply of sugar.

SOMBRA.

A Township in the Western District, is bounded on the east by the township of Dawn, on the west by the River St Clair; on the north by Moore, and on the south by Dover and the Chenail Ecarté. In Sombra 13,476 acres are taken up, 1589 of which are under cultivation. The north branch of Bear Creek runs through the centre of the township, in the south of which it joins the east branch, which flows along near the south border of the township; near the centre of the south of the township, it discharges itself into the Chenail Ecarté. The east and north of the township contain excellent land—that bordering on the lower portion of the St Clair and Chenail Ecarté is rather inclined to be marshy; and there are extensive low plains, very useful for feeding cattle. Walpole Island and St Ann's Island, the former of which is occupied by Indians, are included in the township. The village of Wallaceburgh is situated at the forks of Bear Creek. There are two grist and two saw mills in the township.

Population in 1842, 800, who are a mixture of Canadians and emigrants from Great Britain and Ireland.

Ratable property in the township, £8708.

SOMMERVILLE.

A Township in the Colborne District, is bounded on the east and north by unsurveyed lands; on the west by unsurveyed lands and the township of Bexley; and on the south by Verulam. This township has not yet been correctly surveyed, and little is known of it. It is at present but little settled, and no return has yet been made from it. Fifty-one thousand two hundred and ninety-seven acres of Crown lands are open for sale in Sommerville, at 8s. currency per acre.

SOPHIASBURGH.

A Township in the Prince Edward District; is bounded on the north and east by the Bay of Quinté; on the west by Ameliasburgh and Hillier; and on the south by Hallowell. In Sophiasburgh 43,210 acres are taken up, 18,272 of which are under cultivation. An Island in the Bay, called "Big Island," is included in this township. A small lake, called "Fish Lake," containing about 500 acres, is situated about the centre of the township, and is connected with the bay by means of a creek. The village of Demorestville is situated in the township. From the loose manner in which the last census was taken in this township, it was impossible to ascertain the population with any degree of accuracy.

Ratable property in the township, £51,996.

SOUTHWOLD.

A Township in the London District, is bounded on the east by the township of Yarmouth; on the north by Westminster, Delaware and Carradoc, on the west by Dunwich, and on the south by Lake Erie. In Southwold 51,853 acres are taken up, 15,894 of which are under cultivation. This is a well-settled township, containing many thoroughly-cleared and well-cultivated farms. The River Thames runs through the north-west corner of the township, and it is besides watered by branches of Kettle Creek. In the north of the township the timber is principally hardwood, in the centre and south it is mostly pine. A small portion of Port Stanley is situated in Southwold, as are also the villages of Fingal, Five Stakes, and Selborne. There are two grist and three saw mills in the township.

Population in 1842, 2,890; who are principally Scotch.

Ratable property in the township, £46,844

SPARTA.

A Settlement situated near the south-east corner of the township of Yarmouth, six miles east from the plank road. It contains about sixty inhabitants, two stores, one tavern, chair factory, and blacksmith. There is a Quaker meeting house and a Baptist chapel about midway between Sparta and the plank road

SPEED, RIVER.

A Branch of the Grand River. It takes its rise in the high land either in Erin or Caledon; flows through Eramosa and Guelph, and joins the Grand River in the township of Waterloo. It is an excellent mill stream; and there are several mills (both grist and saw) situated on it.

SPRINGFIELD

A Village in the west corner of the township of Brantford, situated on Whiteman's Creek, a branch of the Grand River, seven miles from the town of Brantford. The plank road from London to Hamilton passes through the village Springfield contains about 250 inhabitants, and a Methodist church

Professions and Trades —One grist mill, one saw mill, carding machine and cloth factory, two stores, two taverns, two waggon makers, one saddler, two blacksmiths, two shoemakers, one tailor, one cooper

SPRINGFIELD.

A Village in the township of Toronto, on Dundas Street, nineteen miles west from Toronto, situated on the River Credit in the midst of some very fine scenery. It contains about 140 inhabitants, and possesses an Episcopal church. There are in the village two taverns, one store, one chair factory, one tailor, and one shoemaker.

Post Office, post every day.

STAG ISLAND, or ISLE AUX CERFS

An Island in the River St Clair, five miles below Port Sarnia; contains about 150 acres, of which about 50 acres are fit for cultivation, the remainder being marsh. It belongs to the Indians, but is leased to one or two farmers.

STAMFORD.

A Township in the Niagara District; is bounded on the east by the Niagara River, on the north by the township of Niagara; on the west by Thorold; and on the south by Crowland and Willoughby. In Stamford 22,049 acres are taken up, 11,303 of which are under cultivation This is an old and well-settled township, containing good land, and numerous beautifully situated farms The Falls of Niagara are opposite this township, and the Whirlpool is also in it. The village of Chippewa is situated partly in Stamford, and partly in the adjoining township of Willoughby, which is separated from Stamford by the Welland River; and the village of Drummondville is also in the township, situated near the falls There are three grist mills in the township

Population in 1841. 2,636, who are a mixture of Canadians, English, Irish, Scotch, and Americans

Ratable property in the township, £46,071.

STANLEY.

A Township in the Huron District; is bounded on the north by the River Bayfield; on the west by Lake Huron, on the south by the township of Hay; and on the east by Tuckersmith The soil of this township is good, with the exception of the land bordering on the lake, which is poor. In Stanley there are leased or sold 16,516 acres, of which 1197 are under cultivation, The village of Bayfield is in this township, at the entrance of the river into Lake Huron.

Population, 737.

Ratable property in the township, £6130. 18s.

STEPHEN

A Township in the Huron District, is bounded on the north by the township of Hay, on the west by Lake Huron and the Sable River, on the south by McGillivray; and on the east by Usborne and Biddulph. The land bordering on the lake, for about a mile in length, is sandy and unfit for cultivation; but most of the rest of the township is good Stephen contains 41,603 acres, 4,150 of which are leased or sold, of which 520 acres are under cultivation.

Population of Stephen, 213.

Ratable property in the township, £1,998 10s.

STONEBRIDGE, or PETERSBURGH.

A Village in the township of Humberstone, situated on the feeder of the Welland Canal, one mile and a half from Lake Erie. It is supported almost entirely by the works on the Canal A detachment of the Coloured Company is quartered here.

Population about 200, exclusive of the laboures on the canal.

Professions and Trades.—One physician and surgeon, one distillery, one foundry, seven stores, one druggist, three taverns, two waggon makers, three blacksmiths, three butchers, four shoemakers, two saddlers, three tailors, one tinsmith.

STORMONT.

A County in the Eastern District. It comprises the townships of Cornwall, Finch, Osnabruck, Roxborough, and, except for the purpose of representation in the Legislative Assembly, the town of Cornwall. It returns a member to the House of Assembly.

STORRINGTON.

A Township in the Midland District; is bounded on the east by the township of Hinchinbrooke; on the north by Kennebec and Olden, on the west by Sheffield; and on the South by Portland. In Storrington 24,249 acres are taken up, 6441 of which are under cultivation. This township has lately been divided off from Hinchinbrooke it is well settled, and contains some good farms. It is watered by branches of the Napanee River. There is one saw mill in the township.
Population in 1845, 1,584.
Ratable property in the township, £17,040.

STOUFFVILLE, or STOUFFERSVILLE.

A small Village in the township of Markham, situated on the town-line between Markham and Whitchurch, eleven miles from Yonge Street. It contains about seventy inhabitants, one physician and surgeon, two stores, two taverns, one blacksmith, one waggon maker, one oatmeal mill, one tailor, one shoemaker.
Post Office, post three times a week.

STREETSVILLE

A Village in the township of Toronto, seven miles from Dundas Street, and twenty-three miles from Toronto It was laid out in 1819 It is prettily situated on the River Credit, in a good farming country, and contains about 550 inhabitants. A stage has been lately started, to run from the village to Toronto daily. Streetsville contains three churches and chapels, viz, Episcopal, Presbyterian, and Methodist; and a court-house.
Post Office, post four times a week

Professions and Trades —Two physicians and surgeons, two grist mills, three saw mills, one carding machine and cloth factory, four stores, one foundry, one druggist, one tannery, one land surveyor, four taverns, two saddlers, one carriage maker, one watchmaker, three waggon makers, one baker, four shoemakers, six tailors, six blacksmiths, six carpenters, two cabinet makers, two coopers, one gunsmith, one wheelwright, one painter.

ST ANDREWS (*See* CORNWALL.)

ST. ANDREWS.

An intended Village in the township of Nissouri, situated on the Governor's road, twelve miles east from London, and fourteen miles west from Woodstock It contains a saw mill and store, and a grist mill is in course of erection About 150 village lots have been sold.

ST. CATHARINES.

A Town in the township of Grantham, situated on the Welland Canal, thirty-six miles from Hamilton, and twelve miles from Niagara. The town is beautifully situated, having a fine view for a considerable distance of the Welland Canal and surrounding country. It is a place of much trade, which arises partly from its contiguity to the Welland Canal, and partly from its extensive water power—an immense quantity of wheat being annually converted into flour. The town is well laid out, and contains some excellent buildings; it was incorporated in the year 1845, and at present contains a mixed population of about 3,500.

Stages pass through the town daily during the winter, from Hamilton to Queenston and Niagara, and to Fort Erie, opposite Buffalo; and three times a week—Monday, Wednesday and Friday—to Dunnville on the Grand River. In summer, daily to Chippewa. and to Niagara, to meet the boats to and from Hamilton and Toronto, and Buffalo. There is a ship-yard and dry dock for the repair of vessels; and the principal office belonging to the Welland Canal is kept here. A fire company is established, with two engines.

The grammar school is a handsome building; and there are also barracks, with one company of Canadian Rifles. A newspaper, the "St. Catharines Journal," is published here weekly.

Churches and chapels, six, viz., Episcopal, Scotch Secession, American Presbyterian, Catholic, Methodist and Baptist.

Post Office, post every day.

Professions and Trades.—Six physicians and surgeons, five lawyers, four grist mills (containing twenty run of stones), one trip hammer, one brewery, three distilleries, one tannery, one foundry, one ashery, one machine and pump factory, two surveyors, one pottery, fourteen stores, two auctioneers, twenty-four groceries, one stove store, one printer, one pail factory, one broom factory, one tallow chandler, eight taverns, three saddlers, three cabinet makers, two booksellers and stationers, three druggists, one gunsmith, two watchmakers, three carriage makers, three bakers, two hatters, two livery stables, seven blacksmiths, one veterinary surgeon, three tinsmiths, one tobacconist, seven tailors, nine shoe makers, one grammar school, four schools for young ladies, three bank agencies—" Upper Canada," " Montreal," and " Commercial."

Principal Tavern " St. Catharines House "

Stage fares from St. Catharines.

	s.	d.
To Hamilton	10	0
" Niagara	5	0
" Buffalo	7	6
" Chippewa	2	6
" Dunnville	10	0
" Queenston	2	6

Quantity of flour shipped from St. Catharines during the season of 1844—70,772 barrels.

ST. DAVIDS.

A Village in the township of Niagara, three miles west from Queenston, situated below the mountain, close to the main road from Hamilton to Queenston. It contains about 150 inhabitants.

Professions and Trades.—Two water grist mills, one steam do., one distillery, one tannery, one brewery, one ashery, one carding machine and cloth factory, two stores, one tavern, one cooper, one blacksmith.

ST CLAIR RIVER.

Receives the waters of Lake Huron, and conveys them to Lake St. Clair Including its windings, it is about thirty miles long, and from three quarters of a mile to a mile and a half broad. Between Lake Huron and Lake St. Clair it divides Canada from the United States. There were formerly, within the memory of persons still living in the neighbourhood, three channels connecting the river with Lake Huron; two of these, however, have become filled up, and a cape has been formed called Point Edward, below which is a considerable bay with deep water, well sheltered by Point Edward, capable of affording accommodation to any number of vessels. There is a large island in the river, opposite the upper portion of the township of Moore; and opposite the settlement of "Sutherlands," near the American shore, is a considerable extent of clay banks (called here "flats"), covered with about four feet of water, where some of the old inhabitants say they recollect the existence of an island, and that when children they used to paddle across in canoes in order to play upon it.

The banks of the upper portion of the St Clair are high; those of the lower portion are lower, and in parts inclined to be marshy The banks of the river generally are well settled, and many of the farms are beautifully situated. The flourishing village of Port Sarnia is situated at the head of the St. Clair, in the township of Sarnia; and Froomefield, Corunna and Sutherlands, in the township of Moore. There are several wharves constructed on the Canadian side of the river, for the convenience of supplying the steamboats passing with wood: large quantities are sold; and, as the land near the river becomes cleared, the commodity rises in value.

In the lower portion of the township of Sarnia is a settlement of Chippewa Indians. These Indians are among the first whom Sir John Colborne endeavoured to settle and civilize Previously to 1830 they were wandering heathens, scattered over the western part of the Upper Province. In 1830 a number of them were collected on this reserve, containing 10,280 acres A number of houses were built for them, and an officer was appointed for their superintendence. Their conversion to Christianity, and their progress in religious knowledge, and in the acquisition of sober, orderly and industrious habits, has been, under the care of missionaries of the Wesleyan Methodist Society, both rapid and uniform. The total number of the Indians up to the year 1839 does not appear to have exceeded 350. Since then their number has increased greatly by immigration, chiefly from the Saginaw Bay in the State of Michigan, and by the settlement of wandering Indians; and in 1842, as many as 741 received presents.

There are two other settlements under the same superintendence; one at the River aux Sables, in the township of Bosanquet, on a reserve of 2650 acres, and another almost adjoining it, on a reserve of 2446 acres, at Kettle Point in the same township, where five families reside.

These Indians also possess a fourth reserve, on the River St. Clair. within the township of Moore, containing 2575 acres Owing to the immigration which has taken place on this portion, since the notice to the visiting Indians of the United States was issued, and the removals which have occurred at these and the other Indian settlements in the neighbourhood, together with the mode in which the returns have been rendered, it is difficult to state with precision the progress and the increase of each settlement

At present they are established chiefly on the front of the upper reserve, having small farms of six and a half chains in width on the River St. Clair. The total number of separate farms is forty-two, on sixteen of which there are good substantial log houses, erected by the government on the first formation of the settlement; but on the lower part of the reserve, where no houses were built by the government, the Indians reside in small log or bark houses of their own erection. There is only one log building resembling a barn , but almost all the Indians have small out-houses or sheds in which they house their crops.

From a return made in 1839, there were twenty families occupying houses, who had 146 acres of land cleared, of which 100 were under cultivation Their stock then consisted of two oxen, three cows, and two pigs, and they possessed three ploughs, two harrows, and nine sleighs At present there are thirty-two families settled on the reserve, who have improved 205 acres of land. four individuals have improved from ten to thirty acres, of the others, fifteen have five acres or more, and the remainder under five acres cleared. There are also five families settled on some land purchased with their annuity, and some held by license of occupation under the government, in Enniskillen. These have

o 2

about forty acres under cultivation, and possess two good log houses, and two small log barns

The Indians of the River aux Sables, have about sixty acres under improvement, and one log house. Those at Kettle Point have twenty acres of improved land, and two log houses. The land on the upper reserve was regularly surveyed and laid out in farms. The chief with the approval of the superintendent, placed most of the present occupants on these lands, but it is not indispensable that he should be consulted, as the members of the tribe may choose any unoccupied spot, when once in possession they are secure from intrusion, but repeated ill conduct or drunkenness would subject them to be expelled from the reserve of the chief

They are decidedly improved in agriculture they now understand ploughing, seeding, harrowing, the management of cattle, &c They possess eight ploughs and four harrows, which each family uses alternately a number of scythes and sickles, two fanning mills, and four cross-cut saws, form part of their general stock, besides which each family possesses an axe, and a sufficiency of hoes, &c. They have nine yoke of oxen, eight cows, and some young stock, besides a large number of horses and pigs They are exceedingly attentive to their cattle, and feed them well during the winter. They cultivate chiefly Indian corn and potatoes, with small quantities of spring wheat, oats and peas The field labour is entirely done by the male adults, but the women do all the lighter work of weeding and hoeing the Indian corn and potatoes.

Their fondness for hunting is much diminished, and they seldom hunt except when obliged to do so by want of meat, their stock at present being insufficient to keep them supplied. They have two excellent fisheries, yielding an abundance of herrings and whitefish, and, during the run of the fish in the spring and fall they devote a great part of their time to fishing. They have seines, which the young men, combining in bands, use alternately. Besides the fish which they retain for their own consumption, they dispose of considerable quantities to the white settlers on the banks of the river

The majority of these Indians are Wesleyan Methodists, all those residing in the upper reserve belong to that community, and attend public worship, which is performed in a capacious meeting-house built for the joint purpose of a church and school-house by the government, and lent to the mission, those at the River aux Sables are either members of the Church of England, or are desirous of being admitted into it There are also one or two families of Roman Catholics, and those residing at Kettle Point are heathens

The members of the Church of England at the River aux Sables to which place they retired about two years ago, have as yet neither a clergyman nor a place of worship. This year a catechist, an Indian by birth, has been appointed by the bishop to the charge of this settlement

There is a school-house at the upper reserve, under the direction of the missionary, which is attended by twenty or thirty scholars of both sexes The health of these Indians is good—their numbers are on the increase, they generally have five children to a family, of whom perhaps three arrive at maturity

Many of these Indians are industrious; some of those at the upper reserve are employed to cut cord-wood by the white settlers, and a few of them will manage to cut and pile three cords of wood per day others employ themselves in making bowls, brooms, rush mats and matting, axe handles, baskets, &c, which they usually manage to dispose of to the white settlers in the neighbourhood of the St. Clair.

ST CLAIR, LAKE

A Lake situated between Lake Huron and Lake Erie. It receives the waters of the upper lakes from the River St. Clair, and discharges them into the Detroit River In the widest part it is about twenty-six miles across, and in length, from the head of the Detroit River to the entrance of the River St. Clair, it is about twenty-five miles. In the upper portion of the lake are several large islands, the principal of which are Walpole Island, which is inhabited by Indians (for a description of which see "Walpole Island"), and St. Anne's Island. All the islands to the west of Walpole Island belong to the Americans. The north-eastern channel, separating the island from the main land, is called "Chenail Ecarté;" and that dividing Walpole and St. Anne's Islands is called "Johnson's Channel.".

Besides the River St. Clair, Lake St. Clair receives the River Thames, Bear Creek, Little Bear Creek, and several smaller streams, which enter it on the west and south sides.

Much of the land bordering on the lake is low and marshy, and in places there are extensive plains, which are useful for grazing cattle.

A great rise took place in the lake in the year 1827, which did great damage to the land bordering on it, laying much of the low land under water, and destroying many fine orchards. It has since been gradually subsiding, and the land is becoming dry again, but the damage to the fruit trees was irreparable.

ST. JOHNS.

A Village on the town-line between Thorold and Pelham (the principal part of the village being in Thorold), situated on the road from Hamilton to the Falls of Niagara. It contains about 400 inhabitants and a Methodist church.

Post Office, post twice a week.

Professions and Trades.—Four grist mills, one foundry, two cloth factories, one machine shop, one store, one tavern, one carriage factory, one waggon-maker, two blacksmiths, one tannery.

ST. LAWRENCE. (*The principal River in Canada.*)

It receives the waters of the great lakes from Lake Ontario and conveys them to the Gulf of St. Lawrence. It is nearly half a mile wide at its commencement, and ninety miles wide at its mouth. The name was originally given to the Gulf, and afterwards extended to the River, by Cartier, an early French navigator, in 1534, in honour of a saint in the Romish calendar. Soon after its commencement, it expands into the "Lake of the Thousand Isles;" a portion of the river, the scenery of which is most beautiful and romantic, being studded with islands, some of which are many acres in extent, and others only a few feet square, and most of which are covered with red cedar; some are only just above the surface of the water, and others are abrupt and craggy rocks, jutting up perpendicularly to the height of thirty or forty feet. Sometimes you pass through a narrow channel, between rocks, where, at a short distance, you would imagine there was scarcely room for a boat to pass. In passing through the lake, during the last summer, in company with a German who had travelled over Germany, Switzerland, and France, he declared that in point of natural beauty, the scenery of the Rhine was not to be compared to it. He acknowledged that the addition of old castles and picturesque ruins, added charms to the scenery of the Rhine, that were wanting in that of the St Lawrence; but that in true *natural beauty*, it was far from equal to the Lake of the Thousand Isles.

There are several rapids in the river, some of which it is difficult, and others impossible for sailing vessels or other craft to ascend; and steamboats and vessels, conveying goods between Kingston and Montreal, have been in the habit of descending the rapids, and returning by the Ottawa River, being towed by steamboats through the Rideau Canal. The principal of these rapids, are the Galoppes Rapids, Point Iroquois do., Rapide Plat do., Parren's Point do., the Long Sault do., the Coteau do., the Cedars do., the Cascades do., and the Lachine do. The Galoppes Rapids are situated at about six miles below Prescott. The current in the river is very strong, varying from six to ten miles per hour. The *first class* steam passage vessels can overcome these rapids, as those at

Point Iroquois, Rapid Plat, and Farren's Point in the natural state of the river; but to enable *trade vessels* generally to ascend the Galoppes, improvements are in progress, which consist of one guard lock, one lock with a lift of between seven and eight feet, and a lateral cut or canal two miles in length. The Point Iroquois Rapids occur at about twelve miles below Prescott; to enable vessels to ascend them, a canal has been constructed about three miles in length, with a lock having a lift of about six feet. This work is not quite finished, but will be completed during the present year. The Rapide Plat Rapids are about nineteen miles below Prescott, and to overcome them, a canal has been made about four miles in length, with a guard lock, and a lift lock having about eleven and a half feet rise. The Farren's Point Rapids are about thirty-three miles below Prescott. The improvements here consist of a canal about one mile in length, with a lock having about four feet lift. The next rapids are those of the Long Sault, these are serious, and may indeed be called insurmountable obstacles to ascending the river; they have been avoided by the construction of the Cornwall Canal, which is about twelve miles in length, and commences at the village of Dickenson's Landing, eleven miles above the town of Cornwall. The next work connected with the St Lawrence is the Beauharnois Canal, the object of which is to open a communication from Lake St Francis to Lake St. Louis, avoiding all the rapids of the Coteau, the Cedars, and the Cascades, which occur in the portion of the St. Lawrence between those lakes.

During the season of 1844 it was stated, and generally believed, that a new channel had been discovered through the Cedars Rapids, with a considerable depth of water, and it was supposed, therefore, that no obstruction existed to the passage of vessels, drawing from eight to nine feet water, down all the rapids to Montreal. However, it appeared that this was a mistake, for as the proprietor of the steamboat St George was endeavouring to take his boat (drawing six feet water) through the newly discovered channel, she struck so heavily in several parts of the Coteau and Cascades Rapids as to make it necessary to run her into the entrance of the Beauharnois Canal, to prevent her from sinking.

The several works of the enlargement of the Lachine Canal are nearly completed, and are expected to be sufficiently so to allow of the passage of first class vessels, which then will be enabled to run up from Montreal to Toronto and Hamilton; and, through the Welland Canal, to Lakes Erie, St. Clair and Huron. Below Montreal, the St. Lawrence is navigable for first class vessels from the ocean.

There are many islands in the St Lawrence, some of large size, and others mere rocks. Of these, the largest above Lake St Francis, are Gore Island, opposite the townships of Leeds and Landsdowne, and Sheek's Island and Cornwall Island, opposite the townships of Cornwall and Osnabruck. Below Lake St Francis, there are many islands, the principal of which is the Island of Montreal; but as these are all in the Lower Province, to which the present work does not extend, it is necessary to omit a description of them. The base of the islands in the St Lawrence is limestone, and they are mostly covered with cedars, and other trees of the pine tribe.

There have been expended on the improvements of the St Lawrence up to the 1st of July, 1844, the latest date to which the returns have been published—

Prescott to Dickenson's Landing	£13,490	19 4
Cornwall, to the time of opening the canal in June, 1843...	57,110	4 2
Do to repair breaks in the banks, since the above period	9,925	16 4
Beauharnois	162,281	19 5
Lachine	45,410	11 2
Expenditure on dredge, outfit, &c., applicable to the foregoing in common	4,462	16 3
Lake St. Peter	32,893	19 3
Total	£325,576	5 11

The amount of lockage and canals on the St. Lawrence, consists of:—

	No. of Locks.	Length of Canal MILES.
The Galloppes	2	2
Point Iroquois	1	2¾
Rapide Plat	2	4
Farren's Point	1	0¾
Cornwall Canal	7	11¼
Beauharnois Canal	9	11¼
Total	22	32¼

The banks of the St Lawrence, above Montreal, are generally rather low, the greater portion of them have been long settled, and bear the aspect of a country which has been long reclaimed from its primeval wildness.

From its commencement, till it reaches the St Regis settlement, the St Lawrence separates Upper Canada from the United States, afterwards it divides Upper from Lower Canada; and it forms the southern boundary of the Johnstown and the Eastern districts

The principal towns and villages on the St Lawrence, are Brockville, the district town of the Johnstown District: Cornwall, the district town of the Eastern District; Prescott, in the township of Augusta; Gananoque, in Leeds; and Milleroches, in Cornwall

ST. JOSEPH ISLE.
An Island in the north-west of Lake Huron.

ST MARY'S.

A Village in the township of Blanshard, situated at the falls of the north branch of the River Thames, twelve miles from Stratford, and twenty-five miles north-west from Ingersol It was laid out in 1844, and contains about 120 inhabitants. There is an excellent limestone quarry close to the village

Professions and Trades—One grist mill, one saw do , one physician and surgeon, two asheries, three stores, one tavern, one shoemaker, one tailor, one cooper, one blacksmith.

STRANGE'S MILL.—(*See* ERAMOSA)

STRATFORD.

A Village on the Huron Road, at the corners of the townships of Ellice, North and South Easthope, and Downie. It is forty-five miles from Goderich. The River Avon, a branch of the Thames, runs through the village.

Stratford contains about 200 inhabitants

Post Office, post three times a-week.

Professions and Trades—Two physicians and surgeons, one grist and saw mill, one tannery, three stores, one brewery, one distillery, one ashery, two taverns, two blacksmiths, one saddler, two wheelwrights, three shoemakers, two tailors

ST. THOMAS.

A large Village in the township of Yarmouth, beautifully situated on Kettle Creek, seventeen miles from London, and nine miles from Port Stanley. It is surrounded by a succession of hill and dale, and in the midst of a fine, well cultivated country It was laid out about thirty years since, and now contains between 7 and 800 inhabitants It is a place of considerable business. The plank road from London to Port Stanley runs through the village, north and south, and the Talbot Road, east and west. Stages from London to Port Stanley pass through the village daily. A weekly newspaper is published here, the "St. Thomas Standard" Churches and chapels, six; viz., Episcopal, Presbyterian, Catholic, two Methodist, and a Baptist.

Post Office, post three times a week.

Professions and Trades—Four physicians and surgeons, three lawyers, one grist and saw mill, carding machine and cloth factory, two foundries, two breweries, two distilleries, ten stores, six groceries, four taverns, one temperance house, two druggists, one printer, four saddlers, one baker, two butchers, one watchmaker, four coopers, eight blacksmiths, three waggon makers, five tailors, four shoemakers, one painter and glazier, one tinsmith, one surveyor. Two bank agencies—" Montreal," and " Gore "

Principal Tavern.—" Ivor's,"

ST. VINCENT.

A Township in the Simcoe District; is bounded on the north by the Nottawasaga Bay; on the west by the township of Sydenham, on the south by Euphrasia, and on the east by Nottawasaga Bay and the township of Collingwood. In St Vincent 17,028 acres are taken up, 1592 of which are under cultivation. This township is beginning to settle up fast it contains good land, and some thriving farms. The principal settlements are a short distance from the bay. There is an Indian village on the bay, near the town line between St. Vincent and Sydenham, the inhabitants of which possess a fine tract of land in the neighbourhood. St Vincent was added to the Simcoe District in 1844, previous to which time, it formed a portion of the Home District. One thousand five hundred acres of Crown lands are open for sale in the township, at 8s. currency per acre. There are two grist and two saw mills in the township.

There has as yet been no return of the population from St Vincent.

Ratable property in the township, £6758

ST. WILLIAMS, or PORT METCALFE.

A Village in the township of Charlotteville, situated on Lake Erie, six miles west from Normandale It contains about 100 inhabitants and a Methodist church, one store, one tavern, one waggon maker, one blacksmith, one tailor, one shoemaker.

STURGEON CREEK.

A small Stream in the township of Mersea, which runs into Lake Erie; on which is a grist mill.

STURGEON LAKE—(*See* Rice Lake)

SULLIVAN

A Township in the Wellington District, is bounded on the east by the township of Holland, on the north by Derby, on the west by unsurveyed lands; and on the south by Bentinck This township has only lately been surveyed and laid out, and no return has yet been made from it Fifty-two thousand two hundred acres of Crown lands are open for sale in it, at 8s. currency per acre.

SUNNIDALE.

A Township in the Simcoe District; is bounded on the north by the Nottawasaga Bay, on the west by the township of Nottawasaga, on the south by Tossorontio and Essa, and on the east by Flos and Vespra In Sunnidale 3144 acres are taken up, 378 of which are under cultivation The Nottawasaga River enters the township at the south-east corner—runs nearly north for rather more than three miles, when it curves to the east, and leaves the township: after passing through the townships of Vespra and Flos, it re-enters Sunnidale, about three miles from the bay, runs west to within a mile of the town line between Sunnidale and Nottawasaga, then makes a bend and runs north-east, parallel with the bay, just within the township of Flos. Much of the land in the township is hilly and broken. Eighteen thousand four hundred acres of Crown lands are open for sale in Sunnidale, at 8s. currency per acre. There is one saw mill in the township.

Sunnidale is as yet but little settled, and in 1842, it only contained 174 inhabitants.

Ratable property in the township, £1461.

SUTHERLAND'S

A Village in the township of Moore, pleasantly situated on the River St. Clair, opposite the American town "St. Clair," or "Palmer." It was laid out in 1833, by Mr. Sutherland, a gentleman from Edinburgh, who has done a great deal to improve the neighbourhood—having cleared a large quantity of land—built a handsome Episcopal church, &c. Here are several wharves for supplying steamboats with wood. Sutherlands is ten miles from Port Sarnia, and contains a comfortable tavern.

Post Office, post three times a-week.

Population, about 100.

Professions and Trades.—One physician and surgeon, three stores, one tavern, two blacksmiths, one tailor, one shoemaker, one school.

SYDENHAM

A Village in the township of Toronto, 14½ miles from Toronto, situated on Dundas Street. It contains about 140 inhabitants. There is a stone chapel, a short distance from the village, free for all denominations.

Professions and Trades.—Steam grist mill and distillery, brewery, one store, one tavern, one tannery, two blacksmiths, two waggon makers, one carpenter, one butcher, one shoemaker.

SYDENHAM

A Township in the Wellington District, is bounded on the north by Owen Sound; on the west by the township of Derby, on the south by Holland, and on the east by St. Vincent. This township has only lately been opened for sale, and no return has yet been made from it. The land is of good quality. A village, called "Sydenham," is commenced on an excellent mill stream, about a mile back from the lake. At present it contains a grist and saw mill, store, and about 150 inhabitants. In Sydenham 81,180 acres of Crown lands are open for sale, at 8s currency per acre.

TALBOT DISTRICT.

Consists of the county of Norfolk, which comprises the townships of Charlotteville, Houghton, Middleton, Townsend, Woodhouse, Windham, and Walsingham, and for all purposes, except that of representation in the Legislative Assembly, and that of registration of titles, the townships of Rainham and Walpole. The Talbot District is bounded on the north-east by the Niagara District and the Gore district, on the north by the Brock District, on the west by the London District, and on the south by Lake Erie. The district is watered by Big Creek, and a small portion of Otter Creek, besides numerous smaller streams, many of which are excellent mill-streams. The land varies in quality; that in the townships of Walsingham, Houghton and Middleton is principally timbered with pine, that in the other townships is hardwood and pine intermixed. Long Point, which is now an island, is included in the district. Much of the land in the district is rolling, and Simcoe, the district town, is very handsomely situated.

The Talbot District is settled principally by Canadians, with a few Scotch,

Irish and English. It improves but very slowly, and between January, 1842, and January 1844, only 2,800 acres of land were brought into cultivation.

Besides Simcoe, the district town, there are in the district, the villages of Port Dover and Port Ryerse in Woodhouse, Normandale, (where is a blast furnace for smelting the iron (bog) ore found in the neighbourhood) Vittoria and St. Williams in Charlotteville, Waterford in Townsend, Port Rowan and Port Royal in Walsingham, and Fredericksburgh in Middleton. There are no Crown lands for sale in the Talbot District.

Population in 1841, 9,626, since when it has probably increased one-sixth.

The following abstract from the assessment rolls will show the rate of increase and improvement in the district:

Date.	No. of Acres Cultivated.	MILLS. Grist.	MILLS. Saw.	Milch Cows.	Oxen, 4 years old and upwards.	Horned Cattle, from 2 to 4 years old.	Amount of Ratable Property.
1842	54,049	10	48	3,846	1,336	3,846	£166,003
1843	54,895	10	53	4,119	1,503	2,002	169,124
1844	56,899	10	50	4,186	1,643	1,649	185,633

Government and District Officers in the Talbot District:

Judge of District Court............	William Salmon.....................	Simcoe.
Sheriff................................	H. V. A. Rapelje	Do.
Clerk of Peace	W. M. Wilson	Do.
Treasurer	H. Webster	Do.
Inspector of Licenses...............	E. P. Ryerse	Do.
District Clerk.......................	J. H. Davis.........................	Do.
Clerk of District Court	W. M. Wilson	Do.
Superintendent of Schools	Rev. W. Clarke	Do.
Crown Lands Agent	D. Campbell	Do.
Warden	J. W. Powell	Do.

Number of Common Schools in operation in the District.—Townsend, 19; Woodhouse, 12; Charlotteville, 10; Walsingham, 8; Houghton, 6; Middleton, 7; Windham, 9; Walpole, 6; Rainham, 4. Total, 81.

TALFOURD'S.—(*See* FROOMEFIELD.)

TALBOT MILLS.—(*See* SELBORNE.)

TAY.

A Township in the Simcoe District; is bounded on the north by Gloucester Bay; on the west by the township of Tiny; on the south by Medonte; and on the east by Matchadash. In Tay 3159 acres are taken up, 489 of which are under cultivation. Gloucester Bay makes several irregular projections into this township, and Penetanguishine Bay completely divides it into two portions. This township is as yet but little settled, most of the inhabitants, with the exception of those belonging to the government establishment on the bay, being half Indian. There are 3,400 acres of Crown lands for disposal in the township of Tay, at 8s. c'y per acre.

Population in 1842, 202.

Ratable property in the township £1,643.

TECUMSETH.

A Township in the Simcoe District; is bounded on the north by the township of Essa; on the west by Adjala; on the south by Albion and King, and on the east by Gwillimbury West. In Tecumseth 40,768 acres are taken up, 11,576 of which are under cultivation. The township is well watered by numerous small streams which unite in the north of the township, forming the Nottawasaga River. A large swamp is situated on the town-line between Tecumseth and West Gwillimbury, which borders the Nottawasaga River, and is joined in the north of the township by another swamp, which extends into Adjala. Tecumseth is well settled, and contains many fine farms; the land is generally rolling, and the timber of good quality. There are in the township one grist and six saw mills. In Tecumseth 8,000 acres of Crown lands are open for sale, at 8s. c'y per acre

Population in 1842, 2,491, who are principally Scotch, Irish, and Americans. Ratable property in the township, £27,790.

TEMPERANCEVILLE

A Settlement in the township of Malahide, on Talbot Street, about ten miles east from St. Thomas, situated on Catfish Creek, or River Barbu. It contains about 100 inhabitants, one store, two taverns, one waggon maker, one tailor, one blacksmith.

THAMES, RIVER.

One of the principal rivers in Canada West, formerly called *La Tranche*. The north, or principal branch, takes its rise in the great swamp, north of the Huron District; passes through McKillop and Logan, into the north corner of Fullarton, where it is joined by a branch from Hibbert. Lower down in the township it is joined by a small branch, it then passes out of the south corner of Fullarton, cuts across the east corner of Blanshard into Nissouri, where it is joined by a branch, called the "Avon," which runs through Easthope and Zorra. It then flows into the township of London, where it is joined by a branch from Usborn and Biddulph. At the town of London it is joined by the east branch, which takes its rise in Easthope forms the dividing line between Blandford and Zorra, separates West from North Oxford, North from South Dorchester, and then flows along the south border of the township of London, separating it from Westminster. After joining the north branch, the united stream continues its course in a south-westerly direction, forming the dividing boundary between the townships of Lobo, Carradoc, Ekfrid, Mosa, Zone, Camden West, Chatham and Dover, on the north, and Delaware, Southwold, Dunwich, Aldboro, Orford, Howard, Harwich, Raleigh, and East Tilbury, on the south; between which last township and Dover, it discharges itself into Lake St Clair. It is joined by many small streams in its course, and at Chatham it is joined by M'Gregor's Creek.

On the *upper* portions of this river are numerous grist and saw mills.

At and above Delaware, it affords fine trout fishing; and below, during the spring, quantities of white fish, pike, pickerel, and maskelonge are taken, with occasionally sturgeon. Several hundred barrels of fish are frequently cured at and in the neighbourhood of Chatham.

The Thames is navigable for steamboats and schooners to Louisville, a village nearly thirty miles from its mouth, and might be made navigable to London, at no very great expense. To Louisville, it is of an average depth of 16 feet, and in breadth from 200 to 300 feet. The river passes through some of the finest country in Western Canada, the banks on the upper portion being high and rolling, while below, for a distance of about thirty-five miles, the land is mostly level and rich, forming some of the best farming land in the Western District, and noted for its superior growth of wheat. Many of the farms on this portion of the river, have been settled for fifty years, and are in a high state of cultivation, with fine orchards.

There are large quantities of fine white oak and black walnut on the banks of the river, and a considerable trade has for some years been carried on in staves, and walnut lumber. The former are floated down the river from the land where they are cut, to Chatham, where they are collected and shipped on board schooners, which are sent from Kingston, and other ports, for that purpose.

At London and Delaware, are handsome bridges lately erected over the river; that at Delaware is particularly admired. A new bridge is expected to be erected at Chatham, during the year 1846. The scenery on many parts of the Thames is very picturesque.

There are three Indian settlements on the Thames, in the townships of Orford, Delaware, and Carradoc, occupied by Indians of the Delaware, Chippewa, Munsee, and Oneida tribes.

The settlement of the Delaware Indians, was one of the first established by Indians in Canada West. In 1792, the principal remnant of the once flourishing congregations of the Moravian, or United Brethren Church, in the United States, was compelled to seek an asylum in Upper Canada, where they were favourably received by the provincial authorities, and were permitted to settle on the River La Tranche, (now called the Thames). By an Order in Council, dated 10th July, 1793, a large tract of land on the river, comprising about 50,000 acres, was granted for their use; on which they proceeded to build a village, called Fairfield, a church, and other premises, at the expense of a voluntary society, established at Bethlehem, in the state of Pennsylvania, in the year 1787, under the name of "The Brethren's Society for the Propagation of the Gospel." By a second Order in Council, dated 26th February, 1799, a survey of this tract was ordered to be made, and the land was appropriated to the trustees of the Moravian Society, "to be reserved for ever to the society, in trust, for the sole use of their Indian converts."

The first settlement was destroyed in 1813, by an invading army of Americans. A severe battle was fought in the village, and the noted Indian chief, Tecumseth, was killed. After which event, the tribe removed to the opposite side of the river, in the township of Orford, in the Western District; where they possess a tract of land, containing about 25,000 acres. At present, there are only two or three families residing on the old battle ground, on the north side of the river. In 1836, these Indians were induced by Sir F. Head to surrender a large portion of their lands, about six miles square, in exchange for an annuity of £150.

The number of Indians who belong to the tribe of the Delawares, was 302 in 1837; but owing to a dissension which arose the previous year, relative to the sale of their lands, a portion of the community retired to Missouri, United States; and their present number is only 153. The settlement in Orford is generally known as Moraviantown.

The Chippewas and Munsees occupy a tract of land, containing about 9000 acres, in the township of Carradoc, in the London District. It is only within the last ten years that the Chippewas have been reclaimed from a wandering life, and settled in their present location. The Munsees have been settled since the year 1800, on land belonging to the Chippewas, with the consent of that tribe. Their village is called "Munsee-town." The present number of Chippewas is 378, and of Munsees 242.

The Oneidas are a band of American Indians, who came into Canada in the year 1840, and have purchased, with the produce of their former lands and improvements, sold to the American Government, a tract of about 5000 acres, in the township of Delaware, in the London District, which is separated by the River Thames, from the Chippewa and Munsee settlements. Their number is 436. There are also several Pottawatamie families, who have fixed their residence among the Chippewas, during the last year; and a band of about 500 Senecas, from Tonawantee, in the state of New York, are expected shortly to form a settlement near their brethren, the Oneidas.

The Chippewas possess an annuity of £600, granted by the government for a surrender of land made in 1832, the Moravians have £150 per annum, in exchange for land ceded to Sir F. B. Head; the Munsees have no annuity.—These three tribes partake of the presents. The Oneidas neither possess an annuity, nor are entitled to presents; but they brought with them into Canada a considerable sum of money, received from the American government in purchase of their lands and improvements, which they lodged in the hands of the chief superintendent.

The Moravian Delawares are collected in a village, which contains one frame and thirty-four log-houses, with ten barns. They have 292 acres under cultivation. Their stock consists of 14 oxen, 40 cows and 47 heifers, 60 horses, 35 sheep, and 200 swine. they possess 8 waggons, 16 ploughs, 5 harrows, 3 fanning mills, &c.

The Chippewas and Munsees live on small farms, scattered over their tract. Some of the Chippewas are settled on surveyed lots of 20 acres each. This tribe occupies 70 log houses and six wigwams, with 25 barns attached. They have 450 acres under cultivation. Their stock consists of 30 oxen, 27 cows, 44 heifers, 82 horses and colts, and 400 swine. Their agricultural implements include 4 waggons and carts, a fanning-mill, 9 ploughs, 9 harrows, &c. They have a blacksmith's forge, and two and a half sets of carpenter's tools.

The Munsees occupy one frame and 50 log houses, to which are attached 10 barns. They have 269 acres under cultivation They possess 14 oxen, 50 cows, 30 heifers, 35 horses and colts, and 250 swine Their implements include 5 waggons, 11 ploughs, 7 harrows, a fanning-mill, &c.

The Oneidas, who are more recently settled, but who brought with them the means of purchasing from old settlers, occupy 6 frame and 48 log houses, with 4 wigwams; they have also 5 frame and 15 log barns. They cultivate 335 acres of land. Their stock consists of 64 oxen, 61 cows, 27 heifers, 17 horses, and 162 swine. They possess 14 waggons and carts, 13 ploughs, 16 harrows, three fanning-mills, two sets of carpenter's tools, &c

Those families who live in wigwams do so from necessity, and not from choice.

A number of the Chippewas are settled on surveyed lots, as already stated, but in general each Indian selects the spot which he wishes to cultivate, and the chiefs do not interfere. The extent of land cultivated by each family varies from one to fifteen acres When a family has no land under cultivation, they depend upon the bounty of their neighbours, who are always ready to share with those in want. They also hunt; and make bowls, brooms and baskets, which they sell to the whites. There is very little decrease in the partiality of these Indians for hunting and fishing. They usually leave their homes towards the end of October, and remain away until the beginning of January · they also spend about a month during each spring in the chase. They resort to the unsettled lands in the London and Western Districts, and it is probable that as soon as these lands are occupied, they will be compelled to abandon the chase The effect of the gradual settlement of the country has been to assimilate their habits to those of the whites, and to attach them to their homes, they now hunt and fish as near home as possible.

With regard to their religious and moral condition, a very decided improvement has taken place within quite a recent period The Delawares have been converted from Paganism since the year 1783; they are all Christians, and belong to the Church of the United Brethren, who maintain a missionary among them. The converted Chippewas and Munsees belong to the Church of England, and the Wesleyan Methodist Church, but some of them remain heathens. The Pottawatamies and Oneidas are for the most part heathens

A clergyman who has ministered among these Indians during the last seven years was appointed missionary in 1840, at a salary of £100, borne upon the parliamentary grant.

The Moravians have a place of worship at their own settlement; the Episcopalians and Methodists have each a chapel in the Chippewa and Munsee settlement, and there is a Methodist chapel in the Oneida settlement.

There is a school in the Moravian settlement; two among the Chippewas and Munsees, and one among the Oneidas. The former is attended by forty-one scholars, of whom twenty-three are boys from five to fifteen years of age, and eighteen girls, from six to fourteen. The schoolmaster is maintained by the Moravian Missionary Society.

The school at Lower Munsee is under the control of the Missionary Society of the Church of England, and the scholars belong to the Chippewa and Munsee tribes. The schoolmaster receives an annual salary of £50 from the annuity of the tribe. The school is attended by twenty-one boys from six to fifteen years of age, and by four girls from six to ten; besides a number of young men and women who attend occasionally.

The second school for the same two tribes is under the control of the Wesleyan Methodist Missionary Society in Canada. It is attended by seventeen boys and eighteen girls, between six and fourteen years of age, and by three young men. The school in the Oneida settlement is also under the control of the Wesleyan Methodist Society; the teacher is an Indian of the Oneida tribe. It is attended by sixteen boys from six to sixteen years of age, and by seventeen girls from five to fifteen.

These tribes are on the increase since their conversion to Christianity. Their health is generally good, although many are stated to die from want of proper nourishment and medical treatment diseases are on the decrease among them. The average number of children born to a couple is eight; of whom about three are reared A small number only are half-breeds.

These Indians are under the general charge of a superintendent of the Indian department, who resides at Delaware.

THAMESVILLE.

A small Settlement in the township of Camden West, situated on the River Thames, fifteen miles east from Chatham. The western road passes through it. It contains about fifty inhabitants, a grist and saw mill, and tavern.

Post Office, post every day.

THORAH.

A Township in the Home District; is bounded on the north by the Talbot River; on the west by Lake Simcoe, on the south by the township of Brock; and on the east by Eldon In Thorah 15,970 acres are taken up, 2501 of which are under cultivation. This township contains excellent land, the timber on which is mostly hardwood. There is a small village on the lake shore, called "Beaverton," where is a post office. The steamboat Beaver stops here, but cannot approach the shore, on account of the shelving nature of the bank; there not being a sufficient depth of water close in shore There are some good, and prettily situated clearings on the banks of the lake. There are one grist and two saw mills in the township.

Population in 1842, 670.

Ratable property in the township, £9470.

THORNHILL.

A Settlement on Yonge Street, eleven miles from Toronto. A branch of the River Don passes through it, on which is a grist and saw mill, and tannery. There are also in the settlement, three stores, a manufactory for making threshing machines and other machinery, one blacksmith, one waggon maker, two shoemakers, one tailor.

THOROLD.

A Township in the Niagara District; is bounded on the east by the township of Stamford; on the north by Grantham and a small portion of Louth; on the west by Pelham; and on the south by Crowland. In Thorold 23,389 acres are taken up, 11,678 of which are under cultivation. The Welland River divides the township from Crowland. This is one of the best settled townships in the Niagara District, containing a great number of excellent, well cleared farms. Most of the land is rolling. The Welland Canal is carried through the township, and has added greatly to its prosperity. The villages of Thorold, Port Robinson, Allanburg, and St. Johns are situated in the township; and there are eight grist and five saw mills in the township.

Population in 1841, 2284; who are a mixture of Canadians, Americans, Irish, Scotch, English, and Welsh.

Ratable property in the township, £49,699.

THOROLD.

A Village in the township of Thorold, situated on the summit of the mountain, four miles from St. Catharines. It was commenced in the year 1826, and now contains about 1000 inhabitants. The Welland Canal runs close past the village. There are three churches and chapels in Thorold, viz., Episcopal, Catholic, and Methodist.

Post Office, post three times a-week.

Professions and Trades.—Two physicians and surgeons, two grist mills, (one do. in progress), one cement mill, one brewery, nine stores, seven taverns, one tannery, one saddler, one chemist and druggist, three waggon makers, three blacksmiths, two painters, two cabinet makers, two tinsmiths, eight shoemakers, one baker, hatter, two barbers, three tailors, one ladies' school.

THURLOW.

A Township in the Victoria District; is bounded on the east by the township of Tyendenaga; on the north by Huntingdon; on the west by Sidney; and on the south by the Bay of Quinté. In Thurlow 46,984 acres are taken up, 18,254 of which are under cultivation. The River Moira enters the township at its north-east corner, passes through the township to its south-west corner, where it enters the Bay of Quinté. This township is well settled, principally by U. E. Loyalists and their descendants, who have very good farms. The town of Belleville is situated in the south-west corner of the township, on the Bay of Quinté. There are eight grist and fifteen saw mills in Thurlow.

Population in 1842 (exclusive of Belleville), 2,649.

Ratable property in the township, (including Belleville), £79,066.

TILBURY EAST.

A Township in the Western District; is bounded on the north-east by the township of Raleigh; on the north by the River Thames; on the west by Tilbury West; and on the south by Romney—the south-east corner of the township having a frontage on Lake Erie. In East Tilbury 16,999 acres are taken up, 1,315 of which are under cultivation. A low, wet prairie or marsh, about three miles in breadth, which is used extensively for grazing, borders on the Thames. Two or three branches of the Thames run through the township. There is a Catholic church in the township, situated on the Thames, about eleven miles below Chatham. Three thousand nine hundred acres of Crown lands are open for sale in the township, at 8s. currency per acre; and about 5000 acres are possessed by the Canada Company.

Population in 1844, 540; nearly half of whom are French Canadians.

Ratable property in the township, 6,550.

TILBURY WEST.

A Township in the County of Kent; is bounded on the east by the townships of Tilbury East and Romney, on the north by Lake St. Clair, on the west by Rochester, and on the south by Mersea. In Tilbury West 10,607 acres are taken up, 707 of which are under cultivation. A wet prairie or marsh, from three to four miles in width, borders on the lake, and extends along the whole breadth of the township this is useful for grazing cattle, but is not fit for cultivation. The remainder of the land is rich and fertile, and the timber is altogether hardwood. Three thousand seven hundred acres of Crown lands are open for sale in Tilbury West, at 8s currency per acre; and the Canada Company possess about 4000 acres in the township.

Population in 1844, 437, nearly two-thirds of whom are French Canadians.

Ratable property in the township, £4,339.

TILSONBURG.

A small village in the south-east corner of the township of Dereham, situated on Otter Creek, fifteen miles from Ingersol. It contains about one hundred inhabitants, who have a Canadian Wesleyan Church.

Post Office, post three times a week.

Professions and Trades.—Grist and saw mill, carding machine and fulling mill, axe factory, one store, one tavern, two tanneries, three blacksmiths, one tailor, one shoemaker.

TINY.

A Township in the Simcoe District, is bounded on the north and west by the Georgian Bay and Nottawasaga Bay; on the South by the township of Flos; and on the east by Tay. In Tiny 8,243 acres are taken up, 892 of which are under cultivation. This is a long irregularly shaped township. A bay, called Thunder Bay, projects for about two and a half miles into the north of the township, and Penetanguishine Bay enters it from the township of Tay, cutting across the town-line, thus dividing the township into two portions. A small lake, containing about 800 acres, is situated near the south line of the township; and there are three smaller lakes in the north of the township. With the exception of the settlers in the village of Penetanguishine, the inhabitants are principally half French half Indian. In Tiny there are 21,200 acres of Crown lands for disposal, at 8s c'y per acre.

Population in 1842, 230.

Ratable property in the township, £4,610.

TORBOLTON.

A Township in the Bathurst District, is bounded on the north and north-east by the Ottawa River, on the south-east by the township of March; and on the south-west by Fitzroy. In Torbolton 7,920 acres are taken up, 1,097 of which are under cultivation. But little is done in this township in the way of agricultural operations, the inhabitants being principally engaged in lumbering. Four thousand six hundred and thirty-three acres of Crown lands are open for sale in Torbolton, at 8s c'y per acre.

Population in 1842, 389.

Ratable property in the township, £3,716.

TORONTO.

A Township in the Home District, is bounded on the east by the township of Etobicoke and a small portion of the Gore of Toronto; on the north-west by Chinguacousy, on the south-west by Trafalgar, and on the south-east by Lake Ontario. In Toronto 59,267 acres are taken up, 28,468 of which are under cultivation. This is one of the best settled townships in the Home District: it contains a large portion of very excellent land, and a number of well cultivated farms. For from two to three miles from the lake the land is light and sandy, and the timber principally pine; afterwards, it becomes rolling, and the timber the best kinds of hardwood. The Rivers Credit and Etobicoke both run through the township. The village of Cooksville is situated in the township on the Dundas Street: and the villages of Springfield, Streetsville, Churchville, and Port Credit, on the River Credit—the first is situated on Dundas Street, and the last at the mouth of the River Credit. There are four grist and twenty-one saw mills in the township.

Population in 1842, 5,377.

Ratable property in the township, £79,585.

TORONTO GORE

A Township in the Home District, is bounded on the east by the township of Vaughan and a small portion of York, on the north-west by Albion, and on the south-west by Chinguacousy and a small portion of Etobicoke. In Toronto Gore 18,206 acres are taken up, 7,784 of which are under cultivation. This is a wedge-shaped township, of small size, with its base towards the township of Albion. It is watered by branches of the River Humber, and contains some good land. It is well settled, principally by Irish and Scotch, with a few Canadians, and a large portion of the township is under cultivation. There is one grist mill in the township.

Population in 1842, 1,145

Ratable property in the township, £16,756

TORONTO

The District Town of the Home District, situated in the south-east of the township of York, on a bay of Lake Ontario. The neighbourhood first commenced settling about fifty years ago, but for some years it advanced very slowly. In 1799 the whole district, which then included a large portion of the surrounding country, which has since been formed into separate districts, contained only 224 inhabitants. In 1817 Toronto (then Little York) contained a population amounting to 1200, in 1826 it had increased to 1,677, and in 1830, to 2860. Since then its progress has been rapid, and in 1842 it contained 15,336 inhabitants, and in 1845, 19,706.

Toronto became the capital of the Upper Province in the year 1797, and remained so till after the union of the Upper and Lower Provinces, when the seat of government was removed to Kingston in 1841 by Lord Sydenham. Had this event taken place ten years sooner, it might have had a serious effect upon the prosperity of the town, but in 1841 Toronto had become a place of too great commercial importance to feel much ill effect from the removal of the government offices, and the loss of the expenditure of a few thousand pounds per annum.

The situation of that portion of the town bordering on the bay is rather low, particularly in the east of the city, towards the River Don, in the west the banks are higher, and the land generally slopes gradually up from the water's edge; so that the farther back from the bay, the higher, drier, and more healthy does the situation become.

Toronto was incorporated in the year 1834. By the act of incorporation the city was divided into five wards, called St. George's, St. Patrick's, St. Andrew's, St. David's, and St. Lawrence's—each ward to have the power to elect two aldermen and two common councilmen, who are to choose the mayor from amongst the aldermen. The corporation to have the power to make by-laws for the regulation of the internal police of the city, &c.

The improvements made in the City of Toronto within the last two years have been astonishing; many new buildings (and those the handsomest in the city) have been erected; and the side-walks, several of which were in a very

P

dilapidated state, and some almost impassable, have been relaid and much improved Toronto now contains ninety-one streets, some of which are of great length; the planked portion of King Street being about two miles long. The extreme length of the city, from the Don Bridge to the western limits of the city, is upwards of three miles. Property which was purchased a few years since for a mere trifle, has increased wonderfully in value, and many houses in King Street pay a ground rent of £100 Rents are generally as high as in the best business situations in London, England, and some houses in good situations for business let at from £200 to £250 per annum

Among the public buildings those particularly deserving of notice are the new front to Osgoode Hall, the banks, and St George's Church The Lunatic Asylum and the Catholic Cathedral, now erecting, will be extensive and handsome buildings Besides these, many of the private buildings have added greatly to the embellishment of the city and its environs The new stores at present erecting in King Street, from the design of Mr Thomas the architect, will be when finished the handsomest buildings of the kind in Canada, and equal to anything to be seen in England

The public buildings in Toronto comprise the Jail, a large stone building, situated in the east end of the town, the Court-house, which is of brick, and contains the district offices, the old Market-house over which are the Newsroom and Athenæum (or Public Library), the new City Hall, where are kept the offices of the corporation officers, and the police office, the Upper Canada College, the old Parliament Buildings (part of which is at present occupied by the officials of King's College), the Hospital, and the Post Office. There are within the city twenty-one churches and chapels, of these five are Episcopal, one Church of Scotland, one Presbyterian Church of Canada, one United Secession Presbyterian, two Roman Catholic, two British Wesleyan, one Primitive Methodist, two Canadian Wesleyan, one Congregational, one Christian, one Unitarian, one Baptist, one Disciples, and two for coloured people—Methodist and Baptist. There are also a House of Industry, Mechanic's Institute, two Fireman's Halls, Fish Market, Custom-house and Barracks

The city is lighted with gas, and there are water-works for the conveyance of water from the bay to the different houses, and there are also in the city regular stations for coaches and cabs Steamboats leave daily for Kingston, Hamilton, Niagara, Queenston and Lewiston, and Rochester calling at Port Hope, Cobourg and other intermediate places, and stages leave daily for all parts of the country. Omnibuses have been established to run regularly to Richmond Hill, Thornhill, Cooksville and Streetsville, and every hour from the market place to Yorkville; and a horse ferry-boat plies during the day between the city and the opposite island

Amongst the different societies and institutions are to be found the Freemasons, who have a provincial grand lodge, the St George's, St Patrick's and St. Andrew's Societies, St Patrick's Benevolent Society, three Odd Fellows' Lodges, a Home District Agricultural Society, Toronto Horticultural Society, the Medico-chirurgical Society, Toronto Athenæum Church Society, Bible Society, Mechanic's Institute, a Dispensary, a Theatre (the performers in which are principally amateurs), a Temperance Reformation Society, a Turf Club, Cricket Club, Curling Club and Chess Club, four Fire Companies with four engines, two Hook and Ladder Companies, a Hose Company, and a Property Protection Company There are also a Home District Savings Bank, a Fire and Life Assurance Company, and a Mutual Fire Insurance Company.— The University of King's College is empowered to grant degrees in the several arts and sciences, the Presbyterians have a Theological Seminary, and the Congregationalists an Academy

Ten newspapers are published in Toronto, viz, *British Canadian, Herald, Patriot, British Colonist, Examiner, Christian Guardian, Star, Mirror, Banner* and *Globe*. The following monthly periodicals are also published here—the *Upper Canada Jurist, British American Cultivator,* and *Sunday-school Guardian.* There are fifteen common schools in operation in the city.

The following Government and District Offices are kept in Toronto —Judge of District Court, Sheriff, Clerk of Peace, Treasurer, Registrar, Inspector of Licenses, Crown Lands Agent, Judge of Surrogate Court, Registrar of ditto, District Clerk, Clerk of District Court, Deputy Clerk of Crown, Superintendent of Schools, Probate Office, Clergy Reserves' Office, Commissariat Office, Ordnance Office, Royal Engineers' Office, Marriage License Office, Indian Office, Emigrant Agent, and Board of Works

Professions and Trades.—Twenty physicians and surgeons, sixty-five lawyers, eighteen wholesale merchants, thirty-four dry goods and general stores, eleven hardware stores, eighty-three grocery and provision stores, two china and glass stores, one stove manufactory, six booksellers and stationers, two apothecaries, one manufacturing chemist, one steam grist mill, nine chemists and druggists, eleven distilleries, four foundries, thirteen breweries, three tanneries one starch maker, four architects, two surveyors, five artists and portrait painters, one wood engraver, three engravers, two drawing masters, four music masters, one dancing master, thirteen printers, three accountants, six land agents, two dentists, one hundred and seven hotels, inns and taverns, eleven boarding houses, one optician, one cloth manufacturer, nine watchmakers, nine gardeners and florists, one wine merchant, one music store, two oil-cloth manufacturers, one silversmith, three jewellers, two coach makers one finding store, sixteen auctioneers, one nail maker, seven axe makers, one patent leather dresser, six curriers, two furriers, eight soap and candle makers, one brass founder, two iron turners, one ivory turner, one paper maker, one fanning-mill maker, one boat builder, hot and cold baths, one bellows maker, one dyer, two dairies, three French polishers, thirteen wheelwrights and waggon makers, seven bookbinders, one brush maker, two broom makers, nineteen saddlers, sixteen builders, two rope makers, four gun makers, one camphine oil maker, two veterinary surgeons, five plumbers, two sail makers, one millwright, one scale maker, ten confectioners, five turners, four picture-frame makers and gilders, one pump maker, seven maltsters, three tobacconists five upholsterers four livery stables, nine shoe stores, nine hatters, forty-nine shoemakers, twenty-five cabinet makers, two cutlers, one sculptor, one chair maker, nineteen bakers, two greengrocers, twenty-three tin and copper smiths, six coopers, two marble workers, thirty-seven blacksmiths, twenty-seven butchers, forty-seven clothiers and tailors, one farrier, one fancy silk worker, three sausage makers, one blacking maker, one basket maker, twenty-seven painters, two locksmiths, twenty-three milliners and dressmakers, four ladies' schools, one custom-house broker Banks—the head quarters of the Upper Canada Bank and Home District Savings Bank, and branches of the Banks of British North America, Montreal, City Bank of Montreal, Commercial and Gore and the following companies have offices here— Home District Mutual Fire Insurance Company, British America Fire and Life Assurance Company, Phœnix Fire Insurance Company (England), Alliance Fire Insurance Company (do), Britannia Fire Insurance Company (do), Eagle Life Insurance Company (do), Montreal Fire and Inland Marine Insurance Company, Marine Insurance Company, Canada Company, Gas and Water Company.

Principal Taverns—" Macdonald's Hotel," " North American Hotel," and " Wellington Hotel,"—besides which there are many excellent inns and taverns, some of which, in point of accommodation and comfort are nearly, if not quite equal to the above.

Principal Boarding Houses—Club House, corner of King and York Streets, Mrs. Henderson, Queen Street, Mrs Cullen, 46 King Street East, Mrs Hutchinson, Adelaide Street, W Hall, 5 King Street East, — O'Brien, corner of Wellington and Bay Streets, John Chipman, Bishop's Buildings, Adelaide Street.

Land Agents—A. B. Townley, 7 King Street East; H. E. Nicolls, 59 King Street East; F. Lewis, 36 King Street West; W. Osborne, corner of King and Jordan Streets; and T. Radenhurst, Front Street.

The following Steamboats are owned at Toronto:

Name.	Tonnage.
Admiral	288
Princess Royal	347
Sovereign	314
Eclipse	198
City of Toronto	349
Chief Justice Robinson	315
Cobourg	317
Traveller	300
Transit	225
America	221
Despatch	186
Queen Victoria	149
Total Tonnage	3209

Besides several schooners, the number and tonnage of which could not be ascertained.

The following are the Rates of Toll at Toronto Harbour:

Description of Property.	Rate. s. d.
Merchandise, per ton, weight or measurement, per bill of lading	1 3
Flour, per barrel	0 2
Oysters in shell, per do.	0 2
Cider, per do.	0 2
Apples and other Fresh Fruit, per do.	0 2
Lime and Gypsum, per do.	0 2
Potatoes and other Vegetables, per do.	0 2
Pork, per do.	0 3
Ashes, per do.	0 3
Salt, per do.	0 3
Whiskey, per do.	0 3
Sheep and Pigs, each	0 2
Horses and Horned Cattle, each	0 6
Wood, per cord	0 4
Stone, per toise	0 10
Lumber, per 1000 feet board measure	1 0

Amount of Harbour Dues collected at the Port of Toronto, during the years 1843 and 1844.

Date.	Total Amount Collected.	Expense of Collection.	Net Revenue.
	£. s. d.	£. s. d.	£. s. d.
1843	571 15 0	94 13 5	477 1 7
1844	712 3 8	121 10 11	590 12 9

Exports from the Port of Toronto for the year 1845.

Flour	153,226	barrels.
Wheat	53,787	bushels.
Ashes	363	barrels
Peas	528	bushels.
Pork	2057	barrels
Beef	300	barrels.
Do.	120	tierces.
Hams	45,500	pounds.
Timothy Seed	861	barrels
Butter	555	kegs
Lard	2	tierces.
Do.	95	kegs.
Wool	2	tons
Sheep Pelts	3380	
Maple Sugar	29	barrels
Calf Skins	12,600	pounds.
Sole Leather	9,540	do
Salted Hides	42	hhds.
Furs and Peltries	£2500	value
Shingles	150	bundles.
Starch	350	boxes.
Lumber	1,550,000	feet.
Estimated Value of Exports	£187,700	

TOSSORONTIO.

A Township in the Simcoe District, is bounded on the north by the township of Sunnidale, on the west by Mulmur, on the south by Adjala, and on the east by Essa. In Tossorontio 3781 acres are taken up, 563 of which are under cultivation. In the south of the township, with the exception of a small cedar swamp, the land is good, farther north it becomes hilly and broken, and continues bad for four or five miles, the timber being principally pine and hemlock, towards the north of the township it improves. The township is well watered. In Tossorontio 8600 acres of Crown lands are open for sale, at 8s currency per acre. There has as yet been no return of the population in this township

Ratable property in the township, £1667

TOWNSEND

A Township in the Talbot District, is bounded on the east by the township of Walpole, on the north by Oakland and a small portion of Brantford, on the west by Windham, and on the south by Woodhouse. In Townsend 47,871 acres are taken up, 16,623 of which are under cultivation. This is a well settled township, containing excellent land, and many well cleared farms. There is no large river in the township, but it is watered by some good mill streams, on which are one grist and eleven saw mills. The village of Waterford is situated a little west of the centre of the township

Population in 1842, 2517

Ratable property in the township. £46,210.

TRAFALGAR

A Township in the Gore District; is bounded on the north-east by the township of Toronto, on the north-west by Esquesing, on the south-west by Nelson; and on the south-east by Lake Ontario. In Trafalgar, 70,115 acres are taken up, 28,180 of which are under cultivation. The township is watered by the Twelve-mile Creek and the Sixteen-mile Creek. Trafalgar is a well settled township, containing numerous well cleared and cultivated farms, most of which have good orchards. The land in general, with the exception of that bordering on the lake, which is light and sandy, is of excellent quality. Timber—principally hardwood, with a little pine intermixed. The villages of Oakville, Bronté, and Palermo are in the township, the two former situated on the lake shore road, and the latter on Dundas Street. There are seven grist and twenty-three saw mills in the township

Population, ———.

Ratable property in the township, £109,789

TRENT, OR TRENT-PORT.

A Village in the south-east corner of the township of Murray, twelve miles west from Belleville, situated at the entrance of the River Trent into the Bay of Quinté It is principally supported by the lumber trade; immense quantities of timber being brought down the river. An excellent bridge has been constructed across the River Trent at this place The Toronto and Kingston stages pass through the village, and, during the season, a steamboat leaves daily for Kingston, calling at Picton, Belleville, Bath, Amherst Island, and other landing places on its route. There are two churches in the village, Episcopal and Catholic.

Population, about 350

Post Office, post every day.

Professions and Trades—One physician and surgeon, two lawyers, eight stores, three taverns, one distillery, three asheries two waggon makers, three blacksmiths, one tinsmith, two tailors, three shoemakers. There is a grist and saw mill about one mile from the village.

TROUT LAKE—(*See* RICE LAKE.)

TUCKERSMITH

A Township in the Huron District, is bounded on the north-east by Hullett and McKillop, on the west by Stanley and Hay, on the south by Usborne; and on the south-east by Hibbert. The land in the greater part of the township is good Two branches of the Bayfield River pass through the township, on which there are two grist and one saw mills Tuckersmith contains 42,308 acres, 15,892 of which are leased or sold, of which 2233 acres are under cultivation

Population, 599.

Ratable property in the township, £8451.

TUDOR

A Township in the Victoria District, is bounded or the east by the township of Grimsthorpe, on the north by unsurveyed lands, on the west by the township of Lake, and on the south by Madoc This township is not yet opened for sale, and no return has yet been made from it.

TURKEY CREEK

A Stream running from east to west, nearly through the centre of the township of Sandwich, into the Detroit River There is a grist mill on it.

TYENDENAGA

A Township in the Victoria District, is bounded on the east by the township of Richmond, on the north by Hungerford, on the west by Thurlow, and on the south by the Bay of Quinté In Tyendenaga 41,226 acres are taken up, 13,717 of which are under cultivation The Salmon River enters the township about the centre of its eastern border, runs across the township to its south-west corner, where it enters the Bay of Quinté. There are two small lakes in the

north-east corner of the township Tyendenaga is well settled, principally by Irish emigrants. The village of Shannonville is in the south-west corner of the township, on the eastern road There are two grist and eight saw-mills in the township.
Population in 1842, 2898.
Ratable property in the township, £34,076

USBORNE

A Township in the Huron District, is bounded on the north and north-east by Tuckersmith, Hibbert, and Fullarton, on the south-east by Blanshard, on the west by Hay, and Stephen; and on the south by Biddulph The greater part of the township is good land. A branch of the River Sable runs through the north of the township. Usborne contains 33,576 acres, 5,650 of which are leased or sold, of which 728 are under cultivation. There are in the township, one grist, and one saw mill.
Population, 283
Ratable property in the township, £3071 8s.

UXBRIDGE

A Township in the Home District, is bounded on the east by the township of Reach; on the north by Scott, on the west by Whitchurch and Markham; and on the south by Pickering. In Uxbridge 14,128 acres are taken up, 3337 of which are under cultivation This township contains some good land, and a portion of it is of very secondary quality There is a large lake near the north-west corner, situated partly in Uxbridge and partly in Whitchurch. Timber, a mixture of hardwood and pine. Two hundred and ten acres of crown lands are open for sale in Uxbridge, at 8s currency per acre There are one grist, and four saw mills in the township
Population in 1842, (including the township of Scott), 810.
Ratable property in the township, £11,951.

VANKLEEK HILL

A Village in the west of the township of West Hawkesbury, eight miles south from the Ottawa River, it contains about 250 inhabitants, who are principally of Dutch or German extraction. There are in the village a steam grist mill, carding machine and cloth factory, saleratus factory, two asheries, one foundry, six stores and two taverns.

VAUGHAN.

A Township in the Home District, is bounded on the east by the township of Markham; on the north by King, on the west by the Gore of Toronto, and on the south by York In Vaughan 60,496 acres are taken up, 19,766 of which are under cultivation This is a township of excellent land, it is well settled and contains numerous well cleared and highly cultivated farms The land is generally rolling, and the timber a mixture of hardwood and pine. The township is watered by branches of the River Humber. The Yonge Street Road separates the township from that of Markham On the road, partly in Vaughan and partly in Markham, are the settlements of Richmond Hill, and Thornhill. There are six grist and twenty-five saw mills in the township
Population in 1842, 4,300
Ratable property in the township, £60,942.

VERULAM

A Township in the Colborne District, is bounded on the east by the township of Harvey; on the north by Sommerville; on the west by Fenelon, and on the south by Emily. In Verulam 9,298 acres are taken up, 956 of which are under cultivation. A large lake called "Sturgeon Lake", stretches across the centre of the township, from west to east. A small lake, situated about the centre of the south border of the township, has a communication with Sturgeon Lake There is much pine timber in this township. Verulam contains a mixed population. There is one grist mill, and one saw mill in the township. 8817 acres of crown lands are open for sale in Verulam, at 8s. currency per acre.

Ratable property in the township, £4296.

VESPRA.

A Township in the Simcoe District, is bounded on the north by the township of Flos, on the west by Sunnidale, on the south by Essa, Innisfil, and Kempenfeldt Bay. In Vespra 13,040 acres are taken up, 1722 of which are under cultivation. The Nottawasaga River runs through the north-west corner of the township, and Willow Creek, a branch of the Nottawasaga, flows through nearly the centre of the township, and might easily be made navigable to within nine miles of Barrie One branch of Willow Creek derives its source from a small lake about four miles from Barrie, in the south-east corner of the township The land on the bay is poor, sandy and stony, but a short distance back it begins to improve, and the interior of the township contains good land. The town of Barrie is situated near the south-east corner of the township, on Kempenfeldt Bay, and the village of Kempenfeldt about two miles below it. In Vespra 11,400 acres of Crown lands are open for sale, at 8s currency per acre. There are in the township one grist and two saw mills, and one distillery

Population in 1842, 571.
Ratable property in the township, £10,873.

VICTORIA DISTRICT

Consists of the County of Hastings, which returns a member to the House of Assembly, and comprises the following townships—Elzevir, Grimsthorpe, Hungerford, Huntingdon, Lake, Marmora, Madoc, Rawdon, Sydney, Tudor, Thurlow, and Tyendenaga It is bounded on the east by the Midland District; on the north by unsurveyed lands, on the west by the Colborne and Newcastle Districts, and on the south by the Bay of Quinte

The district is watered by the Trent, the Moira, and the Salmon Rivers, and their branches, and there are numerous small lakes scattered over it

A large portion of the district consists of excellent land, and the townships of Sydney, Thurlow, and Tyendenaga contain many fine farms

Iron ore of superior quality exists in the townships of Marmora and Madoc; and in the former township a bed of lithographic stone has been discovered, which, after being examined and tested by a lithographer in London (England), was pronounced of excellent quality; but I am not aware if the bed has yet been quarried.

Clearing is going on rapidly in the district, and large quantities of potash are made. Eleven thousand five hundred acres of land were brought into cultivation between January, 1842, and January, 1844

The district is settled principally by Irish and Scotch, U E. Loyalists and their descendants and Canadians

Belleville, the district town, is a thriving place The only other villages in the district are Shannonville, in Tyendenaga, and a small settlement in each of the townships of Madoc and Marmora

Sixty-five thousand and eighty-three acres of Crown lands are open for sale in the Victoria District, at 8s currency per acre, to purchase any of which application must be made to the Crown Lands Agent, at Belleville

Population in 1842, 15,842, since when it has probably increased one-fifth.

The following abstract from the assessment rolls, will show the rate of increase and improvement in the district:

Date.	No. of Acres Cultivated.	MILLS. Grist.	MILLS. Saw.	Milch Cows.	Oxen 4 years old, and upwards.	Horned Cattle from 2 to 4 years old.	Amount of Ratable Property.
1842	61,098	17	30	5564	1850	2342	200,264
1843	63,705	17	37	5753	1985	2617	206,498
1844	72,630	21	39	6124	2026	2609	225,819

Government and District Officers in the Victoria District.

Judge of District Court	Wm. Smart	Belleville.
Sheriff	J. W. D. Moodie	Do.
Clerk of Peace	W. Fitzgibbon	Do.
Treasurer	Philip Ham	Do.
Judge of Surrogate Court	J. B. Crowe	Murray.
Registrar of Surrogate Court	W. Bowen	Frankford.
Do. of County of Hastings	A. McLean	
Deputy Registrar	B. Dougall	Belleville.
Inspector of Licenses	A. Marshall	Do.
Collector of Customs	Henry Baldwin	Do.
Crown Lands Agent	Francis McAnnany	Do.
Inspector of Potash	Thos. Parker	Do.
District Clerk	P. O'Reily	Do.
Deputy Clerk of Crown	W. H. Ponton	Do.
Warden	W. Hutton	Do.
Coroners	P. O'Reily	Do.
	W. H. Ponton	Do.
	John Dougall	Do.

Number of Common Schools in operation in the District.—Thurlow, seven; Sydney, eight; Tyendenaga, sixteen; Rawdon, seven; Huntingdon, six; Hungerford, four; Madoc, five; Marmora, two. Total, fifty-five. The town of Belleville has not come under the late act, not having raised an equivalent to the grant.

VIENNA.

A Village in the township of Bayham, situated on Otter Creek, three miles north from Port Burwell, in the midst of a hilly country. The lumber trade is carried on very extensively in the vicinity, and is the principal support of the village. Vienna was first settled about ten years since, and now contains about 300 inhabitants. Churches and chapels, three, viz., Episcopal and two Methodist; and there is also a Baptist chapel about one mile from the village.

Post Office, post three times a-week.

Professions and Trades.—One grist mill, three saw mills, one physician and surgeon, carding machine and fulling mill, one distillery, one tannery, eight stores, two taverns, two waggon makers, two cabinet makers, four blacksmiths, one saddler, one tinsmith, three shoemakers, two tailors.

Principal Tavern.—" Red Lion."

VITTORIA.

A village situated near the south-east corner of the township of Charlotteville, nearly three miles from Lake Erie, and seven miles from Simcoe. It was laid out in 1816; and was for a short time the district town of the London District till the removal of the district offices to London, in 1826. The registry office for the county of Norfolk is kept here There are three churches and chapels, viz. Episcopal, Presbyterian, and Baptist. A good mill stream runs through the village, on which it is intended to erect two grist mills during the present year. There are two carding machines and fulling mills about half a mile from the village

Population, about 300

Post Office, post six times a-week.

Professions and Trades—Two physicians and surgeons, one lawyer, one distillery, two tanneries, three stores, two taverns, three tailors, four waggon makers, four blacksmiths, four shoemakers, two saddlers, one cabinet maker.

WAINFLEET

A Township in the Niagara District, is bounded on the east by the township of Humberstone; on the north by Pelham, and Gainsborough; on the east by Moulton and a small portion of Caistor and Canborough, and on the south by Lake Erie In Wainfleet 22,357 acres are taken up, 6,404 of which are under cultivation The township is separated from Pelham and Gainsborough by the Welland River, The Grand River feeder of the Welland Canal passes through nearly the centre of the township A large tamarack and cranberry swamp stretches across the township, a little to the south of the feeder. There is a small settlement called Marshville in the south of the township, on the feeder, and there are also two saw mills in the township

Population in 1841, 1147, who are principally Canadians, with a few Dutch, Irish, and English

Ratable property in the township, £19 890

WALLACEBURGH

A Settlement in the township of Sombra, situated at the forks of Bear Creek, nine miles from the River St Clair, and about seventeen from Chatham. The road from Chatham to Port Sarnia passes through it The north and west branches of Bear Creek unite at this spot, and each of them has a depth of from twelve to twenty feet water Wallaceburgh contains about sixty inhabitants, one store, one tavern, one blacksmith

Post Office, post twice a week

WALPOLE

A Township in the Talbot District, is bounded on the east by the township of Rainham, on the north-east by Cayuga Oneida, and Tuscarora, on the west by Townsend and Woodhouse, and on the south by Lake Erie. In Walpole 23,163 acres are taken up, 5,637 of which are under cultivation. The plank road from Hamilton to Port Dover passes through the north-west of the township There are some good farms in the township, and some of the land is of excellent quality, but a large portion of the timber consists of pine There is a small settlement called "Williamsville," situated on Lake Erie, on the town line between Walpole and Rainham; and there are two grist, and five saw mills in the township. There has as yet been no return of the population in the township

Ratable property in the township £17 041

WALPOLE ISLAND

A Large Island situated in the north-east of Lake St Clair, it is about ten miles long, and from three to four miles wide It is a fine island, and is occupied by parties of Chippewa Pottawatamie, and Ottawa Indians These Indians are also known under the name of Chippewas of Chenail Ecarte. The Chippewas who have long hunted over the waste lands about the Chenail Ecarte and Bear Creek, are a branch of the same nation that is settled in Sarnia, and share in the same annuity. The Pottawatamies are recent immigrants from the United States.

The settlement at Walpole Island was commenced at the close of the American war, when Colonel McKie, called by the Indians "White Elk," collected and placed upon this island the scattered remains of some tribes of Chippewas who had been engaged on the British side. Being left for many years without any interference or assistance on the part of the government, they became a prey to the profligate whites settled on the frontier, who by various frauds, and in moments of intoxication, obtained leases, and took possession of the most fertile and valuable part of the island

When the settlement was first placed under the charge of an assistant superintendent in 1839, these Indians possessed scarcely an acre of arable land, but he has succeeded in expelling many of the most mischievous intruders, under the authority of an act of the Provincial Legislature, passed in 1839, and has placed their farms at the disposal of the Indians, who have since become more settled, and have turned their attention more generally to agriculture

The number on the Island has increased considerably since 1839, owing to the influx of several bands of Pottawatamies, and Ottawas, invited by the proclamation of 1837, relative to the discontinuance of presents to visiting Indians Previously to that year they did not exceed three hundred, but in 1842, presents were distributed to one thousand, one hundred and forty, viz

    Chippewas, old residents 319
    Chippewas, arrived within a year . . . 197
    Pottawatamies and Ottawas from Michigan . . . 507
    On their way to settle 117

                    Total . . 1140

The new comers are very different in character and habits from the resident Chippewas The Pottawatamies especially, are skilful hunters, and have long depended solely upon the chase They are wild, turbulent, mendicant and dishonest They possess no land or property. They have been kindly received by the resident tribes, and allowed to settle on their lands, but their roving habits render them averse from settling, they prefer remaining poor, ragged and filthy, to the restraints of civilized life, they are a burthen on their brethren, a nuisance to the white farmers in the district which they frequent, and their arrival in the province is in every respect to be regretted Their chief hunting grounds are near the Thames, and the upper parts of the two branches of Bear Creek They also hunt in the United States, but with some danger to themselves, as the Americans do not allow it

The Indians who are settled upon Walpole Island, occupy the farms and houses hitherto possessed by the white squatters, together with a few houses erected by themselves The present number of dwellings is twenty-eight, of which three are framed, with several more in the course of erection, and four log barns There is no village, the farms being detached, as among the white settlers There are five inferior chiefs among the Chippewas, who live surrounded by their own relations and connections by marriage, and the young men, who though under the controul of the head chief, recognise especially their own leader These, on the expulsion of the squatters, met together, and subdivided the farms and arable land among themselves, according to their numbers. Thus, each separate band cultivates one vast enclosure, each man planting more or less according to his industry It is intended, however, to lay out the fields more regularly

Their acquaintance with agriculture is of recent date, but their progress has been satisfactory In 1839, they planted only Indian corn, and used no other implement but the hoe At present they have nine ploughs, and as many yoke of oxen, besides scythes and sickles in abundance They have also a large number of pigs and horses, and the chief has two cows Steps have been taken to improve the breed of these animals; a large quantity of marsh hay is saved for winter fodder. The extent of cleared land is estimated at 600 acres, and it is annually on the increase. The greatest extent cropped by one Indian may be twelve acres, the smallest, about three acres. At least one hundred heads of families have commenced to till the land within the last two years. When a family has no land in cultivation, its members depend upon the chase and fishing, and the sale of baskets and mats. The chief crop is Indian corn, but they also plant large quantities of potatoes, some oats, buckwheat, and peas. They are about to begin the cultivation of wheat. Much of the lighter part of field labour is still done by the women.

The fondness for hunting and fishing is very much on the decrease among the Chippewas, who seldom indulge in either, except during the winter. The game has almost disappeared in the neighbouring hunting grounds.

All these Indians are heathens, but twenty families have applied for religious instruction. In January, 1841, a missionary of the Church of England was appointed, on a salary of £100, borne upon the parliamentary grant; but whether through the want of a proper interpreter, the distance of the residence, (there being no suitable house on the island) or other circumstances, the Indians have not profited by his labours, and the Bishop has been obliged to appoint another clergyman in his place. It is now intended to erect on the island, with the funds belonging to these Indians, a building adapted for a chapel and school-house, with a house for the missionary, and the plans and estimates have received the approval of the Governor General. A schoolmaster also is to be appointed and paid from the same source. The Indians are anxious for the education of their children, and since the recent death of their old chief, their aversion to become christians has diminished, and may be expected to be gradually overcome.

The health of the settled Indians is very good, and surpasses that of the neighbouring whites, their numbers are also on the increase, but the contrary is the case with the roving Pottawatamies, many of whom have been known to die from the effects of intoxication, or in brawls, and from the effects of severe weather during the winter. The number of children born to a family is about five, and the number raised three. There are no regular half-breeds among them, recognised as such.

WALSINGHAM

A Township in the Talbot District, is bounded on the east by the township of Charlotteville, on the north-west by Middletown, on the west by Houghton: and on the south by Lake Erie. In Walsingham 18,635 acres are taken up, 5,322 of which are under cultivation. A stream called 'Big Creek' runs through the township from north-east to south-west, at the mouth of which is a settlement called Port Royal, where is a steam saw mill. Near the centre of the south of the township is a shipping place called Port Rowan. The principal part of the timber of the township is pine, and large quantities of sawed lumber are exported. There are two grist and six saw mills in the township.

Population in 1841, 1,046
Ratable property in the township, £18,412

WARDSVILLE

A small Village in the township of Mosa, situated on the western road, thirty-six miles from London, it contains 100 inhabitants, an Episcopal church, five stores, one tavern, two blacksmiths.

WARWICK

A Township in the Western District, is bounded on the east by the township of Adelaide, on the north by Bosanquet, on the west by Plympton; and on the south by Brooke. In Warwick 26,448 acres are taken up, 3,080 of which are under cultivation. The north branch of Bear Creek runs through the township, and it is watered besides by branches of the River Aux Sables, and other small streams Warwick contains a large portion of good land, and since the new road has been completed from London to Port Sarnia, it has commenced settling up fast In Warwick 1,400 acres of Crown lands are open for sale, at 8s. c'y per acre

Population in 1843, 1,235, which includes the township of Bosanquet, in which are very few settlers

Ratable property in the township, £11,204.

WARSAW

A Village in the west of the township of Dummer, situated on the Indian River, fifteen miles north-east from Peterborough It contains about seventy inhabitants, grist and saw mill, carding machine, two stores, and two taverns.

WATERDOWN.

A Village in the township of Flamborough East, seven miles from Hamilton It contains about 200 inhabitants, and a Methodist church

Post office, post twice a week

Professions and Trades —Two grist mills, two saw do , carding machine and cloth factory, two stores, one tannery, two taverns, one saddler, one scythe factory, one cooper, one tailor, one shoemaker, one blacksmith.

WATERFORD

A Village in about the centre of the township of Townsend, on the road leading from Simcoe to Brantford, seven miles from Simcoe, and eighteen from Brantford. It is situated in a valley, surrounded by high hills, and the Nauticoke creek runs through the village

It contains about 150 inhabitants, who have a Baptist Chapel

Post Office, post every day.

Professions and Trades —One grist mill, one saw do , one distillery, three stores, two taverns, one waggon maker, one blacksmith, one tailor, one shoemaker, one cooper.

WATERLOO

A Township in the Wellington District, is bounded on the east by the townships of Puslinch and Guelph, on the north-west by Woolwich, on the west by Wilmot, and on the south by Dumfries In Waterloo 82,825 acres are taken up, 30,026 of which are under cultivation This is the best settled and most wealthy township in the Wellington District. It has been settled about forty years, almost entirely by Pennsylvanian Dutch and Germans, most of whom brought considerable capital with them into the country, and their farms are consequently well cleared, and they have excellent houses and farm buildings They are a thrifty set, and are gradually increasing in wealth Many of them cannot speak English The land is mostly rolling, and the farms are generally well situated The Grand River runs through the centre of the township, and in the south of it is joined by the River Speed Numerous other branches of the Grand River are spread over the township The villages of Preston, Waterloo, Little Germany, Glasgow, New Hope, Berlin, and Bridgeport are situated in the township There are eight grist and twenty saw mills in the township

Population in 1841, 4424

Ratable property in the township, £94,759.

WATERLOO

A Village in the township of Kingston, situated on the western road, three miles west from Kingston—the little Cataraqui River runs through it. There is a Methodist church in the village, and a Quaker meeting-house.

Population about 200

Professions and Trades.—Three physicians and surgeons, carding machine and fulling mill and cloth factory, one ashery, one tannery, one store, three taverns, three waggon makers, one saddler, two blacksmiths, two shoemakers, one tailor, one baker.

WATERLOO, or FORT ERIE RAPIDS

A Village in the township of Bertie, situated on the Niagara River, about two miles below the entrance to Lake Erie, and sixteen miles from Chippewa. A steam ferry-boat is established which crosses the river every half hour to the American village, "Blackrock," which is about two miles below Buffalo. There is an Episcopal church in the village, and a custom house

Population, about 180

Post Office, post three times a-week

Professions and Trades.—One grist mill, two stores, two taverns, one grocery, one waggon maker, two blacksmiths, one tailor, one cooper, two shoemakers.

WATERLOO.

A Village in the township of Waterloo, two miles north from Berlin, situated on a branch of the Grand River—contains about 200 inhabitants, principally Germans, who have a Lutheran meeting-house.

Post Office, post twice a-week

Professions and Trades,—One grist and saw mill, one distillery, two stores, two taverns, two blacksmiths

WAWANOSH.

A Township in the Huron District, belonging to the Crown, is bounded on the north by Crown lands, on the west by Ashfield, on the south by Colborne; and on the east by Crown lands as yet unsurveyed. The soil and climate of this township are excellent. The River Ashfield runs through its north-west corner, and the River Maitland runs completely through it from north to south, making several bends in its course. This township is settling fast. In Wawanosh there are taken up 2050 acres, of which 87 are under cultivation. Government price for land in Wawanosh, 8s currency per acre

Population, 133

Ratable property in the township, £593

WAWANOSH, LAKE

A Lake in the north of the township of Sarnia, about half a mile from Lake Huron. It contains about 2000 acres and varies from six to eight feet in depth. The Riviere aux Perches runs through it.

WELLAND.

A County in the Niagara District. It comprises the townships of Bertie, Crowland, Humberstone, Pelham, Stamford, Thorold, Wainfleet, and Willoughby. For the purpose of representation in the Legislative Assembly, it is united to the county of Lincoln

WELLAND CANAL

The Channel of water communication between Lakes Erie and Ontario, constructed to overcome the obstruction in the navigation between the two lakes, caused by the Falls of Niagara. Its entrance from Lake Ontario, at Port Dalhousie, is in the north-west corner of the township of Grantham, it then passes through that township and the centre of Thorold, in the south of which it strikes the Welland River, after leaving which it divides, and one branch runs straight on to Lake Erie, while the other is carried to the Grand River.

The Welland Canal was originally projected by Mr Merritt, in the year 1818, and the work was commenced in 1824

The design at the time was to connect the Welland River, which is a tributary of the Niagara River, and enters that river above the rapids, and the surface of which is ten feet above the level of Lake Erie, with Lake Ontario, from which it is distant only about sixteen miles. This design to connect the two lakes by a canal so short, failed in consequence of the peculiar geological formation of that part of the ridge situated near the village of Port Robinson, through which the canal must pass. This part, which was found to consist of clay upon quick sand, and which after great expense and labour had been incurred, caved in and destroyed the work, is commonly called the deep cut.

The original design having failed, the Grand River was adopted as the feeder, and a summit level assumed, 6½ feet above Lake Erie, and 336½ feet above Lake Ontario, the descent to the former being overcome by one lock, at Port Colborne; and to the latter by thirty-eight locks. These locks were of wood, 110 feet by 20.

The works on the canal having become very much out of repair—the woodwork of the locks decayed and giving way; and the canal itself very inefficient for the accommodation of the increased traffic through it, and constantly requiring repairs, it was determined to make extensive improvements in the canal,— bearing more the character of a new work altogether—than the patching up of the old one.

The canal, according to the present design, will be navigable throughout by vessels 26 feet 4 inches, by 140 feet, the tonnage of which will be about 450 tons. New and magnificent, and substantial locks (of cut stone) have been constructed, the work of which is equal to that of any public work in the world. The canal has been straightened in many places, and from the increased size and capacity of the new locks, it has been found possible to diminish their number.

The Grand River was originally intended as the feeder, and principal channel for the canal, but it was found advisable to take the supply of water from Lake Erie as being less liable to fluctuation in its level, than any river could possibly be. A channel has therefore been formed from the Welland River straight to the lake. This has been a work of enormous labour and expense; a large portion of the cut being formed through the solid rock. This will much diminish the length of the passage, and the cut to Lake Erie will be the principal thoroughfare for all traffic on the canal, passing between the two lakes. The entire length of the canal and its branches will be about fifty-two miles. The harbour at Port Dalhousie is at present very defective, but when the proposed improvements are completed, will be equal to any harbour on the lake.

The original cost of the canal was £450,000, on repairs and other improvements, £250,000 was expended. The construction of the new canal is estimated to cost £750,000. These seem large sums, but when the magnitude and importance of the work is taken into consideration, it will be generally allowed that the money could not have been expended in any way to more advantage to the Province generally, and more particularly so, to that of the country west of the Niagara River.

Great disturbances having frequently occurred along the line of the canal, and many faction fights having taken place amongst the Irish labourers employed on the works, some of which were attended with loss of life, it was found necessary to have an armed force stationed on the canal, in order to overawe the rioters. A company of soldiers was therefore raised from amongst the coloured men settled in the province. In addition to which a party of mounted police were stationed along the line. These measures have had the desired effect, and peace has been since preserved.

The villages on the canal are Port Dalhousie at the entrance, on Lake Ontario, from thence to St. Catharines, 5¼ miles, from thence to Thorold, 4½ miles, from thence to Allanburgh, 3½ miles and from thence to Port Robinson, 2½ miles. From Port Robinson to Lake Erie by the Grand River, to the aqueduct, 4½ miles, from thence to Marshville, 8½ miles, from thence to Dunnville, 13¼ miles, from

Dunnville to Lake Erie, 4¾ miles. From Port Robinson to Lake Erie by the feeder; to Merrittsville, 4 miles, to Helmsport or the Junction, 1 mile, from thence to Stonebridge, 6 miles, and from thence to Port Colborne, 1½ miles.

Comparative Statement of the principal Articles of Property passed through the Welland Canal, from the opening of Navigation to the 30th November, in the years 1841, 1842, 1843, *and* 1844.

Articles.	1841.	1842.	1843.	1844.
Beef and Pork, barrels	30,416	87.394	19,382½	41,976
Flour, do.	213.483	247,602	171,450	305,208
Ashes, do.	268	441	991	3,412
Beer and Cider, do.	81	234	134	50
Salt, do.	156,138	152,533	145,971	209,008
Do. bags	......	......	......	4,204
Whiskey, barrels	1,950	3,142	1,875	931
Plaster, do.	113	310	129	2,068
Fruit and Nuts, do.	246	459	265	470
Butter and Lard, do.	174	1,259	1,133	4,639
Seeds, do.	1,127	609	584	1,429
Tallow, do.	23	......	209	1,182
Water Lime do.	25	316	230	1,662
Pitch and Tar, do.	......	......	282	75
Fish, do.	132	838	1,227	1,758
Oatmeal, do.	75	......	156	132
Bees Wax, do.	......	......	......	36
Oil, do.	......	2	116	96
Saw Logs, number,	11.300	8,885	12,026	10,411
Boards, feet.	3,580,911	4,199,590	2,231,143	7,493,574
Square Timber, cubic feet,	1,155,686	267,242	342,414	406,525
Half Flatted, do.	......	......	1,300	13,922
Round, do.	28.556	7,231	8,360	20,879
Staves, Pipe, number,	1,373,436	1,253,405	649,403	630,692
Do. West India, do.	1,462,725	1,128,506	183,960	1,197,916
Do. Double Flour Barrel, do.	277.277	260,790	9,656	150,596
Shingles, do.	414,500	217,600	61,100	330,400
Wheat, bushels.	1,579,966	1,891,380	1,172,850	2,122,502
Corn, do.	70,474	151,164	92,186	75,528
Barley, do.	1,304	20	......	930
Rye, do.	467	1,764	......	142
Oats, do.	3,619	12,240	13,031	5,653
Potatoes, do.	486	1,050	8,818	7,311
Butter and Lard, kegs,	967	1,917	1,692	4,669
Merchandise, tons,	4.031	3,539	4,392	11,318 16 *cwt.*
Coal, do.	1,422	2.301	1,819	1,689
Castings, do.	91	213	228½	211
Iron, do.	78	237	485	1,748¼
Tobacco, do.	369	277	97¼	140
Grindstones, do.	257	220	99½	151½
Plaster, do.	369	935	422¼	1,491¾
Hides, do.	9	16	66	101½
Bacon and Hams, do.	58	41	164½	307
Bran and Shorts, do.	45	392	29	231
Water Lime do.	......	......	......	441
Stone, toise,	126	311	1,106	738
Firewood, cords,	31	402	1,876½	3,251¼
Passengers, number,	358	1,229	120	3,261½
Small Packages, do.	103	496	315	459
Pumps, do.	20	112	117	102
Schooners, do.	2,056	2,226	1,543	2,121
Steamboats and Propellers, do.	......	34	24	484
Scows, do.	1,063	1,430	824	1,671
Rafts, do.	133	78	......	118
Tonnage, tons.	277,144	304,983	224,408	327,570

Amount of Tolls collected...... £20,210.19s.9d. £23,946.19s.6d. £16,135.7s. 8d. £25,573.3s.10d.

The following are the Rates of Toll upon Persons and Property passing through the Welland Canal:—

DESCRIPTION OF ARTICLES.	QUANTITY OR BULK.	Through the whole line.			From Port Maitland to Dunnville & vice versa.			From Port Maitland, Dunnville, and Port Colborne to Port Robinson, and vice versa.			From Port Robinson to Thorold, and vice versa.			From Thorold to St. Catharines, & vice versa.			From St. Catharines to Port Dalhousie, and vice versa.		
		£	s.	d.	£	s.	d.	£	s.	d.	£	s.	d.	£	s.	d.	£	s.	d.
On Steamboats and Vessels under 50 tons burden	Each	0	10	0	0	5	0	0	5	0	0	2	6	0	1	3	0	1	3
do. do. from 50 to 75 do.	Do.	0	15	0	0	7	6	0	7	6	0	3	6	0	2	0	0	2	0
do. do. from 75 to 100 do.	Do.	0	15	0	0	7	6	0	7	6	0	3	6	0	2	0	0	2	0
do. do. from 100 to 150 do.	Do.	0	15	0	0	7	6	0	7	6	0	3	6	0	2	0	0	2	0
do. do. from 150 to 200 do.	Do.	0	15	0	0	7	6	0	7	6	0	3	6	0	2	0	0	2	0
do. do. from 200 to 250 do.	Do.	0	15	0	0	7	6	0	7	6	0	3	6	0	2	0	0	2	0
do. do. upwards of 250 do.	Do.	0	15	0	0	7	6	0	7	6	0	3	6	0	2	0	0	2	0
Canal Boats under 50 tons for Passengers chiefly	Do.	0	5	0	0	2	6	0	2	6	0	1	3	0	0	7½	0	0	7½
Canal Scows, Boats, Lighters, &c., for freight chiefly	Do.	0	2	6	0	1	3	0	1	3	0	0	7½	0	0	4	0	0	4
1.—GROCERIES AND PROVISIONS.																			
Flour	Barrel	0	0	4	0	0	1	0	0	2	0	0	1	0	0	0½	0	0	0½
Pork and Beef	Do.	0	0	6	0	0	1½	0	0	3	0	0	1½	0	0	0¾	0	0	0¾
Brandy, Gin, Rum, Whiskey, Shrub, Peppermint and Vinegar	Do.	0	0	9	0	0	2½	0	0	5	0	0	2	0	0	1	0	0	1
Wine	Do.	0	1	3	0	0	4	0	0	7½	0	0	3½	0	0	2	0	0	2
Do.	Pipe	0	2	6	0	0	7½	0	0	3	0	0	7	0	0	4	0	0	4
Butter and Lard	Barrel	0	0	6	0	0	1½	0	0	3	0	0	1½	0	0	0¾	0	0	0¾
Do. do.	Keg or Firkin	0	0	1½	0	0	0½	0	0	0¾	0	0	0½	0	0	0¼	0	0	0¼
Cheese	Cwt.	0	0	1½	0	0	0½	0	0	0¾	0	0	0½	0	0	0¼	0	0	0¼
Beeswax and Tallow	Do.	0	0	1½	0	0	0½	0	0	0¾	0	0	0½	0	0	0¼	0	0	0¼
Beer and Cider	Barrel	0	0	6	0	0	1½	0	0	3	0	0	1½	0	0	0¾	0	0	0¾

Rates of Toll.—Continued.

Description of Property.	Quantity or Bulk.	Through the whole line.			From Port Maitland to Dunnville, & vice versa.			From Port Maitland, Dunnville, and Port Colborne, to Port Robinson, and vice versa.			From Port Robinson to Thorold, and vice versa.			From Thorold to St. Catharines & vice versa.			From St. Catharines to Port Dalhousie, and vice versa.		
		£	s.	d.	£	s.	d.	£	s.	d.	£	s.	d.	£	s.	d.	£	s.	d.
Apples (fresh and dried), Fruit and Nuts, Rice	Barrel	0	0	4	0	0	1	0	0	2	0	0	1	0	0	0½	0	0	0½
Oil	Do.	0	0	9	0	0	2½	0	0	5	0	0	2	0	0	1	0	0	1
Fish, salt or fresh	Do.	0	0	9	0	0	2½	0	0	5	0	0	2	0	0	1	0	0	1
Do. dried	Cwt.	0	0	3	0	0	1	0	0	1½	0	0	0½	0	0	0½	0	0	0½
Hams and Bacon, Sugar	Do.	0	0	1½	0	0	0½	0	0	0¾	0	0	0¼	0	0	0¼	0	0	0¼
Tobacco, leaf	Do.	0	0	2	0	0	0½	0	0	1	0	0	0½	0	0	0¼	0	0	0¼
Do. manufactured	Do.	0	0	2	0	0	0½	0	0	1	0	0	0½	0	0	0¼	0	0	0¼
Biscuit and Crackers	Barrel	0	0	6	0	0	1½	0	0	3	0	0	1½	0	0	0¾	0	0	0¾
Oysters	Do.	0	1	0	0	0	3	0	0	6	0	0	3	0	0	1½	0	0	1½
Onions, seeds	Bushel	0	0	1	0	0	0½	0	0	0½	0	0	0¼	0	0	0⅛	0	0	0⅛
Bran, Ship Stuffs	Ton	0	2	6	0	0	7½	0	1	3	0	0	7	0	0	4	0	0	4
2.—Agricultural Produce.																			
Wheat, Indian Corn, Barley, and Rye	Bushel	0	0	1	0	0	0½	0	0	0½	0	0	0¼	0	0	0⅛	0	0	0⅛
Oats and Potatoes, Beans, Peas, Seed, and Vegetables of all kinds	Do.	0	0	1	0	0	0½	0	0	0½	0	0	0¼	0	0	0⅛	0	0	0⅛
Raw Cotton and Wool	Ton	0	2	6	0	0	7½	0	1	3	0	0	7	0	0	4	0	0	4
Hay	Do.	0	2	6	0	0	7½	0	1	3	0	0	7	0	0	4	0	0	4
Hemp and Rags	Do.	0	2	6	0	0	7½	0	1	3	0	0	8	0	0	4	0	0	4
Sheep, Hogs, Calves, Colts	Each	0	0	2	0	0	0½	0	0	1	0	0	0½	0	0	0½	0	0	0¼
Horses, Horned Cattle, Asses	Do.	0	0	6	0	0	1½	0	0	3	0	0	1½	0	0	0¾	0	0	0¾
Flax Seed and all other Seed in barrels	Barrel	0	0	6	0	0	1½	0	0	3	0	0	1½	0	0	0¾	0	0	0¾

3.—Iron, Minerals, Ores, &c.,																			
Salt	Ton	Free																	
Sea Coal	Do.	Do.																	
Gypsum, not ground, in bulk	Do.	0	2	6	0	0	7½	0	1	3	0	0	7	0	0	4	0	0	4
Do. ground, in bulk	Do.	0	3	9	0	1	0	0	2	0	0	0	9	0	0	6	0	0	6
Ground Gypsum and Cement	Barrel	0	0	2	0	0	0½	0	0	1	0	0	0½	0	0	0¼	0	0	0¼
Pot and Pearl Ashes	Do.	0	0	7½	0	0	2	0	0	3½	0	0	2	0	0	1	0	0	1
Pitch, Tar, Varnish and Turpentine	Do.	0	0	6	0	0	1½	0	0	3	0	0	1½	0	0	0¾	0	0	0¾
Brick, Sand, Lime, Clay and Manure	Ton	0	0	5	0	0	1½	0	0	3	0	0	1	0	0	0½	0	0	0½
Grind Stones, Cut do., Iron Ore, and Mill Stones	Do.	0	0	5	0	0	1½	0	0	3	0	0	1	0	0	0½	0	0	0½
Pig & Scrap Iron. Broken Castings, & Wrought Iron	Do.	0	2	6	0	0	7½	0	1	3	0	0	7	0	0	4	0	0	4
Iron Castings, going up	Do.	0	3	9	0	0	0	0	2	0	0	0	9	0	0	6	0	0	6
Do. going down	Do.	0	2	6	0	0	7½	0	1	3	0	0	7	0	0	4	0	0	4
Mineral Coal, American	Do.	0	2	6	0	0	7½	0	1	3	0	0	7	0	0	4	0	0	4
Charcoal, Copperas and Manganese	Do.	0	2	6	0	0	7½	0	1	3	0	0	7	0	0	4	0	0	4
Pig Lead and Bar do.	Do.	0	2	6	0	0	7½	0	1	3	0	0	7	0	0	4	0	0	4
Lead, Manufactured	Do.	0	2	6	0	0	7½	0	1	3	0	0	7	0	0	4	0	0	4
Stones, Unwrought	Cord	0	1	3	0	0	4	0	0	7½	0	0	3½	0	0	2	0	0	2
Fire Wood	Do.	0	0	7½	0	0	2	0	0	3½	0	0	2	0	0	1	0	0	1
Tan Bark	Do.	0	0	7½	0	0	2	0	0	3½	0	0	2	0	0	1	0	0	1
Stone Ware and Earthenware	Ton	0	5	0	0	1	3	0	2	6	0	1	2	0	0	8	0	0	8
4.—Furs, Peltry, Skins, &c.																			
Raw Hides, the Skins of Domestic and Wild Animals	Cwt.	0	0	3	0	0	1	0	0	1½	0	0	0½	0	0	0½	0	0	0½
Furs	Do.	0	0	3	0	0	1	0	0	1½	0	0	0½	0	0	0½	0	0	1½
Dressed Hides and Skins	Do.	0	0	3	0	0	1	0	0	1½	0	0	0½	0	0	0½	0	0	0½
5.—Furniture, &c.																			
Furniture and Baggage	Ton	0	2	6	0	0	7½	0	1	3	0	0	7	0	0	4	0	0	4
Carts, Waggons, Sleighs, Ploughs, Mechanics' Tools, and Farming Implements	Do.	0	2	6	0	0	7½	0	1	3	0	0	7	0	0	4	0	0	4
6.—Lumber, &c,																			
Squared Timber, 12×12 and upw. in Boats or Vessels	per M. C. Feet.	1	0	0	0	5	0	0	10	0	0	4	0	0	3	0	0	3	0
Do. in Rafts	Do.	1	10	0	0	7	6	0	15	0	0	6	0	0	4	6	0	4	6

Q 2

Rates of Toll —CONTINUED

DESCRIPTION OF ARTICLES	QUANTITY OR BULK	Through the whole Line			From Port Maitland to Dunnville, & vice versa			From Port Maitland, Dunnville, and Port Colborne to Port Robinson, and vice versa			From Port Robinson to Thorold, and vice versa			From Thorold to St Catharines, & vice versa			From St. Catharines to Port Dalhousie, and vice versa		
		£	s.	d	£	s	d	£	s	d.	£	s.	d	£	s	d	£	s.	d.
Squared Timber under 12×121, and Round or Flatted Timber in Boats or Vessels	per M L Feet	0	15	0	0	3	9	0	7	6	0	3	6	0	2	0	0	2	0
Do in Rafts	per M C Feet	1	0	0	0	5	0	0	10	0	0	4	0	0	3	0	0	3	0
Small Round Building Timber, Floats and Traverses, in Boats	M. L In Feet	0	5	0	0	1	3	0	2	6	0	1	2	0	0	8	0	0	8
Do. in Rafts	Do .	0	7	6	0	2	0	0	3	6	0	2	0	0	1	0	0	1	0
Boards, Planks, Scantling, & Sawed Lumber, in Boats	M F. In meas	0	1	3	0	0	4	0	0	7½	0	0	3½	0	0	2	0	0	2
Do. in Rafts	Do	0	5	0	0	1	3	0	2	6	0	1	2	0	0	8	0	0	8
Pipe Staves and Headings	per M	0	10	0	0	2	6	0	5	0	0	2	0	0	1	6	0	1	6
West India Staves and Headings	Do.	0	3	6	0	1	0	0	1	6	0	1	0	0	0	6	0	0	6
Headings	Do . .	0	3	6	0	1	0	0	1	6	0	1	0	0	0	6	0	0	6
Shingles	Do	0	0	3	0	0	1	0	0	1½	0	0	0½	0	0	0½	0	0	0½
Saw Logs	Each	0	0	4	0	0	1	0	0	2	0	0	1	0	0	0½	0	0	0½
Cedar Posts	Cord	0	2	0	0	0	6	0	1	0	0	0	6	0	0	3	0	0	3
Posts and Rails for Fencing	Do	0	1	6	0	0	5	0	0	9	0	0	4	0	0	2½	0	0	0½
Empty Barrels.	Each	0	0	1	0	0	0½	0	0	0¼	0	0	0¼	0	0	0¼	0	0	0¼
7.—ARTICLES NOT ENUMERATED.																			
On all Articles of Merchandise not enumerated in the foregoing List	Ton	0	5	0	0	1	3	0	2	6	0	1	2	0	0	8	0	0	8
Firkins, Small Casks, Packets, &c	Each	0	0	1½	0	0	0¼	0	0	0¾	0	0	0¼	0	0	0¼	0	0	0½
Passengers, Adults	Do.	0	0	6	0	0	1½	0	0	3	0	0	1¾	0	0	0¾	0	0	0¾
Do. Children	Do	0	0	3	0	0	1	0	0	1½	0	0	0½	0	0	0½	0	0	0¼

WELLESLEY.

A Township in the Wellington District, is bounded on the east by the township of Woolwich; on the north-east by Peel, on the north-west by Mornington; and on the south by Wilmot. In Wellesley 1,280 acres are under cultivation, only fifty acres are returned as uncultivated. This township formed a part of what was called the Queen's Bush, (crown land, where fifty acre lots were given away to actual settlers) The Canastoga, a branch of the Grand river, runs through the north-east corner of the township.

Population in 1841, 254

Ratable property in the township, £2,884

WELLINGTON DISTRICT.

Consists of the county of Waterloo, which comprises the township of Arthur, Amaranth, Bentinck, Derby, Eramosa, Egremont, Guelph, Glenelg, Garafraxa, Holland, Luther, Mornington. Minto, Maryborough, Melancthon, Nichol, Normanby, Peel, Proton, Puslinch, Sydenham, Sullivan, Waterloo, Wilmot, Woolwich, and Wellesley, and, for the purpose of representation in the Legislative Assembly only, the township of Dumfries, and for all purposes except that of representation in the Legislative Assembly, the township of Erin

The Wellington District is bounded on the east by the Gore, Home, and Simcoe Districts; on the north by the Simcoe District, and unsurveyed lands; on the west by unsurveyed lands, and a small portion of the Huron and Brock Districts, and on the south by the Gore and Brock Districts It is watered by the Grand River and some of its branches, the Saugeen, and numerous small streams, some of which are excellent mill streams. Some portions of the district, (which formerly composed part of the Gore District) have been long settled, as the township of Waterloo, which has been occupied above forty years The more northerly townships, as Guelph, Woolwich, Nichol, &c, have been more recently settled Guelph was laid out nearly twenty years since by Mr Galt, on a block of land belonging to the Canada Company, and Woolwich, Nichol, Eramosa and Erin, have been settled subsequently, and many of the new townships towards Owen Sound have as yet very few settlers in them. A road has lately been opened by the government from Arthur to Owen Sound, and fifty acre lots have been given to settlers, fronting on the road, with liberty to purchase, within a certain time, the fifty acres in the rear According to a return made in 1845, there were settled on this road within the first thirty miles above Arthur, a population amounting to 1111, of these 537 were Irish, 222 Scotch, 182 English, French Canadian eighty-four. Anglo Canadians seventy-eight, Americans eight; and they had under cultivation 2,500 acres of land

There is much fine land in the district, and some of the best farms in the Province may be found in the townships of Guelph, Waterloo, Wilmot, and Puslinch Eramosa, Erin and Woolwich are also well settled Much of the land in the district is timbered with the best kinds of hardwood, maple, beech, Elm, Oak, &c. with a sufficiency of pine for all necessary purposes The township of Waterloo was settled by a number of emigrants from the United States, consisting of Pennsylvanian Dutch, the rest of the district has been settled almost exclusively by English, Irish, and Scotch emigrants Guelph, the district town, is situated in the midst of a rolling country, surrounded by handsomely situated, and well cultivated farms, and it is dry and healthy. There are besides in the district, the villages of Preston, Berlin, Glasgow, and Waterloo, in Waterloo, Haysville and Hamburg, in Wilmot, Fergus and Elora, (the latter of which is beautifully situated on the Grand River), in Nichol, and others of less note. There is some fine scenery in the district; that of the falls of Elora is particularly picturesque. Lime stone is abundant in the district, along the course of the Grand River and its branches. The settlers in this district are generally in good circumstances, and are improving the country fast,

15,000 acres of land were brought into cultivation between January, 1842, and January, 1844. In the Wellington District 307,178 acres of Crown lands are open for sale, at 8s. currency per acre, to purchase any of which application must be made to the Crown lands agent at Elora. A few lots in Amaranth, Erin, Garafraxa, and Melancthon, vary in price from 2s. 6d. to 10s. per acre

Population of the district in 1841, 13,851, since when it has probably increased one fifth.

The following abstract from the assessment rolls will show the rate of increase and improvement in the district.

Date.	No. of Acres Cultivated.	MILLS. Grist.	MILLS. Saw.	Milch Cows.	Oxen, 4 years old, and upwards	Horned Cattle, from 2 to 4 years old.	Amount of Ratable Property.
1842	75,863	12	39	6590	3623	4366	£234,892
1843	82,897	14	43	6872	3602	4572	243,872
1844	90,791	19	47	6973	3785	4515	258,763

Government and District Officers in the Wellington District:

Judge of District Court	A. J. Fergusson	Guelph.
Sheriff	Geo. G. Grange	Do.
Clerk of Peace	Thos. Saunders	Do.
Treasurer	Wm. Hewat	Do.
District Clerk	R. F. Budd	Do.
Inspector of Licenses	James Hodgert	Do.
Clerk of District Court	Robt. Alling	Do.
Deputy Clerk of Crown	Wm. Hewat	Do.
Superintendent of Schools	Alex. Allan	Preston.
Warden	A. D. Fordyce	Fergus.
Coroners	Henry Orton	Guelph.
	Jas. Buist	Fergus.
	Dr. Scott	Berlin.

Number of Common Schools in operation in the District.—Guelph, eight; Waterloo, twenty-four; Wilmot, twenty; Woolwich and Queen's Bush, six; Wellesley, five; Nichol, five; Eramosa, five; Erin, twelve; Puslinch, eight; Garafraxa, six; Amaranth, 1; total, one hundred.

WELLINGTON SQUARE.

A Village in the township of Nelson, pleasantly situated on Lake Ontario, eight miles from Hamilton. It has been settled about twenty years. The steamboats to and from Hamilton generally touch here. Wellington Square contains about 400 inhabitants. There are in the village an Episcopal church and a Free church, A schooner is owned here.

Post office, post every day.

Professions and Trades.—One physician and surgeon, one steam grist mill, one foundry, one tannery, two stores, six groceries, one druggist, one pottery, four taverns, one saddler, one tinsmith, two waggon makers, two blacksmiths, one baker, four tailors.

Principal Tavern—" Ontario House."

Exports from Wellington Square for 1844.

Flour	10,922	barrels.
Timothy Seed	91	do.
Wheat	34,921	bushels.
Butter	26	kegs.

WELLINGTON

A small Village situated in the south-east corner of the township of Hillier, and partly in the township of Hallowell. it contains about 150 inhabitants. There are two churches in the village—Catholic and Methodist. There are three stores in the village.

WENTWORTH.

A County in the Gore District, it comprises the townships of Ancaster, Brantford, Binbrooke, Barton, Glandford, Onandaga, Saltfleet and Tuscarora, and for all purposes, except that of representation in the Legislative Assembly, and that of registration of titles, the townships of Seneca and Oneida, and, except for the purpose of representation in the Legislative Assembly, the town of Hamilton.

WESTERN DISTRICT.

Consists of the Counties of Essex and Kent. It is the most south-westerly district in the Province, and is bounded on the east by the London District and a small portion of the Huron District, on the north by Lake Huron, on the west by the River St Clair, Lake St Clair and the Detroit River, and on the south by Lake Erie. It is watered by the River Thames and the River Sydenham, or Bear Creek, the River aux Sables, and numerous small streams are distributed over the district. This district contains some of the finest land, and the most temperate climate of any portion of the province, the winter is short, and the spring sets in early. The valley of the Thames, as also that of Bear Creek, contain large portions of fine farming land well adapted for raising wheat; as do also the townships of Moore, Sarnia, Plympton, Warwick and Enniskillen, and the soil for about seven miles below Chatham is noted for the superior quality of peas it produces. The County of Essex is well fitted for the cultivation of Indian corn, and tobacco of very good quality has been raised in it.

This district, although possessing the most temperate climate, the shortest winter, and some of the richest land in the province, has hitherto settled up very slowly. This may be attributed to various causes, in the first place, its remoteness, and till very lately, the lack of convenient modes of reaching it. again, many emigrants newly arrived in the country, having very incautiously settled themselves down on the plains or prairies, within convenient distances of extensive marshes, attracted by the greenness of the pasture (not, after all, much greener than themselves), and the ease with which the land could be brought into cultivation, where, as any reasonable person would have anticipated, they soon (from the miasma arising from the marshes) caught ague and fevers. These, removing to other parts of the country, and blaming, not their own folly, as they ought to have done, but the climate of the country generally, deterred other settlers from venturing into it. It is true that in the Western District there are many wet and marshy places, but not more in proportion than in other parts of the province, but most of these may be easily drained, for many of those places which were wet three or four years ago have been effectually drained in making the new roads through the district. No localities can be drier or more healthy than the townships on the upper portions of the Thames and Bear Creek, and on Lake Huron. And, on a hot summer's day, no situation can be more agreeable than that of the settlers on the banks of Lake Huron, in the township of Plympton,—the air is seldom sultry, and there is generally a refreshing breeze from the lake. On the lake shore vegetation flourishes; and the farms, gardens and orchards never suffer from late or early frosts. In the townships of Dover and Tilbury a large portion of the land consists of open plains, partaking very much of the nature of marsh these are very useful for grazing cattle, which thrive very well on them, but no man of common sense would dream of making his habitation on them—those of course who have done so, have suffered the consequences.

The soil of a large portion of the district consists of a deep alluvial soil, very rich, and capable of producing large crops. In some of the townships bordering on Lake Erie the soil is a mixture of gravel and loam; and in Sarnia there is a large extent of oak plains. The timber of the district consists of maple, beech, black-walnut, butternut, hickory, oak, elm, &c.

The southern portion of the district has been long settled, many of the occupants in the County of Essex holding their lands under old French grants, which were confirmed to them by the British government after the conquest of Canada. The present inhabitants, the descendants of the original settlers, are still in every particular essentially French, and are too fond (sometimes too much so for the good of the country) of keeping up old French customs. Thus, on the death of a landowner his property becomes divided amongst his children; and on the decease of each of those children, it again becomes subdivided; so that in the present day, in that portion of the district peopled by French Canadians there is scarcely a good-sized farm to be found. And not only are the farms small and insufficient, but the farming is wretched. Many of these people settled on the lower portion of the Thames, actually build their stables on the banks of the river for the convenience of shovelling the manure into it. The following is an example of the difference between French and English farming: About ten years since an emigrant from England, a Lincolnshire farmer, engaged to rent a farm in the township of Dover East. The owners of the land (French Canadians) having exhausted that portion of the land which was cleared, and being too indolent to clear more, were literally starved out, they were therefore compelled to let the farm. When Mr W took possession he found *nine hundred loads of manure at the barn door*. When he took the farm there were forty-five acres of land cleared (out of a hundred acre lot), and he engaged to pay a rent of $50 per annum. He has now had the farm ten years, has cleared thirty additional acres, and is so well satisfied with the quality of the soil that he has leased it for five years, at an annual rent of $180. Since he has had the farm he has sold 1,300 bushels of wheat from one year's crop.

The farms and other settlements in this district generally have very fine orchards attached to them, and fruit is usually very plentiful in the district. Apples have been sold at Chatham at $3\frac{1}{2}d$ currency per bushel; and peaches have been sold on the shores of Lake Erie at 1s 3d per bushel.

Many of the dwellings on the Detroit and St. Clair Rivers are beautifully situated.

Clearing has lately been going on extensively in the townships of Plympton and Warwick, and large quantities of potash have been made, but so little are the advantages of the district generally known, that cultivated farms are to be bought here for from $10 to $15 per acre, which in any other portion of the province would fetch from $30 to $50 per acre. Thirteen thousand acres of land have been brought into cultivation between January, 1842, and January, 1844.

The towns of Chatham, Sandwich (the district town), and Amherstburg are situated in the district, the former on the Thames, and the two latter on the Detroit River, and there are besides in the district the villages of Windsor on the Detroit River, Port Sarnia, Froomfield and Sutherlands on the St Clair, Errol, in Plympton, and Louisville on the Thames, besides smaller places of less note.

In the Western District 57,850 of Crown lands are open for sale, at 8s. c'y. per acre, to purchase any of which application must be made to the Crown lands agent at Sandwich.

Population in 1844, 27,619, since when it has probably increased one-tenth.

The following abstract from the assessment rolls will show the rate of increase and improvement in the district:

Date.	No. of Acres Cultivated.	MILLS. Grist.	MILLS. Saw.	Milch Cows.	Oxen, 4 years old and upwards.	Horned Cattle, from 2 to 4 years old.	Amount of Ratable Property.
1842	69,335	19	19	8,375	3,148	4,112	£394,711
1843	77,176	14	17	92,14	3,556	4,833	324,221
1844	82,726	15	22	9,624	3,963	4,628	341,354

Government and District Officers in the Western District:

Judge of District Court............	Alexander Chewett..........	Sandwich.
Sheriff................................	George W. Foote............	Do.
Clerk of Peace	Charles Baby..................	Do.
Treasurer	J. B. Baby......................	Do.
Registrar	James Askin....................	Do.
Inspector of Licenses.............	W. G. Hall......................	Do.
Judge of Surrogate Court........	John A. Wilkinson..........	Do.
Registrar of do.....................	James Askin...................	Do.
District Clerk.......................	John Cowan...................	Do.
Deputy Clerk of Crown	S. J. Fluett.....................	Do.
Collectors of Customs...........	R. E. Vidal.....................	Port Sarnia.
	John F. Elliott.................	Windsor.
	William Cosgrave............	Chatham.
	F. Caldwell.....................	Malden.
	—. Cronyn.....................	Rond 'Eau.
Warden	John Dolsen...................	Dover East.
Coroners............................	Hugh Johnston	Moore.
	R. Pegley.......................	Chatham town.
	S. T. Thebo....................	Sandwich.
	W. G. Hall......................	Do.
	James Kevill	Amherstburg.
	A. Young, junior..............	Port Sarnia.
	P. P. Lecroix...................	Sombra.

Number of Common Schools in operation in the District.—Anderdon, two; Brooke, none; Camden, three; Chatham, six; Colchester, three; Dawn, seven; Dover, East and West, three; Gosfield, six; Harwich, eleven; Howard, ten; Maidstone, four; Malden, nine; Mersea, five; Moore and Enniskillen, two; Orford, three; Plympton, three; Raleigh, twelve; Rochester, two; Romney, three; Sandwich, ten; Sarnia, four; Sombra, seven; Tilbury East, three; Tilbury West, three; Warwick and Bosanquet, five; Zone, six. Total, 138.

WESTMEATH.

A Township in the Bathurst District; is bounded on the east by the Ottawa River; on the north-west by the township of Pembroke; on the south-west by Stafford; and on the south-east by Ross. In Westmeath 15,863 acres are taken up, 1,684 of which are under cultivation. Westmeath is as yet but little settled, and 34,200 acres of Crown lands are open for sale in it, at 8s. currency per acre. There are two saw mills in the township.

Population in 1842, 628.

Ratable property in the township, £7,056.

WESTMINSTER.

A Township in the London District; is bounded on the east by the township of South Dorchester; on the north by London, on the west by Delaware, and on the south by Yarmouth and Southwold. In Westminster 56,695 acres are taken up, 16,751 of which are under cultivation. This is an old-settled township, containing good land, a large portion of which is rolling, it is well settled, and contains many fine farms, which are in a good state of cultivation, and have flourishing orchards. The township is watered by branches of the Thames and of Kettle Creek. Westminster is settled principally by Canadians, Americans, and Pennsylvanian Dutch. The village of Westminster, or Hall's Mills, is situated on the old road from Delaware to London, and a settlement called the "Junction," at the meeting of the new Delaware road with the plank road from London to Port Stanley. There are four grist and two saw mills in the township.

Population in 1842, 3,376

Ratable property in the township, £45,656

WESTMINSTER, or HALL'S MILLS.

A Village in the township of Westminster, six miles from London, pleasantly situated on the old road from London to Delaware, in the midst of a fine, well settled country. It contains about 200 inhabitants, who are principally Canadians and Americans.

Post Office, post twice a week.

Professions and Trades.—One grist mill, one distillery, carding machine and cloth factory, one tannery, one tavern, one store, one fanning-mill maker, one blacksmith, one waggon maker, one shoemaker, and one tailor.

WESTON

A Village in the township of Etobicoke, situated on the Humber River, four miles above Dundas Street. It contains about 150 inhabitants, a portion of whom have procured an act authorising them to form a joint stock company for the purpose of making a plank road from the village, five and a half miles in length, to form a junction with Dundas Street. This gives them easy communication with the City of Toronto. There are two churches in Weston—Episcopal and Methodist.

Post Office, post twice a week.

Professions and Trades.—One grist and saw mill, one tannery, two distilleries, two stores, one tavern, two shoemakers, one saddler, one wheelwright.

WESTVILLE, or WILLIAMSVILLE

A small Village in the township of Kingston, situated on the western road, about one mile west from Kingston. It contains about 200 inhabitants, one store, one tavern, one grocery, one bakery, one painter, and one shoemaker.

WHITBY.

A Township in the Home District, is bounded on the east by the township of Darlington and a small portion of Cartwright, on the north by Reach, on the west by Pickering, and on the south by Lake Ontario. In Whitby 61,841 acres are taken up, 28,474 of which are under cultivation. This is a well settled township, containing a large portion of excellent land, which is mostly rolling. The farms are generally well cleared and cultivated, and in good order. The timber is a mixture of hardwood and pine. There are some excellent mill streams in the township. The flourishing villages of Oshawa and Whitby are situated on the main road from Toronto to Kingston, Gibb's Mills, about one mile south from Oshawa, Windsor Harbour on the lake shore; and Columbus and Winchester in the rear of the township, on the plank road from Windsor Bay to Skugog. There are eight grist and twenty-five saw mills in the township.

Population in 1842, 5,714, who are a mixture of English, Irish, Scotch, Canadians and Americans.
Ratable property in the township, £92,077.

WHITCHURCH.

A Township in the Home District, is bounded on the north by the township of East Gwillimbury, on the west by King, on the south by Markham, and on the east by Uxbridge. In Whitchurch 43,462 acres are taken up, 15,330 of which are under cultivation. This is an old settled township, containing many fine farms, which are generally well cultivated, and many of which are beautifully situated, and have excellent orchards attached to them. Most of the land is rolling. Whitchurch was originally settled by Pennsylvanian Quakers, most of whom or their descendants still hold the land. The village of Newmarket is situated in the north-west corner of the township. There are four grist and thirteen saw mills in the township.
Population in 1842, 3,836.
Ratable property in the township, £51,392.

WILLIAMS

A Township in the London District, is bounded on the north by the township of McGillivray; on the west by the River Sable and Bosanquet, on the south by Adelaide, and on the east by Lobo. The River Sable runs through the east and south of this township, till it reaches its south-west corner, when it makes a sharp bend and runs northward, becoming its western boundary. The soil is generally good. In Williams 20,895 acres are leased or sold, of which 2,296 are under cultivation. In the township are one grist and one saw mill.
Population 857.
Ratable property in the township, £9133.

WILLIAMSBURGH.

A Township in the Eastern District, is bounded on the north-east by the township of Osnabruck, on the north-west by Winchester, on the south-west by Matilda, and on the south-east by the River St Lawrence. In Williamsburgh 45,340 acres are taken up, 8,301 of which are under cultivation. The township is watered by branches of the Petite Nation River. It contains a fair proportion of good land, and is pretty well settled. There is a small village called "Cooksville" situated in the north-west of the township, six miles from the St Lawrence, and a settlement called "Mariatown," on the banks of the river. One hundred acres of Crown lands are open for sale in Williamsburgh, at 8s. currency per acre. There are one grist and four saw mills in the township.
Population in 1842, 2,941.
Ratable property in the township £38,935.

WILLIAMSTOWN

A Village in about the centre of the township of Charlottenburgh, situated on the River aux Raisins. It contains about 200 inhabitants.
Professions and Trades—One grist and saw mill, four stores, four taverns, two tanneries, one saddler, two blacksmiths, two shoemakers, two tailors.

WILLIAMSVILLE.

A small settlement on the town line between Walpole and Rainham, situated on the shore of Lake Erie. The Walpole post office is kept here.
Williamsville contains about 30 inhabitants, one store, one tavern, one blacksmith.

WILLOUGHBY.

A Township in the Niagara District, is bounded on the east by the Niagara River, on the north by the township of Stamford, from which it is separated by the Welland River, on the west by Crowland, and on the south by Bertie. In Willoughby 15,036 acres are taken up, 5686 of which are under cultivation. This township contains good land, and some well cleared farms, there is, however, a considerable quantity of low and wet land in it. Part of the village of Chippewa is in the township, the remainder being situated in the adjoining township of Stamford. The greater portion of Grand Island in the Niagara River, is situated opposite Willoughby. There are two saw mills in the township.

Population in 1841, 895, who are principally Canadians and Americans, with a few English; there are also a number of Swiss and German emigrants.

Ratable property in the township, £17,069.

WILMOT

A Township in the Wellington District, is bounded on the east by the township of Waterloo, on the north by Wellesley, on the west by North and South Easthope, and Zorra, and on the south by Blandford. In Wilmot, 51,463 acres are taken up, 15,310 of which are under cultivation. The River Nith, or Smith's Creek, runs through the west of the township from north to south. The villages of Hamburg and Haysville are in the township; the latter situated on the Huron road; and there are also in the township two grist and nine saw mills.

Population in 1841, 2220, who are principally Germans, with a few Canadians.

Ratable property in the township, £43,552.

WINCHESTER

A Village in the township of Whitby, situated near the centre of the township, five miles north from the village of Windsor. The plank road to Skugog passes through it. It was commenced in 1840, and contains about 300 inhabitants.

Professions and Trades.—One physician and surgeon, one grist mill, one ashery, one tannery, seven stores, three taverns, two waggon makers, three blacksmiths, three coopers, three tailors, three shoemakers, one cabinet maker.

WINCHESTER.

A Township in the Eastern District, is bounded on the north-east by the township of Finch, on the north-west by Russel and Osgoode, on the south-west by Mountain, and on the south-east by Williamsburgh. In Winchester 17,606 acres are taken up, 2,461 of which are under cultivation. The Petite Nation River runs through the south of the township, and it is watered besides by several branches of the same river. A large proportion of the timber of the township consists of pine. Four hundred acres of Crown lands are open for sale in Winchester, at 8s. currency per acre. There are one grist and two mills in the township.

Population in 1842, 979.

Ratable property in the township, £10,830.

WINDHAM

A Township in the Talbot District, is bounded on the east by the township of Townsend, on the north by Burford, on the west by Norwich and Middleton, and on the south by Charlotteville. In Windham 31,710 acres are taken up, 11,396 of which are under cultivation. The township is watered by Big Creek, which runs nearly through its centre. This is a well settled township, containing good land, the timber is a mixture of hardwood and pine. There are one grist and two saw mills in the township.

Population in 1841, 1568.

Ratable property in the township, £28,203.

WINDMILL POINT.

A Point of Land on the shore of the St Lawrence, about one mile east from Prescott, so called from the circumstance of a large windmill being erected there Previous to the late rebellion there was a flourishing settlement here, which contained several good stone houses Two battles were fought here during the rebellion, after the last of which the houses were set on fire by the military, and have not since been rebuilt.

WINDSOR

A Village in the township of Sandwich, pleasantly situated on the Detroit River, opposite the city of Detroit, in Michigan It was laid out in 1834, and is a place of considerable business Two steam ferry-boats ply constantly between this place and Detroit The situation is healthy, the town being built on a high bank, from thirty to forty feet above the river, which is here about a mile in width. Windsor possesses barracks, which are occupied at present by a battalion of Rifles In December, 1838 (during the rebellion), this place was attacked by a band of 400 Americans and rebels, who crossed over from Detroit, and burned the steamer Thames, and two or three houses They were charged by a party of militia, eighty in number, who, after firing two shots, completely routed them

Windsor contains about 300 inhabitants

Professions and Trades.—One physician and surgeon, one brewery, one distillery, four stores, three taverns, seven groceries, one baker, two carpenters, two blacksmiths, two tailors, two shoemakers, one tinsmith, one bank agency (Montreal)

Post office, post every day.

List of Exports for the year 1844, *with their estimated value* .

Quantity	Description	£	s	d
4642 Bushels	Wheat	696	6	0
65 Barrels	Flour	65	0	0
61 Do	Potash	290	0	0
434 Do	Pork	1164	0	0
77 Do	Lard	308	0	0
93 Do	White Fish	162	15	0
3 Do.	Furs (value not ascertained)			
98 Tierces	Beef	294	0	0
70 Do.	Hams (value not ascertained)			
22 Hogsheads	Do do			
15 Kegs	Tongues	22	10	0
226 Do	Lard	197	15	0
33 Do	Tobacco	99	0	0
4 Boxes	Bacon	16	0	0

The principal part of the pork, bacon, hams, lard, tongues, and beef were made from hogs and cattle *imported* from the United States, and *slaughtered* and *packed* in Canada.

WINDSOR.

A Village in the township of Whitby, situated on the eastern road, two miles from Windsor Bay, and about thirty-one from Toronto The plank road from the bay to Skugog Lake passes through the village There is a Congregational Church in the village

Population about 500

Post office, post every day.

Professions and Trades—Two physicians and surgeons, two lawyers, eight stores, two druggists, one bookseller and stationer, three taverns, one watchmaker, one ashery, one brewery, three saddlers, two cabinet makers, one chair maker, one fanning mill maker, two waggon makers, one tinsmith, one baker, three blacksmiths, four shoemakers, four tailors

About one mile east from the village is a small settlement called "Windsor East."

WINDSOR HARBOUR.

A Village and shipping place in the township of Whitby, situated on Lake Ontario, about thirty-two miles from Toronto. An excellent harbour has been formed here, by constructing a breakwater and building two piers, within the breakwater is enclosed a basin of about 120 acres in extent, which when completed will have a depth of ten feet. The width of the channel, at its entrance, between the piers, is two hundred and fifty feet, and there is a light-house on the west pier. Up to July 1st, 1844, £15,355 was expended on this harbour. A plank road is in course of formation from the harbour to Scugog Lake.

The Steamboat "America" (a British boat) calls here daily, on her passage to and from Rochester and Toronto. Seven schooners, whose collective tonnage amounts to about 400 tons, are owned here. Windsor Harbour is a port of entry and has a resident collector of customs. There are two churches in the village, Episcopal (built of stone), and Methodist.

Population about 250.

Professions and Trades.—One brewery, three stores, four taverns, one saddler, two blacksmiths, two shoemakers, two tailors, one wheelwright, one baker, one ship carpenter.

Exports from the port of Windsor during the season of 1844.

Flour	21,597 Barrels.
Pork	1,435 Do
Ashes	610 Do.
Oatmeal	285 Do.
Beer	120 Do
Wheat	14,563 Bushels.
Oats	1,682 Do.
Peas	290 Do.
Grass Seed	1,175 Do.
Potatoes	1,240 Do.
Butter	32 Firkins.
Lard	32 Kegs
Hams	14,000 lbs
Lumber	646,000 Feet.

WINDSOR EAST

A small settlement in the township of Whitby, about half a mile east from Windsor. It contains one saddler, two tailors, one cabinet maker, one waggon maker, one blacksmith.

WOLFE ISLAND.

A large Island situated in the north-eastern extremity of Lake Ontario, near the entrance of the River St. Lawrence. Its western portion is opposite the town of Kingston. It is a long, irregularly shaped island, having numerous small bays running into it. It forms a township of the Midland District. In Wolfe Island 24,449 acres are taken up, 6152 of which are under cultivation. Wolfe Island is well settled, and contains some good farms. There is one saw mill on the island.

Population, 1289.

Ratable property in the township, £17,323.

WOLFORD.

A Township in the Johnstown District, is bounded on the north-east by the township of Oxford, on the north-west by Montague, on the south-west by

Kitley, and on the south-east by Elizabethtown and Augusta. In Wolford 25,243 acres are taken up, 6477 of which are under cultivation. The Rideau River and Canal separate the township from Montague, and the township is also watered by branches of the Rideau River. The timber is a mixture of pine and hardwood. In Wolford 300 acres of Crown lands are open for sale, at 8s. currency per acre. There is a grist mill and a saw mill in the township.

Population in 1842, 2422

Ratable property in the township, £21,384.

WOODHOUSE.

A Township in the Talbot District, is bounded on the east by the township of Walpole, on the north by Townsend; on the west by Charlotteville, and on the south by Lake Erie. In Woodhouse 28,226 acres are taken up, 10,232 of which are under cultivation. This is a well settled township, containing excellent land, and many well-cleared and cultivated farms. The land is generally rolling, and most of the farms are handsomely situated. Simcoe, the district town, Port Dover on Lake Erie, at the mouth of Patterson's Creek, and a small shipping place called ' Port Ryerse," are situated in the township. The plank road from Hamilton to Port Dover, passes through the township. The timber in Woodhouse is a mixture of pine and hardwood. There are three grist and eleven saw mills in the township.

Population in 1841, 1694, who are principally Canadians and Americans.

Ratable property in the township, £41,864.

WOODSTOCK.

The District Town of the Brock District, in the south-west corner of the township of Blandford, thirty-two miles from London, and forty-six miles from Hamilton, pleasantly situated on a rising ground in the midst of a rolling country. It forms one long street of about a mile in length, and is divided into East Woodstock, and West Woodstock. It became the district town in the year 1840, (before which time the county of Oxford formed a portion of the London District.) It contains six churches and chapels, viz Episcopal, (of brick, and in which is a tolerable organ,) Presbyterian, Baptist, British Wesleyan, Canadian Wesleyan, and Christian. There is a jail and court house, built partly of brick, and partly framed. Two newspapers are published here weekly, the "Monarch," and "Herald." There is a Mechanics Institute, and a cricket club.

Population, 1,085

Post Office, post every day.

The following Government and district offices are kept in Woodstock:—Judge of district court, sheriff, clerk of peace, judge of surrogate court, registrar of ditto, treasurer, inspector of licenses, district clerk, clerk of district court, deputy clerk of crown, district superintendent of schools.

Professions and Trades.—Two grist mills, one saw mill, carding machine and fulling mill, brewery, distillery, two tanneries, four physicians and surgeons, two lawyers, one foundry, ten stores, seven groceries, one bookseller and stationer, five taverns, five cabinet and chair makers, four waggon makers, two watchmakers, one soap and candle factory, two livery stables, one glover, one turner, six blacksmiths, ten shoemakers, three bakers, four butchers, four saddlers, two coopers, one tinsmith, one barber, three painters, eight tailors, one printers, one school, one bank agency "Gore."

Principal Tavern.—"Woodstock Hotel."

Land Agent, J. F. Rogers.

WOOLWICH.

A Township in the Wellington District, is bounded on the east and north-east by the townships of Guelph and Nichol, on the north-west and west by Peel and Wellesley, and on the south by Waterloo. In Woolwich, 32,327 acres are taken up, 9100 of which are under cultivation. This is a large township and it is as yet but thinly settled. Much of the land in the township is of excellent quality, and the timber principally hardwood. The Grand River runs through the township. In the north of the township is a large block of land, containing 20,000 acres, belonging to the estate of the late General Pilkington. The village of Woolwich is situated in the township, and there are also in Woolwich two grist and two saw mills, one of which is situated on the Canastoga, a branch of the Grand River. There is an Episcopal church in the township, near the village of Elora.

Population in 1841, 1009.

Ratable property in the township, £22,315

WOOLWICH.

A small Settlement in the township of Woolwich, seventeen miles from Galt; it contains two churches, Presbyterian and Methodist, a post office, post twice a week, a tavern and a blacksmith.

WOOPPOOSE ISLAND.

A small Island in Prince Edward's Bay, in Lake Ontario, between the forks of the township of Marysburgh. It is not inhabited.

YARMOUTH.

A Township in the London District, is bounded on the east by the townships of Malahide and Dorchester; on the north by Westminster, on the west by Southwold, and on the south by Lake Erie. In Yarmouth 70,758 acres are taken up, 22,350 of which are under cultivation. The township is watered by Catfish Creek which separates it from the township of Malahide, and by Kettle Creek, which separates it from Southwold, both of which are good mill streams. The land in the township is generally of excellent quality, and most of it rolling. The township has been long settled, and contains many fine farms, well cleared and cultivated, with good orchards. It is the most thickly settled township in the London District. The north of the township is settled principally by Highland Scotch, and the south mostly by Quakers.

The villages of St. Thomas and Port Stanley are situated in the township (the former on the plank road from London, and the latter at the mouth of Kettle Creek) as are also the settlements of Jamestown and Sparta. There are five grist and ten saw mills in the township, from which large quantities of sawed lumber are exported, much of the timber on the creeks being pine.

Population in 1842, 1239.

Ratable property in the township, £70,057.

YONGE

A Township in the Johnstown District, is bounded on the east by the township of Elizabethtown, on the north by Bastard and Kitley, on the west by Lansdowne; and on the south by the river St. Lawrence. In Youge, 38,214 acres are taken up, 15,017 of which are under cultivation. The great Gananoque Lake extends into this township from the township of Lansdowne, and there are also three smaller lakes in the township, one of which is in the north, another near the centre of the township, and the third nearly midway beteween the two, the whole of these are connected by means of small streams with the Gananoque Lake. There are two marshes in the south of the township, both of which discharge themselves into the St Lawrence. This township is well settled, and contains good farms. In the north of the centre of the township is a settlement called "Farmersville," and in the north-east of the township a settlement called "Charleston." There are in the township five grist and twelve saw mills. In Yonge 200 acres only of Crown lands are open for sale at 8s. currency per acre

Population in 1842, 4036, who are principally Scotch and Irish.

Ratable property in the township, £46,673.

YORK

A Township in the Home District, is bounded on the east by the township of Scarborough, on the north by Vaughan, on the west by Etobicoke, and a small portion of Toronto Gore, and on the south by Lake Ontario In York 55,236 acres are taken up, 24,238 of which are under cultivation This is an old settled township, and much of it has been long under cultivation It is watered by the Humber and the Don rivers, and their branches The land in the south of the township, bordering on the lake, is poor and sandy, in the rear of the township it improves in quality. There is a considerable quantity of pine in the township, and a large portion of the township is timbered with a mixture of hard wood and pine

The City of Toronto is situated in the south of the township, on the Bay of Toronto, and there are eight grist and thirty-five saw mills in the township.

Population in 1842, 5,720

Ratable property in the township, £82,682.

There were shipped at the Humber during the year 1845

Flour	54,625 barrels,
Potash	84 "
Pork	127 "
Timothy Seed	8 "
Bran	60 tons,
Lumber (sawed)	20,000 feet,
Woollen Cloths	1,600 pounds,
Pot Barley	58 barrels,
Buckwheat Flour	3 "
Peas	48 "

YORK

A Village in the township of Seneca, pleasantly situated on the banks of the Grand River, five miles from Caledonia, and nineteen from Hamilton Considerable business is done here in the lumber trade A grist mill, saw mill, and shingle factory were burned down in December 1844, which are about being rebuilt. York contains about 150 inhabitants. Churches and chapels, two, viz Episcopal and Wesleyan Methodist

Post Office, post three times a week

Professions and Trades.—One physician and surgeon, two saw mills, (one of which has a gang of twelve saws,) three stores, three taverns, two waggon makers, two blacksmiths, three tailors, two cabinet makers, four shoe makers

YORK, COUNTY OF (See HOME DISTRICT.)

ZONE

A Township in the Western District, is bounded on the east by the township of Mosa; on the north by Brooke, on the west by Dawn, and on the south by Camden West and the River Thames In Zone 29,177 acres are taken up, 5,340 of which are under cultivation The River Sydenham (Bear Creek) crosses the township from its north-east corner to its south-west corner This is a fine township, containing excellent land, the greater portion of which is covered with the best kinds of hard wood, maple, oak, elm, beech, black walnut, &c On Bear Creek, and also on the Thames, are many beautiful situations for farms There are many well cleared and cultivated farms in the township On the bank of the Thames is a salt spring, where salt has been made, but its capa-

R

bilities have never yet been thoroughly tested and brought into operation The settlements of "Zone Mills," or "Van Allen's Mills," and "Smith's Mills," are situated on Bear Creek; and on the Thames is the site of the old Moraviantown, the battle ground where Tecumseth, the Indian Chief, was killed, in the year 1813 In Zone 800 acres of Crown lands are open for sale at 8s currency per acre. There are two grist and two saw mills in the township.

Population in 1845, 1231, who are principally emigrants from Great Britain and Ireland, with a few Canadians.

Ratable property in the township, £15,230

ZONE MILLS.

A Settlement in the township of Zone, pleasantly situated on the east branch of Bear Creek, nine miles from the western road and the River Thames It contains about 100 inhabitants; grist and saw mill, carding machine and fulling mill, one store, one waggon maker, one blacksmith

Post Office, post twice a week.

ZORRA

A Township in the Brock District, is bounded on the east by the township of Blandford, on the north-west by South Easthope and Downie, on the west by Nissouri, and on the south by North Oxford and part of Blandford In Zorra 60,220 acres are taken up, 10,627 of which are under cultivation. This township contains very excellent land, and the timber is generally hard wood, maple, oak, elm, beech, &c On the west side of the township, near its centre, is a spring, from which issues a large body of water, forming at once a creek of considerable size. The village of Embro' is situated a little south-west, and the village of Huntingford a little south-east of the centre of the township. There are one grist and three saw mills in the township

Population in 1842, 2722, who are principally Highland Scotch.

Ratable property in the township, £35,120.

CANADA;

ITS FIRST SETTLEMENT AND EARLY HISTORY, CLIMATE AND PRODUCTIONS.

CANADA;

ITS FIRST SETTLEMENT AND EARLY HISTORY, CLIMATE AND PRODUCTIONS

The first settlement made by Europeans in Canada, was in 1535, by Jacques Cartier, a French navigator, who sailed up the river of Canada, (which he named the St. Lawrence, as far as the island of Montreal, where he found a settlement of Huron Indians, called Hochelaga, to which island he gave the name of Mont Royale, (afterwards called Montreal.) He took possession of the territory, which he called New France—built a fort—and wintered in the country. On this expedition he carried off a chief of the natives, and conveyed him to France, where he lived about four years, was converted to Christianity, and died there.

In 1540, an expedition, consisting of five ships, under the command of Cartier, was fitted out by command of François de la Roque, Lord of Robervall, who had been appointed Viceroy of Canada by the King of France; and who himself intended to follow with two additional ships. His departure, however, was postponed till the year 1542. When he arrived in Canada, he built a fort, and wintered about four leagues above the island of Orleans. In 1549, the same nobleman, accompanied by his brother, and a numerous train of adventurers, again embarked for Canada; but they were never afterwards heard of, which so discouraged the government and people of France, that for more than thirty years no further measures were taken to communicate with the settlers who remained in Canada.

In 1576, Martin Frobisher was sent out by Queen Elizabeth, with three small ships, and discovered Elizabeth Foreland, and the straights which still bear his name. He entered a bay in north latitude 63°, and carried off one of the natives. In this voyage he discovered what he supposed to be gold, which encouraged a society of adventurers to send him out the following year, with three other ships, to explore the coast of Labrador and Greenland, with an ultimate view of discovering a passage to India, but he returned without success. He brought away with him nearly two hundred tons of the ore supposed to be gold; which however, to their disappointment turned out to be some other mineral. In 1578, he sailed again for the continent of North America, with no less than fifteen ships, in search of gold; and carried home immense quantities of the same glittering substance, to the complete ruin of many of the adventurers.

In 1581, the French trade to Canada was renewed, after an interruption of more than thirty years, and in 1583, three ships were employed in the trade to the continent.

In 1598, the Marquis de la Roche received a commission from Henry the Fourth, of France, to conquer Canada; but returned without doing anything of consequence, and shortly afterwards died of vexation. On the death of La Roche, his patent was renewed in favour of M. De Chauvin, who made a voyage up the St. Lawrence, as far as Tadousac, where he left some of his people, and returned with a freight of furs. The following year he sailed again, and proceeded as far as Trois Rivières. In 1603, Pierre du Gast, a gentleman of the bed-chamber to the same king, received a patent, constituting him Lieutenant General of the American territory, from the fortieth to the forty-sixth degrees of north latitude, with power to colonise it, and subdue and convert the natives to Christianity. In 1608, Champlain was sent out with three ships for the purpose of making a permanent settlement, and after having examined all the most eligible situations along the coast of Nova Scotia, (then called Acadia), and the River St. Lawrence, fixed upon the present site of Quebec, where he laid the foundation of what he intended to be the future capital of the country.

In 1627, in the reign of Louis XIII, Canada, then called New France, was, by direction of Cardinal Richelieu, placed together with its trade, under the management of a company, called the " Company of One Hundred Associates," at the head of which was the Cardinal himself. A commission having been given by Charles I to David Kertk, and his kinsmen, to conquer the American dominions of France; Kertk attacked Canada, in July, 1628, and continued to carry on his military operations with vigour. In 1630, he appeared again off Point Levi, and sent an officer to Quebec to summon the city to surrender. Champlain, then in command, knowing his means to be inadequate to a defence, surrendered the city by capitulation. The terms of the capitulation were favourable to the French colony, and they were so punctually and honourably fulfilled by the English, that the greater part of the French chose to remain with their captors, rather than return as had been stipulated to France. In 1632, Charles I, by the treaty of St. Germain, resigned the right which he had claimed to New France and Acadia, as the property of England, to Louis XIII, King of France.

In 1635, Rene Rohault, having become a Jesuit, resumed a project which had been interrupted by the English conquest of Quebec, of founding a college in that city, an institution that had been planned ten years before. In this year, M. Champlain died at Quebec.

In 1640, the French king vested the property of the island of Montreal in thirty-five Associates, of whom Maisonneuve, a gentleman of Champaign, was one; and who on the 15th October, 1641, was declared governor of the island; and brought over with him several families to Montreal.

The French in their trade with the neighbouring Indians, being much obstructed by the Mohawks, then a powerful tribe, and being unable to subdue them without assistance, in 1647, sent M. Marie, a Jesuit, as an agent to solicit aid from Massachusetts, with offers of liberal compensation for assistance, which the government of the English colony refused, on the ground that the Mohawks had never injured them.

In the following year, the colonists of Newfoundland sent to the Governor and Council of Canada a proposal of perpetual peace between the colonies, even though the mother countries might be at war. Although the French were much pleased with the proposal, and anxious to conclude an agreement of the kind, the business terminated without success, because the English were firm in their determination not to assist the French against the Iroquois (or Five Nations.)

In 1649, in the month of March, a party of Iroquois, about one thousand in number, attacked the Huron village of St Ignatius, containing four hundred persons, all of whom, with the exception of three only, were massacred. About five years afterwards, the Eries, a numerous tribe of Indians inhabiting the borders of Lake Erie, were so effectually exterminated by the Iroquois, that were it not for the name of the lake, we should have no memorial of their existence.

In 1665, M. de Courcelles, being appointed governor of New France, transported the regiment of *Calignan Salieres* to Canada; it consisted of one thousand foot, and they were accompanied besides by numerous families, with mechanics, hired servants, horses (the first ever seen in Canada), cattle and sheep. The one hundred associates in whom the property of the colony was vested, had grown weary of the expense of maintaining the colony, and from the year 1644 abandoned the fur trade to the inhabitants, reserving to themselves as their right of lordship an annual payment of one thousand beavers. Reduced at length to the number of forty-five associates, they made a total resignation of all their rights in 1662, to the French King, who soon afterwards included New France in the grant which he made of the French colonies in America, in favour of the West India Company formed by the great Colbert.

The Mohawks having greatly annoyed the French were attacked in the following year by a French army of twenty-eight companies of foot, and the whole militia of the colony. This formidable body of troops marched upwards of seven hundred miles, in the depth of winter, from Quebec into the country of the Mohawks, with a view of utterly destroying them, but the Indians retired with their women and children into the depth of the woods, leaving only a few ancient sachems in the villages, who chose rather to die than desert their habitations. These were murdered by the French, and their villages burnt, but nothing was gained by the expedition. In the following year, peace was at length established between the French and the Five Nations, which continued for several years, and they cultivated a mutual trade. In 1670 the small pox broke out amongst the Indians in the northern parts of Canada, and swept off whole tribes, particularly the tribe of Athkamegues, which has never since been heard of. Tadusac, the chief mart of the Indian fur trade with the French, was deserted, as was also Trois Rivieres, where the small-pox carried off 1,500 Indians at once. In 1671, a grand congress of the French and of many Canadian Indians was held at the Falls of St Mary, where the Indians professed submission to the king of France in a formal manner. In 1672, M de Courcelles, governor of Canada, commenced building a fort on the north side of the outlet of Lake Ontario (near where Kingston now stands), as a barrier against the Iroquois, which was completed in the following year by Count Frontenac, who called it after his own name. The French likewise built a fort at Michilimackinac. In 1674 Quebec was made a bishopric. In 1678 M. de Sale rebuilt the Fort Frontenac with stone, he also launched a bark of ten tons on Lake Ontario, and in the year following another vessel of sixty tons on Lake Erie, about this time he also enclosed a little spot of ground at Niagara with stockades intended for a fort. In 1683, the French erected a fort between the Lakes Erie and Huron, and in the following year M de la Barre with a large army from Canada made an unsuccessful expedition into the country of the Five Nations, and found it necessary to conclude his campaign with a treaty. He was met at the place appointed by the Oneidas, Onondagas, and Cayugas, the Mohawks and Senecas refusing to attend. Seated in a chair of state, surrounded by his own Indians, principally the Hurons of Lorette, and the French officers, he addressed himself to Garangula, an Onondaga chief, in a very haughty speech, which he concluded with a menace to burn the castles of the Five Nations, and destroy the Indians, unless the satisfaction which he demanded was given. Garangula, who sat at some little distance before his men, with his pipe in his mouth, and the great Calumet of peace before him, did nothing but look at the end of his pipe during this harangue. when it was finished, after walking five or six times round the circle in silence, he stood perfectly upright, and thus addressed the French general. "Onnuntio, I honour you, and all the warriors who are with me honour you. Your interpreter has finished your speech, I now begin mine. my words make haste to reach your ears, hearken to them. Onnuntio, in setting out from Quebec, you must have imagined that the scorching beams of the sun had burned down the forests, which rendered our country inaccessible to the French, or that the inundations of the lakes had shut us up in our castles, but now you are undeceived, for I and my warriors have come to assure you that the Senecas, Cayugas, Onondagas, Oneidas and Mohawks are yet alive." After ascribing the pacific overtures of the general to the impotence of the French, and repelling the charges brought against his countrymen, he thus concludes " My voice is the voice of all the Five Nations; hear what they say; open your ears to what they speak. The Senecas, Cayugas, Onondagas, Oneidas and Mohawks, say, that when they buried the hatchet at Cataracuay, in the presence of your predecessor, in the very centre of the fort, and planted the tree of peace in the same place, it was then agreed that the fort should be used as a place of rendezvous for merchants, and not as a refuge for soldiers. Hear, Onnuntio, you ought to take care, that so great a number of soldiers as appear now, do not choke the tree of peace, planted in so small a fort, and hinder it from shading both your country and ours with its branches. I do assure you that our warriors shall dance to the Calumet of peace under its leaves, and that we will never dig up the axe to cut it down, until the Onnuntio or the Corlar shall either jointly or separately endeavour to invade the country which the Great Spirit has given to our ancestors This belt confirms my words, and this other the authority which the Five Nations have given me"

In 1685, according to a return made by order of the Government, the inhabitants of Canada amounted to 17,000, three thousand of whom were supposed to be capable of bearing arms

In 1687 M Denonville, who had succeeded De la Barre, took the field at the head of 1500 French and 500 Indians, in order to attack and destroy the Senecas, who had refused to attend at the late treaty, and were known to be firmly attached to the English. He commenced his march from Cataraqui in June; and the scouts of the French army advanced as far as the corn of the Indian settlements, without seeing a single Indian, although they passed within pistol shot of 500 Senecas, who laid on their faces, and suffered them to pass and repass without attacking them. At length, when the invading army had approached within a quarter of a league of the chief village of the Senecas, they raised the war shout, accompanied with a discharge of fire arms from all sides This surprise threw the French into confusion, and the Senecas fell upon them with great fury, but the French Indians being rallied, repulsed them in the end In this action about a hundred French, ten French Indians, and eighty Senecas were killed The next day Denonville continued his march, with the intention of burning the village, but he found it already in ashes, the Senecas had burnt it and fled Two old men only were found in the village, who were cut into pieces and boiled to make soup for the French allies Before Denonville returned into Canada he built a fort with four bastions at Niagara, in which he left a garrison, but it was soon afterwards abandoned

In 1689 Denonville was recalled, and Count Frontenac came over as governor of Canada On the 26th of July in this year a body of 1200 Indians of the Five Nations invaded the Island of Montreal, burnt all the plantations, and made a horrible massacre of men, women and children, throwing the whole French colony into the utmost consternation, insomuch that Valrennes, the commandant at Cataraqui, was ordered by Denonville to abandon that place In this attack 1000 French are said to have been slain, and twenty-six carried off and burnt alive

In the following year an attack was made on Quebec by an English fleet, under the command of Sir W Phipps, which proved unsuccessful. Between this time and the year 1698, when the Count Frontenac died, the war between the French and Indians still continued, with varying fortunes, neither party gaining any very signal advantage over the other, and on the arrival of M de Callieres in 1699, who succeeded Count Frontenac as Governor of Canada, he terminated the disputes with the Indians by agreeing to an exchange of prisoners, which treaty of peace took place at Onondaga.

In 1705 the loss of a large and richly laden ship bound to Quebec (which was captured by the English), compelled the colonists to raise their own hemp and flax, which by permission of the French court they manufactured into linens and stuffs

In 1714 the whole number of men capable of bearing arms, between the ages of fourteen and sixty, that could be raised in Canada, only amounted to 4,484; and in 1749 the population had increased so much, that the militia of Canada numbered 12,000.

In 1759 Quebec was taken by General Wolfe, and Niagara was captured by Sir W. Johnston, and on the 8th September, 1760, Montreal, Detroit, Michilimackinac, and all other places within the government of Canada, were surrendered to his Britannic Majesty, and the destruction of a fleet ordered out from France in aid of Canada, completed the annihilation of the French power on the continent of North America As a reward to those soldiers and officers who had fought during the late war, the governors of the British possessions in North America were empowered to grant to each field officer 5000 acres of land, to a captain, 3000, to a subaltern or staff officer, 2000, to a non-commissioned officer, 200, and to each private 50 acres of land At this time Canada contained upwards of 65 000 inhabitants, and the exports for the year from Great Britain to Canada amounted to £8,623

In 1791, by an act of parliament, the Province of Quebec was divided into two separate provinces, to be called the provinces of Upper and Lower Canada, and the first parliament of the Upper Province met at Niagara on the 17th Sept 1792. In 1797 the second parliament met at Little York (now Toronto), which place continued to be the capital of the Upper Province till after the re-union of the two provinces in the year 1841, when Lord Sydenham removed the seat of government to Kingston, where it remained till 1844, when it was again removed to Montreal When the two provinces were re-united their designation was changed from Upper and Lower Canada, to Canada West and Canada East. Canada East is inhabited principally by the descendants of the old French settlers, with the exception of Quebec and Montreal (which, being the principal shipping places and commercial depots of the Lower Province, have amongst their population many English, Irish and Scotch merchants, and other persons connected with the trade and shipping interests of the province and Great Britain), and the Eastern townships, which the British American Land Company have been for some time engaged in trying to settle with British emigrants.

The Upper Province, or Canada West, (to which province this work is limited), is settled principally by emigrants and the descendants of emigrants from Great Britain and Ireland There are also large numbers of U E Loyalists (or persons who fought on the side of Great Britain during the American war, a mixture of all nations) and their descendants, and in particular localities there are large settlements of Pennsylvanian Dutch, and there are also many Americans scattered over the country. The Irish have rather a majority in the province, and next to them the English

Much has been written against, and strange notions are prevalent in Britain respecting, the climate of Canada Most persons on the other side of the Atlantic imagine that the winter is so severe, and the snow so deep, that it is impossible for any one to stir out of doors without being wrapped up to the eyebrows in furs or woollens, nor even then without the risk of being frozen to death, or lost in the snow. This is a very erroneous idea, and persons after being a short time in Canada are not a little surprised to find the climate very different to what they had expected, and to what it had been represented Emigrants from England find but little difference between the climate of Canada and that which they have left, except that the former climate is much drier, much more so indeed than any one would be led to expect, considering the immense bodies of water distributed over it and by which it is surrounded. Persons in Upper Canada generally clothe themselves much more lightly than they have been accustomed to, do at home and many persons who in England always wore both cloak and great-coat in winter, in Canada seldom put on either. It matters little how low the thermometer may be, if there is no wind, a person taking exercise does not feel the cold, the atmosphere being remarkably clear and bracing, with a cloudless sky, the weather is generally very pleasant; and the finest winter's day the author was ever out on, was spent in travelling between Barrie and Penetanguishene, the mercury in the thermometer being early in the morning down to twenty-eight degrees below zero. Indeed in Upper Canada, parties are heard much more frequently complaining of the heat than of the cold, and (which seems rather singular, considering their colour) the Indians say they suffer much more from the heat in summer than from the cold in winter. To convey a more definite idea of the severity of a winter in Upper Canada, it may be mentioned that the chain of shallow lakes which are distributed over the Newcastle and Colborne districts are seldom or never frozen over hard enough to bear a man with any heavy burden before Christmas, and they are generally open again before the middle of April. Lake Simcoe is seldom ventured upon with sleighs before the end of January, and farther west the winter is still shorter. Owing to the want of proper explanations, and misstatements by travellers and others who have attempted to describe the country (some of whom have seen very little of it), an idea has been formed in England that the great lakes are frozen over in winter, which is entirely a mistake. Lake Erie alone, which is very shallow, is said to have been frozen over two or three times within the last forty years; which, however, is very doubtful. The earth is seldom frozen to a greater depth than from twelve to eighteen inches, and the snow does not generally lie deeper than from eighteen inches to two feet. The length of the winter and the depth of snow vary very much according to the latitude of the locality, for instance, in the south of the Western District there is at least six weeks less winter than in Montreal, and while the snow at Sandwich or Amherstburg is seldom more than a foot in depth, at Penetanguishene it is frequently four feet deep. East or north of London there is generally sufficient snow for sleighing by about the third week in December, this usually lasts for two or three weeks, sometimes a little longer, when a thaw (called from its regular periodical appearance the January thaw) takes place, which continues for a few days, when it is succeeded by a fresh fall of snow, and the sleighing then continues good till the end of February or the beginning of March, when it breaks up altogether. In Upper Canada the occurrence of winters with scarcely any snow at all is not unfrequent, and such seasons are generally found to be injurious to the fall crops of wheat, and are besides considered to be a great misfortune, as they are found in many places to be a serious hindrance both to business and pleasure travelling, the snow when well beaten making the worst road in the province fully equal to a railroad. In fact, the winter is *the* season for travelling on the roads in Canada, in summer the principal part of the travelling is performed by steamboat. There is a material difference between the climate of Upper and Lower Canada. In Upper Canada a man can, if he chooses, work out of doors at all seasons of the year; but in the Lower Province there are occasionally days in the winter when the cold is so severe that it would be impossible for him to work in the open air.

It is something rather singular with respect to the climate of Canada, that the weather generally changes every three days, for instance there is seldom more than three days of severe weather at one time, and if the weather continues fair for three days, and does not change on the fourth, there is almost certain to be a continuation of fine weather for two days longer. In summer the thermometer seldom rises above eighty-five degrees, and the heat is generally moderated by pleasant breezes from the lakes. By the following statement from the minutes of the Trinity House at Quebec, it will be seen that navigation never opens later, even there, than the sixth of May, and seldom later than the latter end of April, and the steamboats on the St Lawrence and Lake Ontario, seldom cease running till nearly Christmas, and from Toronto to Niagara they frequently continue to run (weather permitting) through the whole winter.

Statement, from the minutes of the Trinity House at Quebec, of the dates of the opening of navigation, and of the arrival of the first steamboat from Montreal, in each year, from 1817 to 1844.

| NAVIGATION OPENED. || ARRIVAL OF FIRST STEAMBOATS. ||
Year	Date.	Date.	Names of Boats.
1817	May ... 6	May ... 7	Malsham.
1818	April ... 28	April ... 27	Do.
1819	No minute	May ... 2	Telegraph.
1820	"	April ... 24	Lady Sherbrooke.
1821	"	May ... 3	Quebec.
1822	"	April ... 29	Lady Sherbrooke.
1823	April ... 25	" 27	Quebec.
1824	" 20	" 21	Swiftsure.
1825	" 19	" 17	Do.
1826	No minute	" 22	Laprairie.
1827	April ... 14	" 16	Waterloo.
1828	" 15	" 12	Chambly.
1829	" 18	" 20	Lady of the Lake.
1830	" 16	" 17	Do.
1831	No minute .	" 21	Do.
1832	May ... 1	" 29	St. Lawrence.
1833	April ... 19	" 18	Do.
1834	" 18	" 17	Lady of the Lake.
1835	May ... 4	May ... 4	Canada.
1836	" 10	" 11	Do.
1837	" 2	" 1	British America.
1838	" 1	April ... 28	St. George.
1839	April ... 23	" ... 21	British America.
1840	" 21	" ... 19	Lady Colborne.
1841	May ... 4	May ... 1	Queen.
1842	April ... 26	April ... 21	Lady Colborne.
1843	May ... 5	May ... 5	Canada.
1844	April ... 23	April ... 23	Alliance.

From the greater dryness of the climate, persons suffer far less from coughs and colds than they do in England; and many persons frequently expose themselves to the weather with impunity, in a manner that in any part of Great Britain would be fraught with great danger. Almost every work on the subject of Canada has a chapter or two devoted to that never-ending and ever-fruitful theme—*ague.* An emigrant comes out, and (contrary to the advice of every one capable of giving it) thoughtlessly settles himself down in the immediate neighbourhood of a swamp; as might naturally have been anticipated, he catches the " *ager,*" and forthwith he condemns the country—unfairly so: he had previously been warned, but was unwilling to take the advice of those who knew better than himself, and he suffers the consequence of his folly. As well might the whole climate of England be condemned, because the fens of Lincolnshire, Cambridgeshire and Essex produce ague. The Indians are as liable to suffer from ague as the whites.

In consequence of the dryness of the climate, the surface of the country, in the latter part of the summer and autumn, has not that beautiful, verdant appearance that is so attractive in a moist climate like that of England; but this want is amply compensated for by the magnificent appearance, and the beauty of the tints of the forest trees in the autumn, when their leaves are changing. Here every variety of colour may be noticed, intermingled one with another—crimson, orange, yellow, and every variety of brown, the whole forming one of the richest scenes that can well be imagined.

Canada may properly be said to have but three seasons—summer, autumn, and winter; indeed were it not for the change in the appearance of the foliage, it would be difficult to say where summer ends and autumn commences. Generally, as soon as the snow disappears, warm weather sets in, and vegetation is exceedingly rapid, so much so, that although the spring is about a month later than in England, by the end of June vegetation of all kinds is as far advanced as in the latter country. It occasionally happens that frosts occur in May, which do a great deal of mischief, but these are only occasional, and the farmer may always reckon upon fine weather for his harvest. Corn, on an average, is ready for cutting about a fortnight or three weeks earlier than in England, and the grain, when once ripe, dries so fast, that it is not at all unusual for corn to be cut and carried on the same day.

From the warmth of the seasons, and the absence of summer frosts, many fruits that can only be raised under glass in England, such as melons, are grown in the greatest perfection in the open ground. In the southern portions of the province, fruit is grown in such plenty, that peaches have been sold in the Western District, on the shores of Lake Erie, at a quarter of a dollar per bushel, and apples have been sold on the Thames at three-pence halfpenny per bushel. Pumpkins and squashes grow in the open fields to an enormous size; from fifty to eighty pounds weight is not at all unusual. All the vegetable productions of England flourish under proper cultivation, apples, pears, plums, peaches, cherries, raspberries, currants and strawberries, damsons are not yet much cultivated and gooseberries have had but little attention paid them. Cabbages, peas, beans, celery asparagus, lettuces, onions, turnips, carrots, parsnips, tomatoes, cucumbers, rhubarb, and spinach grow luxuriantly; and almost every other description of vegetable, necessary or desirable for the table, may be cultivated with very little trouble.

Of the natural productions of the country, amongst the monarchs of the forest may be found, white and red pine, the former of which will frequently be found one hundred feet high to the first branch, and will occasionally reach two hundred feet in height; the average size of the timber cut for the Quebec market, will be in logs of about twenty inches square, and sixty feet in length; white oak, which will cut to about eighteen inches square, and about fifty feet in length, although sticks of both timbers are occasionally cut considerably larger. Of both these kinds of timber immense quantities are annually sent to England, and large quantities of white oak are split up into staves for the manufacture of puncheons, hogsheads, barrels, &c, for the supply of the English and West Indian markets. There are several kinds of ash, white ash, which is valuable for making oars, swamp ash, and prickly ash (or black ash, as it is frequently called), which is an ornamental wood, some of which is very handsome, and is used for making furniture, black and white birch, with the bark of the latter of which the Indians make their light and beautiful canoes; beech, elm, hickory, sugar maple, from the sap of which immense quantities of excellent sugar are made (some families occasionally making as much as two thousand five hundred pounds), and the beautiful birds-eye or curled maple, butternut is also a tree the wood of which is highly ornamental, and the fruit of which is very good eating, it is rather larger than the walnut, richer, but the flavour not quite so delicate. The black walnut, which furnishes the most beautiful wood for cabinet work grown on the continent of America; this wood is as yet but little known in Europe, but it richly deserves to be so; it is much used for the best kinds of furniture in America, sawn into veneers; much of it is most beautifully veined, and some of it is richer in colour, and far more beautiful in appearance than the finest specimens of rosewood. The wild cherry tree (the Laurus Cerasus, or cherry laurel), is very abundant and is much used for common furniture, it is a hard and durable wood. The bass-wood or lime tree; on rich moist ground, the white sycamore and button-wood tree; in the marshes, alder, spotted alder, willow and varieties of thorn, and in the swamps red and white cedar, tamarack and hemlock; from the tamarack the gum is obtained with which the Indians cement and make water-tight the seams of their bark canoes besides which there are the spruce fir, pitch pine (or Scotch fir), larch, black oak, and several other varieties, the cedar is a most useful wood for many purposes, and very lasting. Of shrubs there are many varieties, amongst which are the sumach and leather-wood tree.

Of the wild fruits of the country may be mentioned the wild cherry, which is principally used for flavouring spirits, wild grapes, few of which however are to be found sufficiently sweet for eating, black currants, which although not equal to the cultivated, make a very good preserve, red currants, several kinds of gooseberries, red, green and black, the fruit of most of which is covered with prickles, and is only usable when young, raspberries, which are of a fine flavor; and nearly equal to the cultivated, black raspberries; cranberries, which make a most delicious preserve, and large quantities of which are exported; none of these however reach England in a state of perfection, the reason of which is that the berries are gathered much too early, long before they are ripe, through the jealousy of the Indians, each of whom is afraid he shall not get his share; they therefore generally pick them in August, although they are not thoroughly ripe till October, when they are allowed to hang on the bush through the winter, and are gathered in the spring, they are a very rich fruit. These cranberries grow in marshes, which are generally much infested with rattlesnakes, therefore the white settlers seldom venture into them, but depend for their supply of the fruit upon the Indians. Besides these there are wild plums; strawberries, which grow in great abundance in particular localities, and which are about equal to the English wild strawberry; blackberries and hazle nuts, and many other kinds of wild fruit.

The flowers are almost innumerable, early in the summer the woods are literally clothed with them; amongst which will be found many beautiful varieties which are cultivated in the English gardens, such as the scarlet lobelia, blue lupin, purple gentian, columbine, violets (without scent), fleur de lis, the beautiful white water lily, two varieties of dog's-tooth violet, scarlet and other honey suckles, wild rose (rosa canina), dogwood, arbutus, diosma crenata, sweet briar, asclepias (two or three varieties), campanula, lychnis, golden rod, michaelmasdaisy, hyoscyamus niger, hydrastis Canadensis, pyrola (or winter green), hare bell, mimulus, phlox, Solomon's seal, calceolaria, &c. To give, however, a detailed list of the botanical productions of Canada would occupy a volume. Hops grow wild, and in great perfection.

The living, breathing denizens of the forest are various; but their numbers are fast diminishing before the destructive progress of civilization. When they shared the sovereignty of the land with the red man, they were comparatively but little disturbed; but as the country became settled up they were either gradually destroyed, or were obliged to retreat before the advancing footsteps of their common foe. On this subject there has been much misrepresentation in all works published on Canada. Game of all kinds has generally been represented as so plentiful, that no person would so much as dream of starting for Canada without at least *one* gun; and emigrants on their arrival, generally keep glancing from side to side as they walk up the streets, expecting every instant to see a bear or a wolf dart out from the doorways; and in strolling into the country, they walk very cautiously along, lest they should inadvertently tread upon and crush some poor partridge, hare, or turkey. In the present day, bears and wolves are only to be found in the more unsettled neighbourhoods, and it is very seldom that they are seen, unless regularly hunted after, and sometimes the hunters will be out several days before they can find a bear; and wolves are still more difficult to come at. Both these occasionally commit depredations in the farm yards bordering on the woods; and the Legislature in consequence established a premium or head money, payable for the head of each wolf. Formerly it was only necessary to take the scalp (i. e., the skin from the top of the head, and the ears) to a magistrate, who granted a certificate entitling the applicant to the premium. But this was found to lead to abuses, as some of the Indians were in the habit of breeding a cross between the wolf and their own curs, which when sufficiently old were killed for the sake of the premium; and many instances have occurred of *foxes'* scalps being substituted by white settlers for those of *young wolves*. A new regulation was consequently made, and the party claiming the premium was compelled to present the whole head. The beaver is now seldom found within reach of the white settlements, and the panther, lynx and wild cat have emigrated far to the north. Foxes, both silver grey, cross and red, raccoons, otters, fishers, martens, minks and muskrats, still remain in diminished numbers, and large quantities of fur are still annually exported.

Of the game—deer have become gradually destroyed, and but few comparatively now remain. In some localities, as in the Western District, they were tolerably plentiful till the winter of 1842-3, when a numerous band of Pottawattamie Indians came to the province from the United States. These were noted hunters, and the winter being favourable for the pursuit, immense numbers of the deer were slaughtered. The Indians do not generally kill more than they want for use, but this roving band appeared to hunt merely for the sake of destroying, as many a deer was left where it fell to be devoured by the wolves. In Canada, large numbers of deer are killed, at what are called "deer licks," these are wet swampy places, the water of which is strongly impregnated with salt, and which places the deer are in the habit of visiting at night, during certain seasons of the year. In order to get within shot, the Indians usually build up a kind of platform in the branches of a neighbouring tree, and watch there, rifle in hand, for the arrival of the deer, whose doom is soon sealed. Occasionally the deer, when hunted, will take to the lakes, and swim out sometimes more than a mile, the hunters generally follow in canoes or skiffs, and a desperate water fight ensues, which usually ends in the destruction of the poor quadruped. Previous to the winter of 1842, wild turkeys were also plentiful in the Western and London Districts, but the severity of that winter, and the great depth of snow, caused them to be completely starved out of the woods, and immense numbers were killed in the farm yards, whither they had ventured in search of food. This was complete murder, as most of them were little better than skin and bone. Had they been fed and taken care of during the winter, and allowed to escape in the spring, the breed would have been effectually preserved; whereas in consequence of the wholesale destruction practised amongst them, not a single turkey was met with during the following year. Last year, two or three flocks were seen, therefore there are still hopes of their continuing to exist in the province. In particular localities, and at certain seasons of the year, the partridge or pheasant, for by both names is it known, (which is in reality a kind of grouse), is tolerably plentiful in the woods. Woodcocks and snipes are not so numerous, but may occasionally be met with. There is also a species of hare, which turns white in the winter. Pigeons are very plentiful in the spring and autumn, and are killed by hundreds. Of ducks there are many varieties, some of them are very beautiful, they are excellent eating, and being found in great numbers, particularly about the marshy parts of the lakes and rivers, afford excellent sport. Wild swans are occasionally seen, and wild geese very commonly. Amongst the smaller animals the squirrels must not be omitted, as they are in great numbers, and form the principal *game* of Canada. Of these there are four varieties, the black squirrel, the largest and most numerous; the grey squirrel, which is seldom met with, the red squirrel, and the ground squirrel or chipmonk; these when properly cooked are excellent eating, and most persons prefer them to pigeons.

For the purpose of preserving the game of the province, and in order to endeavour to prevent its utter destruction, a bill was lately brought into parliament by Colonel Prince (himself a keen sportsman), the enactments of which are as follows :

"That no person or persons shall, within this province, from and after the passing of this act, hunt, shoot, take, kill or destroy any wild swan, wild goose, wild duck, teal, widgeon or snipe, between the tenth day of May, and the fifteenth day of August, in any year.

"That no person shall hereafter trap or set traps, nets or snares for any grouse or quail, or kill, or hunt, or go in quest after the same at night, within this province.

"That if any person shall hunt, shoot, take, kill or destroy any wild swan, wild goose, wild duck, teal, widgeon or snipe between the tenth day of May, and the fifteenth day of August in any year, or shall sell, offer for sale, buy, receive, or have in his or her possession, any of the above mentioned birds, between those periods, (such birds having been taken or killed after the said tenth day of May, the proof to the contrary whereof shall be upon the party charged,) or if any person shall trap or set traps, nets or snares, for any grouse or quail, or shall kill or hunt, or go in quest after the same at night, (that is to say, between sunset and sunrise,) on any such person being convicted of any or either of the said offences, before a justice of the peace, upon the oath or affirmation of one or more credible witness or witnesses, (which oath or affirmation the justice is hereby authorized to administer,) or upon view had of the offence by the said justice himself, shall pay a fine or penalty not exceeding five pounds, nor less than five shillings, current money of this province, together with the costs and charges attending the conviction."

It is to be feared, however, that no enactment of the kind will have much effect in preserving the game, as its provisions cannot be extended to the Indians, who are the principal hunters in the province, few other persons having much time or inclination for the sport.

Among the smaller feathered tribe are many beautiful birds the jay, which is about the size of the English jay, but the whole of whose plumage is blue, and beautifully marked, several varieties of woodpecker, the largest of which is called the "cock of the woods," a bird nearly the size of a rook, with black plumage, and a tuft of scarlet feathers on his head, a smaller one, with the body and wings black and white, the head and neck of a glossy black shaded with green, and a crimson spot on the top of the head, another, about the same size, spotted over with black and white, with one or two other varieties. The scarlet taniger, a scarlet bird with black wings, and a very sweet note, the bluebird, nearly as large as a blackbird, of a most beautiful blue, with a red breast, the indigo bird, a smaller bird of a deeper blue, three varieties of blackbirds, one of which has scarlet shoulders, the American canary, or flax-bird a bird much resembling the canary both in plumage and note, the only difference in the former being that the wings are black, and there is also a patch of black feathers on the top of the head. The robin, a bird something resembling the English robin in appearance, but more than double the size, the meadow lark, (a different bird to the English sky lark), the thrush, the kingfisher, the whippoor-will, the sandpiper, several varieties of fly catchers, and tree creepers, the swallow; two varieties of plover; the curlew; two species of humming birds, one of which is of a golden green, and the other has a crimson throat, with many other species, some of which are equally handsome. Some of these birds, however, only spend the summer with us, coming in the early spring, and migrating to the south in the autumn. Besides these, we have the bald-headed eagle, a noble bird; the kite, the large fishing hawk, the sparrow hawk, the large horned owl, and two or three smaller varieties, the heron, the bittern and the crow.

In the lakes and rivers, the principal fish are the sturgeon, which is frequently taken of from eighty to a hundred pounds weight, the lake or salmon trout, which grows to the size of from ten to forty pounds, the whitefish, (the most delicious fish in the lakes), and herrings, of these three many thousand barrels are annually taken and salted, a large portion of which is exported to the United States There are also pike, of large size, pickerel, three varieties of bass; maskelonge, a magnificent fish; cat-fish, suckers, perch: and occasionally eels; and in most of the rivers and mill streams may be found the speckled trout In the St Lawrence, and rivers running into Lake Ontario, large quantities of fine salmon have formerly been taken during the migration of the fish in the spring and autumn In the river Credit, in particular, a waggon load has frequently been taken by two or three persons in one night, but for the last two or three seasons the fish have almost deserted the streams running into Lake Ontario, the reason of which is supposed to be, the great number of dams erected across them, for the purpose of securing a supply of water for the grist and saw mills, which have much increased in number within a few years, and the immense quantity of saw-dust which is consequently constantly floating down them. It being considered desirable to preserve the salmon if possible, and prevent their being altogether exterminated or driven from the lake, an act was passed, which provides as follows

"That from and after the passing of this act, it shall not be lawful for any person or persons at any time between the tenth day of September in any year, and the first day of March in the succeeding year, to take, catch or kill any salmon or salmon fry, in any manner whatsoever.

" That it shall not be lawful for any person or persons at any time to take, catch or kill in any manner, in any district in Upper Canada, any salmon or salmon fry nearer the mouth of any of the rivers or creeks emptying into Lake Ontario or the Bay of Quinté, than two hundred yards, or within two hundred yards up from the mouth of any such river or creek as aforesaid , Provided always, that nothing herein contained shall be construed to prevent the taking of salmon with a seine or net at any place along the shores of Lake Ontario between the first day of February and the first day of August

' That it shall not be lawful for any person or persons to take, catch or kill, or to attempt to take, catch or kill any fish whatsoever, in any river or creek within Upper Canada, by torch or fire light within one hundred yards of any mill which may now or hereafter be erected on any such river or creek as aforesaid.

" That from and after the passing of this act, it shall not be lawful for any person or persons to buy, receive or have in his or their possession, under any pretence whatever, any salmon taken or caught during the period in which persons are hereby prohibited from taking or attempting to take or catch salmon within Upper Canada , and the proof that any salmon was not so taken or caught, shall lie on the person or persons in whose possession any such salmon shall be found

" That if any person or persons shall be convicted of any offence against this act, before any one or more of her Majesty's justices of the peace within the district in which the offence shall have been committed, upon the oath of one or more credible witness or witnesses, such person or persons shall upon conviction, as aforesaid, forfeit and pay a sum not exceeding ten pounds, nor less than five shillings, for the first offence at the discretion of the justice or justices before whom such conviction shall be had, with all reasonable costs both before and after conviction , and for every subsequent offence of a like nature, the sum of five pounds, with costs as aforesaid , and upon any such conviction, it shall be lawful for the said justice or justices before whom such conviction shall have been made, to issue his or their warrant of distress against the goods and chattels of the offender or offenders "

Two varieties of turtle are plentiful in the rivers and ponds—the common and the snapping turtle The North American porcupine should not be forgotten, it is considerably smaller than the South American porcupine, and the quills are both shorter and more slender , they are naturally of an opaque white; and the Indians dye them of many beautiful colours, and use them extensively in ornamental work.

Snakes are numerous; but venomous kinds are not so plentiful as in the country more to the south (in the United States); of the latter are the rattle-snake, adder; and the copper-head is also said to exist. The water-mocassin is also said to be venemous. Those which are harmless consist of the large black snake, the small brown snake, and the garter snakes. Great numbers of the snakes are destroyed by the large hawks, which seem to consider them a very delicious morsel. Frogs (or Canadian nightingales) exist in great numbers in the ponds and ditches. Wild bees are also numerous: they make their comb in a hollow tree, and occasionally a tree (called a bee tree) is felled, in the hollow of which will be found two or three hundred weight of honey.

Of entomological specimens many beautiful varieties are to be met with, and mosquitoes are apt to form an early and sometimes rather *too intimate* an acquaintance with the newly arrived emigrant.

Minerals, and those of the most valuable kinds, are very abundant in the province. Iron ore of the richest description (which is said to produce iron equal to the Swedish) exists in the townships of Madoc and Marmora, in the Victoria District; in Bathurst, and in the Bathurst District, and in other places; and bog iron ore is found in great plenty in many places, and is used extensively for making stoves and other castings. Silver, tin and lead are known to exist in various parts of the Province, beautiful specimens being frequently seen in the possession of the Indians, but the exact locality of the mines is not known, and the Indians are not willing to discover them. Copper has lately been discovered on the Canadian side of Lake Superior, and gold is also said to have been found. Marble of many beautiful varieties—pure white, green and yellow striped, spotted black and white, grey and black—exists in great plenty in the Eastern, Bathurst, Johnstown, Midland and Victoria districts, and also on Lake Huron. Lithographic stone in the townships of Marmora and Rama, freestone, limestone and granite are also abundant. Gypsum (or plaster of Paris) is also found in large quantities on the Grand River and other parts. And in various parts of the province salt has been made from brine springs, the water, however, has not generally been found sufficiently impregnated with salt to make the operation profitable.

DIVISIONS AND EXTENT OF THE UPPER PROVINCE:

ITS PROGRESS AND IMPROVEMENTS, RESOURCES, TRADE AND AGRICULTURE, EDUCATION, ADVICE TO EMIGRANTS, &c

---

Canada West commences about twenty miles above the confluence of the St Lawrence and the Ottawa Rivers, and the settled portion extends towards the west and south-west as far as Lake Huron, the River St Clair, Lake St. Clair, and the Detroit River, and on the south it is bounded by the River St. Lawrence, Lake Ontario, the Niagara River, and Lake Erie. From the dividing line between Upper and Lower Canada to the Detroit River, the distance is about 500 miles in a straight line.

Canada is generally described as a flat country; but it is only called so by those who have travelled over very little of it. Most persons who have written

S

descriptions of the country have only travelled along the regular stage roads (which are always carried over as much level ground as possible), and have seen very little of the interior of the country. The surface of the greater portion of the Upper Province is rolling; and there are many portions that are very hilly. A range of hills or ridges, that may almost be termed mountains, runs through the townships of Albion and Caledon, and on to Lake Huron, terminating in the Blue Mountains on the Georgian Bay one of these mountains is said to be about 2000 feet above the level of the lake. By looking at the map of the country, and noticing the sources and the courses of the streams, it is easy to form a tolerably correct judgment of the relative height of the land. Thus it will be seen that the ridge of land running through the townships north of Toronto must be considerably above Lake Ontario, as the rivers taking their rise in it, and which flow into Lake Simcoe, after passing down the falls of the Severn, through the Georgian Bay and Lake Huron, the rapids of the River St. Clair, Lake St. Clair and Lake Erie, the rapids and the Falls of the Niagara River, enter Lake Ontario, and, after performing a circuit of nearly 800 miles, pass down within from twenty to thirty miles of their source.

The following is the quantity of land surveyed in Upper Canada, and the manner in which it has been disposed of, together with the estimated quantity still remaining unsurveyed.—

	Acres.
There were originally surveyed in Upper Canada, including the surrenders by Indian tribes	18,153,219
Which has been appropriated and disposed of as follows	
For support of Protestant Clergy	2,407,687
For Education—King's College, Toronto	225,944
" Upper Canada College	63,642
" Grammar Schools	258,330
To the Canada Company	2,184,413
U. E. Loyalists, and for various claims	10,404,663
Indian Reservations not disposed of	808,540
Land remaining on hand	1,500,000
Unsurveyed Lands in Upper Canada	13,592,320

Of the unsurveyed land 9,119,260 acres are supposed to be of a sufficiently good quality for cultivation; and 4,472,960 acres bad land, unfit for cultivation.

Canada West is divided into twenty districts, which are again subdivided into counties, ridings and townships. The districts vary in size, as do also the townships, the Western District containing twenty-nine townships, and the Prince Edward District only six. As the large districts become settled up, and contain a sufficient population to form two districts out of one, they are generally divided; thus the Colborne District was formed from the Newcastle, the Simcoe from the Home, and the Huron from the London. Some townships contain as many as 90,000 acres, and others not more than 20,000. Most of the townships are laid out in square blocks, but some of them are divided in a manner that defies description—leading one to form the conclusion that the original surveyors seldom commenced their work until *after* dinner. The townships are divided into concessions, which are generally supposed to run north and south, or east and west, but these vary very much according to circumstances. When a river runs through or bounds a township, the front lots are always laid out to face the river, no matter in what direction its course may lie. The concessions are again subdivided into lots of 200 acres each, and half lots of 100 acres.

About half the surveyed lands of Upper Canada has been purchased from the Indian tribes since the year 1818, the dates and quantities of which, together with the remuneration received by the Indians for them, are shown in the annexed statement.

Statement of Lands surrendered by the Indians for Annuities, shewing the dates of the surrenders, the names of the different Tribes, their present numerical strength, the number of Acres ceded, and the amount of the Annuities :—

Date of Surrender.	Name of Tribe.	Present Numerical Strength.	Number of Acres ceded.	Amount of Annuity in Currency. £ s. d.	Conditions.
20th July, 1820	Mohawks of the Bay of Quinté	415	33,280	450 0 0	£2. 10s. to each member of the Tribe, but not to exceed £450.
31st May, 1819	Mississagas of Alnwick	218	2,748,000	642 10 0	£2 10s. to each member of the Tribe, but not to exceed £642 10s.
28th Oct, 1818	Mississagas of the River Credit	245	648,000	522 10 0	If the Tribe decreases one-half, the annuity is to decrease in the same proportion; the original number specified in the deed is 440 souls.
5th Nov., 1818	Mississagas of Rice and Mud Lakes	345	1,951,000	740 0 0	
17th Oct, 1818	Chippewas of Lakes Huron and Simcoe	540	1,592,000	1200 0 0	
26th April, 1825	Chippewas of Chenail Ecarté and St. Clair	1129	2,200,000	1100 0 0	
9th May, 1820	Chippewas of the River Thames	438	580,000	600 0 0	£2 10s. to each member of the Tribe, but not to exceed £600 yearly.
25th Oct, 1826	Moravians of the River Thames	184	25,000	150 0 0	
9th August, 1836	Saugeen Indians*	348	150,000	1250 0 0	£2 10s. to each member of the Tribe; not to increase, but to decrease with its diminut'n.
	Total number of Acres		9,927,280		

* This Tribe did not commence receiving their annuity until the 1st January, 1840. They are resident in the two villages situated at the mouth of the Saugeen, and at Owen Sound.

243

Writers on Canada and the United States, who take a very superficial view of the subject, are apt to institute a very unfair comparison between the two countries, and always draw a conclusion unfavourable to Canada. In the United States every thing is said to be bustle and activity, progress and improvement; whilst the contrary is said to be the case in Canada. If this were really so, no one need be surprised when he takes into consideration the immense sums that have been borrowed from England, for the purpose of constructing the public works in the United States; which works may be said to have cost them nothing, as but little of the principal, and not much more of the interest has been paid. If we could get the cash on as easy terms in Canada, we should have no difficulty in "going a-head" quite as fast. But has Canada really been standing still all these years, while the States have been making such progress? Let us look at the facts and see. Within the last twenty-five years the Rideau Canal, the Welland Canal, and the St Lawrence Canals, some of the most magnificent and important undertakings in the world, have been commenced and completed. In the year 1799, the Home District only contained 224 inhabitants, and in 1845, the City of Toronto alone contained 19,756. Twenty years ago, Hamilton, London, Bytown, and Cobourg, scarcely had an existence, now they are flourishing towns, containing handsome houses and public buildings, and their outskirts are studded with elegant villas. About forty years since, the first settlers entered the Gore and Wellington Districts (then united in one), at that time a mere wilderness, now they contain some of the finest farms in the Province. Forty years ago there was a post established from Niagara to Amherstburg once in six months, which was carried by a man on foot; after a time this was increased to four times a year, then once a-month, afterwards every week; till at length letters reach Amherstburg every day, with the exception of Wednesday, which omission is caused by the post not leaving Toronto on Sunday. In the year 1796, Toronto is described by the Duc de Rochefoucauld as being a mere swamp, containing only a fort and twelve log huts, and without a single settlement within a hundred miles of it, now the three great thoroughfares—the western, the northern, and the Kingston roads—are each planked or macadamised for about twenty miles, and for the same distance nearly every lot fronting on the roads is taken up, settled, and under cultivation. Three years ago the voyage from Montreal to Kingston, by the Rideau Canal, occupied five or six days, now, by the St Lawrence, the journey may be performed in twenty-eight hours, and from Kingston to Montreal in twenty-four hours.

As a proof that improvements have not been going on so very slowly, the following sums have been expended on the public works at present in progress, or lately finished, up to the first of January, 1846 —

	£	s	d
Welland Canal	551,646	17	4
Cornwall Canal	71,724	1	2
Williamsburgh Canals	156,347	13	10
Burlington Bay Canal	46,650	4	8
Hamilton and Dover Road	40,104	9	4
Newcastle District, &c	8,303	7	0
Crooks' Rapids	10,004	16	6
Heeley's Falls	9,113	17	7
Middle Falls	4,851	10	8
Rauney Falls	10,749	9	5
Harris' Rapids	1,647	3	3
Rice Lake Road	7,206	19	2
Seymour Bridge	613	2	5
Buckhorn Bridge	453	14	1
Whitla's Rapids	6,210	0	5
Chisholm's Rapids	7,728	2	6
Seugog Rapids	6,706	17	9
Fiddler's Island	220	15	0

River Trent	338	14	0
Windsor Harbour	24,242	18	7
Dover Harbour	7,136	17	1
Long Point Lights	2,899	8	2
Windsor and Scugog Road	8,624	16	10
Port Stanley Harbour	16,423	6	3
Rond 'Eau Harbour	6,971	1	1
Ottawa Improvements	45,906	15	9
Main North Toronto Road	8,147	9	7
Brantford Road	49,501	6	3
Chatham, Sandwich, &c, Road	41,968	7	2
Owen's Sound Road	220	0	2
Scugog and Narrows' Road	54	10	2
Surveys, Canada West	379	0	8
Amherstburg and Sandwich Road	559	19	10
Cornwall and L'Orignal Road	28	0	0
Toronto Custom House	1,102	3	10
Kennebec Road	211	4	8
Grand River Swamp Road	2,295	11	0
Rouge Hill Road and Bridge	992	2	9
L'Orignal and Bytown Road	160	8	8
Belleville Bridge	564	7	11

Besides large sums expended on the works in Lower Canada.

Canada is also said to be a *poor* country: no one could travel over it and long retain that impression. The beauty and substantial nature of the public buildings—the handsome banks, stores, and elegant mansions—the beauty and superior excellence of the steamboats—the mills and rapidly increasing manufactories—the extensive and well cultivated farms, are all sufficient evidences of her wealth. In 1844 there were in the Upper Province 2,017,115 acres of land under cultivation; 175,604 milch cows, 139,584 oxen and other horned cattle over two years old, and the ratable property in the province amounted to £7,390,345. But these, it should be remembered, were only the numbers and amount *returned to the assessors*, and, as few persons ever return anything like the whole amount of their property, at least five-and-twenty per cent. may fairly be added to this amount, and the only articles of property assessed consist of land cultivated and uncultivated, houses, water grist and saw mills (steam mills are not assessed), merchants' shops, store-houses, horses, milch-cows, cattle over two years old, distilleries, and pleasure waggons; so that there is a vast amount of property of which no account whatever is taken. Land under cultivation is rated at £1, and uncultivated land at 4s currency per acre which is much under its real value, as many farms in the province could not be purchased at £10 or £12 per acre, and in some situations from $10 to $15 per acre is asked for wild land.

With regard to the population it is difficult to arrive at a true statement; with the exception of two or three districts, no census has been taken since that of 1842, which in many districts was taken in so careless a manner that but little dependence was to be placed upon it. However, the fault rested more with those who planned than with those who had to carry out the task. Enormous sheets of paper containing 121 columns were given out to be filled up, some items of which, in the first place, were very inquisitorial, and many of the people were not inclined to give the information required, many of them also believing that the object in collecting the returns was for the purpose of imposing additional taxes upon them, wilfully made false statements, and, in the second place, from the nature and size of the sheet to be filled up, no man of common intelligence could be supposed to avoid occasionally inserting an item in a wrong column.

To give anything like a correct account of the quantity of produce of various kinds—wheat, flour, pork, beef, &c —raised and exported, would be under the present order of things absolutely impossible, as no entry is made of articles exported. It is most extraordinary that no provision is made by the provincial government for collecting some account of the grain and other farming produce exported from the province, in order that its capabilities and progress might-be made public and known to the world. At present, except in some locality where the produce shipped is liable to harbour dues, there is no possibility of arriving at a knowledge of the exports except from the shipping merchants. A statement has lately been published by the House of Assembly of certain returns made to it, which contains very little real information on the subject; thirteen pages, or about half the pamphlet being taken up with *imports* at the little port of St Johns In this return the exports of wheat and flour from Montreal and Quebec in 1844 are stated at—Flour, 415,467 barrels, and wheat, 282,183 bushels Now, as the quantity of flour and wheat that passed through the Welland Canal, the Desjardins Canal, with that shipped from Hamilton, alone amounted to—of the former, 448,958 barrels, and of the latter, 2,141,022 bushels, it is manifest that this amount must be incorrect, or what becomes of the immense quantity of both wheat and flour shipped from the various ports along the coast of Lake Ontario, including Wellington Square, Oakville, Port Credit the Humber, Toronto, Windsor Bay, Oshawa, Bond Head, Brighton, Port Hope, Cobourg, Colborne, Trent, Belleville, the Prince Edward District, and the Johnstown District? unless the whole of this large quantity is required for the consumption of the inhabitants of Lower Canada, which will hardly be pretended Large quantities of barrelled beef and pork, butter, peas, pot and pearl ashes, furs, wool, lumber and staves are exported, the aggregate value of which, if its amount could be ascertained, must be enormous.

In consequence of the suicidal policy of many of the importing merchants in Montreal, and the forwarders, the former in demanding too large profits, and the latter in making enormous charges for freight, the imports of many heavy articles from Great Britain are falling off, particularly of heavy groceries, such as tea, coffee, sugar, spices, &c , the western merchants finding that they can go to New York and make their purchases (even paying the additional duties upon the articles on account of their being foreign goods), at a greater advantage than they can buy them in Montreal. This has been particularly the case since the diminution of the duty upon tea imported from the United States, thus, in 1842 the quantity of tea imported into Quebec and Montreal amounted to 1,380,940 lbs, and in 1845 it had fallen off to 770,615 lbs In 1844 the number of vessels employed on the lakes and rivers above Quebec amounted to 86 steamboats, whose aggregate tonnage amounted to 12,808 tons, and 794 sailing vessels, barges, &c , the tonnage of which was 72,842 tons, and the

Property insured by the St. Lawrence Inland Marine
  Assurance Company for the season amounted to . £445,176 0 5
The premium on which amounted to 4,857 11 2
The amount of losses during the year paid by the Company 3,293 7 1
Additional losses not yet settled, but estimated at … … . 1,430 0 0

For many years the agriculture of the province generally was at a very low standard, but within the last few years it has begun to make great advancements, and is beginning to keep pace with the improvements introduced into England and Scotland. The emigration into the country of scientific agriculturists, with the establishment of agricultural societies, have been mainly instrumental in producing this great change, stock of a different and better description has been imported, and much land that was previously considered by the old proprietors worn out, has been improved and brought back, by means of judicious treatment, to its old capabilities.

In order to give an impetus to the progress of improvement in agriculture, and for the encouragement of agricultural societies in Upper Canada, an act was passed, which provides—

"That when any agricultural society, for the purpose of importing any valuable stock, or whatever else might conduce to the improvement of agriculture, shall be constituted in any district in Upper Canada, and shall make it appear, by certificate under the hand of the treasurer of such district society, that the sum of not less than £25 has been actually subscribed and paid to the said treasurer by the several agricultural societies of such district, the president of the said society shall make application, enclosing the said certificate to the governor, lieutenant-governor, or person administering the government in this province, for and in support of the said society, it shall and may be lawful for the governor, lieutenant-governor, or person administering the government in this province, to issue his warrant to the receiver general in favour of the treasurer of the said society for treble the amount that shall have been paid or subscribed in such district as aforesaid: Provided always, that the annual sum to be granted to each district shall not exceed the sum of £250 currency.

"That in the event of there being county, riding, or township agricultural societies established, there shall not be more than one county or district society in each county or riding of any district within this province, and a proportion of the district bounty shall and may be granted to each county, riding or township agricultural society, and paid to them by the district society in proportion to the money that each county, riding or township agricultural society shall have subscribed: Provided nevertheless, that the whole sum granted to the district and county societies together shall not exceed the sum of £250 in each year; that, in the event of more than £50 being subscribed by the several societies in any district, the said grant of £250 shall be divided to each society in due proportion according to the amount of their subscriptions respectively.

"That each agricultural society shall and may elect such officers and make such by-laws for their guidance as to them shall seem best for promoting the interests of agriculture, according to the true intent and meaning of this act.

"That the treasurer's account of the receipts and expenditure of the preceding year shall, after the first year, always accompany the application for grants in aid of the said agricultural societies.

"That if the treasurer of any township society shall on or before the first day of July in each and every year, pay any sum of money into the hands of the treasurer of the district or county societies, he shall be entitled to receive the same again so soon as the legislative grant shall have been received, with a portion of the legislative grant equal to the amount so paid, or in proportion to what shall fall to their share upon an equal division being made, in proportion to the sums paid by the several societies in the district or county.

"That the secretary of each society shall annually transmit to the three branches of the Legislature, within fifteen days after the opening of each session of the provincial parliament, a report of its proceedings, showing the amount of the subscriptions received in the course of the year, and the amount received out of the public chest, the expenses of the society, the names of the persons to whom it shall have granted premiums, the objects for which such premiums were obtained, and all such other observations and information as he shall deem likely to tend to the improvement of agriculture."

Every district now has its agricultural society, and premiums are given for the best articles of live or dead stock exhibited at the annual show; and at some of these agricultural meetings stock is occasionally exhibited which would be no disgrace to the great cattle show at Smithfield. In many districts there are also branch societies in connection with the district society.

With respect to the provision made for public education, from a return made by the Hon. Mr. Macaulay, of the 10th of August, 1841, for the general board of education, it appears that the

Total quantity of land originally set apart for school purposes was		546,861½
Of which were appropriated—		
For the King's College	225,994	
For Upper Canada College	66,000	
		291,944
Leaving reserved for Grammar Schools		254,917½
Sold under the management of the General Board of Education, up to 31st December, 1840	52,930½	
Sold by Col. Talbot under his former instructions, from Jan. 1st, 1841, to Dec. 31st, 1843	1,932	
		54,862½
Amount of Grammar School Lands remaining disposable on January 1st, 1845		200,055

For the purposes of education a district or grammar school is established in each district town, the master of which receives an annual grant of £100 from the government. In addition to which each township is divided into school districts, the number varying according to the size of the township and the amount of the population. Each school district has a school house erected in it, and the schoolmaster receives from the district (in addition to what he is paid by the pupils) a certain sum per quarter in proportion to the number of his scholars. The schools in each district are under the general superintendence of a district superintendent. For the support of these schools a small tax is levied upon the inhabitants.

The following is the amount paid towards the support of common schools in Upper Canada, for the year 1844:

	£	s.	d.
Brock District	706	1	10
Bathurst do	907	9	0
Colborne do	564	10	8
Dalhousie do	628	11	8
Eastern do	1,287	4	1
Gore do	1,811	15	7
Home do	2,952	9	3
Huron do	257	3	8
Johnstown do	1,302	15	9
London do	1,325	6	4
Midland do	1,373	18	6
Newcastle do	1,217	6	11
Niagara do	1,459	1	9
Ottawa do	326	6	8
Prince Edward do	601	10	4
Simcoe do	561	11	2
Talbot do	485	14	11
Victoria do	587	4	1
Wellington do	612	19	11
Western do	1,030	17	4
Total	£19,999	19	5

It is most extraordinary, so long as Canada has been settled, that its great natural advantages should still be so little known; that so many persons who are either compelled by necessity to emigrate, or who do so from choice, should continue to pass it by and go on to the west of the United States, or otherwise emigrate to the more distant colonies of the Cape, New South Wales, or New

Zealand; and yet such is the case. Much of the emigration to the United States, however, is caused by the writings of English authors. Every now and then a traveller starts for the United States with a pocket full of money, travels over them at that season of the year when the appearance of the country is most captivating, becomes enchanted with the beauty of its scenery, the length of the summer, the ease with which an existence may be obtained; and straightways returns home and writes a book on the subject, painting everything *couleur de rose* "One fool makes many;" and many persons whose judgments are led astray by the fascinating descriptions of travellers, emigrate there, and it is not till too late, when the property they took with them has been all expended, and their constitutions ruined, that they find out their mistake, but unfortunately they discover it too late, for they are left without the means of removing. Each state in its turn has been an *el dorado*, a perfect paradise. Thirty years ago it was Ohio and Indiana, then Illinois, then Michigan and Missouri, within the last five or six years, Wisconsin and Iowa; and now the current is beginning to set in strongly towards Oregon and California.

Birkbeck's "Letters from Illinois," published about twenty-seven years ago, induced many families of respectability to emigrate to the valley of the Wabash, who have since bitterly cursed his folly and their own. Many of them took out large sums of money, which they invested in land, or deposited in United States' banks; and many of them have of course lost their all, and Birkbeck's own family are scattered to the four winds of heaven. Birkbeck himself, according to his own account, used to keep his carriage in England. He took out with him to Illinois £5000 or £6000, and one of his sons, previous to his death, was actually earning a livelihood by working in a brick-field. Stewart again, some years since, followed the example of Birkbeck, and wrote very flattering accounts of the south-west, and with the same results, but he himself was not simple enough to remain there.

In what respects will the advocates of emigration to the United States pretend to say that any portion of that country is superior to Canada. Is it in the climate? A tree may be judged of by its fruits, and very many of the native Canadians, in point of robust appearance and complexion, might be taken for English emigrants. Will any one venture to make the same assertion respecting a native of Ohio, Indiana, Illinois, or Missouri? And of what avail is it that the climate will grow cotton and tobacco, if the settler neither has the strength to cultivate them, nor a market in which to dispose of them, when grown? In the winter and spring of 1841-2, pork (a staple article of the State,) was selling in Illinois, at from a dollar to a dollar and a half per 100 lbs, and at that price it was almost impossible to obtain cash for it, wheat at a quarter dollar, and indian corn from five to ten cents per bushel, butter, fifteen and sixteen pounds for a dollar, fowls, half a dollar per dozen, and other farming produce in proportion. At such prices farming could not be very profitable. A man certainly might live cheaply, and cram himself with bacon and corn bread till he brought on bilious fever, but he could *make nothing* of what he raised. And a farmer having a fat ox, has even been known after killing it, to take from it the hide and tallow, and drag the carcase into the woods to be devoured by the wolves, finding from the small price the beef would fetch, that it was more profitable to do so than to sell the whole animal!

Is it from the nature of the government, that the States are so much more desirable as a place of residence—where the only law is mob law, and the bowie knife is the constant companion of the citizens, and is used even in the halls of legislature themselves? Or is New Zealand much to be preferred, where the settler in taking his morning ramble, to acquire an appetite for his breakfast, frequently receives a "settler" himself, and instead of returning to his morning's meal, is roasted for the breakfast of some native chief, and his interesting family. Canada, on the contrary, suffers under none of these disadvantages and annoyances. The government and constitution of the country are English, the laws are English; the climate is fine and healthy, the Indians are tolerably civilized, none of them at any rate are cannibals, and few of them are even thieves; and bowie knives are not "the fashion." The settler, unless he has been guilty of the folly of planting himself down beyond the bounds of civilization and of roads, may always command a fair price and cash for whatever he can raise—he need never be beyond the reach of medical attendance, churches, and schools—he can obtain as much land as he need wish to purchase, at a fair and moderate rate—he knows that whatever property he acquires is as secure as if he had it in England—his landed property, if he possesses any, is gradually increasing in value—and if he is only moderately careful and industrious, he need have no anxiety for the future—his sons, growing up in and with the country, and as they grow, acquiring a knowledge of the country and its customs, and the various modes of doing business in it, if steady, will have no difficulty in succeeding in any business they may select, or may be qualified for.

Much has been written on the subject of emigration, and many speculations entered into as to *who* are the proper persons to emigrate? The only answer that can be given to this question is—*those who are obliged to do so*. Let no person who is doing *well* at home, no matter what may be his profession or occupation, emigrate with the expectation of doing *better*,—let him not leave his home and travel over the world, in search of advantages which he may not find elsewhere. But those who are *not* doing well, who find it difficult to struggle against increasing competition, who fear the loss in business of what little property they possess, or who find it difficult with an increasing family to keep up appearances as they have been accustomed to do, and find it necessary to make a change—all these may safely emigrate, with a fair prospect of improving their condition. Persons of small, independent incomes may live cheaply in Canada, particularly in the country, and enjoy many comforts, and even luxuries, that were not within their reach at home. Retired military men do not generally make good settlers. They usually, when they leave the army, sell out, instead of retiring on half pay; and when they emigrate they are apt to squander their property in purchasing land and in building, till at length they come to a stand for want of the means to proceed, frequently with their buildings half-finished, from being planned on too large a scale; although, if they had been asked in the commencement how they intended to *live* when the ready money was expended, they would have been unable to give an intelligible answer. If they succeed in getting some government office, the emoluments of which are sufficient for their support, they will manage to get along very well; otherwise they will sink gradually lower and lower, and their children are apt to get into idle and dissipated habits. The idle and inactive life to which they have been accustomed while in the army, particularly during these "piping times of peace," totally incapacitates them for making good settlers in the backwoods. *A lounger, unless independent, has no business in Canada.* Naval officers, on the contrary, make settlers of a very different character. They have been accustomed, when on service, to a life of activity; and if they have been long on service, they have generally seen a great deal of the world—they have their half-pay to fall back on, which fortunately for them they cannot sell—and they generally make very excellent settlers. Lawyers are not wanted: Canada swarms with them; and they multiply in the province so fast, that the demand is not by any means equal to the supply. Medical men may find many openings in the country, where they will have no difficulty in making a tolerable living; but they will have to work hard for it, having frequently to ride fifteen, twenty-five, or even thirty miles to see a patient! And in the towns, the competition is as great as in England.

Weavers are generally supposed to be, from the nature of their previous occupation, unfitted to turn farmers in the backwoods. This is entirely a mistake. Although they may not for some time make good choppers, as no old-countryman does at first (and some never acquire the art), still they are very capable, as soon as they have got a little insight into the proper mode of managing and working a farm, of taking and cultivating cleared or partially cleared farms—which may always be obtained to rent, or farm on shares. A good proof of this occurred a short time since in the Western District, where two young men, (weavers from Paisley), took a farm on shares, on the River Thames, and before it had been in their occupation a year and a half, it was cleaner and in better condition than any farm within miles of them.

Mechanics of all kinds can always find employment at good pay; and at present, building is going on extensively—much of it in the towns of stone, and stone-cutters, particularly those capable of executing ornamental work, such as cornices, figures, heads, &c, are much in demand.

There are many kinds of establishments much wanted in the province, and large sums of money are annually sent to the States for work that might as well be executed in Canada. For instance, one or two engraving establishments, capable of executing maps of the largest class, are much wanted in Toronto. Within the last year, several large works have been sent from the province, through the impossibility of getting them executed in it. Amongst these are—Bouchette's large Map of Canada, seven feet by four; Raikin's large Map of the Niagara, Gore, and Wellington Districts; Billiard & Paris' Map of the Western District; and I was compelled to lithograph the map for the Gazetteer, on account of the absolute impossibility of meeting with an engraver capable of executing the work, within reach. This is a branch of the arts much wanted in Canada. Maps are in great demand, and are difficult to procure, in consequence of the trouble of getting the plates engraved, it being necessary at present, with all large works, to get the plates engraved at New York, and also to get the impressions struck off there, which, from the distance, is both a great expense and inconvenience. But an establishment of this kind in Toronto should be capable, not only of engraving, but should also have every convenience for, and workmen capable of printing maps of the largest class, and should also bring out with them printing presses, copper, and every other article necessary for the art, as these things are not to be procured here. One or two extensive lithographic establishments are also much wanted. An establishment for printing in colours, embossed cards, &c, in the manner introduced in England within the last few years, for placards and showbills, would also succeed very well. With many other branches of the arts, of which it is impossible to give a catalogue.

Many persons emigrating lay out what spare cash they can collect together in any articles that they imagine will prove a good speculation in the country to which they are journeying, fancying that they are coming into the backwoods, where goods are scarcely procurable, and that any articles they can bring out, will command a large profit. They are not aware that business of every kind is carried on extensively in Canada, and that most articles are to be bought as cheap there as in England, with merely the addition of the expense of carriage, and as on many articles the duty is considerably lower in Canada than in England, they are to be purchased at a less price. One wholesale house alone, is understood to have imported goods during the season of 1844, to the amount of £120,000. Other parties, supposing that furniture must necessarily be expensive in a new country, bring out all the old lumber they can lay their hands on. Some even carry their folly to the extreme of carrying out with them their heavy kitchen tables and dressers, long school-room desks, &c—(do they fancy timber is *scarce* in Canada?) and find, to their astonishment and vexation when they arrive at Toronto, or wherever may be their place of destination, that it would have cost them far less to purchase the articles where they intended to settle, than the mere expense of transport, and that it would have been much more to their advantage to have made a bonfire of their goods and chattels than to have brought them across the Atlantic. Common furniture of all kinds is remarkably cheap, and that of a superior kind is considerably lower in price than the same quality in England.

Emigrants coming out to Canada, usually commit some very great mistakes; these are, loitering about the large towns, purchasing land before they know its value, buying more land than they are able to cultivate properly, and entering into speculations they know nothing whatever about. We will take these in order as they stand, In the first place, an emigrant, coming out with perhaps a large family and small means, wishes to purchase land with the intention of farming, and of course wants it as cheap as he can procure it, at the same time it is an object with him to spend as little in looking for it as possible. He does not consider that by staying in a large town he defeats these objects, as his expenses in a large town are considerably higher than they would be in the country, and he is apt to be led insensibly into extravagancies, which in the country he would avoid In a large town he cannot stay in a first-rate tavern for less than from a dollar to a dollar and a half per day, while in the country he may board in a house equally respectable, with accommodation in every respect equal, and a good table, for from two and a half to three dollars per week; again, in a town he has not the opportunities of hearing of land to be purchased cheap, and land in the neighbourhood of large towns is always rated higher, than land of the same, or perhaps better quality, situated a few miles distant. No emigrant, unless he has plenty of money to spare, should stay a single day upon the road till he arrives at Toronto, unless he has previously made up his mind to settle in the Victoria, Newcastle or Colborne districts, (or has friends residing east of Toronto whom he wishes to visit), in which case he should make his way as quickly as possible to Belleville, Cobourg, Port Hope, or Peterborough. If he wishes to settle in the neighbourhood of Toronto, he should take up his quarters in a respectable tavern on Yonge Street, or Dundas Street, where by remaining quiet and looking about him, he will soon hear of something likely to suit him, and he may visit Lloydtown in the township of King, Markham in Markham, Newmarket in Whitchurch, or any other of the villages in the neighbourhood. Should he prefer going further northward, and feel inclined to take the pure bracing atmosphere of the Simcoe District as a compensation for its more lengthy winter, he may proceed to the Holland Landing, and from thence make his way either by the road, or across Lake Simcoe to Barrie or Orillia If he wishes to go westward and settle in the Gore, Niagara, or Wellington districts, let him take his passage either to Hamilton or Niagara From the former place he may make easy journies to Dundas, Brantford, Galt, Paris, and Caledonia, (all of which except the first are on the Grand River,) in the Gore District, and he may also visit the villages on the river below Caledonia, and to Guelph, Preston, Elora, and Fergus in the Wellington District, in all of which neighbourhoods he will be likely to hear of land to suit him If he feels a desire to see the Niagara District, he may proceed direct to Niagara or Queenston, by steamboat from Toronto, or when at Hamilton he may visit the villages along the road from Hamilton to Niagara, and also along the Niagara River and the Welland Canal. Should he prefer the Talbot or Brock Districts he may proceed by stage from Hamilton to Caledonia, and from thence to Port Dover on Lake Erie, from whence he may visit Simcoe, Vittoria, and other villages in the neighbourhood. Should he find nothing to suit him there, he may retrace his steps to Hamilton or Brantford, and look over the Brock District, to do which he should make his head quarters at Woodstock, Beachville, or Ingersoll Should he however, at starting, intend to proceed farther west and settle either in the London or Western districts, he should not waste his time and means in wandering over that portion of the country where he has no intention of fixing himself, but proceed at once to London or Chatham From London he may visit Delaware, St. Thomas, Port Stanley, Kilworth, Westminster, Wardsville, the settlements on the road to Chatham, on that to Port Sarnia, and on that to Goderich; in all of which localities he will have no difficulty in meeting with excellent land, either wild or partly cleared, at a moderate price From Chatham he may extend his inquiries to the settlements on the banks of the Thames, he may look along Bear Creek, the townships bordering on Lake Erie, the River St Clair, and the southern portion of Lake Huron, in every township of which he may purchase land of the finest quality, at a very low rate To look over the latter portion of the district he should fix his quarters at Port Sarnia.

In the second place, no emigrant should purchase land till he has been sufficiently long in the country to know its value. A person purchasing land immediately on his arrival is certain to pay at least one-third more for it than he would after he has been in the country for some time. If he has capital, and can afford to remain idle for six months, let him establish himself at some respectable tavern in a village in that part of the country he thinks he would prefer residing in, he will there have an opportunity of looking about him, and seeing the quality of the land in the neighbourhood, and learning its relative value. By mixing among the farmers, he will get an insight into the mode of farming in the province, the cheapest method of clearing land, and the value of labour; all very essential things for him to know   And he will find after a time, when he has acquired all this knowledge, that the money he has expended has been well laid out, as in the subsequent purchase of his farm he will save considerably more than he has spent in looking about him   If he understands farming, but has no capital, or not sufficient to enable him to live for a time without employment, let him either rent a farm for a year (which he may readily do for a dollar per acre for the cleared portion of the land), or he will have no difficulty in obtaining a cleared farm to work on shares, that is, the owner of the land will find the whole or a portion of the stock and seed, and, by way of rent, take a share of the produce. In this case he can lose very little or nothing; he may live off the farm, and in a year or two he is certain to hear of some farm in his immediate vicinity which may either be purchased at a bargain (perhaps for half what it would have cost him had he purchased immediately on his arrival), or obtained on lease at a low rent. If he has no capital, or knows nothing of farming, let him engage himself to some farmer for a time, where he may learn everything connected with the business, and be paid something for his services besides   After staying on a farm for a year or two, and becoming capable of managing one himself, he will have no difficulty in procuring one to rent or farm on shares, and in course of time, if he is careful and industrious, he will be enabled to purchase one for himself   He will have acquired his knowledge and experience of the subject without any expense to himself, and will be the better able to take advantage of what he has learned.

In the third place, a farmer, who in England would consider that to farm well and profitably he ought to have a capital to start with of at least £4 or £5 for each acre of land he intended to cultivate, will emigrate with the remnant of his property, amounting to perhaps £400 or £500, or £600. This would enable him to take a farm in Canada, stock it well, and farm it well, to live comfortably, pay the rent, keep his produce till the state of the markets enabled him to sell it at a profit, and in the course of five or six years to save sufficient to *purchase* a good cleared farm, free from all incumbrances   But this will not suit him, the man who has been accustomed all his life to rent land, the moment he places his foot on American soil, becomes possessed with the mania for purchasing land, nothing will do but he must have a farm of his own —he must become a *landed proprietor*. The consequence is, that finding land easily acquired, he purchases a farm worth three, or four, or five times the amount of the whole of his capital, pays an instalment on it, and then has not sufficient cash left to stock his farm properly   He is consequently compelled to purchase live stock of an inferior quality, and insufficient in number—he is unable to employ labour on his farm, when it would be profitable for him to do so—he is obliged to go into debt to the stores, and consequently must part with his grain the moment it is off the ground, in order to satisfy the demands of his creditors, and must take whatever he can get for it,—and he has to struggle hard for years to provide the instalments on his land as they fall due. This is perfect folly, and he might have saved himself the toil and anxiety of all these years, and been in possession of a good farm much sooner, had he only been satisfied in the first instance to rent, instead of purchasing   No person should purchase more land than he is able to pay for; and, above all things, he should avoid purchasing land on long credits. Many persons again, with small capital, who know nothing whatever of farming or clearing land, immediately on their arrival, purchase a lot of wild land, looking merely at the cheap rate at which it is to be bought, without any consideration of what it is likely to cost them before the stumps are out. These generally find in the end that it would have been much better for them had they purchased land partially cleared. But it is exceedingly difficult to convince a newly arrived emigrant of this fact.

"A man convinced against his will,
Is of the same opinion still"

And so it proves. Many of them are not willing to profit by the experience of other people, but require to pay dearly for the lesson. A few acres well cultivated are more profitable, even in Canada, than a larger quantity half or badly cultivated.

The fourth and last, although not the least important part of our subject, relates to those persons who come out with a certain amount of capital which they wish to invest profitably in business. These immediately commence speculating in something which they do not understand—perhaps purchase some concern which the owner has found to be unprofitable, and is therefore glad to part with, and in a short time they are obliged in their turn to sell out, after having incurred a heavy loss. Emigrants may rest assured that those who have been in the country a few years, know much better what speculations will answer, than those who have been out only a few weeks, or at most months, and are not likely to part with any really profitable concern without receiving its full value for it, and a business that may afford a very good return to one accustomed to the mode of doing business in the province, may turn out to be a very losing concern in the hands of a stranger. In general, emigrants with capital who, have growing up sons, will find it far better to invest their capital in good securities, and live upon the interest, while they place their sons in some good houses of business, and in the course of a few years, when these sons have acquired a knowledge of the commercial affairs of the province, they will be enabled to realize handsome profits on the capital, which, if their fathers had speculated with, they would most assuredly, have lost.

With respect to those portions of the province in which it is desirable for the emigrant to purchase land, much will depend upon various circumstances; as, if he is either English, Irish, or Scotch, he will most likely prefer settling among his own countrymen. Something also will depend upon the amount of capital he has to invest. There is one point however, of great importance, that I should wish strongly to impress upon the *newly-arrived* emigrant in particular, (because no other is likely to fall into the mistake), and that is, let him on no account whatever, no matter what the price, or the apparent advantages held out to him may be, be induced to purchase land at a distance from good roads and a good market, as nothing tends so much to keep back the settler, and frequently to dishearten him, and prevent his getting on as fast as he otherwise would do, as that feeling of loneliness that frequently oppresses him, when he finds himself alone in the woods and no neighbours within convenient reach. He is apt in such a case to be away from home more than is profitable either for himself or his farm. And there is no occasion for this, as in no district of the province need a man buy land at a greater distance than a mile from a cleared farm. By making proper inquiries the emigrant is always sure to hear of some one willing to sell within easy distance of a good market; and he may take this as a general rule, that one hundred acres within seven miles of a place where he can sell his produce at a fair price, and obtain cash for it, is worth more than four times the quantity, at twice or three times the distance, and at the end of ten or twelve years, he will generally find that the 100 acres has increased in value more than the 400. People in general have a great penchant for purchasing land either on a road or a river; and the difference in price on that account, is consequently very great; although frequently the land in the back lots will be of better quality than that in front.

To such an extreme is this carried, that land facing on a road will frequently be valued at twelve or fifteen dollars per acre, while that in the next concession (little more than a mile) back, may be purchased at from 1½ to 3 dollars. Land in Canada is valued, not according to its quality, but entirely according to its locality and other circumstances. Thus, if a few wealthy settlers fix themselves in any particular locality, and make considerable improvements, the neighbourhood becomes *aristocratic*, and land in the vicinity rises in value accordingly Thus, farms in the neighbourhood of Woodstock have been sold at from $30 to $50 per acre; while farms equal in quality of soil, and superior as regards facility of getting to markets, may be purchased in the London and Western Districts for less than half the sum

All lands in the possession of the Crown, with very few exceptions, are sold at 8s. currency per acre, which may be paid for either in cash or scrip This scrip is usually to be purchased (and the emigrant, if a stranger, may ascertain where it is to be met with by inquiring of some respectable merchant or storekeeper) at a discount of twenty, twenty-five and sometimes thirty per cent. If he gets it at a reduction of twenty-five per cent, his land (supposing he purchases Crown lands) will only cost him 6s c'y per acre, which is 3d per acre *less* than the government price of land in the United States The reader should particularly notice this fact, as great stress is laid by writers on the United States, upon the *low price* at which land is to be bought of the government there, while the Crown lands in Canada are really to be bought at a less price, and there are about 2,300,000 acres in Upper Canada alone, already surveyed to be disposed of at this price, exclusive of the clergy reserves An agent appointed for the sale of these lands in each district, whose name will be found under the head of the district, and the quantity of land for sale in each township will be found under the head of the township.

For the guidance of emigrants, it may be as well to state the average value of land in each of the districts which they will be most likely to settle in—premising that these are the prices at which the land is to be purchased of private individuals, and that frequently a farm may be obtained at a considerably lower rate In the Victoria District land near the front may generally be purchased at from four to ten dollars per acre for wild land, and for cultivated farms (including buildings) from twenty to thirty-five dollars per acre, and in the back townships at from one to four dollars for wild land, and from eight to twenty for cultivated In the Newcastle District, in the first range of townships, wild land will be worth from five to ten dollars and cultivated from twenty to thirty; and in the back townships, from two to five dollars for wild land, and from twelve to twenty-five for cultivated—some few farms in the neighbourhood of Port Hope and Cobourg, may be valued as high as forty or fifty dollars In the Colborne District wild land in the neighbourhood of Peterborough will be worth from five to fifteen dollars, and cultivated from ten to thirty, according to situation and distance from the town, and wild land at a distance may be obtained at from one to three dollars In the townships of Whitby, Pickering, Scarborough, Markham, Whitchurch, York, Vaughan, the front of King, Toronto and Chinguacousy, cleared farms will range from twenty to fifty dollars per acre, according to situation, &c, and wild land at from ten to twelve—with the exception of the townships of York, Toronto and Scarborough, where the wild land is valuable for the wood, on account of their vicinity to the City of Toronto In the northern townships of the district wild land may be bought at from one to four dollars, and cleared at from ten to fifteen dollars, and the same prices will apply to the Simcoe District In the Gore District, with the exception of the north of the townships of Nassagweya and Esquesing, land will be generally rather high, wild land will range from six to fifteen dollars, and cleared farms from twenty-five to fifty dollars In the Wellington District cleared farms in the townships of Guelph, Waterloo and Puslinch, will be worth from fifteen to forty dollars, and wild land from five to fifteen, and in the northern townships they will vary, according to their remoteness, from one to four dollars for wild, and from ten to twenty-five for cultivated. In the Niagara District wild land will vary from three to ten, and cultivated farms from ten to forty dollars per acre. In the Talbot District from two to six dollars for wild, and from eight to twenty-five for cleared land. In the Brock District, from four to eight dollars for wild land, and from twenty to fifty for cultivated. In the Huron District prices vary according to locality, with the exception of the two government townships (Ashfield and Wawanosh), where all the land (wild) is rated at 8s. currency. In the London District, in the neighbourhood of London, Delaware and Westminster, and along the road to Port Stanley, wild land will be worth from five to eight dollars, and cultivated from twenty to forty; in the more remote townships the price will be about half. Along the road from London to Chatham, and on the banks of the Thames, wild land may be purchased at from two to six dollars, and cleared farms at from ten to fifteen; and at one or two concessions back they are to be bought for half. In the back townships between the Thames and Lake Erie, and also in those on Bear Creek, land of fine quality may be purchased at from one to three dollars per acre. On the River St. Clair there is but little wild land, at least, close to the river, and that is worth ten dollars per acre, the wood being in demand for the steamboats. In the townships of Plympton and Warwick, wild land of the best quality is to be bought at from two to three dollars per acre.

By *cleared farms* is generally understood those which have from seventy to eighty acres cleared out of a hundred, and it is for such farms that these prices are calculated; and of course the price will always vary according to the quantity of land cleared and under cultivation and the value of the buildings. At the same time it must be borne in mind, that in every district there may be some farms in particular situations that would be held considerably higher.

All emigrants in want of information or employment on their arrival at Kingston, are directed to apply at the office of Mr. A. B. Hawke, chief emigrant agent for Canada West. The government agents whose names are hereunto annexed will also direct emigrants in want of work to places where they may find it; as well as furnish information as to the routes, distances, and rates of conveyance to those parts of the province to which settlers may be desirous of proceeding.

Emigrant Agents.—G R. Burke, Bytown; W. J. McKay, Cobourg and Port Hope; E. McElderry, Toronto; J. H. Palmer, Hamilton; A. B. Hawke, junior, Port Stanley.

All indigent emigrants requiring medical assistance may obtain it gratis, on application to Dr. E. V. Cortlandt, Bytown; Dr. T. W. Robison, Kingston; General Hospital, Toronto; or Dr. W. G. Dickinson, Hamilton.

In order to guard against all misapprehension as to the assistance which the emigrant agents are authorised to grant, emigrants are distinctly informed, that the claims of the destitute who land in Canada during the current season only will be admitted, and that no able-bodied person, unless burthened with a helpless family, will be entitled to assistance in any form.

The following is a statement of the number of emigrants who arrived at Quebec, from the year 1840 to 1845, both inclusive:—

Places of Departure.	1840.	1841.	1842.	1843.	1844.	1845.
England and Wales	4567	5970	12191	6499	6380	Proportions fm the different parts of the kingdom not yet ascertain'd
Ireland	16291	18317	25532	9728	9528	
Scotland	1144	3559	6095	5006	5720	
New Brunswick, Nova Scotia, and Ports on St. Lawrence	232	240	556	494	582	
Continental Ports	...	...	...	...	...	
	22234	28086	44374	21727	22210	26280

POST OFFICE LIST.

LIST OF POST OFFICES IN CANADA WEST.

Name of Office.	Name of Town, Village or Township.	District.	Name of Postmaster.	Toronto.	Kingston.	London.	Cobourg.	Chatham.	Goderich.	Barrie.
Adolphustown	Adolphustown, t'p.	P. Edward.	S. Griffiths	173	32	311	67	342	328	233
Adjala	Adjala, t'p.	Simcoe	James Hart	54	222	169	130	235	198	39
Albion	Albion t'p.	Home	S. B. Sterne	53	230	145	125	216	208	56
Aldborough	Aldborough, t'p.	London	E. M'Kinlay	184	361	47	256	113	162	244
Alexandria	Lochiel, t'p.	Eastern	R. Chisholm	323	146	451	251	490	476	383
Ameliasburgh	Ameliasburgh, t'p.	P. Edward.	T. McMahon	115	76	248	38	314	306	170
Amherstburg	Amherstburg, t	Western	James Kevill	269	442	138	328	70	197	323
Amiens	Caradoc, t'p.	London	Jas. McKirdy	158	334	20	230	76	78	237
Ancaster	Ancaster, v.	Gore	James Chep.	55	232	83	127	136	106	115
Arnprior	Bathurst, t'p.	Bathurst	Isaac Gregory	367	154	401	251	467	460	430
Asphodel	Asphodel, t'p.	Colborne	Thos. Walker.	119	114	257	47	323	316	179
Aylmer	Malahide, t'p.	London	P. Hodgkinson	137	150	30	209	91	89	292
Ayr	Ayr, v.	Gore	Jas. Jackson	36	258	120	153	186	94	141
Amherst Island	Amherst Island, t'p.	Midland	Unknown	166	11	166	92	232	319	234
Ballinafad		Wellington.	T. C. Stephens	42	218	138	113	204	197	101
Berlin	Berlin, v.	Do.	Geo. Davidson	82	259	114	151	180	94	139
Barrie	Barrie, t.	Simcoe	John McWatt.	60	237	208	132	274	274	...
Bath	Bath, v.	Midland	W. J. Mackay.	159	18	297	87	363	314	219
Bayham	Bayham, t'p.	London	Joseph Bowes.	129	306	37	201	103	143	187
Beachville	Beachville, v.	Brock	W. Merigold.	102	294	36	189	101	122	177
Beamsville	Beamsville, v.	Niagara	J. B. Osborne.	71	248	113	143	176	130	131
Beaverton	Thorah, t'p.	Home	James Ellice	73	210	170	105	274	228	133
Belleville	Belleville, t.	Victoria	— Menzies	118	59	256	46	319	273	178
Beverly	Eastard, t'p.	Johnstown.	P. Schofield	259	82	397	87	460	414	329
Bloomfield	Hallowell, t'p.	P. Edward.	J. Thirkell	122	44	323	59	334	277	192

LIST OF POST OFFICES IN CANADA WEST.

DISTANCES IN MILES FROM

Name of Office.	Name of Town, Village or Township.	District.	Name of Postmaster.	Toronto.	Kingston.	London.	Cobourg.	Chatham.	Goderich.	Barrie.
Bond Head	Bond Head, v.	Simcoe	J. F. Robinson	42	210	181	100	223	186	27
Bradford	Bradford, v.	Do.	John Peacock	37	214	185	109	238	192	23
Bruntford	Brantford, t.	Gore	W. Richardson	73	250	65	145	131	124	133
Brighton	Brighton, v.	Newcastle	Jos. Lockwood	98	79	181	26	276	163	158
Brockville	Brockville, t.	Johnstown	Henry Jones	233	56	371	169	434	388	293
Brock	Brock, t'p.	Home	Thos. Hill	59	207	198	94	208	224	220
Brougham	Pickering, t'p.	Do.	N. Howell	29	162	176	59	226	184	89
Burford	Burford, t'p.	Brock	W. Whitehead	83	260	55	153	121	134	143
Burritt's Rapids		Johnstown	S. Burritt	113	136	446	187	512	413	339
Bytown	Bytown, t.	Dalhousie	G. W. Baker	328	142	466	256	532	483	388
Caledon	Caledon, t'p.	Home	Geo. Bell	58	225	141	121	207	168	126
Caledonia	Caledonia, t'p.	Ottawa	W. Parker	341	164	497	269	563	556	419
Camden East	Camden East, t'p.	Midland	S. Clarke	157	32	343	137	409	402	217
Canboro'	Canboro', t'p.	Niagara	Wm. Fitch	83	260	125	123	191	142	143
Carleton Place	Carleton Place, v.	Bathurst	R. Bell	299	122	434	227	500	454	359
Castleford	Horton, t'p.	Do.	Thos. O'Neil	376	166	428	224	494	531	436
Cavan	Cavan, t'p.	Newcastle	J. Knowlson	88	133	226	30	292	243	148
Chinguacousy	Chinguacousy, t'p	Home	P. Howland	34	211	126	106	192	153	90
Chippewa	Chippewa, v.	Niagara	J. Hepburn	110	287	160	182	226	166	170
Churchville	Churchville, v.	Home	D. Perry	25	202	135	102	201	166	85
Clarke		Newcastle	John Beavis	54	123	192	17	258	209	122
Clearville	Oxford, t'p.	Western	D. Gesner	189	366	52	261	31	167	249
Cobourg	Cobourg, t.	Newcastle	Thos. Scott	72	103	210		276	227	132
Colborne	Colborne, v.	Do.	J. A. Keeler	88	89	226	16	292	243	148
Colchester	Colchester, t'p.	Western	G. Buchanan	259	436	132	381	80	227	132
Coldwater	Coldwater, v.	Simcoe	Edmund Moon	99	276	247	171	313	254	39
Consecon	Hillier, t'p.	P. Edward	Robert Beggar	107	59	245	35	311	262	367

Cooksville	Cooksville, v.	Home	F. B. Morley	16	191	124	81	190	140	74
Cornwall	Cornwall, town	Eastern	G. C. Wood	294	117	432	222	498	449	354
Credit	Springfield, v.	Home	J. Magrath	19	193	110	90	176	137	78
Crowland	Crowland, t'p	Niagara	W. Vanalstein.	99	272	139	169	205	156	157
Darlington	Bowmanville, v.	Newcastle	R. Fairbairn	43	134	181	29	247	198	103
Dawn Mills	Dawn, t'p	Western	W. Taylor	197	374	69	289	15	139	277
Delaware	Delaware, v.	London	John Drake	149	326	12	221	54	72	209
Demorestville	Demorestville, v.	Pr. Edward	T. Demorest	137	49	328	70	394	292	197
Dereham	Dereham, t'p	Brock	B. VanNorman	109	295	22	183	88	132	342
Dickenson'sLand'g	Osnabruck, t'p	Eastern	W. Colquhoun.	282	105	420	210	486	437	342
Drummondville	Stamford, t'p	Niagara	S. Falconbridge	107	287	150	179	216	163	167
Dundas	Dundas, v	Gore	B. Ewart	52	229	94	124	160	103	112
Dunnville	Dunnville, v.	Niagara	A. S. St. John	90	297	118	192	184	275	180
East Oxford	East Oxford, t'p.	Brock	Alex. Daly	93	270	45	165	111	124	133
Edwardsburg	Edwardsburg, t'p.	Johnstown	W. S. Akin	254	77	392	182	458	408	314
Ekfrid	Ekfrid, t'p	London	Jas. McIntyre.	103	340	26	235	38	131	228
Eldon	Eldon, t'p	Colborne	A. Campbell	87	189	181	88	247	240	145
Elora	Elora, v.	Wellington	James Ross	82	289	143	173	209	114	161
Embro	Zorra, t'p	Brock	D. Matheson	124	301	37	182	103	145	184
Emily	Emily, t'p	Colborne	J. L. Hughes	103	163	254	58	320	241	176
Eramosa	Eramosa, t'p	Wellington	Geo. Forster	61	271	136	166	202	107	154
Ericus	Raleigh, t'p	Western	J. W. Little	214	391	77	286	14	282	274
Erin	Erin, t'p	Western	W. Cornock	47	224	144	119	210	159	104
Errol	Plympton, t'p	Western	Thos. Laing	196	372	58	267	71	118	255
Esquesing	Esquesing, t'p	Gore	J. Lynd	33	210	130	105	196	145	93
Etobicoke	Etobicoke, t'p	Home	W. Gamble	9	186	131	81	197	146	69
Farmersville	Yonge, t'p	Johnstown	W. Landon	249	72	387	175	453	404	309
Fenelon Falls	Fenelon, t'p	Colborne	James Wallis	109	198	289	93	355	264	211
Fergus	Wellington	J. McQueen		102	279	144	174	210	115	162
Finch	Finch, t'p	Eastern	A. Cochburry	302	125	440	230	506	457	362
Fitzroy Harbour	Fitzroy Harbour, v.	Bathurst	G. Learmouth	358	145	410	242	476	513	389
Flos	Flos, t'p	Simcoe	John Craig	78	255	226	150	294	233	18
Fort Erie	Bertie, t'p	Niagara	James Kerby	126	303	108	192	174	182	186
Frankford	Sidney, t'p	Victoria	W. Bowen	116	81	254	44	320	271	184

LIST OF POST OFFICES IN CANADA WEST.

DISTANCES IN MILES FROM

Name of Office.	Name of Town, Village or Township.	District.	Name of Postmaster.	Toronto.	Kingston.	London.	Cobourg.	Chatham.	Goderich.	Barrie.
Franktown	Beckwith, t'p.	Bathurst	E. McEwen	290	104	428	218	494	445	350
Fredericksburg	Fredericksburg, t'p.	Midland	W. A. Anderson	168	27	306	82	372	323	228
Galt	Galt, v.	Gore	A. Shade	71	248	75	143	131	84	131
Gananoqui	Gananoqui, v.	Johnstown	L. McDonald	207	24	332	129	398	356	261
Georgina	Georgina, t'p.	Home	J. O. Bouchier	53	230	150	125	216	208	58
Goderich	Goderich, town	Huron	Thos. Kydd	155	332	59	227	125		205
Gosfield	Gosfield, t'p.	Western	J. Strong	246	423	109	318	48	175	319
Grimsby	Grimsby, v.	Niagara	F. Nelles	65	242	107	139	174	190	125
Guelph	Guelph, town	Wellington	R. Corbett	87	264	129	159	195	100	147
Haldimand	Grafton, v.	Newcastle	John Taylor	81	96	219	8	285	236	141
Hamilton	Hamilton, town	Gore	E. Ritchie	48	225	90	120	156	107	108
Hawkesbury	Hawkesbury, t'p.	Ottawa	C. Hersey	344	167	482	227	548	499	404
Hillier	Hillier, t'p.	Pr. Edward	P. Flagler	111	55	334	44	400	266	171
Holland Landing	Holland Landing, v.	Home	W. J. Sloane	36	209	180	104	233	187	28
Howard	Howard, t'p.	Western	D. Warner	197	374	60	269	126	175	257
Humber	York, t'p.	Home	R. Bowman	7	193	122	88	188	139	76
Huntley	Huntley, t'p.	Dalhousie	John Graham	321	144	459	249	525	446	381
Hornby	Hornby, v.	Home	W. McKindsay	30	297	127	101	193	144	89
Houghton	Houghton, v.	Talbot	B. M. Brown	127	304	72	198	138	185	140
Indiana	Indiana, v.	Niagara	R. Brown	71	272	137	144	203	154	155
Innisfil	Innisfil, t'p.	Simcoe	B. Ross	50	228	167	118	233	224	9
Jordan	Jordan, v.	Niagara	W. Bradt	91	268	120	162	186	123	150
Katesville	Adelaide, t'p.	London	R. Brown	164	341	27	237	67	132	224
Kemptville	Oxford, t'p.	Johnstown	W. H. Bottum	269	92	436	197	502	423	329
Keswick	N. Gwillimbury, t'p.	Home	S. Goode	47	224	195	119	261	202	43
Kilmarnock	Montague, t'p.	Johnstown	J. Maitland	302	99	440	230	506	457	362
King	King, t'p.	Home	D. McCallum	29	230	190	104	256	208	48

Kingston	Kingston, t.	Midland	Robt. Deacon	177		315	105	381	532	237
Kitley	Kitley, t'p	Johnstown	W Chamberlain	253	76	395	181	461	408	313
Lanark	Lanark, t'p	Bathurst	John Hall	288	111	426	216	492	443	348
Lancaster	Lancaster, t'p	Eastern	R. McDonald	310	133	448	238	514	466	370
Lloydtown	Lloydtown, v.	Home	A. Eastwood	43	220	180	115	246	198	46
Lochiel	Lochiel, t'p	Eastern	D. McLeod	330	153	468	272	534	607	390
London	London, t.	London	G. J. Goodhue	138	315		210	66	59	198
L'Orignal	L'Orignal, v.	Ottawa	T. H. Johnson	350	173	488	278	554	699	410
Loughboro'	Loughboro', t'p	Midland	H. Madden	192	16	331	120	397	348	253
Louisville	Louisville, v.	Western	Jno. Crow	191	354	60	263	6	119	245
McGillivray	McGillivray, t'p	Huron	J. Moody	158	335	20	230	86	40	218
McKillop	McKillop, t'p	Do.	A. Meyer	133	310	80	200	146	26	189
McNab	McNab, t'p	Bathurst	Jas. Morris	353	176	438	234	504	541	408
Madoc	Madoc, t'p	Victoria	D. McKenzie	160	77	298	64	354	292	220
Maitland	Maitland, v.	Johnstown	W. Garvey	238	61	390	166	456	392	312
Mara	Mara, t'p	Home	M. McDonagh	66	218	178	113	244	220	31
March	March, t'p	Dalhousie	Thos. Read	340	163	478	266	544	495	400
Markham	Markham, t'p	Home	A. Barker	22	199	160	94	226	177	58
Mariposa	Mariposa, t'p	Colborne	Jacob Ham	79	187	278	84	344	278	200
Marmora	Marmora, t'p	Victoria	J. Fidler	148	89	286	76	352	280	208
Marshville	Wainfleet, t'p	Niagara	E. Lee	116	282	158	188	224	173	195
Martintown	Martintown, v.	Eastern	A. McMartin	307	130	445	235	511	630	367
Matilda	Matilda, t'p	Do.	G. Brouse	260	83	398	188	464	415	320
Merrickville	Merrickville, v.	Johnstown	E H Whitmarsh	282	105	446	236	512	440	368
Mersea	Mersea, t'p	Western	F. A. Ambridge	207	414	98	309	32	367	297
Middleton	Middleton, t'p	Talbot	N. Eagles	110	287	60	182	126	169	170
Milford	Marysburgh, t'p	Pr. Edward	W. Y. Church	135	47	326	72	392	290	195
Milton	Trafalgar, t'p	Gore	Jas. Gordon	32	221	118	116	184	135	104
Mill Creek	Ernestown, t'p	Midland	P. S. Timerman	165	12	327	93	393	344	249
Mohawk	Brantford, t'p	Gore	A. Cook	78	253	70	159	136	129	138
Mono Mills	Mono, t'p	Simcoe	A. Lewis	60	239	154	134	220	177	122
Moira	Do.	Victoria	W. Mullett	135	76	283	63	349	286	195
Moore	Moore, t'p	Western	Jas. Baby	237	414	82	289	47	130	279
Mosa	Mosa, t'p	London	Unknown	173	350	36	245	28	228	233

LIST OF POST OFFICES IN CANADA WEST.

DISTANCES IN MILES FROM

Name of Office.	Name of Town, Village or Township.	District	Name of Postmaster.	Toronto.	Kingston.	London.	Cobourg.	Chatham.	Goderich.	Barrie.
Moulinette	Cornwall, t'p	Eastern	T. McCosh	287	110	439	215	505	442	347
Mulmur	Mulmur, t'p	Simcoe	John Little	69	264	154	161	220	183	49
Murray	Murray, t'p	Newcastle	Chas. Biggar	101	65	239	99	305	256	161
Nanticoke	Walpole, t'p	Niagara	John S. Gray	114	288	87	169	153	252	157
Napanee	Napanee, v	Midland	A. McPherson	147	30	285	75	351	302	207
Nassagiweya	Nassagiweya, t'p	Gore	A. Campbell	70	247	142	127	208	133	115
Nelson	Nelson, t'p	Do.	T. Cooper	32	209	106	104	172	123	92
Newboro'	North Crosby, t'p	Johnstown	B. Tett	274	97	412	198	478	429	344
Newmarket	Newmarket, v	Home	W. Roe	30	207	168	102	234	185	33
Niagara	Niagara, t	Niagara	A. Davidson	93	270	135	165	201	152	173
North Augusta	Augusta, t'p	Johnstown	S. J. Bellamy	249	72	401	177	467	404	317
North Port	Sophiasburgh, t'p	Pr. Edward	S. Solmes	142	54	333	75	399	297	202
Norval	Esquesing, t'p	Gore	W. Clay	37	214	134	109	200	149	97
Norwich	Norwich, t'p	Brock	Thos. Wallace	95	272	58	167	124	127	163
Nottawasaga	Nottawasaga, t'p	Simcoe	A. Campbell	94	272	215	127	281	228	30
Normandale	Charlotteville, t'p	Talbot	Jno. Tolmie	108	284	91	179	157	166	167
Oakland	Oakland, t'p	Brock	Jno. Joyne	83	258	75	155	141	134	159
Orillia	Orillia, v	Simcoe	G. Alley	85	262	233	157	299	240	25
Oakville	Oakville, v	Gore	R. K. Chisholm	26	203	124	98	190	141	86
Oro	Oro, t'p	Simcoe	E. Ryall	72	249	220	144	286	297	12
Osgoode	Osgoode, t'p	Ottawa	D. Cameron	303	163	491	281	556	458	413
Osnabruck	Osnabruck, t'p	Eastern	J. Bockus	281	104	419	209	485	436	341
Otonabee	Otonabee, t'p	Colborne	Thos. Carr	110	123	228	18	294	248	150
Otterville	Norwich, t'p	Brock	J. H. Cornell	101	278	53	173	119	133	161
Oxford	Oxford, t'p	Do.	Jas. Ingersoll	110	287	28	182	94	88	170
Oshawa	Oshawa, v	Home	Edw. Skae	35	142	173	37	239	190	95
Pakenham	Pakenham, v	Bathurst	A. Dickson	310	133	472	247	538	474	379

Palermo	Palermo, v.	Gore	A. S. Newbury	27	204	111	99	177	128	99
Paris	Paris, v.	Do.	G. Macartney	79	256	59	161	125	92	139
Pelham	Pelham, t'p	Niagara	J. S. Price	100	272	153	170	219	225	155
Penetanguishine	Penetanguishine, v.	Simcoe	J. M. Hamilton	105	282	230	177	264	260	45
Percy	Percy, t'p	Newcastle	A. Splatt	136	97	285	39	351	275	194
Perth	Perth, t.	Bathurst	F. Allen	275	98	413	203	479	430	335
Peterboro'	Peterboro', t.	Colborne	E. Sanford	101	148	230	37	296	256	161
Pickering	Duffin's Creek, v.	Home	F. Leys	22	155	169	54	235	177	82
Picton	Picton, t.	Pr. Edward	W. Rorke	127	39	318	64	300	282	187
Plantagenet	Plantagenet, t'p	Ottawa	P. McMartin	351	174	468	279	534	600	429
Point Abino	Bertie, t'p	Niagara	Jno. Haun	119	314	139	189	205	171	197
Port Burwell	Port Burwell, v.	London	J. P. Bellairs	137	314	45	209	111	105	197
Port Colborne	Port Colborne, v.	Niagara	Jas. Black	108	283	143	179	209	165	166
Port Dalhousie	Port Dalhousie, v.	Do.	N. Pauling	87	264	125	159	191	242	147
Port Dover	Port Dover, v.	Talbot	R. Jenkins	104	281	79	176	145	259	164
Port Hope	Port Hope, t.	Newcastle	D. Smart	65	112	216	7	282	220	125
Port Robinson	Port Robinson, v.	Niagara	D. McFarland	90	271	136	166	202	153	154
Port Sarnia	Port Sarnia, v.	Western	Geo. Durand	210	387	72	281	138	132	269
Port Stanley	Port Stanley, v.	London	J. Bostwick	157	334	26	235	92	85	217
Port Talbot	Dunwich, t'p	Do.	M. Burwell	165	342	27	287	90	86	225
Portland	Bastard, t'p	Johnstown	Unknown	269	92	386	99	452	415	337
Prescott	Prescott, t.	Do.	A. Jones	245	68	383	173	449	399	305
Preston	Preston, v.	Wellington	A. Ferrie	74	254	113	146	179	87	134
Princeton	Blenheim, t'p	Brock	W. Grinton	89	206	40	171	106	102	149
Petersburg		Wellington	Jno. Ernest	93	267	134	164	200	105	152
Port Credit	Port Credit, v.	Home	W. R. Raines	20	195	120	90	186	148	78
Port Rowan	Port Rowan, v.	Talbot	A. McClellan	129	293	65	217	131	175	197
Queenston	Queenston, v.	Niagara	Jno. Stayner	100	277	142	172	208	159	160
Rainham	Rainham, t'p	Talbot	C. Williams	99	277	128	200	194	285	190
Raleigh	Chatham, t.	Western	Jas. Read	173	378	66	273	......	125	261
Ramsay	Ramsay, t'p	Bathurst	J. Wylie	298	121	442	235	508	446	367
Rawdon	Rawdon, t'p	Victoria	E. Fidlar	133	74	271	65	337	288	201
Reach	Reach, t'p	Home	Jas. Leitch	48	173	185	58	251	203	103
Richmond	Richmond, v.	Bathurst	Geo. Lyon	307	130	445	235	511	460	367

LIST OF POST OFFICES IN CANADA WEST. DISTANCES IN MILES FROM

Name of Office.	Name of Town, Village or Township.	District.	Name of Postmaster.	Toronto.	Kingston.	London.	Cobourg.	Chatham.	Goderich.	Barrie.
Richmond Hill	Richmond Hill, v.	Home	J. Sinclair	16	208	155	89	221	172	43
Romney	Romney, t'p	Western	Thos. Renwick	228	405	91	300	157	358	288
River Trent	Trent, v.	Victoria	W. Robertson	206	71	244	34	310	161	274
St. Andrews	Cornwall, t'p	Eastern	D. McDonell	301	124	440	229	506	426	361
St. Catharine's	St. Catharine's, t.	Niagara	W. H. Merritt	82	259	124	154	190	141	142
St. George	Dumfries, t'p	Gore	G. Stanton	69	246	103	141	169	120	129
St. John's	Pelham, t'p	Niagara	Jno. Davis	92	269	150	164	216	222	152
St. Thomas	St. Thomas, t'p	London	E. Ermatinger	149	326	17	227	83	77	215
St. Vincent	St. Vincent, t'p	Simcoe	W. Stephenson	124	306	184	200	250	194	69
Sand Hill		Home	H. Yeoman	57	238	137	122	203	175	121
Sandwich	Sandwich, t.	Western	P. H. Morin	253	430	115	325	52	175	313
Scarboro'	Scarboro', t'p	Home	A. McLean	12	165	150	84	216	167	72
Seneca	Oneida, t'p	Niagara	J. Little	62	239	104	134	170	121	130
Seymour East	Seymour East, t'p	Newcastle	Jno. Rainie	155	83	280	62	346	279	231
Seymour West	Seymour West, t'p	Do.	H. Rowed	168	86	285	67	351	300	205
Shannonville	Shannonville, v.	Victoria	R. McMichael	127	50	265	58	331	282	187
Sharon	Sharon, v.	Home	J. Hogaboom	37	212	152	107	218	190	34
Sheffield	Beverley, t'p	Gore	W. Churchill	65	242	91	137	157	90	133
Simcoe	Simcoe, t.	Talbot	G. Campbell	97	247	69	169	135	156	157
Smith's Falls	Smith's Falls, v.	Bathurst	G. Mittleberger	273	92	411	201	477	428	333
Smithville	Smithville, t'p	Niagara	J. Forsyth	75	252	117	147	183	134	135
South Gower	South Gower, t'p	Johnstown	W. Bower	265	88	403	193	469	419	325
Sparta	Yarmouth, t'p	London	D. Wilson	165	337	38	238	104	88	204
Stanley's Mills	Toronto Gore, t'p	Home	R. Woodill	18	195	134	90	200	157	78
Stoney Creek	Stoney Creek, v.	Niagara	J. Williamson	55	232	97	127	163	114	115
Stouffville	Whitchurch, t'p	Home	Jno. Boyer	48	181	155	100	221	183	88
Stratford	Stratford, v.	Huron	J. C. W. Daly.	110	286	72	181	138	46	169

Streetsville	Streetsville, v.	Home	W. H. Paterson	20	197	130	92	196	161	80
Sunnidale	Sunnidale, t'p.	Simcoe	A. Gillespie	85	261	184	156	250	239	24
Tecumseth	Tecumseth, t'p.	Simcoe	D. Evans	50	227	187	100	253	192	33
Thamesville	Thamesville, v.	Western	N. Cornwall	185	365	47	257	113	243	277
Thornhill	Thornhill, v.	Home	W. Parsons	12	189	150	84	216	167	48
Thorold	Thorold, v.	Niagara	P. Keefer	86	263	128	158	194	145	146
Toronto city	Toronto city, t.	Do.	C. Berezy	..	177	138	72	204	155	60
Trafalgar	Trafalgar, t'p.	Home	A. Proudfoot	20	197	118	92	184	135	80
Tuckersmith	Tuckersmith, t'p.	Gore	R. Thwait	155	364	49	193	115	12	217
Tyrconnell	Danwich, t'p.	Huron	J. Patterson	173	350	35	245	111	101	233
Uxbridge	Uxbridge, t'p.	London	J. Boscom	44	222	200	99	266	199	235
Vankleek Hill	Vankleek Hill, v.	Home	N. Stewart	337	160	489	373	555	492	304
Vaughan	Vaughan, t'p.	Ottawa	G. Stegman	22	199	189	94	205	157	58
Vienna	Vienna, v.	Home	J. Saxon	134	311	42	212	108	102	200
Vittoria	Vittoria. v.	London	S. McCall	103	280	95	175	161	162	163
Wallaceburgh	Wallaceburgh, v.	Talbot	L. H. Johnson	215	393	88	311	154	158	286
Walpole	Walpole, t'p.	Western	W. Mudie	137	292	96	193	162	292	197
Walsingham	Walsingham, t'p.	Niagara	E. Dickenson	116	290	60	217	126	172	176
Waterford	Townsend, t'p.	Talbot	James Green	89	268	83	169	149	142	151
Warwick	Warwick, t'p.	Western	C. R. Nixon	182	358	44	253	110	104	241
Waterdown	Waterdown, t'p.	Gore	J. Barnard	67	244	97	127	193	114	115
Waterloo	Waterloo, t'p.	Wellington	D. Snyder	85	260	127	157	193	98	145
Welland Port		Niagara	L. Cavers	105	282	143	189	209	235	145
Wellington	Hallowell, t'p.	P. Edward	A. McFaul	122	50	239	50	305	246	201
Wellington Square	Wellington Square,v	Gore	H. Smith	38	215	112	110	178	129	98
West Flamboro'	West Flamboro',t'p.	Do.	W. Colclough	57	234	97	127	163	156	125
Westmeath	Westmeath, t'p.	Bathurst	C. Bellows	406	238	458	254	524	501	466
Westminster	Westminster, t'p.	London	C. Hall	145	320	6	217	60	65	205
Whitby	Whitby, t'p.	Home	A. McPherson	31	146	169	41	235	186	91
Williamsburg, E.	Williamsburg, t'p.	Eastern	M. Pillar	272	95	389	200	455	427	328
Do. N.	Do.	Do.	W. Bell	275	98	392	203	470	430	343
Do. W.	Do.	Do.	J. Holden	268	91	406	196	472	423	332
Williamstown	Charlottenburg, t'p.	Do.	D. McNichol	316	139	454	244	517	471	376
Wilmot	Wilmot, t'p.	Wellington	R. Hays	91	268	109	163	175	64	151

POST OFFICES IN CANADA WEST.

DISTANCES IN MILES FROM

Name of Office.	Name of Town, Village or Township.	District.	Name of Postmaster.	Toronto.	Kingston.	London.	Cobourg.	Chatham.	Goderich.	Barrie.
Wilton	Ernestown, t.p	Midland	S. Warren	150	23	337	82	403	314	263
Windsor	Windsor, v.	Western	T. Ritter	250	432	116	327	50	197	315
Woodstock	Woodstock, t.	Brock	H. C. Barwick.	113	290	32	185	98	91	173
Woolwich	Woolwich, t'p	Wellington.	D. Davidson	87	264	126	159	192	100	147
Weston	Weston, v	Home	Unknown	10	186	129	81	195	166	51
Williams	Williams, t'p	Huron	D. McIntosh	168	345	20	240	86	40	238
Warsaw	Dummer, t'p	Colborne	T. Clevate	114	161	252	56	269	260	174
Yonge	Yonge, t'p	Johnstown.	Robert Harvey	243	46	381	171	447	398	303
York	York, v.	Niagara	A. Scobie	67	244	109	139	175	154	127
York Mills	Milton, v.	Home	W. Hamilton	6	197	144	78	210	161	54
Zone Mills	Zone, t'p	Western	J. Van Allen	198	365	60	280	24	234	266

266

LISTS OF MAGISTRATES IN CANADA WEST.

These Lists comprise only the Magistrates who have actually qualified, and are capable of acting, with the exception of those for the Ottawa, Western, and Johnstown Districts—which include the whole number of names in the commission—the names of those magistrates who had actually qualified, not having been returned, up to a late date, to Montreal.

Magistrates who have qualified in the Bathurst District.

John G. Malloch..	Perth.	Jno. L. McDougall	Horton.
Alex. McMillan...	Do.	Alex. McDonell	MacNab.
Rod'k Matheson...	Do.	John Bell	Perth
Alex. Fraser	Do	Wm Wallace	Ramsay
Anthony Leslie	Do	John Doran	Perth
Henry Glass	Do	Thos McCaffray..	Drummond.
John Ferguson	Do.	W. G. Wylie	Ramsay.
Donald Fraser	Lanark	Patrick Campbell.	Bathurst.
Matthew Leach	Do	Henry Aith	Horton.
Geo. Tenant	Do	Wm. Allan	Drummond.
John Hall	Do	Geo. Kerr	Perth
John Smith	Do.	John Balderson	Drummond
James Wylie	Ramsay	Robert Davies	Beckwith
Joshua Adams	Bathurst.	Colin McLaren	Do.
W. P. Loucks	Elmsley.	Wm Houston	Ramsay
W. Brooke	Burgess	Wm Richards	Drummond.
James Shaw	Elmsley.	H Ayton	Do
Wm. Simpson	Do.	Wm Halfpenny	Lanark.
John Haggart	Perth	Jno Robertson	Darling
James Rosamond..	Beckwith.	Wm Rae	Ramsay.
Peter Macgregor..	Do	John Canboy	Beckwith
Robert Bell	Carleton Place		

Magistrates who have qualified in the Brock District.

J Vining	Nissouri.	G W Whitehead.	Burford
John Scatchard	Do.	R. Rounds	Do
Philip Graham	East Oxford.	L Daniels	Do
John Hatch	Do.	James Oswald	Do
Arch Burtch	Do	John Moore	Do
C. Martin	West Oxford.	L Butler	Blandford
E Harris	Do	R R Hunter	Do
John G Vansittart	Do	John Arnold	Do
E Deedes	Do	J Bodwell, Jun	Dereham
P. Carroll	Do	B Van Norman	Do
F. D Fauquiere	East Zorra	John Eddy	Oakland
R Riddell	Do	M Johnston	Blenheim.
John Harrington.	Do.	N Pickle	Do
J D Dent	West Zorra.	J Jackson	Do
W. Gordon	Do	J Woodrow	Norwich
John Carroll	Do	J. G. Losee	Do.

Magistrates who have qualified in the Colborne District.

Jos. L. Hughes	Emily.	Chas Rubidge	Peterboro'.
William Dixon	Smith.	Richard Birdsall.	Asphodel.
Wm Best	Emily.	Francis Connin	Otonabee
John Gilchrist	Otonabee.	Hon T A Stewart	Douro
Samuel Davidson	Mariposa.	Thomas Need	Verulam.
Patrick Sullivan	Ennismore	Andrew S. Fraser	Peterboro'.
James Foley	Asphodel.	Thomas Choat	Dummer.
Stephen Nicholls	Smith.	James Wallis	Peterboro'.
Alex Campbell	Eldon	Adam Stark	Otonabee.
John Langton	Fenelon	Robert P. Madge	Do
Robt. Denistown	Do		

Magistrates who have qualified in the Dalhousie District.

W. Thompson	Nepean.	Stephen Collins	Nepean.
John Richey	Fitzroy	Arch McDonell	Osgoode.
W. Campbell	Marlborough	G Lyon	Richmond.
John McNab	Osgoode.	W H Thompson	Bytown.
W B Bradley	Huntley.	John Buckham	Torbolton.
W Stewart	Bytown	Daniel O Connor	Bytown.
Ed M Barrie	Smith's Falls.	John Chitty	Bytown.
Alex McDonell	Osgoode	Donald McArthur	Bytown.
Daniel Burrit	Marlborough	Simon Fraser	Bytown.
James Stevenson	Bytown.	Robert Sherriff	Fitzroy.
Henry Harmer	Osgoode	Fred Bearman	Nepean.
G. W. Baker	Nepean.	John McNaughton	Bytown.
Hamnet Pinhey	March	John Eastman	Marlborough.
David McLaren	Torbolton.	W B Bradley, jun.	Huntley.
John B. Lewis	Richmond.		

Magistrates who have qualified in the Eastern District.

George S Jarvis	Cornwall, town	William Mattice	Cornwall, town.
Phil Vankoughnet	Do	Martin Carman	Williamsburgh.
John McGillivray	Charlottenburgh	Hugh McCargar	Mountain
John Chrysler	Finch	Jacob Brouse	Matilda.
Duncan McDonell	Charlottenburgh	George Markley	Williamsburgh.
Guy C Wood	Cornwall, town	Isaac Keeler	Matilda.
A Blackwood	Do township	Robert K Bullock	Osnabruck
Hugh McGillis	Charlottenburgh	D E McIntyre	Charlottenburgh.
Peter Shaver	Matilda	John McRae	Do
John McDonald	Cornwall, township	D A McDonald	Lochiel.
John McLennan	Lancaster	Alexander Fraser	Do
John Cameron	Charlottenburgh	Alexander M Lean	Cornwall, town
John Archibald	Osnabruck	Adam Cockburn	Finch
D. E. McDonell	Cornwall, township	Isaac N Rose	Williamsburgh.
William Clevi	Do town	Charles J Fox	Winchester.
John McBean	Lancaster.	George Laing	Do.
Donald Cattanach	Kenyon.	B G French	Cornwall, township.
Alexander McNab	Lochiel	Hon Alex. Fraser	Legislative Council.
Angus Cattanach	Lancaster		

Magistrates who have qualified in the Gore District.

Alex. Roxburgh	Hamilton.	John Aikman	Ancaster.
Arthur Bowen	Do.	W. McKay	Nelson.
H. T. Harwood	Trafalgar.	N. Bell	Do
D. K. Servos	Barton	J W Williams	Oakville
Alfred Digby	Brantford.	Thos Hummill	Ancaster.
John Williamson	Saltfleet.	P. Cooley	Do
James Racey	Brantford	John A Wilkes	Brantford.
John Secord	Barton	James Winniett	Do
W B Proctor	Do	P Kenney	Trafalgar.
John Willson	Saltfleet	E C Griffin	Flamboro' East.
Hugh Creen	Esquesing	George Chalmers	Trafalgar
James B Ewart	Dundas	Thomas Racey	Dundas
Andrew T Kirby	Flamboro' West.	Alex Robertson	Esquesing
Hiram Smith	Wellington Square.	Robert Heslop	Ancaster.
Elisha Ringham	Glandford	James Cleaver	Nelson
Wm Gourlay	Saltfleet.	Geo Hogaboom	Ancaster.
Thomas Fyfe	Esquesing.	C C. Ferrie	Hamilton
Alex. Proudfoot	Trafalgar.	W Bowman	Dundas
Hugh Willson	Saltfleet	John Winer	Hamilton
George Stanton	St. George.	John Young	Do
Andrew Steven	Hamilton	Archibald Kerr	Do.
Henry Morgan	Binbrook.	David Buchan	Paris
Ed. Thomas	Nelson.	Edward Jackson	Hamilton
Alex McCann	Nassagaweya.	John White	Trafalgar
John Smith	Paris	C Hopkins	Nelson
Robert Holt	Dundas	G Hopkins	Flamboro' East.
John T. Howell	Trafalgar.	Samuel Bowman	Trafalgar
D R Springer	Nelson	James Applebee	Do
Charles Sovereign	Trafalgar	Edward Evans	Flamboro' East
William Walker	Brantford	P D Hart	Brantford
Joseph Spencer	Dundas	Wm Macklem	Barton
John Paterson	Do	J C Wyld	Do.
J S Wetenhall	Binbrook	H Smith	Do
A K Smith	Do	A Shade	Galt.
A Cook	Brantford.	W. Barber	Esquesing
Samuel Mills	Hamilton.	B McKay	Do
Ebenezer Stinson	Do	H Capron	Paris
Samuel Clarke	Trafalgar	P. Spaun	Barton
G H Armstrong	Hamilton	John Buck	Trafalgar
Nathan Gage	Brantford	George Brown	Milton
John W Hunter	Do	P. Fisher	Nelson
L Willson	Trafalgar	Edmund Richie	Hamilton
W B Vanevery	Barton	H Biggar	Brantford
Charles Kennedy	Esquesing	J P. Gage	Wellington Square
Henry Moyle	Brantford,	D McNab	Hamilton
Elijah Secord	Barton	A Elliott	Galt
Alex Buchanan	Brantford	George Chalmers	Trafalgar.
John Wetenhall	Nelson	William Craigie	Hamilton

Magistrates who have qualified in the Home District.

Wm Allison	Markham	S Holden	Markham	
John Button	Do	C J Baldwin	Toronto Gore	
C Chauncey	Do	Alex. Burnside	Do	City.
Robert Campbell	Do	Charles Berczy	Do.	
R C Gapper	Do	Thos Bell	Do.	

W. A. Baldwin	Toronto City.	P. Whitney	Whitby.
Daniel Brooke	Do.	W. Corley	St. Vincent.
James Beaty	Do.	T P. Cooper	Do
R E Burns	Do.	Thomas Fisher	Etobicoke.
J. G. Chewitt	Do	W Gamble	Do
G T. Dennison	Do.	John Grubb	Do.
John Doel	Do	P Shaver	Do.
P. Freeland	Do	J. Graham	East Gwillimbury.
J G. Howard	Do	S. Harrold	Do
Thos Hellıwell	Do.	J Æ. Irving	Do.
S G Lynn	Do	W Reid	Do.
J Lesslie	Do	A Huid	Reach.
George Monro	Do	W. Johnson	Georgina.
James Nation	Do.	Robert Johnston	Do.
M. J. O'Beirne	Do.	Thos. Mossington	Do.
W. L Perrin	Do.	M. McDonagh	Thorah.
T J Preston	Do.	A. McMillan	NorthGwillimbury.
J Radenhurst	Do.	John Prosser	Do.
Thos. G Ridout	Do	A Smalley	Do.
Geo. P. Ridout	Do.	James Monkman	Albion.
Robert S. Jameson	Do	S. B Steine	Do.
John Eastwood	Do.	James Patterson	Streetsville.
J Rogers	Do.	John Sanderson	Do.
L O'Brien	Do.	S. E Phillips	King.
H. Scobie	Do	N Pearson	Do.
J M Strange	Do	H Stewart	Do
W Wakefield	Do.	J Cook	Toronto township.
Geo Bell	Caledon.	J Gardiner	Do.
Wm. Clark	Do	John Hawkins	Do
D McQuarrie	Do.	B Monger	Do.
J. Brett	Mono Mills.	W. B Reeve	Do
John Boyer	Whitchurch.	A Silverthorn	Do.
John Bogart	Do	W Thomson	Do.
M P. Empey	Do.	J. W Taylor	Port Credit
James Gamble	Do.	E W. Thomson	Toronto township.
John Maclem	Do	J. Cummer	York.
E. Birrell	Pickering.	W Campbell	Do
A Campbell	Do	James Davis	Do
Wm. Dunbar	Do.	J Dennis	Do.
L Mackey	Do	F. Jackes	Do.
F Campbell	Chinguacousy	P. Lawrence	Do.
John Lynch	Do	John S Macaulay	Do
W. Crewe	Cooksville.	W C. Rotchford	Do.
W. Clarke	Scarboro'.	Charles Thompson	Do
W. Davinish	Do	John Willson	Do
P Secor	Do	W. Bagshaw	Brock.
John Thom	Do	M Cowan	Do.
John Campbell	Whitby.	James Rickey	Do.
James Dryden	Do.	John Truax	Do
W. Dow, Jun	Do.	F. Boyd	Vaughan.
John Farquharson	Do	R. Burr	Do.
A Farewell	Do.	John W Gamble	Do.
A Mason	Do.	W R Graham	Do.
W. F. Moore	Do.	H McQuarrie	Do.
Edward Skae	Do	D McDougall	Do.
Robert Spears	Do.	A McKechnie	Do.
J T. Somerville	Do	A Thorne	Do.
J. B Warren	Do.	A Bagshaw	Uxbridge.

Magistrates who have qualified in the Huron District.

Arthur Acland	Goderich, town.	William Chalk	Tuckersmith.
William Dunlop	Colborne.	Arch. Dickson	McKillop.
W. B Rich	Goderich, town	James Murray	Hay.
John Bignall	Goderich, township	E T Ledyard	Tuckersmith.
H Ransford	Do	W H DeLa Hooke	Stanley.
J. C. W. Daly	Stratford	George Brown	Goderich, towns'p.
T M Jones	Goderich, town.	Charles Widder	Goderich, town.
James McArthur	Williams.		

Magistrates in the Johnstown District.

George Malloch	Brockville.	Dr. T. Gainfort	Prescott.
Alex. McMillan	Johnstown.	Samuel Crane	Do
W. H. Bottom	Oxford.	Matthew Howard	Elizabethtown.
Truman Hurd	Do.	Palmer Lee	Yonge.
Philip Dulmage	Augusta.	John Crow	Edwardsburg
John Weatherhead	Brockville.	John Booth	Yonge.
Archibald McLean	Yonge.	Thomas Purvis	Do
Dunham Jones	Augusta.	Peter McSweeny	South Gower.
William Brown	Wolford.	James Brooker	Yonge.
James Morris	Elizabethtown	George Dougherty	Oxford
Basil R Church	Wolford	William Gailey	Maitland.
James Mellmoyle	Edwardsburg.	W. Chamberlain	Kitley.
Peter Schofield	Bastard.	Richard Holmes	Do
John Leggatt	North Crosby	Peter Adams	Edwardsburg.
Robert Powell	Elizabethtown.	John Brennan	Kitley.
William Freeland	Augusta.	Samuel J. Bellamy	Augusta.
Paul Glassford	Elizabethtown.	William Simpson	Elmsley South.
John L Reade	Wolford	Walter McCrae	Wolford
H. D Jessup	Augusta	William Riddell	Elmsley South.
Henry Bradfield	Elizabethtown.	S. H Merrick	Wolford
James L Scofield	Brockville.	William Green	Lansdowne or Y.
Nicholas Horton	Elizabethtown	Jesse Delong	South Crosby
Thos Sheffield, jr	Crosby.	Robert Romanes	Elmsley South.
John Kilburn	Do or Wolford	W W Howard	Lansdowne.
James Shaw	South Crosby.	James McDonell	Bastard
Richard Johnston	Lansdowne.	Arthur Fox	Yonge.
Joseph Goff	Elizabethtown	John Ketchum	Elizabethtown.
Nicholas Brisee	Bastard	Elisha Landon	Elmsley.
Alexander McCrie	Wolford	John Holden	Prescott
Milo McCargar	South Gower.	Joseph Adams	South Gower
Samuel Reynolds	Brockville	John S Archbold	Do.
Ephraim Dunham	Do	George W. Arnold	Brockville
Philemon Pennock	Augusta.	H. W Blanchard	Elizabethtown
Thomas McCargar	Oxford	Richard Bolton	Wolford
John Bleakley	Bastard	Henry Bolton	Edwardsburg.
Benjamin Tett	Crosby.	William Briant	Wolford.
W S McDonald	Gananoque	Adminden Burritt	Augusta.
Ephraim Webster	Do	Edmund Burritt	Wolford.
James Sabine	Elizabethtown.	William Campbell	Oxford.
John McLean	Do.	Andrew Carson	Do
William Buell	Brockville	Duncan Clarke	Edwardsburg
John G Booth	Elizabethtown	Roswell Cook	Do
Joshua Bates	Yonge.	Elisha Coller	Wolford
Joseph Wiltse	Do.	John Craig	Oxford.
Aaron Merrick	Wolford.	Peter Davis	Elizabethtown.

William Earl	Lansdowne.	J L. McDonald	Gananoque.
Samuel S Easton	Wolford.	Thomas Newson	Beverley.
James Edgar	Kitley.	Richard Osborne	Yonge
Henry Farre	Elizabethtown.	Peter O'Brien	Augusta.
Robert Ferguson	Kitley	John Patton	Do
John Forrester	Edwardsburg.	William Parkins	Brockville.
John S French	Oxford	J. W. Parmenter	Gananoque.
James Froomis	Edwardsburg	Albert Parsons	Augusta.
William Gibson	Do	Robert Peden	Brockville.
Asa H. Giffin	Wolford.	Richard Preston	South Crosby.
Ogle R Gowan	Brockville.	Robert Putnam	Wolford.
Edward Green	Leeds	John Reid	Brockville.
Robert Headlem	Augusta.	John Rogers	Bastard
James Higgins	Prescott	Robert Rorison	North Crosby.
Thomas Hill	Elizabethtown	Abel Russell	Leeds.
Timothy Hogan	Augusta.	Robert Shepherd	Augusta.
Noah Holliday	North Crosby.	George Sherwood	Brockville.
Alfred Hooker	Augusta	Hial Sliter	Leeds.
Adam Horton	New Dublin.	Septimus Soper	Kitley.
Henry Johnston	Lansdowne	John Spencer	Elizabethtown.
John Johnston	Escott	Cleveland Stafford	Lansdowne.
William Johnston	Kitley.	Allan Sweet	Leeds
James Keeler	Edwardsburg.	Sam P. Thomas	Augusta
Robert Kernehan	Oxford.	James Thompson	Escott.
Thomas Kidd	Escott	John Vanston	Escott.
Andrew Laidlow	Edwardsburg	William Webster	Lansdowne.
Heman Landon	Elizabethtown	Isaac Brock Wells	Augusta.
Thomas Mair	Brockville	E H Whitmarsh	Wolford
Ira Mallory	Yonge	Joseph Wright	Augusta.
William Meneally	Augusta	John Yonge	Yonge.
William Moses	South Gower.	William Young	Bastard.
William Moulton	Yonge		

Magistrates who have qualified in the London District.

Henry Allen	London.	W B Wrong	Bayham
D McKenzie	Do	G Wrong	Malahide
L. Lawrason	Do.	C. Beer	Do.
Thomas H Ball	Do	P Hodgkinson	Do.
Alex Anderson	Do	A McCausland	Do
S Morrill	Do.	B Wilson	Yarmouth.
Adam Telfer	Do	E Mihell	Do
Edward Matthews	Do	J B Clench	Carradoc
Thos C Dixon	Do	Wilson Mills	Do
James B Strathy	Do.	W Livingstone	Do
John H Caddy	Do	Ed Ermatinger	St Thomas
W. J. Geary	Do township	J K Woodward	Port Stanley.
Charles Monserrat	Do.	M McKenzie	St Thomas
John Harris	Do.	B Springer	Delaware
John Geary	Do	R Webb	Do
John Kent	Do	John Johnstone	Do
L. Patterson	Dunwich	W McKenzie	Adelaide.
Thomas McCall	Do	J S Buchanan	Do
John Bostwick	Port Stanley.	R Pegley	Do.
Andrew Dobbie	Bayham	G B Iver	Do.
J Draper	Do	R. W Branan	Do
J W. Wrong	Do	W. McK. Johnston	Do
L Burwell	Do	John Lang	Do

G Munro.	Aldborough.	John K Labatt	Westminster.
J. P. Bellairs	Port Burwell.	John McDougall	Lobo.
Alex Saxon	Do	James McArthur	Williams
John Shore	Westminster.	George Robb	Southwold.
C. Hall	Do	L Fowler	Do
Alex Strathy	Do.	William Hatalie	Mosa.
J. L Odell	Do.	John D Anderson	Do
Thomas Baty	Do	A McGregor	Dorchester
J J. Manning	Do	D Doty	Do.
H. Shenick	Do.		

Magistrates who have qualified in the Midland District.

A McDonell	Kingston.	Jacob Rambough	Camden.
W. Beamish	Do.	E Huffman	Do
J. Ashley	Do.	Edw. Shewell	Do
J. F. Kingston	Bedford	Benj Tett	Newborough.
A. Manahan	Kingston.	C. H Millar	Camden
J. M. Rorison	Do	J. P. Bower	Kingston
W. McCuniffe	Do.	B Ham	Ernestown
M. Clarke	Ernestown	S. Warner	Do
J. Allen	Adolphustown	J B Marks	Pittsburgh.
S Casey	Do.	A Caton	Richmond.
P V. Darland	Do.	A. Schermahan	Do.
John Church	Fredericksburgh.	Richard Hitchins	Amherst Island.
R Lowe	Adolphustown	Benjamin Seymour	Bath
D C Smith	Ernestown.	J Spring	Loughborough.
E. Switzer	Do	J Shibley	Portland.
S. Clark	Camden.	W J. Fairfield	Ernestown.
J. Macfarlane	Kingston.	A. Campbell	Adolphustown.
W. Wilson	Do	D Buth	Kingston
O. Hancox	Bath.	H Yeomans	Do
T. W. Robison	Kingston.	H Gildersleve	Do
J. Fraser	Ernestown	James Sampson	Do
A McNeil	Richmond	A Cameron	Wolfe Island.
Samuel Dorland	Adolphustown	J Counter	Kingston.
David Roblin	Fredericksburgh.	C. McKenzie	Bath.
W. Holditch	Loughborough.	M Shorey, Sen	Fredericksburgh.
F. A Harper	Kingston.	Matt Ruttan	Adolphustown
J Mowatt	Do.	Thomas Scott	Amherst Island
W. Garratt	Do	W. Radclif	Do
M. Asselstone	Ernestown.	Henry Sadlier	Kingston.
John Asselstone	Do.	A. McPherson	Richmond.
Samuel Campbell	Loughborough.	W Simkins	Loughborough.
Alex Cowan, Sen	Pittsburgh.	James Wilson	Richmond.
Thomas Askew	Kingston.		

Magistrates who have qualified in the Newcastle District.

Porter Preston	Manvers.	James Lang	Hope.
D F Burke	Darlington.	Asa F. Waldbridge	Clarke.
Robert Waddell	Monaghan.	Allan Wilmot	Darlington.
George Perry	Cobourg	John D. Smith	Port Hope
James Cummin	Murray	James Goslee	Cramahe
Charles Hughes	Port Hope.	Henry Munro	Clarke
Alex. Macaulay	Murray.	Robt. P. Boucher	Seymour
Myndert Harris	Hope.	Sheldon Hawley	Murray.

U

Andrew Jeffrey	Cobourg.	E W Myers	Do.
Thomas Scott	Do.	D Smart	Port Hope.
Ozem Strong	Cramahe.	A. Macdonald.	Hamilton.
John Barnard	Monaghan.	James G Rogers	Haldimand.
J C. Procter	Cramahe.	E Perry	Cobourg.
James Robertson	Port Hope.	John P Murphy	Murray.
John Beavis	Clarke.	A A Burnham	Cobourg.
Chas. W Spencer	Do.	John Lister	Darlington.
Edward Clark	Do	John Landon	Seymour.
John Middleton	Do	William Lowden	Hamilton.
John Simpson	Darlington	John T William	Hope.
W. H. Allen	Hope	John Steele	Haldimand.
Moses Blackstock	Cavan.	Wm. Robertson	Murray.
John Lamb	Murray	H LeVisconte	Seymour.
John Blair	Percy	Patrick Maguire	Cavan.
F.C A Holdsworth	Hamilton.	Alex Fletcher	Darlington
Alex. Broadfoot	Hope	Henry S Reed	Do
W. F. H. Kelly	Haldimand	John Thomson	Cavan.
S Young	Murray.	Charles Short	Murray.
John Smart	Darlington.	George Hughes	Cavan.
H. McCarty	Cobourg.	J A Keeler	Cramahe.
Thomas Eyre	Do	W McKyes	Haldimand
W. Weller	Do.	John Knowlton	Cavan.

Magistrates who have qualified in the Niagara District.

Ed. M Hodder	Niagara.	George Keefer	Thorold
Dan McDougal	Do	John Turney	Do
W. H Dickson	Do	John Graybiel	Wainfleet.
W. B Robinson	St Catharines.	Jacob Ker	Caistor.
Thomas Butler	Niagara	Henry Fitch	Willoughby.
Henry Smith	Grimsby.	W H Merritt	St. Catharines.
Lewis Wilson	Pelham	George Lykert	Do.
John C Ball	Niagara township	J. Hellems	Crowland.
J. W O Clark	Louth	William Steel	Walpole.
James Tisdale	Caistor	William Bradt	Louth.
A Bradshaw	Canboro'	O Buchner	Crowland
J M Lockhart	Sherbrooke	R Martin	Indian Reserve.
R McKinnon	Indian Reserve	D McF Field	Walpole.
J Kennedy	Gainsborough.	R Kilborn	Clinton.
E S. Adams	St Catharines	W McMicking	Stamford.
J B Jones	Grantham	Arch Thompson	Do.
P. B Nelles	Grimsby	John McMicking	Do.
D McFarland	Thorold	W Lowell	Do.
J. Keefer	Do	J Garner	Do.
Robert Hobson	Do	John Radcliff	Thorold.
A Morse	Grimsby.	P DeLatre	Stamford.
John Kirk	Moulton.	John Lemon	Do.
W H Nelles	Grantham.	James Cummings	Chippewa
George Secord	Gainsborough	T C. Street	Stamford.
Edmund Riseley	Bertie.	H. Mittleberger	St Catharines
J Brookfield	Crowland	Robert Melville	Niagara.
L. Misner	Wainfleet	John McLean	Clinton.
W. M. Ball	Niagara.	P B Clement	Niagara
John McGlashan	Pelham.	John Gibson	Grantham.
Daniel P. Brown	Crowland	J R. Benson	Do.
Robert Henry	Clinton.	A K. Boomer	Do.
Samuel Street	Stamford.	James Davis	York.

A. P Farrell	Dunnville.	J. N Pauling	Port Dalhousie
T Hixson	Clinton.	J B O'Reilly	Wainfleet.
William Adams	Louth.	D. Woolverton	Grimsby.
William Smith	Waterloo	J P. Bridgman	Do
John Jarron	Moulton.	Andrew Thompson	Moulton.
W. Nelles	Haldimand.	George Rowe	Stamford.
J. Misner	Wainfleet.	William Powell	Bertie.
Edward Evans	Rainham.	John Ker	Grantham.
H. Howey	Stamford.	W. J Imlach	Dunn.
G P M. Ball	Louth.	D Thompson	Indiana.
James Little	Seneca	William Ford	Do
Owen Ferris	Humberstone.	John W Ball	Niagara township
J. S. Hann	Bertie.	John Jackson	Indian Reserve.
Robert H Bruce	Cayuga	John Scholfield	Pelham
Daniel Beamer	Louth	John Clark	Port Dalhousie.
J. T. Cooper	Walpole.	Richard Brown	Indian Reserve

Magistrates in the Ottawa District.

George McDonell	L'Orignal.	John Brady	Alfred
Alexander Grant	Do	Thos Blackadder	L'Orignal.
John McDonell	Hawkesbury, East	Richard B Hatt	Chesserville(Plan)
David Pattee	Do West	D R McDonald	Longueil
Chauncey Johnson	Longueil	Charles Hersey	L'Orignal
Josiah P. Cass	Do	F Robertson	Hawkesbury, East
Elisha Cass	Do.	Duncan McDonell	Vankleek Hill
John Kearnes	Plantagenet	Kenneth Fletcher	Plantagenet.
James Molloy	Do	Edward St Julien	Canadian Settlem't.
John Chesser	Do	Wm McDonald	Hawkesbury East.
Neil Stewart	Hawkesbury West	Peter Van Kleek	Do West
Daniel Wyman	Do East	John McMaster	Caledonia
Elisha F Loucks	Russell.	Peter McLaurin	Do Scotch Mills
Hugh McLachlan	Hawkesbury, West	Archibald McBean	Hawkesbury, East.
Charles A Low	Do	Thomas Higginson	Do.
William Cothn	Do	William Parker	Caledonia.
Peter Stirling	Caledonia	Humphrey Hughes	Alfred
Elijah Kellog	Longueil	Alexander McCaul	Clarence.
Archibald Stirling	Hawkesbury,West	Ralph Wilson	Cumberland
William Wait	Longueil.	Allan Cameron	Do
Archibald Petrie	Cumberland.	Archibald Loucks	Russell
Nicholas Giffard	Clarence	Peter Peel	L'Orignal.
Hiram Wyman	Hawkesbury, East		

Magistrates who have qualified in the Prince Edward District.

A Gukison	Picton	David Stinson	Hallowell
David Conger	Wellington	Abraham Lazier	Sophiasburgh.
Wilson Bentley	Athol	Peter W Ruttan	North Port
W A Palin	Do	Simon Washburn	Picton
Conrad Bongard	Marysburgh	Benjamin Hubbs	Hallowell
E. W. Wright	Do	Wm Dougall	Picton
John O'B Scully	Wellington	Samuel Solmes	North Port.
Archibald McFaul	Do	John P Roblin	Amelasburgh
Caleb Williams	Bloomfield	James Cotter	Demorestville
Thomas Flagler	Hillier	James T Line	Hillier
P. C Valleau	Hallowell.	D B Stevenson	Picton
John Allison	Sophiasburgh.	John Howell	Demorestville.
John Lane	Marysburgh	John Thirkell	Bloomfield

U 2

John Stapleton	Hillier.	Henry Vandusen.	Milford
John Murney.	Picton.	George Drewry.	Sophiasburgh.
Norman Ballard	Do.	Henry Dingman.	Marysburgh.
Jacob Howell	Demorestville.		

Magistrates who have qualified in the Simcoe District.

James R Gowan	Barrie	Wm Campaigne	Mulmur.
Edward O'Brien	Toronto	Alexander Lewis.	Mono
George Lount	West Gwillimbury.	Benjamin Ross	Innisfil
John Dawson	Do.	Thomas West	West Gwillimbury.
Elmes Steele	Medonte.	John Craig	Flos.
John Thompson	Orillia	Richard Drury	Oro.
Frederick Stephens	Tecumseth	Andrew Moffatt	Orillia.
John Moberly	Barrie.	William Armson.	West Gwillimbury.
James Wickens, sr	Vespra	P. White	Vespra.
George Wilson	Medonte.	Charles Partridge	Oro.
J Æ Irving	West Gwillimbury	David Soles	Innisfil
Frederick Dallas	Orillia.	John Garbutt	West Gwillimbury.
Charles Thompson	Toronto	M Ryan	Adjala
A Goodfellow	West Gwillimbury	Joseph Hodgson	West Gwillimbury.
W C Hume	Orillia	B West	Do.
W Richey	Sunnidale.	A Cunningham	Do
Mathew Coates	Barrie.	W. Stephenson	Collingwood

Magistrates who have qualified in the Talbot District.

Henry Webster	Simcoe.	G A Killmaster	Do.
Thos J Mulkins	Do	J. B. Hutchinson	Do
J. B. Crouse	Do.	Wm Backhouse	Do.
George H. Parke	Do.	Jacob Wood	Vittoria.
James Walker.	Do.	W. Anderson	Do
Isaac Gilbert	Do.	J Covernton	Do.
James Graham	Do.	J Potts	Do.
David Marr, junior	Do.	L. H Huns	Windham
P O Carr	Do.	A. A Rapelje	Charlotteville.
William Salmon	Do.	R VanNorman	Do
Edward Gilman	Do	J Tisdale	Do.
Henry Waters	Port Dover.	W. Walker	Townsend.
J W. Powell	Do.	W. Mathews	Do.
E P Ryerse	Vittoria	D Duncombe	Do
John Wallace	Middleton.	M. W. White	Houghton.
D W. Freeman	Do	James Brown	Middleton.
John Roach	Do	Wm. McLennan	Do.
H J Killmaster	Walsingham	James L Green	Townsend.
D Schermerhorn	Do	A Boulby	Do.
Titus Williams	Do		

Magistrates who have qualified in the Victoria District.

Benjamin Dougall.	Belleville	John Gilbert	Belleville
A Marshall	Do.	W. Ketchison	Sidney.
John Turnbull	Do	W Bowen	Do.
G N Ridley	Do.	E Ketchison	Do
Benj Ketchison	Do.	S Hawley	Do
P Ham	Do	R Purdy	Do.
B F Davy	Do	H. Hagerman	Do
R Holden	Do	W. Hutton	Do.

G. Turner	Sidney.	E Fidlar	Rawdon.
J. N. Lockwood	Do.	W Chard	Do
C. Gilbert	Do.	W. Bowen	Do.
P. White	Do	S Johns	Marmora.
John Pout	Tyendenaga	W. Campion	Do.
T. D. Appleby	Do.	R. A McCameron	Hungerford.
J Davis	Do	George Bleecker	Thurlow.
J. Sweeney	Do.	D McLellan	Do.
S W. Robinson	Do.	W. Fairman	Do.
M. Nealon	Do.	J. Canniff	Do
C. L. Herchimer	Do	J. Anderson	Huntingdon.
J. Osburn	Do.	J Ketchison	Do.
D McKenzie	Madoc.	O. Durken	Do
J. O'Hara	Do.		

Magistrates who have qualified in the Wellington District.

A. A. Ferguson	Guelph.	Archibald Paterson	Do.
William Hewat	Do	John McKee	Garafraxa.
William Clark	Do.	Alex. Drysdale	Do
Edward Murton	Do.	Thomas Webster	Do
Benjamin Thurtel	Do	James Webster	Nichol.
Charles J. Mickle	Do.	Alex D Fordyce	Do
Thomas Hodgskin	Do.	William Burst	Do.
Richard Jackson	Do.	William Reynolds	Woolwich.
Edw F. Heming	Do	Jacob Bottschin	Wilmot.
John Inglis	Do	William Hobson	Do.
George Armstrong	Eramosa.	James Cowan	Waterloo.
Henry Strange	Do.	James Phinn	Do.
Joseph Parkinson	Do	George Davidson	Do
Henry Trout	Erin.	A M J. Durnford	Arthur.

Magistrates in the Western District.

Alex. Chewitt	Sandwich.	William Baby	Sandwich
Charles Eliot	Do.	George Duck	Howard.
J. B Baby	Do	D H Gesner	Orford.
W Duff	Amherstburg.	R Wingfield	Anderdon.
John Dolsen	Dover	W. Taylor	Dawn
Duncan McGregor	Raleigh.	James Ruddle	Howard.
W. E. Wright	Moore.	William Cosgrave	Dover.
John Prince	Sandwich.	T W Smith	Do.
Joseph Woods	Chatham.	J G Weir	Chatham
A P Toulmin	Plympton.	George Ironsides	Manitoulin.
George Durand	Sarnia.	William Fletcher	Sombra.
Prideaux Girty	Gosfield.	L. H. Johnson	Do.
J. W. Little	Raleigh.	D T McDonald	Do
James Read	Chatham.	Thomas Williams	Chatham.
T. McCrae, jun	Do	Charles R. Nixon	Warwick.
J. A Wilkinson	Sandwich.	John Sloan	Anderdon
Robert Lachlan	Colchester.	George Wilson	Sault Ste Marie.
Robert Reynolds	Amherstburg	John Ballenden	Do
John Ferriss	Colchester.	Joseph Wilson	Do.
Benjamin Lavallie.	Grand Cote	Paul Darling	Manitoulin.
Samuel Gardiner	Windsor.	Thomas L Ritter	Sandwich.
Robert Mercer	Do	Joseph Promcher	Do
Thomas Renwick	Romney.	L J. Fluett	Do.

John A. Ray	Do.	J. W. Sanford	Gosfield.
P. H Morin	Do	Ralph Foster	Mersea.
J. B. La Liberte	Malden	Jonathan Wigfield	Do
F. A. Lafferte	Do.	Alex S Stockwell.	Do
R B. Elliott	Do.	Theodore Malott.	Do.
J B. Fillion	Do.	Giant Duncan	Maidstone.
F Caron	Do.	William Gatfield	Anderdon.
J G Buchanan	Colchester.	Henry Wright	Do.
Mathew Ferris	Do	George Hyde	Plympton.
Richard Thornton	Gosfield.	Froome Talfourd	Moore.
Martin Bower	Do.	Joseph Biddle	Do.

LIST OF MINISTERS OF VARIOUS DENOMINATIONS IN CANADA WEST.

Episcopalian Ministers.

Bishop of the Diocese of Toronto and Archdeacon of York—The Hon. and Rt. Rev John Strachan, D D, LL D.
Archdeacon of Kingston—The Venerable George O'Kill Stuart, LL D.
Examining Chaplain and Secretary to the Bishop—Rev H J Grasett, M.A.
Diocesan Professor of Theology—Rev. A N Bethune, D D

HOME DISTRICT.

City of Toronto	John Strachan, D D, LL D.	Thornhill	D. E Blake, A.B.
	H J Grasett.	Markham and Vaughan	V. P Mayerhoffer.
	H Scadding, M A	Newmarket	G C Street
	W H Ripley, B A	Georgina	John Gibson
	Harvey McAlpin.	Brock	Vacant
	— Ruttan	Whitby	J Pentland, B.A.
Etobicoke	T. Phillips, D D.	Scarboro'	W S Darling.
Toronto township	J. Magrath, M A	Lloydtown	H Bath Osler.
York Mills	Alex. Sanson	Chinguacousy	G. Steven J. Hill.
Streetsville	R J MacGeorge.		

SIMCOE DISTRICT.

Barrie & Shanty Bay	S B, Ardagh, A.M	Orillia	John McIntyre.
Tecumseth and W. Gwillimbury	F. L Osler, M.A.	Penetanguishine	Geo. Hallett, B A. Charles Ruttan.

WELLINGTON DISTRICT

Guelph	A Palmer, A B	Travelling Miss'y	James Mockridge.

GORE DISTRICT.

Hamilton	J. Gamble Geddes.	Wellington Square	T. Greene, A.B.
Saltfleet and		Galt	M. Boomer, A.B.
Binbrook	J. L. Alexander.	Paris	William Morse.
Ancaster & Dundas	W. McMurray.	Oakville	G. Winter Warr.
Brantford	J. C. Usher.	Trafalgar	George Graham.

Missionaries to the Six Nation Indians on the Grand River—Abraham Nelles and Adam Elliott.

NIAGARA DISTRICT.

Niagara	Thomas Creen.	Fort Erie	John Anderson.
Grimsby	G. R. F. Grout.	St. Catharines	A. F. Atkinson.
Chippewa, Stamford, Queenston & Drummondville	W. Leeming.	Louth	G. M. Armstrong.
		Dunnville, &c.	Adam Townley.
Thorold	Thos. B. Fuller.	Settlements on the Grand River	B. C. Hill, M.A.

TALBOT DISTRICT.

Simcoe......... Francis Evans and George Salmon.

LONDON DISTRICT.

London	Benj. Cronyn.	Port Burwell	T. Bolton Read.
London township	C. C. Brough, A.B.	Travelling Missionaries	George Petrie.
St. Thomas	M. Burnham, B.A.		James Stewart.
Adelaide	Arthur Mortimer.		John Hickie.
Carradoc	Rich. Flood, A.M.		

BROCK DISTRICT.

Woodstock	W. Bettridge, B.D.	Oxford	Vacant.

HURON DISTRICT.

Goderich	R. Campbell, M.A.	Devonshire Settle't	H. C. Cooper, B. A.

WESTERN DISTRICT.

Sandwich	William Ritchie.	Moore	Alex. Pyne, A.B.
Amherstburg	Frederick Mack.	Walpole Island	Andrew Jamieson.
Colchester	F. Gore Elliott.	Dawn, &c.	John Gunne.
Chatham	W. H. Hobson.	Raleigh, &c.	F. Wm. Sandys.
Warwick	Vacant.		

NEWCASTLE DISTRICT.

Cobourg	A. N. Bethune, D.D.	Clarke &c.	T. S. Kennedy.
	J. G. D. McKenzie	Grafton, &c.	John Wilson.
Port Hope	Jonathan Shortt.	Travelling Miss'y.	Robert Harding.
Cavan	Samuel Armour.		

COLBORNE DISTRICT.

Peterboro'	R. J. Taylor, M.A.	Fenelon Falls	Thomas Fidler.
Emily	Vacant.		

VICTORIA DISTRICT.

Belleville.................. John Grier, M.A.

PRINCE EDWARD DISTRICT.

Picton	Wm. Macaulay.	Carrying Place	Philip G. Bartlett.

MIDLAND DISTRICT.

Kingston	G. O'Kill Stuart.	Bath	W. F. S. Harper.
	W. M. Herchmer.	Adolphustown	Job Deacon.
	R. Vashon Rogers.	Mohawk, &c.	Saltern Givins.
	J. H. Bartlett, M.A.	Amherst Island	J. Rothwell, A.B.
	John Pope, M.A.	Camden, Loughborough & Portland	Paul Shirley.
Wolfe Island	J. Antisell Allen.		

JOHNSTOWN DISTRICT.

Brockville	. ... E. Denroche, A M.	Prescott	Robert Blakey.
Lamb's Pool . .	. W. Gunning, A B	Kemptville ...	. Henry Patton.

BATHURST DISTRICT.

Perth	. M. Harris, A.M	Smith's Falls ...	F. Tremayne.
Carleton Place	Vacant.	Pakenham, &c ..	Hannibal Mulkins.
Franktown ...	. J. W. Padfield.	Travelling Miss'y	Ebenezer Morris.

DALHOUSIE DISTRICT.

Bytown . . .	S Spratt Strong.	March	Matthew Ker.
Richmond .	. John Flood.		

EASTERN DISTRICT.

Cornwall . .	J. G. B. Lindsay	Osnabruck	Romaine Rolph.
Williamsburgh	.. E. Jukes Boswell.		

Manitoulin Island . ... Frederick Augustus O'Meara, A B.

Travelling Missionary in the Diocese... Richard Garrett

Presbyterian Ministers in connexion with the Church of Scotland.

PRESBYTERY OF BATHURST

Brockville ..	. John Cruikshank	Pakenham	Alexander Mann
Beckwith	... John Smith	Richmond..	David Evans
Smith's Falls .	. George Romanes	Bytown..	Alexander McKid
Perth .	... William Bell	Lanark ..	Thomas Fraser
South Gower	Joseph Anderson	Cumberland ...	. George Bell

PRESBYTERY OF KINGSTON.

Kingston .. . John Machar.
Queen's College T Liddell, Principal and Professor of Divinity.
" . P. C. Campbell, Prof of Classical Literature.

PRESBYTERY OF TORONTO.

Toronto Township	Andrew Bell	Markham	Geo Galloway
Esquesing ...	. Peter Ferguson	Eldon	John McMurchy
Scarboro' .	James George	Pickering & Whitby,	James Lambie
Chinguacousy.	.. Thos Johnston	Monroe .	.. Alexander Lewis
King ..	. John Tawse	Toronto City .	.. John Barclay

PRESBYTERY OF GLENGARY.

Williamstown	. John McKenzie	Williamsburgh...	. John Dickey
Cornwall .	... Hugh Urquhart	Osnabruck ..	Isaac Purkis
Lochiel ..	.. ... John McIsaac	Lancaster . ..	Thos McPherson
Indian Lands	. Daniel Clark	Dalhousie Mills ...	D Sinclair
Martintown .	John McLaurin	L'Orignal	Colin Grigor

PRESBYTERY OF HAMILTON.

Niagara ...	... Robert McGill.	Grimsby	Daniel Eastman.
Nelson ..	... William King	Woolwich	Alexander Ross.
Mount Pleasant .	John Bryning.	Simcoe	Thomas Scott.
Beamsville ..	, George McClachy.		

Presbyterian (Free Church) Ministers.

HAMILTON AND TORONTO PRESBYTERY.

Toronto — Dr. Burns.
Henry Esson.
James Harris.
Streetsville .... William Rintoul
Dundas & Ancaster Mark Y Stark
Hamilton............ Alexander Gale
Zorra .... Donald McKenzie.
Galt .... John Bayne
Stratford............. Daniel Allan.
Thorold and St. Catharines ..... A McIntosh.
Williams .... Duncan McMillan
Puslinch .... William Meldrum.
Port Sarnia......... Wm. Macalister.
Saltfleet .... George Cheyne.
Ayr .... Robert Lindsay.
Fergus .... George Smellie
Amherstburg ..... Robert Peden

Missionaries—Messrs. Macaulay, Steele, Grahame, and Kingan.

COBOURG PRESBYTERY.

Peterboro'& Cavan John M. Rogers
Cobourg .... Thos Alexander
Grafton & Colborne William Reid.
South Cavan ...... James Douglass

KINGSTON PRESBYTERY

Gananoque .... Henry Gordon.
Demorestville.... James Rogers.
Picton .... Alex. McLean.
Camden .... Thos Wightman.
Brockville .... William Stuart
Prescott .... Robert Boyd

Missionary—John Corbet

Congregational Ministers.

Tutor of the Congregational Academy, George Street, Toronto—Rev Adam Lillie

Port Sarnia........ J. Nall
Adelaide .... J Hart.
London .... E Ebbs
St Thomas ...... W P. Wastell
Southwold........ J. Silcox.
Simcoe .... Wm Clarke.
Burford .... Wm Clarke, jun.
Brantford .... Thomas Baker
Hamilton .... J Osborne.
Glandford ...... S Finton
Trafalgar........ H Denney
Esquesing ...... J. Armour
Caledon .... Stephen King
Guelph .... L McGlashen.
Eramosa .... E Martin.
Vaughan .... T Hodgkin.
Toronto .... John Roaf.
Markham ...... D. Kribs
Newmarket .... James Vincent.
Innisfil .... John Climie
Oro .... Ari Raymond
Whitby .... Thomas Machin.
Darlington .... J Climie jun
Brock .... A McKechnie.
Cobourg .... Joseph Harris
Asphodel ..... J Durrant.
Belleville ..... J Woods
Port Dover ... Joseph Marr.

Baptist Ministers.

Chairman of the Canada Baptist Union—Rev. J M Cramp, A.M.
Corresponding Secretary—Rev. F Bosworth, A M

Toronto .... R. A. Fyfe
Do. .... W. Christian.
Hamilton ...... A Booker
Kingston ...... A Lorimer, A B
Brantford ..... J Winterbotham
St. Catharines . W Hewson.
Brockville .... Robert Boyd.
Woodstock ... N Bosworth
Peterboro' .... John Edwards
Do .... John Gilmour.
Beamsville ... George Silver
Bronté .... John Oakley
Whitby .... Israel Marsh.
Hope .... Samuel Tapscott.
York Mills .... James Mitchell
Pickering ..... Thomas Gostick.
Queenston .... J B Vrooman.
Lanark .... Robert Dick.
Waterford .... A Slaght.
Simcoe .... W Rees
Perth .... W Cooper
Breadalbane .. W Fraser
Tuscarora .... W H Landon.
Osgoode ..... D. McPhail
Loho .... D Sinclair
Williamsburg . C Klutz.
Kitley .... H. Nichols
Augusta ...... J. Fay.

Baptist Ministers—Continued.

Beverley	—. McEathron	Oxford	E Elliott
March	M Kerr	Cornwall	A. McLean.
Dundas	J Clutton.	Grafton	J Holman.
Niagara	A Underhill.	Caledon	J Campbell

British Wesleyan Methodist Ministers.

(In consequence of the annual changes to which the Methodist ministers are subject, their circuits are not inserted)

W M Harvard	Ephraim Evans	Henry Lanton	William Case.
Edmund Botterell	E Stoney	Wm. Andrews	William Scott.
James Booth.	John Bredin.	John Gundy	John Sunday.
Robert Cooney	Henry Byers	William Steer.	Thomas Fawcett.
John Douse	Edward Sallows	John C Davidson.	

Canadian Wesleyan Methodist Ministers.

MINISTERS AND PREACHERS.

Henry Wilkinson	John Law	John Baxter	Ozias Barber
William Ryerson.	Wm Willoughby	Wm Coleman.	Michael Fawcett.
John Ryerson	Peter Ker	Benjamin Jones	Erastus Hurlburt.
Richard Jones.	William Philp	William Glass	William Haw.
John Carroll	Matthew Whiting.	G Smith	Francis Coleman
James Musgrove	R E. Tupper	Horace Dean	John Lever
Anson Green	Thomas Demorest.	J W Cawthorne	S Huntingdon.
George F Playter.	Thomas Rattray	Wm McCullough.	G B Butcher
E Ryerson, D D.	Jonathan Scott	Conrad Vandusen.	Matthew Conner.
A McNab, A M	Joseph Messmore	David B Madden.	Thomas Bevitt.
Edwy M Ryerson	Luther O Rice	Asahel Hurlburt	W H Williams.
Corn Flumerfelt	Thomas Cosford	John Sanderson.	J W McCollum.
George Kennedy.	John Goodfellow	Wm McFadden	Joseph Hill.
Matthew Holtby.	Sylvester Hurlburt	Thomas Cleghorn	Wm Pollard.
J E Ryerson.	Joseph Shepley	Robert Darlington	Geo Goodson.
Samuel Philp	John K Williston.	Daniel Wright	James Greener.
David Hardy.	G R. Sanderson	Isaac B Howard	George Beynon.
William Dignam	George Young	Cyrus R Allison	Charles Taggart.
Thomas Williams	Samuel Rose	John Williams	John Armstrong.
Solomon Snyder	William Price	John Gemley	Benj Nankevill
George Pool	C W M Gilbert.	Samuel P LaDow.	Thomas Hannah.
Charles Lavell	James Spencer	Abraham Dayman	James Hughes
K Creighton	James Hutchinson	I B Aylesworth	John Tuke
Rowley Heyland	David Wright	Lachlin Taylor	Joseph Reynolds
Thomas Jeffers	David Jennings	Welington Jeffers	John Howes
Lewis Werner	Alvan Adams	V B Howard	Henry Slater.
Francis N English	Ezra Adams	John Black	Wm Morton.
E Shepherd	George Carr.	George Case	James Elliott
E B Harper			

SUPERNUMERARY PREACHERS

John Culham	John Beatty	Daniel McMullen	Peter Jones.
	Moses Blackstock	Thomas Harmon.	

MISSIONARIES

Solomon Waldron	Horace Dean	William Herkimer.	Robert Robinson.
Abraham Sickles	J W. Cawthorne	John Neelands	Robert Lochhead
David Sawyer	Samuel Belton	Gilbert Miller.	Stephen Miles
Hamilton Biggar	Peter Jones, super	Richard Phelps	Robert Corson.
Alexander Green			

TABLE OF DISTANCES.

Western and South-Western Route.

From Toronto to Lambton, 8—Sydenham, 14½—Cooksville, 16—Springfield, 19—Palermo, 30—Flamborough, 38—Dundas, 40—Hamilton, 45—Ancaster, 51½—Brantford, 68½—Woodstock, 91—Beachville, 96—Ingersol, 101—London, 123—Delaware, 136—Wardsville, 159—Thamesville, 174—Louisville, 183—Chatham, 189—Windsor, 239—Sandwich, 241—Amherstburg, 257

From Toronto to Hamilton by the Lake Shore Road—To Port Credit, 14—Oakville, 26—Bronte, 30—Port Nelson, 35½—Wellington Square, 37—Hamilton, 43.

From Hamilton to Galt, 25—Preston, 28—Stratford, 65—Goderich, 110—Guelph, 42—Fergus, 55—Elo, 55—Arthur, 67—Paris, 27

From Hamilton to Caledonia, 14—Port Dover, 36½—Simcoe, 43½—Vittoria, 49

From Hamilton to Stoney Creek, 7—Grimsby, 17—Beamsville, 22—Jordan, 28—St. Catharines, 36—Niagara, 48—Queenston, 47—Chippewa, 56—Waterloo, 72.

From Brantford to Caledonia, 20—Seneca, 21—York, 25—Indiana, 32—Cayuga, 35—Dunnville, 50—Port Maitland, 55—Paris, 6—Galt, 18—Waterford, 17—Simcoe, 24

Distances on the Welland Canal—From St Catharines to Port Dalhousie, 5—Thorold, 4½—Allanburg, 8—Port Robinson, 10—Merrittsville, 14½—Helmsport, 15½—Stonebridge—21½—Port Colborne, 23.

From London to the Junction, 6—St. Thomas, 17—Port Stanley, 26—Westminster, 6—Kilworth, 8—Delaware, 13—Port Sarnia, 61—Goderich, 59—Temperanceville, 27—Aylmer, 29—Richmond, 37—Vienna, 42—Port Burwell, 45

From Chatham to Louisville, 6—Wallaceburgh, 17—Dawn Mills 15—Zone Mills, 24—Sutherland's, 50—Froomefield, 55½—Port Sarnia, 60—Errol, 73—Rond 'Eau, 14.

Northern Route.

From Toronto to Thornhill 11—Richmond Hill, 16—Holland Landing, 32—Bradford, 36—Barrie, 64—Penetanguishine, 104

From Toronto to Markham 20—Newmarket, 30—Lloydtown, 42—Sharon, 35—Boucher's Mills, 55—Coldwater, 95—Orillia, 92—Sturgeon Bay, 100

Eastern Route.

From Toronto to the Rouge, 12—Duffin's Creek, 23—Windsor, 31—Oshawa, 33—Bowmanville, 42—Newcastle, 47—Newton, 52—Port Hop, 65—Cobourg, 72—Grafton, 80—Colborne, 88—Brighton, 96—Trent, 108—Belleville, 118—Shaunonville, 127—Napanee, 147—Mill Creek, 164—Waterloo, 174—Kingston, 177—Gananoque, 193—Brockville 233—Prescott, 245—Moulinette, 287—Milleroche, 289—Cornwall, 294—Martintown, 307

From Port Hope to Peterborough, 30

From Peterborough to Keene, 13—Warsaw, 15—Norwood 25

From Kingston to Picton, 39—Bloomfield 44—Consecon, 59—Milford, 47—Wellington, 50

From Perth to Lanark, 12—Pakenham, 40—Smith's Falls, 14—Oliver's Ferry, 7

From L'Orignal to Hawkesbury, 4—Caledonia, 9—Vankleek Hill, 8.

From Brockville to Frankville, 22—Chamberlain's Corner, 24—Perth, 40.

Distances on the Rideau Canal.—From Bytown to Merrickville, 47—Smith's Falls, 60—Oliver's Ferry, 72—The Isthmus, 87—Brewer's Mills, 109—Kingston, 126.

LIST OF HOTELS, BOARDING-HOUSES, BANKS, FORWARDERS, &c., AT MONTREAL.

Hotels and Inns.

Rasco's Hotel, 65, St Paul Street; Orr's Hotel. 90, Notre Dame Street; Tetu's Hotel, 23 and 25, Great St. James Street, Sword's Hotel, 2, St. Vincent Street; Ottawa Hotel, McGill Street, Adelphi Hotel, Place D'Armes, Rialto, 49, Notre Dame Street; Victoria Hotel, 10, Place D'Armes; Serafino's Hotel, Fabrique Street, New Market, Eagle Hotel, McGill Street, City Hotel, corner of St. Paul and St. Joseph Streets, Caledonia Hotel, 234, St. Paul Street; Commercial Hotel, corner St Joseph and Commissioners Streets, Feller's Hotel, 231 St Paul Street; Gould's Hotel, College Street, Grant's Hotel, St. Henry Street, Hondlow's Hotel, corner McGill and Lemoine Street; Exchange Coffee House, Exchange Court, St. Paul Street, King's Arm's Inn, St. Charles Street, New Market, London Coffee House, 19, St. Vincent Street, Queen's Arms Inn, 63, St. Paul Street, Dolly's Chop House, St. François Xavier Street

Boarding Houses.

Mrs Armstrong, 23, Chenneville Street; George Dowker, 3, Little St James Street; Mrs Farrel, 4, Chenneville Street, Mrs. L. Gosselin, Recollet, near St. Helen Street; Mrs McEwen, College Street, near the College

Banks.

Hours of Business at all the Banks—from 10, A M, to 3, P M

Bank of British North America, Great St James Street, Bank of Montreal, do ; City Bank, Place d'Armes, Banque du Peuple, St François Xavier Street, Bank of Upper Canada, 11 Great St James Street; Commercial Bank of the Midland District, 37 Great St. James Street.

Forwarders.

Macpherson, Crane & Co, Common, near Dalhousie Street; Murray & Sanderson. Common, near Nazareth Street, H Jones & Co Common, near Dalhousie Street, Hooker, Holton & Co, Common, near Canal Wharf, Ross, Matthie & Co, Common, near Nazareth Street, George Smith, corner George and Common Streets, Alex. Ferguson (Agent of the Quebec Forwarding Co), corner Common and Prince Street, G P Dickson, corner Common and Queen Street.

Government Offices.

Civil Secretary's Office, Government House, Notre Dame Street; Provincial Secretary's Office, do , Receiver General's Office, do ; Inspector General's Office, do , Surveyor General's Office, 55 Notre Dame Street, Board of Works, 45 Notre Dame Street, Crown Lands Office, do.; Provincial Registrar's Office, 60 Notre Dame Street; Emigrant Office, Commissioners' Street—facing the steamboat wharf.

Custom House—St. Paul Street.
Post Office—15, Great St James Street.

Assurance Offices.

Alliance (of London), Auldjo's Buildings, St. Paul's Street, Britannia (do), 24 St François Xavier Street, Eagle (do.), corner St François Xavier and St. Sacrament streets; Globe (do), Gillespie's Buildings; Lloyd's Agents (do.), Ryan, Chapman & Co , Gillespie's Buildings, Minerva (do), corner Recollet and St. Helen Streets; Montreal, 177 Notre Dame Street; Inland Marine Insurance Company, Lemoine Street; Mutual (Montreal), corner St. Sacrament and St François Xavier Streets, National Loan Fund, 51 Great St. James Street, Phœnix (London), 134 St. Paul Street; Quebec, 24 St. François Xavier Street.

Stage Offices.

Albany Stage Office, (via Burlington), Duclos' Hotel, McGill Street, Upper Canada Stage Office, McGill Street, Quebec Stage Office, 22, St. Jean Baptiste Street

The following places were accidentally omitted in their proper order :—

ADELAIDE.

A small Village in the township of Adelaide, situated on the road from London to Port Sarnia, eighteen miles from London. It contains about 120 inhabitants, and an Episcopal Church.

Professions and Trades—One distillery, two stores, two taverns, one waggon maker, one blacksmith, one shoemaker, one tailor.

STONEY CREEK.

A Village in the township of Saltfleet, pleasantly situated on the road from Hamilton to St Catharines, seven miles from Hamilton. Stoney Creek flows through the village. There is an Episcopal Church a short distance from the village.

Population, about 160.

Post Office, post every day.

Professions and Trades—One grist mill, one saw do., two stores, three taverns, three blacksmiths, three waggon makers, two tailors, one shoemaker.

ERRATA.

Barryfield, in the township of "Pittsburgh," should be, in the township of "*Kingston*."

Binbrook, in the "Niagara District;" should be, in the "*Gore District*."

Germany Little, "nine miles south-west," should be, "*nine miles north-east.*"

Oakville, "sixteen miles" west from Toronto, should be, "*twenty-six miles.*"

Torbolton, in the "Bathurst District," should be, in the "*Dalhousie District.*"

"Boucher's Mills," should be, "*Bouchier's Mills.*"

ADVERTISEMENTS.

NIAGARA FALLS MUSEUM,
NEAR TABLE ROCK.

THE Proprietor, grateful for the support he has received from the ladies and gentlemen visiting the Falls, begs leave to announce to them, that his collection has undergone an entire alteration this spring, and a numerous variety of fresh specimens has been added to the rooms The Galleries are classically arranged with the rarest and finest specimens the country can produce.

THE COLLECTION CONTAINS
AN ENTIRE FOREST SCENERY,
Arranged with such taste as to display the nature of every object, exhibiting most of the native Birds and Animals.

In this splendid collection of natural and artificial curiosities will be found upwards of SIX THOUSAND interesting specimens, principally collected in this vicinity; and it must be gratifying to visiters to become acquainted with the Birds, Quadrupeds, Reptiles, Fish (from Lakes Ontario and Erie), Lake Shells, Insects, Plants, Minerals, Indian Curiosities, &c, which are found in this part of America, including the finest specimens of Bald Eagle, with all the Falcon order, an extensive variety of rare and beautiful specimens of the Duck and Diver tribe, a great family of Owls, and a vast variety of other species of rare and fine plumaged birds

QUADRUPEDS,
Comprising the Moose (the largest species of the Deer tribe), two large Elks or Stags, a white Virginian Deer, a Pied Deer, with a large specimen of the common colour, the Lynx, Wild Cat, Red and Grey Wolves, many different varieties of Foxes, Porcupines, Opossums, Otters, Beavers, Marmots, Skunks, Raccoons, Muskrats, and a great variety of Hares and Rabbits, Martins or Sables, Ermines, Squirrels of all colours, White Rats, Mice, &c

LIVING RATTLE-SNAKES, BIRDS, AND ANIMALS.

Some very interesting Skeletons—the Eagle, Humming Bird, Rattle Snake, Ducks, Divers, Birds and Animals of various kinds

Bark of Trees worn by the natives in different parts of the world. Fine specimens of the saw of the Sawfish, and sword of the Swordfish, jaws of a Shark, the whip of a Sea Spider. A number of different species of foreign Fish.

A Rich Collection of Roman, Greek, Egyptian and Polish Coins.

A numerous variety of rare and beautiful Birds, Animals, Reptiles, Sea Shells, Minerals, Fossils, Indian Curiosities, &c, from all parts of the world, among which are worthy of notice, a fine specimen of the Barbary Lion, the Glutton, Civet, Antelope or Gazelle, Agouti, Coatimondi, Leopards, Badger, Duckbilled Platipus, the Alligator and Crocodile, Greenland Dog, various kinds of Monkies, Seal, Guana, Green Lizard, the Boa or Ox-Serpent.

A CAMERA OBSCURA
Is attached to the Museum, without extra charge to visiters.

The best general view of the Falls is obtained from the verandah of the Museum·

Birds, Insects, Minerals, Canes, Indian Curiosities, &c.
FOR SALE.

The Museum will be open all hours through the day. Admittance to the whole, 1s. 3d.; children half-price.

THOMAS BARNETT.

ADVERTISEMENTS.

GREAT BARGAIN

IN THE

WESTERN DISTRICT.

THAT Valuable Property, containing 206 acres of choice Land, situated on both sides of the River Sydenham, at the junction of the east and north branches of that river.

The following is a short description of its locality and advantages:—

Twenty acres on the margin of the east branch are laid out by survey, as the town-plot of "Wallaceburgh;" sixty acres have been cleared, and are under good cultivation, and well fenced The remaining 126 acres are covered with valuable white oak and walnut timber.

This location possesses the advantage of an uninterrupted water communication with all parts of the Province. The River Sydenham is navigable for the largest schooners, from twelve to sixteen miles above Wallaceburg, on each of its branches, where inexhaustible fields of oak and walnut timber are to be found.

Any party wishing to enter into a general business connected with the lumber trade, would find this location one of the best in America for such purposes. The whole or a part of the property will be sold a great bargain. Apply to

GILLESPIE, MOFFATT & Co.,
Montreal.

Or to

EBERTS, WADDELL & Co.,
Chatham.

THE ROYAL EXCHANGE HOTEL;

Chief Stage and Steamboat House for the Town of Chatham.

W. & W. EBERTS,

Proprietors.

This fine building is offered for sale, with furniture, or to rent for a term of years   Apply to

THE PROPRIETORS.

EBERTS, WADDELL & Co.,
OF CHATHAM, WESTERN DISTRICT,
General Merchants and Forwarders.

WILL be happy to furnish any information, and render all the assistance in their power to parties wishing to settle in the Western District.

ADVERTISEMENTS.

NORTH AMERICAN HOTEL,
PORT DOVER.

HENRY McCRACKEN

HAS the honour to inform the travelling public, that he has taken the above House, which he has fitted up with every convenience, and hopes to make all those comfortable who may honour him with their patronage.

LONDON PORTER ALWAYS ON HAND.

A Line of Covered Stages leaves the North American Hotel every morning at eight o'clock, for Hamilton, by way of the plank road.

Fare...................... 2s. 6d., currency.

HOPE HOTEL,
CORNER OF DUNDAS AND TALBOT STREETS,
London, C. W.

THE Subscriber having fitted up and furnished the above Hotel, is prepared to receive visitors, and to offer them every comfort which a well conducted House can afford.

WILLIAM BALKWILL.

N.B.—Good stabling and careful hostlers.

HOUSE, LAND, AND GENERAL AGENCY OFFICE.

IMPROVED FARMS, WILD LAND, AND HOUSES PURCHASED, SOLD OR LEASED;
PATENT DEEDS OF LAND PROCURED;
Lands which belonged to persons deceased, claimed, and the Deeds obtained for their Heirs and Assigns.
Deeds, Leases, Bonds, Agreements, Petitions, Wills, Mortgages, &c., prepared;
Debts and Rents collected;
And all other Agency Business transacted on moderate terms, by

WILLIAM OSBORNE,
Notary Public and Land Agent, No. 16, King Street West, Toronto.

RICHARD SCORE,
MERCHANT TAILOR,
No. 1, Chewett's Buildings, Toronto.

BEGS respectfully to acquaint his Customers, and the Public generally, that his Stock of

WEST OF ENGLAND CLOTHS, CASSIMERES,

SUMMER COATINGS AND RICH VESTINGS,

Is now very complete, and hopes for a continuance of the very liberal support hitherto extended to him.

N.B.—University work done in all the different orders; also, Judges', Queen's Counsel's, and Barrister's Robes, in the most correct styles, and on moderate terms.

ADVERTISEMENTS.

STOVES.

TORONTO FURNACE.

The Subscribers have erected a Foundry on

QUEEN STREET,

A FEW STEPS EAST OF YONGE STREET,

And have commenced the manufacture of

STOVES AND HOLLOW-WARE;

And are now prepared to fill orders

AT WHOLESALE AND RETAIL,

On as favourable terms as any other establishment in the Province.

AMONG THEIR STOVES MAY BE FOUND THE FOLLOWING PATTERNS :—

Bacon's improved Railway	6 boilers.
Burr's do Stove	5 do.
Premium do. do. Nos. 2, 3, and 5, ...	3 do.
Do. do. do.	4 do.
Hathaway do. do Nos. $2\frac{1}{4}$, $2\frac{1}{2}$.	

TOGETHER WITH A GREAT VARIETY OF

PARLOUR, AIR-TIGHT AND SIX PLATE STOVES.

OFFICE AND WARE-ROOMS,

No. 5, ST JAMES'S BUILDINGS, KING STREET,

TORONTO.

GEO. H CHENEY & Co.

Toronto, June, 1846.

ADVERTISEMENTS.

MACDONALD'S HOTEL.

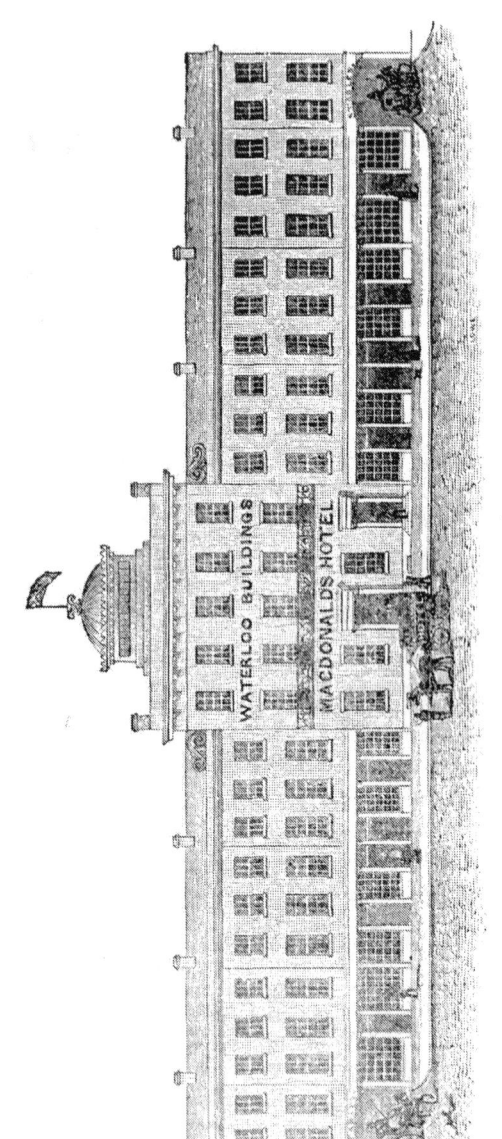

KING STREET, TORONTO.

PASSENGERS CONVEYED TO AND FROM THE BOATS FREE OF CHARGE.
OBLIGING AND ATTENTIVE PORTERS ALWAYS IN ATTENDANCE.

ADVERTISEMENTS.

J. G. JOSEPH,
OPTICIAN, JEWELLER, AND MATHEMATICAL INSTRUMENT MAKER,
56, *King Street, Toronto,*

BEGS leave to inform the Public generally, that he manufactures and keeps for sale a good assortment of articles in the above LINES, which he will dispose of on as reasonable terms as any house in the Province, and WARRANT them. *Instruments, Watches, Jewellery, Silverware, Spectacles, &c*, repaired, or taken in exchange. Orders taken for the most modern GLOBES.

CHARLES ROBERTSON,
GROCER,

Has always on hand a large supply of

GROCERIES, LIQUORS, AND PROVISIONS.

ALSO,

Salt, Plaster of Paris, Field and Garden Seeds, &c.,
AT HIS OLD STAND,
MARKET BUILDINGS,
TORONTO.

LEWIS & BRADBURNE,
COMMISSION MERCHANTS, LAND AGENTS, &c,
8, WELLINGTON BUILDINGS,
TORONTO.

LEWIS & BRADBURNE are now prepared to receive any description of property on consignment, for sale, by auction, or private contract, and to make *liberal cash advances* on the same.

They will also procure any description of goods from the United States, or Great Britain, at a moderate commission, and they feel confident that persons in the habit of purchasing in those markets, will, upon trial, find that they can effect a great saving by buying through them.

They will also attend to the buying and selling, or valuing Real Estate; effecting Mortgages, and the purchase or sale of the same; buying and selling Bank and other Stocks, and the general management of estates.

Deeds procured from Government, and Land Claims prosecuted.

Conveyancing in all its branches accurately attended to.

Toronto, July, 1846

ADVERTISEMENTS.

GENUINE PATENT MEDICINE STORE.

THE SUBSCRIBER respectfully informs his customers, and others, that he is appointed GENERAL AGENT in Canada, for the sale of the following MEDICINES, Wholesale and Retail:—

Bristol's Sarsaparilla—Established 14 years.

THIS INVALUABLE MEDICINE IS THE ORIGINAL AND GENUINE ARTICLE. It has stood the test of time, and has cured diseases heretofore deemed incurable. Certificates of the most inveterate and long-standing cases of Scrofula, Cancer, Leprosy, Chronic Fever and Ague, the frightful diseases caused by Mercury, Dry Gangreen, Prolapsus Uteri, Secondary Syphilis Cutaneous affections of all kinds, Chronic Rheumatism, Liver Complaint, Erysipelas, Ulcers in the Stomach, Chronic Inflammation of the Eyes, Hip Complaint, Lupus or Noli-metangere, Tic-Douloreux, Dyspepsia, Piles, Dropsy, Pimples in the Face, Tetter, Scald Head, Pain in the Bones and Joints, Lumbago, Ring Worm, &c. &c, in many instances of which, the patient had been given up by the faculty, are in the possession of the proprietor, and have been before the public in various publications. In all these complaints, and many others not enumerated, Bristol's Sarsaparilla is a safe and certain remedy, and in some of them, the *only one* that can be relied on for a prompt and permanent cure

☞ By calling on the agent, copies of letters from several of the faculty, in commendation of this medicine, shall be furnished gratis

Dr. Rush's Infallible Health Pills.

A very superior Vegetable Medicine, suitable in price to the times, and to all ages, sexes, seasons, constitutions, and climates ☞ Please give a fair, honest, trial, and if not satisfactory, your money shall be returned.

Circassian Balm.

Unrivalled and unequalled for the cure of *Burns* and *Scalds, Chilblains, Corns, Tetter, Ring Worm, Salt Rheum, Barber's Itch, Broken Breast, Sore Nipples,* and for cleansing and preserving the *Teeth*, and purifying the *Breath*, also for *Shaving*, for the *Toilet*, and *Nursery*, and for *removing paint from Cloth, &c.*

Wild Cherry Bitters.

For Nervous Weakness and General Debility. The Wild Cherry is one of the most valuable alteratives and sedatives in the vegetable kingdom, uniting with its tonic properties the power of calming irritation and diminishing nervous excitability.

These Bitters are highly serviceable in all dyspeptic affections; they assist digestion, restore the tone of the stomach, stimulate the liver, and create an appetite. They are unsurpassed in removing languor or lassitude, (or want of energy to move,) and effectually throw off the drowsiness incident to the spring, or warm season.

Fahnestock's Vermifuge—Warranted Genuine.

In universal demand for the destruction of Worms.

S. F. URQUHART,
Wholesale and Retail Agent.
Temperance Buildings, Yonge Street, Toronto

ADVERTISEMENTS.

SMITH'S
POCKET
COMMERCIAL AND TRAVELLING
MAP OF CANADA WEST.

NOW IN COURSE OF ENGRAVING.

IN consequence of the Universal demand for a Map of this description, which would be at the same time comprehensive, correct, portable, and at a reasonable price, (all Maps of Canada hitherto published being either on too large a scale, or very incorrect), the author of the *Canadian Gazetteer* has made arrangements for publishing a MAP, which in point of correctness and quantity of matter contained in it, will be superior to any Maps of the Province hitherto published; while from the immense sale anticipated, he will be able to furnish it to the public at the low price of 3s. 9d. currency.

It will be engraved on copper, in the very best style—will contain all the Towns and Villages, the Principal Roads, with a Table of Distances; and will be put up in stiff covers of a convenient size for the pocket.

To be ready for delivery as early as it can be engraved and printed.

Orders for the Map will be taken by all Agents for the *Gazetteer*, Booksellers, Storekeepers and Postmasters.

H. & W. ROWSELL,
BOOKSELLERS AND STATIONERS,

HAVE always on hand a large and varied Stock of Account Books, Writing Papers, Drawing Papers, and

EVERY DESCRIPTION OF

PLAIN AND FANCY STATIONERY,

ALSO,

PRINTED BOOKS,

CONSISTING OF

WORKS IN EVERY DEPARTMENT OF LITERATURE AND SCIENCE,

And including all that are required for the various branches of study pursued at the *University of King's College*, Toronto.

SCHOOL BOOKS IN GREAT VARIETY,

Being all those in use at *Upper Canada College*.

THE IRISH NATIONAL SCHOOL BOOKS,

And also the various other kinds, both ENGLISH and CANADIAN EDITIONS, in use in this Colony.

Account Books made to order; Books bound in any style; Copper-Plate Engraving and Printing; Book and Job Printing neatly executed on the most reasonable terms, and on the shortest notice. Lithographic Printing executed in a superior manner—this mode of printing is well adapted for Maps, Plans, &c.

Books of all kinds, or any article connected with the business, procured to order from England or the United States.

ROWSELLS AND THOMPSON, PRINTERS, TORONTO.

UNIVERSITY OF CALIFORNIA LIBRARY

Los Angeles

This book is DUE on the last date stamped below.

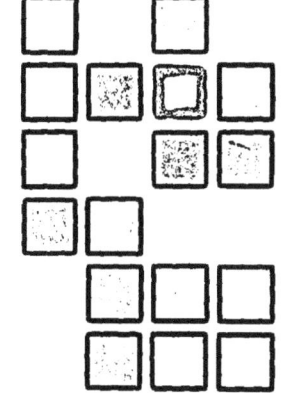